The Letter of the Law

The LETTER
OF THE LAW

*Legal Practice and
Literary Production
in Medieval England*

EDITED BY
EMILY STEINER AND
CANDACE BARRINGTON

CORNELL UNIVERSITY PRESS
Ithaca & London

First published 2002 by Cornell University Press
First printing, Cornell Paperbacks, 2002

Printed in the United States of America

Library of Congress Cataloging-in-Publication Data

The letter of the law : legal practice and literary production in
medieval England / edited by Emily Steiner and Candace Barrington.
    p. cm.
   Includes bibliographical references and index.
   ISBN 0-8014-3975-2 (cloth : alk. paper)—ISBN 0-8014-8770-6 (pbk.
: alk. paper)
    1. English literature—Middle English, 1100–1500—History and
criticism. 2. Practice of law—England—History—To 1500. 3. Law and
literature—History—To 1500. 4. Law—England—History—To 1500. 5.
Law in literature. 6. Law, Medieval.   I. Steiner, Emily. II.
Barrington, Candace.
  PR275.L35 L47 2002
  820.9'355—dc21

                              2001006097

Cloth printing   10 9 8 7 6 5 4 3 2 1
Paperback printing   10 9 8 7 6 5 4 3 2 1

To Robert and Marilyn Steiner
and
Fred and Connie Barrington

Contents

The Letter of the Law

Introduction

EMILY STEINER AND CANDACE BARRINGTON

Scholars have long recognized the pervasive presence of the law in medieval English literature, from depictions of Christ as a litigious *redemptor* in the Wakefield plays, to the itinerant mystic Margery Kempe's collection of safe-conducts, to the startling legal imagery in *Piers Plowman*, such as the image of Truth's pardon. Several decades ago John Alford argued compellingly that the omnipresence of legal culture in Middle English literature, both in its material and conceptual forms, was more than simply a logical extension of the Augustinian concept that "all law is one law." As different legal spheres became more sharply defined—the common law and canon law, manorial and king's courts, written and oral transmission—and developed competing jurisdictional claims, medieval writers found it increasingly difficult to subscribe to notions of a unified law.[1] Alford's essay successfully, if not immediately, alerted literary scholars to the rich possibilities of this kind of comparative work, especially regarding the later medieval period. Yet the curious intersection of law and literature in late medieval England would seem to point to something more than the anxious and haphazard recording of larger cultural phenomena within literary contexts; as the essays in this volume attempt to show, it suggests broader implications for the re-formation of a vernacular literary tradition in England. But as Richard Firth Green rightly notes in *The Cambridge History of Medieval English Literature*, most medievalist literary criticism of the last few decades generally has been limited either to tracking down representations of legal practices in literary texts or to ex-

---

[1] John Alford, "Literature and Law in Medieval England," *Publications of the Modern Language Association* 92 (1977): 941–51.

posing the narrative strategies and creative silences of legal texts. Both approaches have been enormously productive; nevertheless, Green suggests, the new challenge for readers of medieval English literature is to understand law and literature as "parallel forms of discourse."[2]

This challenge, of course, may be leveled at law-and-literature studies more generally and indeed at any criticism that claims to be interdisciplinary. Too often, as several legal scholars have argued, law and literature are assumed to be separate disciplines, a post-Romantic assumption that programmatically distributes law and literature into oppositional categories, such as the scientific and the expressive or the instrumental and aesthetic, prior to formulating an analogy between the two.[3] The resultant analogy more often than not capitalizes on "paradoxical" similarities in order to posit the literary as a corrective to the legal text, either in its capacity to represent legal practice or in the ethical challenge that it poses to legal hermeneutics. Medievalists, however, are enviably placed to make new inroads into the subject of law and literature, in part because of the inherently interdisciplinary nature of medieval law, inseparable as it was from political theory and theology. For example, Elizabeth Fowler's incisive work on medieval contract and dominion and Karma Lochrie's study of the moral, economic, and legal implications of secrecy have gone beyond merely acknowledging the instability of modern disciplines or the reciprocal influences of law and literature to focus on the larger intellectual debates and ideological conflicts that occupied medieval legislators and poets alike. As Lochrie rightly observes about medieval legal terms, "If we are to gauge their cultural significance we need to account for the semantic company they keep, as well as their specific relationship to medieval laws and customs."[4] Indeed, Lochrie's astute observation points to another factor that may enable medievalists productively to reshape law-and-literature studies, namely, the peculiar linguistic, rhetorical, and generic affinities between medieval law and literature. Jody Enders has cogently argued that the relationships between medieval literary genres on the one hand and classical and medieval rhetoric on the other may be brought into focus by the legal underpinnings of medieval drama: "The study of the performance of such social institutions as law, drama, and religion thus facilitates a better understanding of the role of ritualized discourse in the advent of literary genres that differ yet are nonetheless intertwined."[5]

---

[2] Richard Firth Green, "Medieval Law and Literature," in *The Cambridge History of Medieval English Literature*, ed. David Wallace (Cambridge: Cambridge University Press, 1999), 407–31.

[3] See, for example, Guyora Binder, "The Law-as-Literature Trope," in *Law and Literature*, ed. Michael Freeman and Andrew D. E. Lewis (Oxford: Oxford University Press 1999), 64–67; the other essays in the collection speak eloquently to these issues as well.

[4] Elizabeth Fowler, "Civil Death and the Maiden: Agency and the Conditions of Contract in *Piers Plowman*," *Speculum* 70 (1995): 760–92; and "Chaucer's Hard Choices," in *Medieval Crime and Social Control*, ed. Barbara Hanawalt and David Wallace (Minneapolis: University of Minnesota Press, 1998), 124–42. Karma Lochrie, *Covert Operations: The Medieval Uses of Secrecy* (Philadelphia: University of Pennsylvania Press, 1999).

[5] Jody Enders, *Rhetoric and the Origins of Medieval Drama* (Ithaca: Cornell University Press, 1992), 10.

As the essays in this volume demonstrate, new histories of insular law have also helped to renegotiate the relationship between law and literature by uncovering issues significant to the conditions of medieval literary production: political and ethical authority, coercion and social class, competing local and royal jurisdictions, communal negotiations, the rise of literate professions, and the status of the written record.[6] To take just a few representative examples, John Bellamy's and Norman Doe's studies of common law courts illustrate the tensions between theory and practice in the common law's various claims to authority.[7] Anthony Musson's insightful analysis of accusations and convictions in *The Local Adminstration of Criminal Justice, 1294–1350* reveals them to be constructed narratives and subjective representations.[8] In his controversial study Robert C. Palmer argues that Edward III's government responded to the social upheavals caused by the plague by using the law to coerce people to fulfill their responsibilities.[9] Philippa Maddern likewise has shown the ways in which dominant classes used violence to maintain their social and ideological positions, even through what would seem the antithesis of violence: law and order.[10] In her study of the mixed jury, Marianne Constable reveals the history of insular law to be a series of negotiations between communities, each with a different stake in the juridical mix.[11] Concerning the relationship between literate technologies and legal history, Richard Firth Green in *The Crisis of Truth*, building on Michael Clanchy's landmark *From Memory to Written Record*, traces the conflict between "trouthe" (communal coherence founded on ethical truth) and "truth" (written and verifiable evidence) in late medieval English culture.[12] Still other historians, building on the work of Paul Brand for an earlier period, have begun to figure out how

[6] John Baker's survey remains an excellent entry point into the intricacies of medieval common law (*An Introduction to English Legal History*, 3rd ed. [London: Butterworths, 1990]). For a helpful outline of medieval England's legal institutions, its courts and professions, see John Hudson, *The Formation of the English Common Law: Law and Society in England from the Norman Conquest to Magna Carta* (London: Longman, 1996). For a bibliography of scholarship before 1989, readers are directed to Richard Allen, "Writings in the Medieval Period," in *English Legal History: A Bibliography and Guide to the Literature*, ed. W. D. Hines (New York: Garland, 1990), 9–36.

[7] John Bellamy, *The Criminal Trial in Later Medieval England: Felony before the Courts from Edward I to the Sixteenth Century* (Toronto: University of Toronto Press, 1998). Norman Doe, *Fundamental Authority in Late Medieval England* (Cambridge: Cambridge University Press, 1990).

[8] Anthony Musson, *The Local Administration of Criminal Justice, 1294–1350* (Woodbridge, Suffolk: Boydell, 1996). See also Noël James Menuge, "The Wardship Romance: a New Methodology," in *Tradition and Transformation in Medieval Romance*, ed. Rosalind Field (Cambridge: Boydell and Brewer, 1999), 29–43. For another excellent history of late medieval justice, see Anthony Musson and W. M. Ormrod, *The Evolution of English Justice: Law, Politics, and Society in the Fourteenth Century* (Basingstoke: Macmillan, 1999).

[9] Robert C. Palmer, *English Law in the Age of Black Death, 1348–1381* (Chapel Hill: University of North Carolina Press, 1993).

[10] Philippa Maddern, *Violence and Social Order: East Anglia, 1422–1442* (Oxford: Clarendon Press, 1992).

[11] Marianne Constable, *The Law of the Other: The Mixed Jury and Changing Conception of Citizenship, Law, and Knowledge* (Chicago: University of Chicago Press, 1994).

[12] Richard Firth Green, *A Crisis of Truth: Literature and Law in Medieval England* (Philadelphia: University of Pennsylvania Press, 1999), 38–39. Michael Clanchy, *From Memory to Written Record: England, 1066–1307* (Oxford: Blackwell, 1993).

legal knowledge was transmitted and lawyers were trained in the poorly documented fourteenth century.[13] All of these studies, in short, have the effect of removing English legal history from institutional isolation and placing it in the midst of other social and cultural developments.

Inspired by recent literary studies and aided by significant advances in medieval legal history, the nine contributors to this volume strive to rethink the analogy between law and literature by developing innovative approaches to medieval texts as varied as Chaucer's *Knight's Tale*, fifteenth-century Robin Hood ballads, and William Thorpe's report of his own heresy trial. Taken together, they suggest that Middle English literature (understood here as encompassing approximately 1225 to 1475) developed in *dialogue* with legal discourse, practices, and material culture, and further, that insular law and English literature were bound up together in larger processes of institutional, linguistic, and social change. Or, to put it another way, they argue that the re-articulation of an English literary tradition—of both poetry and prose—was conditioned from the thirteenth century by broad and discreet encounters with the law. These encounters, in their turn, significantly determined explorations of character, negotiations of discursive and linguistic boundaries, definitions of genre, the positioning of disciplinary and spiritual authority, the notion of a literary career, the status of the material text, and the conceptualization of linguistic truth. Each essay aims to preserve the historical and textual contingencies of each comparative moment, thereby presenting medieval texts as unique legal worlds related indirectly, if critically, to the procedures and terminology recorded in handbooks, yearbooks, parliamentary reportage, charters, court proceedings, and chronicles. They demonstrate, in other words, the ability of Middle English writers to engage creatively with legal discourse without becoming overwhelmed by the law's powerful structures of meaning: what one contributor, Bruce Holsinger, has coined a "vernacular legality." In so doing they ask what might be particularly medieval or, perhaps more contentiously, what might be perceived as being distinctly English about the relationship between law and literature.

Christine Chism ("Robin Hood: Thinking Globally, Acting Locally") and Jana Mathews ("Land, Lepers, and the Law") show how medieval literary texts resist legal abuses or capitalize on legal exclusions by inventing narrative strategies that in some sense become legal systems themselves. Chism valuably corrects the nostalgia of Bakhtinian and folkloric readings, arguing that the Robin Hood ballads interrogate the crucial collaboration between institu-

[13] Paul Brand, *The Origins of the English Legal Profession* (Oxford: Blackwell, 1992). Other important studies include J. H. Baker, *The Third University of England*, Selden Society Lecture (London: Selden Society, 1990); the articles collected in *Learning the Law: Teaching and the Transmission of Law in England, 1150–1900* (London: Hambledon, 1999); and Brand's article collection *The Common Law Tradition: Lawyers, Books, and the Law* (London: Hambledon, 2000). For the later history of lawyers, see, e.g., Christopher W. Brooks, *Lawyers, Litigation, and English Society since 1450* (London: Hambledon, 1998).

tionalized unity and an essential "misrecognition" on the part of the governed (following Bourdieu). That is to say, what is at stake in the ballads is the way in which those who govern and those who are governed reproduce symbols that legitimate self-serving appeals to community and common profit. Thus, it is not simply that the Robin Hood ballads do not resist legal institutions but rather that they also suggest how socio-judicial authority should properly be exercised both throughout the national arena and within the politically ascendant northern marches.

Like Chism, Mathews explores the manner in which literary texts devise formal and ideological alternatives to exclusive legal practices, but she is interested less in the capacity of the literary for resistance than in how it might borrow from legal practice to formulate theories of character. In her examination of Robert Henryson's *Testament of Cresseid*, a fifteenth-century "sequel" to Chaucer's *Troilus and Criseyde*, Mathews reads the *Testament* as a study in the problem of legal personhood. Whereas previous criticism of the *Testament* has focused on Henryson's refiguration of Chaucerian morality, classicism, or gender politics, she shows that Henryson draws from Scottish land law to reimagine the problem of Cresseid in terms of legal devaluation and revaluation. In addition to using land law to contextualize the relationship between agriculture and abjection, Mathews further explores Henryson's devaluation and revaluation of Cresseid: first, in terms of late medieval leprosy laws; and second, in terms of the medieval last will and testament, the means by which Cresseid successfully reemerges by the end of the poem as a legal person.

Andrew Galloway, like Mathews, explores how legal developments register legal abuses and exclusions by inscribing "unnamed trace[s] or oblique assessment[s]" onto textual narratives. In "The Literature of 1388 and the Politics of Pity," he explains that the parliamentary trials of Richard II's reign, and especially the Merciless Parliament and its aftermath, turned the ethical notion of pity into a menacing legal instrument, as registered both within contemporary chronicles, such as Thomas Favent's, and in the shifting narrative strategies of the prolific London poet John Gower. Galloway focuses on two of Gower's later literary works, the Ricardian *Confessio amantis* and the Henrician "epic," the *Cronica tripertita*, both of which are preoccupied in different ways with the ethical nature of pity and its legal abuse, specifically the unreliability and implicit violence of royal pardon. By charting Gower's difficult literary response to the changing legal roles of royal pity, Galloway instructively redefines the relationship between legal and literary production as well as the trajectory of medieval literary careers. In the appendix to this volume, Galloway newly translates Favent's record of the 1386 Parliament, thereby providing a more accurate and accessible account than previously available.

Other contributors focus on the ways in which literary texts restage the performances of medieval courts. Richard Firth Green, in "Palamon's Appeal of Treason," argues that Chaucer's *Knight's Tale*, through its grand enactment of a trial by battle, dramatizes the overreaching tendencies of the late medieval international Court of Chivalry. Green shows that certain alterations the *Knight's Tale* makes to its original, Boccaccio's *Teseida*, shift the whole thrust of the combat between the two young Thebans away from the chivalric and toward the judicial. This move was a response to disquieting signs in the early 1380s that the Court of Chivalry was beginning to extend its jurisdiction from martial law and the conduct of English combatants overseas to domestic disputes, reintroducing into English civil process a disturbing form of action virtually extinct for seventy or eighty years: trial by combat. But as Green so persuasively proves, the *Knight's Tale* does not merely dramatize the excesses of the Court of Chivalry. It also reveals in that dramatization two larger jurisprudential issues at stake in that court's transformation: the threat it posed to the older quasi-legal ethos of negotiation and compromise, and the dangerously increased powers it offered to any potentially autocratic ruler.

Like Green's essay, Emma Lipton's "Language on Trial" investigates the literary reenactment of trials, but from the perspective of performance rather than judicial practice. Recent dramatic criticism has examined the N-Town "Mary and Joseph" play, which dramatizes the apocryphal story of Mary's trial for adultery, through a Foucauldian lens of bodily spectacle and punishment. Lipton, by contrast, innovatively combines dramatic and linguistic theories of performance to suggest that the play simultaneously enacts and queries the institutional evaluation of different kinds of truth claims. Specifically, it uses the miracle of the Immaculate Conception to expose the inefficacy and indeterminacy of public rumor. In the place of rumor (a perfectly legitimate mode of proof in medieval courts), the play, not unlike the *Knight's Tale*, offers an archaic model of proof—the ordeal—that relies (like the Virgin Birth) on divine intervention rather than on the inherent performativity of legal language alone. In offering such an alternative, the play simultaneously calls attention to affinities between legal and dramatic performances and promotes drama as a source for legal theory and reform.

Still other contributors approach questions of authorship, discursive boundaries, and textual authority from the perspective of the materials and rhetoric of the law. Maura Nolan, for example, explores the ways in which medieval legal careers offered models for and challenges to a particularly English idea of authorship. In "'Acquiteth yow now,'" she critiques the problems of textual criticism surrounding the *Man of Law's Tale* and the resultant failure of critics to identify the legal discourse that the Man of Law represents. She points out that textual critics, by canonizing the "practical" textual difficulties of the Prologue to the *Man of Law's Tale*, have ceded further analysis of that tale and its teller to a theoretical literary criticism falsely divorced from questions of textual contradiction. Likewise, the critical focus on the Man of Law as tale-teller has ignored the "genuine historical tension or incongruity" between law and poetry. In contrast to previous criticism, then, Nolan argues that the textual inconsistencies in the Man of Law's Prologue stem from the tensions between law and poetry—amounting to a poetic "philosophy of law"—which first appear in the *General Prologue* (in the Host's contract with the tale-tellers) and inform much of the *Canterbury* frame. And she suggests further that the Man of Law competes with Chaucer himself, in part because the tale-telling project has appropriated a legal vocabulary, and in part because the language of the law provided late medieval authors with an appropriable and secularized vocabulary of legitimacy.

Bruce Holsinger and Emily Steiner, in turn, show how the literary appropriation and transformation of legal vocabularies (jurisdictional and documentary) gave medieval poets an extremely versatile discourse with which to negotiate liturgical and interpretive boundaries. Holsinger argues that the very subject of the early thirteenth-century debate poem *The Owl and the Nightingale* is jurisdiction, specifically conceived as jurisdiction over liturgical boundaries. The poem is not explicitly concerned, in other words, with the well-known contests between secular and canonical law documented by the jurist Henry Bracton, but rather it draws creatively from that jurisdictional discourse to delineate, separate, and regulate modes of musical and liturgical authority (as embodied in the emergent musical genre the *conductus*). Holsinger coins the phrase "vernacular legality" to explain the process by which the language of jurisdiction is linguistically and ideologically transformed by the author of *The Owl and the Nightingale*: "A working notion of vernacular legality will allow us to address not only the ways in which vernacular writers recruit official legal vocabularies and institutions for their own purposes, but also, and perhaps most importantly, those means by which certain writers infuse the vernacular with a juridical and forensic authority that would otherwise be restricted to the agents of official legal culture."

In "Inventing Legalities: Documentary Culture and Lollard Preaching," Steiner reconsiders Holsinger's formulation of a "vernacular legality" in a very different context: the fifteenth-century trials of the accused Lollards William Thorpe (1407) and Margery Baxter (1428). She maintains that late medieval documentary culture (charters, seals, coffers, etc.) produced an alternative version of itself, which could be pressed into the service of both mainstream vernacular piety and heterodox polemic. As a result, documentary culture provided a crucial "intergeneric" framework for discussions about textual authority, a hot issue in the early fifteenth century preoccupying orthodox and heterodox writers alike. Lollard preachers and polemicists were notoriously hostile to legal documents, but Steiner shows how they borrowed documents—both fictive and real—to challenge orthodox notions of textual authority. She suggests first that they borrowed the popular image of Christ's charter to contest indulgences and to describe a particularly Lollard ideal of spiritual community. She then goes on to show how Lollards on trial appropriated the rhetoric of legal documents to extricate Lollard polemic from the evidentiary language of ecclesiastical trial documents and to restore a distinctly Lollard hermeneutic.

Finally, Frank Grady, like Galloway, is concerned with the implications of parliamentary trials for the invention of literary traditions. In "The Generation of 1399," however, he turns from legal rhetoric to legal genres, arguing (alongside Steiner) that documents and parliamentary proceedings offered alternatives to early fifteenth-century writers. He bases his argument on a trio of partisan Lancastrian poems depicting the final years of Richard II's reign— *Richard the Redeless*, *Mum and the Sothsegger*, and Gower's *Cronica tripertita*— which deliberately eschew the visionary authority of their literary exemplars (the *Piers Plowman* tradition and Gower's *Vox clamantis*) in favor of a documentary or legal authority. Grady suggests that, in the wake of the 1399 deposition of Richard II and the Lancastrian usurpation, visionary authority seemed to promote a critique of legal and political institutions dangerously abstracted from the institutions themselves, but the measure of immediacy and immanence lost by abandoning the dream-vision was recovered by adopting a documentary model. Rather than considering texts Lancastrian simply by virtue of their chronology, then, Grady uses the legal document to show how political allegiances might reconfigure the formal characteristics of literary texts. Or, to put it another way, the instruments of the law, through their formal exchangeability and specific claims to spoken and written authority, offered early fifteenth-century poets a means of aligning themselves politically while still advertising the critical viability of vernacular poetry.

Of course, to insist on the historical, geographical, and linguistic contingencies of medieval English law and literature is to ignore the trilingual character of insular law—specifically, Anglo-Norman or "law French." Yet it could be argued that it is precisely the failure of England's other vernacular to maintain a working relationship between the legal and the literary that illustrates what is finally at stake in the resurgence of English as a literary medium. If Anglo-Norman in 1066 inexorably linked the administrative and cultural interests of a new ruling class,[14] by the late thirteenth century it had begun to give way, at least in the domestic (as opposed to the increasingly centralized administrative) spheres, to English. To be sure, meditative and historical works continued to be produced in Anglo-Norman throughout the thirteenth and fourteenth centuries, but by 1300, writers such as Robert of

---

[14] To cite a familiar example, Robert of Gloucester's metrical chronicle (ca. 1300) describes the aftermath of the Conquest as a problem of *diglossia:*
þus com lo engelond in to normandies hond
& þe normans ne couþe speke þo bote hor owe speche
& speke french as hii dude atom, & hor children dude also teche;
So þat heiemen of þus lond of hor blod come
Holdeþ all þulke spreche þat hii of þom nome.
(7537–41)
Albert C. Baugh and Thomas Cable, *A History of the English Language*, 4th ed. (Englewood Cliffs, N.J.: Prentice Hall, 1993), 111–12.

Gloucester and the author of the *Cursor Mundi* were proclaiming the universality of English and the elitism or esotericism of Anglo-Norman.[15] As Anglo-Norman was declining as a language of personal and literary expression, moreover, it took on a new incarnation as law French, a dialect that effectively replaced Latin as the language of legal pleading, parliamentary debates, and royal administration.[16] The relationship of Anglo-Norman to institutional authority was consequently redefined. Whereas in the past it had signaled the direct authority of its Norman speaker, as law French it now signaled the channeled authority of the aristocracy's representatives, the lawyers and legal clerks of Westminster and the courts (those who, not incidentally, would form a kind of "coterie" of poets reshaping a tradition of English letters).[17] Anglo-Norman became, in other words, the provenance of legal technicians rather than legal actors, and, perhaps as a result, was often criticized as

[15] How long the language of William the Conqueror continued to be spoken among members of the aristocracy remains a matter of debate. For several centuries following the Conquest, Anglo-Norman was surely the language of culture and administration within aristocratic households (including, of course, the royal household), but most likely by the beginning of the thirteenth century, few Englishmen of any class learned to speak Anglo-Norman "fram tyme þat a buþ yrokked in here cradel" (John of Trevisa's translation of Higden's *Polychronicon*, from Kenneth Sisam, ed., *Fourteenth-Century Verse and Prose* [Oxford: Clarendon Press, 1921], 149). For a balanced account of the debate, see Glanville Price, *The Languages of Britain* (London: Edward Arnold, 1984), 217–31. For more recent discussions of spoken Anglo-Norman, see Cecily Clark, "The Myth of 'the Anglo-Norman Scribe,'" in *History of Englishes: New Methods and Interpretations in Historical Linguistics*, ed. Matti Rissanen, Ossi Ihalainen, Terttu Nevalainen, and Irman Taavitsainen (Berlin: Mouton de Bruyter, 1992), 117–29; and Douglas A. Kibbee, "*For to Speke Frenche Trewely*": *The French Language in England, 1000–1600: Its Status, Description, and Instruction* (Philadelphia: John Benjamins Publishing, 1991), 39–41.

[16] This shift to "law French" had already been anticipated by the gallicized entries in the Domesday Book, and brought into focus by Henry III, whose 1258 confirmation of the privileges of Oxford was drawn up in French and English, as well as Latin. By the reign of Edward I, however, a professional class of lawyers conducted all their legal pleadings in Anglo-Norman, which, around the same time, also became the language of record for the *Statutes of the Realm*, the *Rotuli Parliamentorum*, and some town and guild records. See William Rothwell, "Language and Government in Medieval England," *Zeitschrift für Franzosische Sprache und Literatur* 93 (1983): 258–70, and "The Legacy of Anglo-French: *Faux Amis* in French and English," *Zeitschrift für Romanische Philologie* 109 (1993): 16–46. Woodbine proposed that the upsurge in written Anglo-Norman was the result of Henry III's conscious policy to reintroduce French into England. Accordingly, fourteenth-century "Anglo-Norman" was not a descendant of Norman but a continental French that quickly decayed. His speculation has never gained wide acceptance. See George E. Woodbine, "The Language of English Law," *Speculum* 18 (1943): 395–436; and John B. Collas, ed., introduction to *Yearbooks of Edward II*, Selden Society no. 70 (London: Selden Society, 1953), xix–xxi, for a refutation of some assumptions on which Woodbine's argument rests.

[17] It is telling, in this respect, that the colossal rise of English as a literary language after 1350 was shortly followed by the Englishing of legal forms of a confessional or declarative nature such the last will and testament after 1370, indentures of retaining, and the deliberately Englished "confessions" of the duke of Gloucester and Richard II. For the notion of a Westminster and London coterie of poets, see Katherine Kerby-Fulton and Steven Justice, "Langlandian Reading Circles and the Civil Service in London and Dublin, 1380–1427," *New Medieval Literatures* 1 (1997): 59–83. For an incisive history of the relationship between London factionalist politics, written legal culture, and English poetic careers, see Sheila Lindenbaum, "London Texts and Literate Practice," in Wallace, *The Cambridge History of Medieval English Literature*, 284–309.

being specialized and unintelligible, as fourteenth-century parliamentary directives suggest.[18] The gradual institutional and bureaucratic marginalization of Anglo-Norman is witnessed by the trajectory of the last three literary texts recorded in Anglo-Norman: Duke Henry of Lancaster's 1350 meditative treatise *Le Livre de seyntz medicines*,[19] in which he apologizes for his poor "French"; the lawyer and poet John Gower's allegorical satire *Mirour de l'omme* (ca. 1370s), in which the narrator assumes the role of legal advocate; and the Chaucerian poet and Privy Seal clerk Thomas Hoccleve's *Formulary* (1408), a collection of model letters in which Anglo-Norman's "imaginative" functions had been almost completely eclipsed by its institutional ones.[20]

By way of conclusion, then, we may say that this very briefly sketched history of Anglo-Norman has at least two important implications for the relationship between Middle English literature and medieval legal culture. First, Anglo-Norman, broadly speaking, may have modeled for English letters a powerful relationship between the imaginative and legal—or, in the case of Anglo-Norman, between the domestic culture of aristocratic letters and royal or national governance—by linking both through dialect to specific class interests and institutions of power. To be sure, later medieval writers invoked the supposed universality or commonness of English to justify writing in Middle English. But in doing so they were reacting to an older Anglo-Norman tradition in which dialect designates a social and discursive realm, a realm that retains within its purview both the legal and the imaginative while at the same time marginalizing other available dialects.[21] Nevertheless, the

[18] As anyone who has read law French knows, however, it has a "double character": it is technically difficult for a French speaker, but often closely follows English syntax and vocabulary, and consequently is not at all difficult for any "pragmatic" English speaker to understand. This double character of Anglo-Norman may account for its survival in parliamentary record keeping through the fifteenth century despite its radical demise in the courts. On this point, see William Rothwell, "The Trilingual England of Geoffrey Chaucer," *Studies in the Age of Chaucer* 16 (1994): 45–67. For the directive of 1318 (against "obscure archaic terminology"), see idem, "The Problem of Law French," *French Studies* 46 (1992): 267, referring to *Rotuli Parliamentorum Anglie Hactenus Inediti*, 86; For the directive of 1362 (against legal pleading in law French), see A. R. Meyers, ed., *English Historical Documents* (Oxford: Clarendon Press, 1969), 4.483, from *Statutes of the Realm*, 2.375.

[19] Henry of Lancaster, *Le Livre de seyntz medicines*, ed. E. J. Arnould (Oxford: Basil Blackwell, 1940), 239.

[20] The formulary has been edited by Elna-Jean Young Bentley as "The Formulary of Thomas Hoccleve" (Ph.D. diss., Emory University, 1965). As Ethan Knapp has explained, the near-anonymous initials "T. H." discreetly inscribed at the bottom of a few of the letters suggest how Anglo-Norman legal forms might offer a literary discourse with which to express the petitioning subject; yet Hoccleve's real engagement with legal and bureaucratic culture nevertheless took place in his English "autobiographical" poems ("Bureaucratic Identity and the Construction of the Self in Hoccleve's *Formulary* and *La male regle*," *Speculum* 74 [1999]: 369). It may seem ironic that the same secular professionals who conducted their daily business in law French were instrumental in producing the first waves of court poets writing in Middle English.

[21] As Susan Crane cogently points out, "When writers in English reassert the prestige of French alongside their own counterclaim to universality, prestige slides towards marginalization, forecasting the definitive passage of French from a 'language of culture' into a foreign language" ("Anglo-Norman Cultures in England," in Wallace, *The Cambridge History of Medieval English Literature*, 52).

slow demise of Anglo-Norman as a discourse and a practice, and its eventual marginalization—if not diminution—in the written record, offered late medieval English poets a space to recuperate the relationship between the legal and the imaginative. In other words, both the possibilities and failures of Anglo-Norman indirectly gave Middle English writers the right to respond to legal practices and to reshape legal discourse. It is our aim in this volume to explain how they did so.

1 Robin Hood

Thinking Globally, Acting Locally in the Fifteenth-Century Ballads

CHRISTINE CHISM

The earliest Robin Hood ballads are marauders at a peculiar inter-section: the place where the reinvention of social order merges with the ad-ministration of justice.[1] This essay examines three late medieval ballads, *Robin Hood and the Monk*, *Robin Hood and the Potter*, and *A Gest of Robin Hood*, argu-ing that they confront the ways in which socio-judicial authority was exer-cised within local and national arenas, and specifically how that authority reconstructed profitable networks of community, association, and representa-tion. Although many of the ballads may have been composed much earlier than the fifteenth century, they are as incisive against later abuses as they are against earlier ones.[2] These outlaw ballads critique the exercise of judicial au-

---

[1] I have used Stephen Knight's and Thomas Ohlgren's edition, *Robin Hood and Other Outlaw Tales* (Kalamazoo: Medieval Institute, Western Michigan University, 1997). All three ballads are cited from this edition by line number in the text.

[2] The precise dating of the genesis of these ballads (let alone putative historical Robin Hoods) is a thorny question based mostly on internal evidence. The weight of recent arguments, how-ever, seems to be toward later and later origins; proponents of thirteenth-century origins have grown quieter. J. R. Maddicott argues for a date as early as the 1330s for the *Gest* (which exists only in later printed copies), linking it to the activities of the Folvilles in the period of disorder at the end of Edward II's reign ("The Birth and Setting of the Ballads of Robin Hood," *English His-torical Review* 93 [1978]: 276–99). Richard Firth Green also assumes a fourteenth-century prove-nance for the *Gest* (*A Crisis of Truth: Literature and Law in Ricardian England* [Philadelphia: Uni-versity of Pennsylvania Press, 1999], 194–98). None of the manuscripts, however, can be dated earlier than 1450, and most are from at least fifty years later. In a useful and thorough study of the ballads (and of the Robin Hood tradition as a whole), Stephen Knight ("Robin Hood in the Ballads," in *Robin Hood: A Complete Study of the English Outlaw* [Oxford: Blackwell, 1994], 44–97) argues for a mid fifteenth-century dating for the *Gest*, remaining noncommittal about *Robin Hood and the Monk*, *Robin Hood and the Potter*, and *Robin Hood and Guy of Gisborne*, which Francis James Child places early (*The English and Scottish Ballads*, vol. 3 [New York: Dover, 1965], 89–91).

thority in a variety of ways, yet the very pluralism of the ballads reveals just how textured and contested were the topographies of late medieval jurisdiction.

This essay focuses on a particular late fourteenth-and fifteenth-century socio-judicial development crucial to the Robin Hood ballads: the localization of law enforcement that accompanied the centralization of monarchical authority over the law. This development gave local officials the power legally to represent the monarch and gave the gentry and locally prominent citizens more influence within the evolving system of courts. As a result, the already sinewy local networks that bound together the provincial elite could exercise even more leverage than before. The localization of law enforcement also strengthened the connections between these officials and the central authority they represented, thereby making the king much more aware of how his representatives were exercising his authority, and giving the representatives improved prospects at the royal court, in parliament, and within judicial courts.

The *Gest* takes issue both with the networks that bound the provincial elite and with the newly forged ties between local officials and royal authority. In the story of Sir Richard, for example, the ballad highlights the local monopoly formed by the abbot, the sheriff, the local lordlings, and the king's justice. Its strategy of attack is, however, unusual: it takes aim at their mutually pleasurable association not just because it is corrupt, but because it is deficient in affection; it is an association of meager desires and poor friendships. Later the *Gest* reveals a similar deficiency in King Edward, who fails to command the hearts of his representatives as surely as Robin Hood can. The *Gest*, in effect, works simultaneously as an ethical and as an affective condemnation of local and monarchical legal authority, and this suggests that it is precisely the deficiency of the affective that renders authority impotent. The *Gest* further suggests that this impotence results from the unchivalric need to play things safe, to anchor networks of association with hard cash, rather than to distribute the kind of continually renegotiated largesse that animates the economy of the greenwood (where no association is entirely safe, but where many prove beyond expectation to be true).

This affective critique becomes more playful in *Robin Hood and the Potter*, which promotes risky, mock-chivalric masculinity as an effective resistance strategy. Here, the sheriff becomes a model of established masculine author-

---

Knight bases his argument on linguistic analysis and the *Gest*'s internal reference to Edward, "our comely king," whom he reads as Edward IV rather than any of his predecessors, arguing that the fifteenth century was the time when previously oral popular ballads began to be written down and circulated to the new reading audiences nurtured and exploited by publishers such as Caxton. This fifteenth-century investment in the production of such manuscripts is significant and foregrounds the ongoing relevancy of the ballads to fifteenth-century audiences. In support, A. J. Pollard refers to fifteenth-century interest in the Robin Hood ballads and plays, especially among the gentry ("Characteristics of the Fifteenth-Century North," in *Government, Religion, and Society in Northern England, 1000–1700* [Phoenix Mill: Sutton Publishing, 1997], 131–43).

ity: he has a wife to rule as well as a city, and stages archery contests in his home. Yet his own masculinity is abrogated by the end of the ballad, not because Robin Hood's is superior, but because Robin Hood recognizes that masculinity—and by extension any authority—must be riskily, strategically, and playfully reenacted rather than institutionally safeguarded.

Robin Hood and the Monk takes particular aim at the systems of hierarchical representation that link judicial periphery to center, local representative to monarch, and servant to master. As Little John beguiles his way along the chain of representation from sheriff to king in order to rescue his master, we see how the chain of representation that binds king to local representative resembles the provincial conspiracies of the *Gest* in its anxious reliance on established institutions, endowed rewards, and safely unified interests.

Each of these slightly different critiques is concerned with the ways in which legal and social authorities symbolically join hands to make one another safe and secure but, at the same time, try to cinch their "friendships" with ties of profit and reward, offices and institutional affiliations. Each ballad thus comments cogently on late medieval discourses of community, friendship, and association, revealing them to be nothing more than strategies for re-creating, policing, and enforcing selected kinds of social order.[3] Or, to put it another way, each ballad reveals communities to be not com-unities of fellow feeling and trust but rather "gated communities" fenced in fear—and therefore irresistible to an enterprising marauder.

Law, Community, and Resistance

Throughout the late fourteenth and fifteenth centuries in England, the desire for social order was prompting legal innovations that knit local jurisdiction to royal authority with unprecedented intimacy. As numerous studies have elaborated, the fourteenth century marked a watershed in the organization of law under the central authority of the king.[4] Paradoxically, however,

---

[3] Much recent historical work elaborates the fifteenth-century reshaping of community at many social levels. Nationally, Alan Harding shows how courts of law reshape and reinforce both "the communities of England and the class-divisions of English society, to create an increasingly dominant national community" that culminates under the Tudors (*The Law Courts of Medieval England* [New York: Barnes and Noble, 1973], 115). On a more local level, Marjorie K. McIntosh discusses how, within village and manorial courts, regional jurors increasingly dealt with problems such as nightwalking, gaming, eavesdropping, and scolding, which did not fall under either traditional secular or ecclesiastical court jurisdiction, by appealing to a language based on ideas of social harmony and unity ("Finding Language for Misconduct: Jurors in Fifteenth-Century Local Courts," in *Bodies and Disciplines: Intersections of Literature and History in Fifteenth-Century England*, ed. Barbara A. Hanawalt and David Wallace [Minneapolis: University of Minnesota Press, 1996], 87–122). For a revealing discussion of fifteenth-century changes in local communities as they emerge in village courts, see Sherri Olson, *A Chronicle of All That Happens: Voices from the Village Court in Medieval England* (Toronto: Pontifical Institute of Medieval Studies, 1996).

[4] Harding, *Law Courts*, 49–85; Edward Powell, *Kingship, Law, and Society: Criminal Justice in the Reign of Henry V* (Oxford: Clarendon Press, 1989); Richard Firth Green, *A Crisis of Truth: Litera-*

this expansion of royal power relied on the cooperation of locally prominent citizens, gentry, and nobility, who provided the justices of the peace, sheriffs, and jury members required to staff the system. Thus, throughout the four-teenth century, structural centralization of the law was accompanied by the effective localization of its administration. It would be several centuries be-fore kings could afford to keep a professional police force or standing army, especially given the military expenditures that accompanied the expansion of warfare at this time.[5] Edward Powell describes, for example, how the preco-cious expansion of royal jurisdiction under kings from Henry II to Edward III required the cooperation of local barons and magnates throughout England and, consequently, how profitable this collusion was for all parties. To be sure, the instruments of royal legal superintendence altered over time, from the lucrative circulations of the general eyres instituted by Henry II to the *trailbaston* and *oyer* and *terminer* commissions of the fourteenth and fifteenth centuries, but their exercise invited mutually profitable negotiations among king, parliament, and regional landowners.[6]

This profitability—and for a while the king's unwillingness to disturb the balance of power in legal affairs—partly explains why powerful or oppor-tunistic locals, notoriously jealous of their traditional prerogatives, tolerated monarchical encroachment on their jurisdictions in the first place. Yet the in-creasing centralization of legal power under the monarch created opportuni-ties for a wide spectrum of classes and occupations. Granted, the chance to participate in royal jurisdiction attracted the regionally powerful; but even the non-landed classes could appreciate the promise of the kind of accessible, speedy, and impartial justice that kings promulgated so effectively from the twelfth century on.

The very inventiveness and expedience with which English kings adminis-tered order, however, and the unprecedented force with which they invested their instruments of judicial reform, generated new forms of aggression among enterprising gentry, who, as K. B. McFarlane has shown, found the law at least as powerful as the sword in promoting self-interest.[7] Richard

---

ture and Law in Ricardian England (Philadelphia: University of Pennsylvania Press, 1999), 121–64.

[5] Richard Kaeuper, *War, Justice, and Public Order* (Oxford: Clarendon Press, 1988), 11–133.

[6] "The general eyre of the twelfth and thirteenth centuries was primarily a device to investi-gate the king's rights and translate them into money, and it did much to fill the coffers of the Angevin kings. In the fourteenth century, trailbaston inquiries became notorious for their puni-tive financial exactions, and under Edward III Parliament consistently sought to buy off the threat of eyres and trailbastons in return for grants of taxation. . . . Of course the profits of justice were as much a part of seigneurial income as of the Crown's. This was particularly true immedi-ately after the Black Death, when landowners sought to compensate for a decline in other sources of revenue by increasing judicial exactions in manorial courts, and when some lords were able to appropriate for themselves the fines levied for breaches of the Statutes of Labourers within their estates." Powell, *Kingship, Law, and Society*, 111.

[7] See K. B. McFarlane, *The Nobility of Later Medieval England* (Oxford: Clarendon Press, 1973), 115. The power and rapidity of apparatus such as commissions of *oyer* and *terminer* made them

Kaueper describes the profound conflicts engendered by the increasing appointments of local gentry as justices of the peace. The law, in sum, became more vulnerable to local networks of influence, patronage, and maintenance, and became a powerful economic weapon in the construction of regional, familial, and professional solidarities, what Kaeuper calls "the business of justice": "Justitia magnum emolumentum est."[8]

In these studies it is clear that the medieval legal administration was continually subject to very interested local appropriations. Pierre Bourdieu points out that the success of authority depends on its deployment of institutionalized symbols (such as the "king's peace," the "common weal," or the "king's law"). These symbols—so apparently universalized and impartial—charm a crucial misrecognition from those who are governed.

> The language of authority never governs without the collaboration of those it governs, without the help of the social mechanisms capable of producing this complicity, based on misrecognition, which is the basis of all authority. . . . The symbolic efficacy of words is exercised only in so far as the person subjected to it recognizes the person who exercises it as authorized to do so, or, what amounts to the same thing, only in so far as he fails to realize, that in submitting to it, he himself has contributed, through his recognition, to its establishment.[9]

The Robin Hood ballads target with precise ferocity a similar institutionalization of social unity and community. In Bourdieu's terms, these ballads not only withhold collaboration but also mount counterattacks. They do not misrecognize judicial authority as already established, secure, and impartial; instead they pin it down at the moments it seeks to secure itself for its own ends. These ballads reveal that, at the same time late-medieval officials such as sheriff, justice, and king are assuming a veil of long-standing legal tradition to persuade collaboration, they are innovating underhandedly to enforce obedience and reap a profit. By calling attention, moreover, to the maneuverings of official authority, they reveal that authority is bound up in continual performances and, even further, that its performances, far from bearing the weight of past traditions, may be as opportunistic as those of the outlaws themselves.

Robin Hood's band holds up a funhouse mirror to late medieval discourses

---

appealing instruments of entrepreneurial self-interest for kings themselves as well as for their subjects. Richard Kaeuper discusses the case of Edward II, who, in his prosecution of Bishop Walter Langton, instructed his chancellor to consult with others to pursue "all the ways and means by which one can trouble the said bishop by the law and custom of our realm." The conventional phrase "by the law and custom of our realm," which mobilizes ideologies of legal impartiality, is inverted into "do all damage possible under formal cover of law" (780–81). See also Richard Kaeuper, "Law and Order in Fourteenth-Century England: The Evidence of *Oyer* and *Terminer*," *Speculum* 54 (1979): 734–84.

[8] Kaeuper, *War, Justice, and Public Order*, 140.

[9] Pierre Bourdieu, *Language and Symbolic Power*, trans. John B. Thompson (Cambridge: Harvard University Press, 1993), 113, 116.

of community and social accord, revealing their pretensions by caricaturing them. To a modern reader brought up on the appealing but neotenous camaraderies of Howard Pyle and Errol Flynn, the outlaw world of the early ballads comes as a shock. Despite the rhetoric of fellowship, there is very little community, utopian or otherwise, to the life in the forest as the oldest surviving ballads describe it. In the fifteenth century, the merry men spend far more time skirmishing than in merrymaking; and although Robin and John reaffirm their fidelity to each other with almost tedious regularity, they also quarrel incessantly about their relative status and draw swords over trivial wagers. In fact, the only time we see solidarity among Robin Hood's men is when he impresses his prisoners by whistling up his "seven score of wight young men / all in a row"(*Gest*, 915–16, 1555–56). Yet this instantaneous nonspeaking cast of extras resembles more the predatory systems of livery and maintenance than it does any organic greenwood community.

The apparent disorganization of Robin Hood's company contrasts with the clubbiness of Robin's political enemies, such as the friars of St. Mary's or the sheriff of Nottingham. These different regulatory agencies take part in conspiracies and collusions that seem at once so naturalized and menacing that their fragility nearly goes unnoticed. In the *Gest*, for example, when the knight Sir Richard goes to St. Mary's Abbey to pay back his loan, he finds not only the abbot but also the sheriff, and with them the high justice of England, ready to back the abbot's seizure of goods. In *Robin Hood and the Monk*, Robin goes into Nottingham to hear a Ladymass and is recognized by a "gret-hedid munke"(75), who shares with the sheriff a personal grievance against the outlaw and immediately runs to notify him. In *Robin Hood and Guy of Gisborne*, an itinerant warrior and bounty hunter, Guy of Gisborne, is prepared to enforce the sheriff's authority and becomes part of a two-pronged attack on the outlaws. And the people who conspire to bring about Robin Hood's death in the later *Death of Robin Hood* are the prioress of Kirklees Abbey and her lover, Sir Roger of Donkesly. The most negative image of institutionalized community in the ballads—the *Gest*'s sullen confraternity of St. Mary's Abbey—underlines the profitability of being on the administrative side of the law: these friars are united chiefly by their legally armored endowments and have the king's justice in their pockets.

By describing these class- and institution-crossing conspiracies, the fifteenth-century Robin Hood ballads show how at the local level, civic administration, law, and church connive to enrich themselves and destroy their common enemies. In effect, by assuming an outsider's perspective, the ballads diffract late medieval ideals of public order and community into their practical antitypes: tightening networks of legalized corruption and economic predation. Thieving their language and symbolism from court and battlefield, monastery and town, these ballads seek to engender a community based not on anxious institutional collaboration and mutually profitable collusion but on risky performance and continual contest.

The *Gest* and the Pleasures of Conspiracy

A Gest of Robyn Hood explores the pleasures and profits of legal alliance at every social level, as its hero distresses networks of local and national authority. Throughout the eight fitts of the *Gest*, Robin challenges authorities at increasingly consequential social intersections, ranging from regional power-mongers like the abbot and the justice he retains to back his accumulation of property, to the sheriff of Nottingham, and even to the king himself. Most interesting in this range of brief encounters is the lability of the outlaw: at every stage Robin Hood both opposes his enemies and mimics them. For example, even as he supports with seigneurial generosity a poor knight's battle against his rapacious creditors, Robin frets about the return of his investment with the cupidity of the moneylending abbot himself. When the sheriff gathers "men of armys stronge" (1268) to besiege Richard of the Lea's castle and later ambushes him in revenge for sheltering Robin and the wounded Little John, Robin Hood and his men retaliate and, sparing neither "hedge ne dyche" (1367), enter Nottingham and behead the sheriff in his own streets. And surprisingly, when the king comes to Nottingham to punish Robin, he is entertained by a Robin Hood who has suddenly become an alternate king of the woods with his own affinity, commanding a loyalty that the king comes to envy. In a striking reversal of king and outlaw—seigneury and violence—Robin Hood acknowledges the physical power of the king's buffet, while the king craves a suit of Robin Hood's green livery. And finally, even as Robin Hood submits and is brought temporarily back into society, the sight of his retinue (now encompassing that of the re-liveried king) briefly suffuses the entire world with a greenwood exuberance. For a terrifying or utopian instant, when the people of Nottingham look out their windows and see "nothynge but mantels of grene / That covered all the felde" (1707–8), they cannot help but conclude that Robin Hood has slain the king and is returning to take his place.

Robin Hood's social agility behooves a figure whose effect on his enemies is often that of a universal social solvent—dissolving the networks through which their authority is enacted. His mimicry calls attention to his enemies' anxious pursuit of prestige, security, and seigneurial pleasure as they cultivate networks of influence through both lateral alliances and hierarchical affiliation. Moreover, the ballads' particular focus on the socio-legal pleasures of such conspiracies not only shows that they drive the law (a psychoanalytic assumption),[10] but also draws attention to the desirable social power gained by manipulating medieval common law. The law invited as many possibilities for individual advancement and enrichment as did the battlefield, and for a much broader social constituency. This breadth of appeal emerges in the variety of

---

[10] Louise O. Fradenburg, "Needful Things," in *Medieval Crime and Social Control*, ed. Barbara Hanawalt and David Wallace (Minneapolis: University of Minnesota Press, 1999), 49–69.

its social expressions. It drove the late fourteenth-century reinvention and politicization of both new and traditional legal venues (in the Court of Chivalry, for instance, as described in this volume by Richard Firth Green); it drew the litigious gentry to courts both local and monarchical; it made opportunistic justices of the peace notorious in the shires and made the king's lawyers equally notorious in London. The narrator of *London Lickpenny* paints a vivid picture of exuberant legal barter which merges London's courts (the King's Bench, Rolls, Chancery, and Westminster) with London's marketplaces. From this lively legal trade he is excluded for want of money, and his hood—a symbol of his status and self determination—is stolen into the bargain. Despite its satire, *London Lickpenny* teems with a covert enjoyment of the law-peddling, food-stuffing, cloth-trading, goods-fencing marketplaces to which the narrator craves entrance. The Robin Hood ballads take a different line of attack, however, when they target the law's profitable pleasures as intrinsically deficient. They make visible the poverty of the desires that drive those systems, their pinched and morbid pleasures in harnessing law to accumulation, friendship to scheming, delight to profit, and leadership to arrogance. Robin's enemies enter the *Gest* exulting in their social power; they emerge from it superlatively *mean*—mean-spirited, trivial, fearful, and avid, qualities opposed to the brawling excess that animates the economy of the greenwood.

The *Gest* assays the power and pleasures of local alliances most devastatingly when Sir Richard confronts his creditors in the abbey.[11] Richard is met at the abbey door by a porter who admires his horse with such ill-concealed avidity that the knight sensibly refuses to have it stabled. The porter informs him that the abbot is feasting "and so is many a gentyll man, / For the love of the [thee]" (395–96), a comment that suggests how legal and/or economic predation might be troped as a kind of love—a troping that, in turn, simultaneously mocks Richard's helplessness to resist his creditors' desires and hints at the pleasurability of their exercise of this power. And when Richard enters the abbey, he enters not a spare refectory, as might be expected, but that conventional scene of aristocratic plenitude, a baronial feasting hall, which allies the lords of the church with the nobility: "Lordes were to mete isette / In that abbotes hall" (405–6).

The abbot soon reveals, however, that it is not largesse but cupidity that actuates his seigneurial display. The abbot has arrayed against the knight a collusion of church, law, local government, and nobility for all of their collective profit and enjoyment: we are told that the "fyrst word the abbot spake [was] / 'Hast thou brought my pay?'" (411–12). Answered in the negative, the abbot turns to the chief justice, whom he has expensively retained to ensure the legality of his seizure of the knight's property, saying, "Sir justyce, drynke to

---

[11] Judgments on the profits and pleasures of conspiracy among Robin Hood's enemies are everywhere in the ballads. For a brief listing, see the beginning of this section.

me" (416). Ten lines later we discover that the sheriff is in on this plot as well. We soon find out, moreover, that the abbot has actually usurped a power reserved to the king alone by retaining the justice "both with cloth and fee" (426). According to Stephen Knight and Thomas Ohlgren, "the practice of giving and receiving robes for such purposes was considered a conspiracy in the legal code of King Edward I (1305–6); in another statute of Edward III, dated 1346, justices were required to swear that they would accept robes and fees only from the king."[12] By including this detail, the ballad not only shows its understanding of the legal meaning of conspiracy but also underlines the abbot's considerable power and resources in buying off a chief justice, as well as the extent to which the king's power is being appropriated at the local level.[13]

In what follows, the knight tests the solidarity of the conspiracy by pleading separately with the abbot, sheriff, and justice. Here again, the language of love and affection infiltrates the network of monetary relations: "Now, good syr justice, be my frende, / And fende me of my fone!" (423–24). The sheriff is also asked for friendship, but the plea to the abbot himself is the most earnest of all:

> Now, good syr abbot, be my frende,
> For thy curteysé,
> And holde my londes in thy honde
> Tyll I have made the gree!
> And I wyll be thy true servaunte,
> And trewely serve the,
> Tyl ye have foure hondred pounde
> Of money good and free.
> (429–36)

Here the knight is not simply pledging his land; he is willing to mortgage himself in a transaction that for all its language of courtesy and truth speaks more to the contingencies of contract than to old-style feudalism.[14] The knight's abasement here only intensifies the pathos of his attempt to imbue a monetary relationship with love and trust: the abbot is to hold the knight's

---

[12] Knight and Ohlgren, *Robin Hood and Other Outlaw Tales*, 156 n. 426.

[13] The actual retaining of justices was more prevalent in the first half of the fourteenth century than it was subsequently, when monarchical and parliamentary legislation forced such alliances to take subtler forms; Edward III's 1346 ordinance itself bespeaks its acknowledgment as a problem and is one of several attempts to control it. See J. R. Maddicott, "Law and Lordship: Royal Justices as Retainers in Thirteenth- and Fourteenth-Century England," *Past and Present Supplement* 4 (1978).

[14] Green has read Robin Hood and the knight as nostalgic throwbacks to older systems both of feudalism and folk law (*Crisis*, 165–205). These readings correctly identify an undertone of nostalgia (i.e., the archaism implicit in a flight from society to a realm of more "natural" temporality), but I wish also to emphasize the outlaws' pragmatic, flexibly up-to-date strategies: they work with and within current systems and are as quick to seize a contractual advantage (as the knight does here) as they are to mimic more thoroughgoing conservatisms.

land in his hand, not just to wield power over it but to protect it as a friend. The failure of this plea for friendship emerges in the knight's bitter conclusion that "it is good to assay a frende / Or that a man have need" (447–48). Notably, what the knight proposes is less a return to old-style feudalism than an entrance into what the abbot has already formed, a circulation of mutual service, friendship, and enrichment. But he falters before the abbot's inhospitable dive to the bottom line. Whatever pleasurable conspiracies are forming in the provinces, the knight is going to be left out of them. He will be their slave rather than their servant. When he is rejected, however, he is quick to show his own teeth, threatening to make the abbot's seizure of land a prize not worth the venture. Having tested the conspiracy to reveal its steely heart, the knight declares that he will never make "abbot, justice, ne frere" (475) his heirs—simultaneously asserting the complex of legalism and intimacy implicit in the relationship they are usurping, even as he bars them from it—and produces the money that Robin Hood has lent him. The frustrated abbot immediately turns on the justice and demands the return of his retaining fee, which the justice flatly refuses. The knight, disgusted, leaves them to their bickering.

That the ballad passes not only a legal but also an affective judgment on the gratifications of such conspiracies at once links it to, but also crucially distinguishes it from, other late medieval discourses in which love, politics, and legal corruption are linked together to do the social work of those in power. The technical word for bribery in the fourteenth and fifteenth centuries was *embracery*. According to the *Oxford English Dictionary*, Edward III's statute 38, st. 11, cap 12 provided penalties for "les embraceours demesner ou procurer tielx enquestes" (bribers who instigate or procure such (fraudulent) inquests); *embracery* could also refer to the process of illicitly influencing a jury. But the word contained erotic connotations as well, producing a complex of meanings in which love, association, crime, and money were merged in fascinating and condemnatory ways. David Wallace, writing on the pleasures, profits, and paranoias surrounding associational forms in late medieval London, has shown, for example, that the *Cook's Tale* delegitimizes associations of masterless men by linking them with prostitution, a connection made by fourteenth-century letter-books as well.[15]

In the fifteenth century, however, "association" did not need the language of illicit sexuality to make it dangerous. Historically, it had worked as a double-edged sword, especially in the wake of the Rising of 1381, when the problem of dividing "good" from "bad" forms of association became a matter largely of where the divider stood. Some forms of association were basic; they were the glue that held society together, and the means by which truth and loyalty could be constructed and collectively performed. Oaths of obedience

---

[15] David Wallace, *Chaucerian Polity: Absolutist Lineages and Associational Forms in England and Italy* (Stanford: Stanford University Press, 1997), 170.

and of truthfulness were fundamental not only to political structure but also to law, which had traditionally been based on customs of pledging and oath-taking. But as Alan Harding points out, "communal oaths of obedience to established authority had always been in danger of becoming oaths of communal solidarity against the authorities,"[16] and, in fact, "association" became an accusation, as early as the late thirteenth century, when it first appeared directed not against the lower classes but against the lords.[17] Late in the fourteenth and into the fifteenth century, however, it was most often being used by the gentry against those lower than themselves. In the aftermath of the Rising, this strategy for condemning and controlling the political, legal, and social power of the commons acquired even more virulence and energy.[18]

These changes in the rhetoric of association were partly due to changes in the demographics of legal participation over this time. Throughout the fourteenth and fifteenth centuries, not everyone was eager to take advantage of the evolving and newly documentary court system, either by using it or by serving within it, and this was the case at just about every social level, from the village (where there are numerous records in court rolls of refusal of office) to London bureaucracies.[19] To a large extent the legal system depended on voluntarism for local administration, which laid it open to manipulation by the social groups best served by participation. Thus, even more insidious than the law's adaptation as a weapon of individual entrepreneurship was its acculturation to the class interests of its most immediate administrators: the regional country gentry who staffed its juries and became the notorious late-fourteenth-century justices of the peace. Harding shows how "as justices rather than simple peace-keepers, the country gentry became the moral arbiters of society, enforcing their values in the courts," both by targeting the people who most plagued them (extortionate clergy or royal officials, for instance) and by determining the language of indictment.[20] Troubled by post-plague labor shortages, the gentry—the commons in parliament, and the landlords at home—empowered justices of the peace to enforce the punitive labor legislation, which attempted wholesale and draconian control of all those considered socially inferior. Particularly resented was the Ordinance and the Statute of Laborers, which not only fixed wages at pre-plague levels

---

[16] Alan Harding, "The Revolt against the Justices," in *The English Rising of 1381*, ed. R. H. Hilton and T. H. Aston (Cambridge: Cambridge University Press, 1984), 190.

[17] Harding, "Revolt against the Justices," 188.

[18] When activated by the problem of the Rising, the evolving concept of conspiracy was mobilized to construct terrifying (to the landed classes) visions of organized, purposive social reorganization from below. Harding describes how "allegations of secret councils in the woods were widespread. At Scarborough, the rioters were said to have bound themselves 'with one assent' by oaths as well as liveries (like the chief justice's 'robe and fee') to support one another's quarrels, and to have forced people to swear loyalty to them and to the commons of all England." Ibid., 192.

[19] For a useful discussion of the refusal of office in the context of village officialdom, see Olson, *Chronicle of All That Happens*, 103–31.

[20] Harding, "Revolt against the Justices," 165–93.

but also legalized the practice of impressing into service any able-bodied person not immediately occupied on another lord's business. Harding stresses that labor laws could be effectively administered only by local justices who had an intimate knowledge of the inhabitants of their regions: "Only truly local justices could regulate local society in this detail." Throughout the late fourteenth and fifteenth centuries, the gentry were in effect, able to use the law to reorganize society and erect new class barriers between themselves and the common people.[21]

The 1381 rebels resisted this development, and the fifteenth-century Robin Hood ballads do so as well—but differently. There is much evidence that the 1381 rebels appropriated and redirected against their social superiors the languages of licit organization (obedience to oaths, loyalty to masters) and illicit conspiracy.[22] Their ability to do this was aided not only by the difficulty of controlling persecutory discourse but also by the longevity of cultural memory. The language of illicit association had once been used against the powerful; it could still be used against them. One incident in the Rising shows especially vividly how the rebels might throw back at their persecutors accusations of illicit association, and in this respect the incident contrasts usefully with the *Gest*. Both Walsingham and the chronicler of Bury St. Edmunds describe a vicious incident staged at Bury during the Rising, their accounts demonstrate not only their own judgments against the apparent barbarity of the rebels, but also, more surprisingly, the rebels' social acumen. In the Bury chronicler's account, the rebels decapitate the prior of the abbey and his powerful associate John Cavendish, the chief justice of King's Bench, whom they have found hiding in a nearby village. Before exhibiting the heads over the stocks—an action that combines idioms of the civic shaming of felons (displayed in the stocks) and the royal punishment for traitors (heads impaled on stakes)—they place the heads on spears and stage a grisly drama of corrupt association for the edification of the populace: "They put the head of the prior to the justice's head, now to his ear as though seeking advice, now to his mouth as though showing friendship, wishing in this way to make a mockery of their friendship and counsel which was between them during their lives."[23]

---

[21] Ibid., 182. Steven Justice notes how, for precisely this reason, the 1381 rebels targeted for violent harassment "the gentry and prosperous burgesses who served as sheriffs and who chose and sometimes served as shire knights, the jurors, and the men of law" (*Writing and Rebellion: England in 1381* [Berkeley: University of California Press, 1994], 58).

[22] For more extensive discussion of this kind of audacious redeployment, see Green's discussion of the rebels' parodic and carnivalesque seizure of the oppressive symbologies of their persecutors (*Crisis*, 198–205). Steven Justice argues for a kind of "assertive literacy" (*Writing and Rebellion*, 24) on the part of the rebels which also bears out this pattern; see also his discussion of John Ball as a willful but extremely canny reader of *Piers Plowman* (102–39).

[23] "Capitibus igitur illudentes, caput prioris applicuerunt ad caput justitiarii, nunc ad auriculam, quasi consilium postulando, nunc ad os ejus, quasi amicitias ostendendo, volentes pro hoc eis improperare de amicitias et consiliis quæ inter se invicem vita comite habuerunt" (*Memorials of St. Edmund's Abbey*, vol. 3, ed. Thomas Arnold, Rolls Series no. 96 [New York: Kraus Reprint, 1965–67], 128). Translation is from Powell, *Kingship*, 42.

Walsingham's account of this incident makes the illicitness of the heads' friendship even racier: their heads are placed "next to each other with the greatest disrespect as if they were whispering to each other or exchanging kisses."[24] In addition to dramatizing the rebels' anger at the corruptibility of legal officials, this scene also blurs the boundaries between conciliar and affectionate bonds. It shows a keen awareness that the law is a network of alliances contiguous with other powerful networks within and between church and state, working for the advantage as well as for the mutual society, help, and comfort that one ought to have of the other. This gruesome puppet show, in other words, opens up the underworld of estate theory, holding up a dark mirror to the web of mutual exchanges that hold society together. And it is here that the rebels appropriate and redirect the heinous association of love, council, and conspiracy.

The *Gest* follows a different strategy. Rather than shaming the elite for mixing law, pleasure, and profit, the *Gest* intimates that they are not affectionate enough for true profit. It exposes the cowardice implicit in self-interested associational formations, and it critiques the reliance on static systems of maintenance, whether lateral or hierarchical. And this critique, though less sadistic than that of the Bury rebels, is even more devastating. Robin Hood's enemies are shown to be feeble and fearful, interested in hoarding rather than in hazarding. They impoverish themselves by rejecting the endlessly self-productive and profitable free venture of friendship, such as the one that Sir Richard offers them. They are, finally, less honorable, because they risk less and, in grasping at surety, lose even what they have.

Robin Hood substitutes for such power-husbanding conspiracies social contests of a particularly masculine kind: the displays of strength between him and Little John; the combats between him and the potter, the sheriff, and the friar of St. Mary; and John's battles with the monk. These associations thrive on venture, danger, and dissent, and their participants, in the process of losing (which they often do), gain more than they ever hoped to win. Many critics and historians have noted the masculine associations of Robin's chief pastimes: hunting, poaching, and archery, the last a skill that every able-bodied man was supposed to practice in order to be ready to defend the realm.[25] But the ballads' performance of masculinity is also socially and generically multivalent—much more so than the knuckle-and-staves virility of the sixteenth-century Robin Hood plays—it draws inventively from courtesy literature, emerging market economies, yeoman fraternities, anti-fraternal writing,

---

[24] Walsingham, *Historia* 2:3, cited and translated in Green, *Crisis of Truth*, 204. Green places this incident in the context of other grisly exhibitions of public fury against the officials and documents of written law (198–205). For another useful account of this incident, see Powell, *Kingship*, 41–44.

[25] Barbara Hanawalt, "Men's Games, King's Deer: Poaching in Medieval England," *Journal of Medieval and Renaissance Studies* 18.2 (1988): 175–93; Dean A. Hoffman, "With the shot Y wyll / All Thy Lustes to Full-fyll: Archery as Symbol in the Early Ballads of Robin Hood," *Neuphilologishe Mitteilungen* 86 (1985): 494–505.

devotional tracts, and medieval romance.[26] Whether Robin is out-husbanding the sheriff, out-largessing the king, or teaching patient poverty to the friar by inducing him to join his men in a night of spartan discomfort, he continually parodies, in Judith Butler's sense, the appurtenances of masculinity in its different social guises.[27]

One of the most important guises is chivalric, the system of performed honor and reputation that justifies, finally, a knight's right to social authority and monetary reward by dramatizing the risks that he incurs. In his mid-fourteenth-century treatise *Livre de chevalerie*, Geoffroi de Charney castigates cowards (who act much like the authorities in the ballads):

> They are eager to grab whatever they can whenever they can, and are so miserly in spending that they will only shell out to maintain their bodies in comfort, at which the devils will rejoice. . . . If they are threatened by anyone, they fear greatly for their physical safety and dread the loss of the riches they have amassed in such a discreditable way. . . . And while the cowards have a great desire to live and a great fear of dying, it is quite the contrary for the men of worth who do not mind whether they live or die, provided that their life be good enough for them to die with honor. And this is evident in the strange and perilous adventures which they seek.[28]

Yet there is a difference between what a knight does when he seeks adventure in chivalric romance and what Robin Hood's men do in the forest. In the forest of the Robin Hood ballads, "maistery," or performed masculinity, is continually available but never permanently retained. If Robin wins the gold-headed silver arrow at the sheriff's archery contest, it is only as a prelude to the sheriff's nearly fatal shooting of Little John. Robin himself routinely loses his contests, not just to noble enemies such as the king, but also to John, to his own men, even to the potter from whom he has demanded a toll and by whom he is taught a painful lesson. The point of "maistery" is not that you win, or even how you play the game—many of Robin Hood's and Little John's games are vicious and bloody—but rather *that* you play the game, maintaining a continual exchange of jokes, disguises, services, and blows. Victory in these games grants only a temporary "maistery," entirely independent of traditionally conceived structures of associational or hierarchical social legitimacy. Masculine performance in the ballads, therefore, helps to unbind chivalric homosociality from its foundational underpinnings of custom, lineage, and land. The ballads do what the medieval Robin Hood never actually

---

[26] Knight, *Robin Hood: A Complete Study*; Richard Tardiff, "The 'Mistery' of Robin Hood: A New Social Context for the Texts," in *Words and Worlds: Studies in the Social Role of Verbal Culture*, ed. Stephen Knight and S. N. Mukherjee (Sydney: Sydney Association for Studies in Society and Culture, 1983), 130–45.

[27] Judith Butler, *Gender Trouble* (New York: Routledge, 1990), 112–40.

[28] Richard W. Kaeuper and Elspeth Kennedy, *The Book of Chivalry of Geoffroi de Charney: Text, Context, and Translation* (Philadelphia: University of Pennsylvania Press, 1996), 125–27.

does—steal from the rich to give to the poor—by making honorable masculinity available to any rank willing to undertake adventurous risks and keep oaths.

But masculine performance in the ballads does even more radical work than when it subjects stultified cultural systems to high-spirited "natural" energies. It is no accident that both *Robin Hood and the Potter* and *Robin Hood and the Monk* begin with two of the most lyrical invocations of the joys of nature in late medieval poetry:

> In somer, when the shawes be sheyne,
> And leves be large and long,
> Hit is full mery in feyre foreste
> To here the foulys song,
>
> To se the dere draw to the dale,
> And leve the hilles hee,
> And shadow hem in the leves grene,
> Under the grene wode tre.
> (*Robin Hood and the Monk*, 1–8)

Here, not just the delights but the sheltering shadows of the forest are crucial; the deer clearly metonymize the outlaws, whom we will soon see rising to greet the day and venturing forth to make the sheriff of Nottingham's life a living hell. The fragility of the deer (and Robin Hood's own vulnerability) finally do not matter; they stand for the resilience and fecundity of the greenwood as a whole.[29] How better to move an object that constructs itself as immovable than with a force which fantasizes itself as irresistible? Nadine Gordimer, in a postcolonial context, highlights the ways in which "natural" energies may accompany or buttress more overtly political forms of resistance: "In societies where domination by an outside power exists or has existed, the *occupation of the national personality* is resisted not by obvious means alone—political opposition and rebellion, religious fervor, cultural assertion—but also, perhaps, by the display of sexual energy as a force that has not been, cannot be, touched by alien authority: the life-force itself."[30] In this passage, the very desperation implicit in the attempt to render *some* space (in this case sexuality) immune to colonial infiltration ("has not been, cannot be") attests to the allure of the fantasy of disruptive, naturalized, performed masculinity. And this is precisely the fantasy that the Robin Hood ballads activate

---

[29] But just as nature is also a realm of unceasing contest, physical risk, and radical contingency, the outlaw's life in the greenwood will never be a peaceful utopian brotherhood. In this poem, the first thing Robin Hood and Little John do upon waking up is to start a quarrel over who won at shooting, and it is Robin Hood who cheats Little John, provokes him further by striking him and calling him a liar, and incites him to leave his service.

[30] Nadine Gordimer, "Zaabalawi: The Concealed Side," in *Writing and Being* (Cambridge: Harvard University Press, 1995), 53.

when they make a virtue of the peculiarly anti-foundational prowess of their outlaw heroes, an anti-foundationalism so profoundly naturalized *as* "life-force" that it succeeds in denaturalizing the power structures it opposes.

Robin Hood's iconoclastic "maistery" works by revealing the self-legitimizing constructedness of any authority but its own openly contingent one. By taking on any number of disguises, from forest lord to inept salesman, from king's servant to murderous renegade, from feudal despiser of capitalist economies to wage-buster and delighted profiteer, and from bowman to hart, Robin Hood and Little John simultaneously infect and parody the socially legitimated authorities of their enemies. *Robin Hood and the Potter*, for example, mischievously underlines the transgressive class-crossing nature of Robin's masculinity when Robin Hood in the disguise of a potter is invited to dinner at the sheriff's house, where he wins a postprandial archery contest:

> The screffes men thowt gret schame
> The potter the mastry wan;
> The screffe lowe and made god game,
> And seyde, "Potter, thow art a man.
> Thow art worthey to bere a bowe
> Yn what plas that thow goe."
> (209–14)

The sheriff's compliment reflects his surprise that a lowly and rather dimwitted craftsman could achieve a compensatory masculine skill and the worthiness to bear its symbol. But his ironic permission to the "potter" to bear a bow "In what plas that [he] go" is about to backfire. The ersatz potter tells the sheriff that in fact he doesn't need his accolade; he has a bow already, given to him by Robin Hood, with whom he often shoots in the woods. The sheriff's eyes light up with lust for the chase, and when the potter offers a personal introduction to Robin Hood himself, the sheriff swallows the bait and follows the potter into the forest. There, of course, the sheriff is surrounded, ambushed, robbed, and figuratively unmanned. Robin Hood sends him back home to his wife with the additional present of a white palfrey, effectively displacing the sheriff as lord and provider.

That the sheriff is unmanned by his very eagerness to assume the masculine role of lawful hunter and king's representative draws attention to these roles' contrivance. Robin Hood's social polymorphousness likewise invites suspicion of the naturalized social associations represented by the sheriff, and suggests further that these associations must always be reproved and re-proven, not through fear but through continuous, venturesome self-invention. Not even the king is exempted from the implications of this economy. When Robin Hood or Little John takes aim at the king as the ultimate guarantor of the abuses of his underlings, they enter on their most iconoclastic undertaking, venturing away from the traditional romance trope of chivalric nostalgia and into the contractual entrepreneurialism that marks all levels of fifteenth-century society.

Anxieties of Maintenance

The need to collect and control worthy retainers preoccupies both the local and the monarchical authorities whom Robin Hood confronts, and in this respect the figure of Little John is crucial to the ballads' critique of the collusions that bind local legal authorities to the monarch. While Robin Hood shadows, mimics, and beguiles the masters of the world, Little John shadows, mimics, and beguiles their contractually bound servants, testing in the process the desires that bind servants and masters together. Judicial power, in these ballads, becomes a two-way street rather than a profitable franchise granted conditionally by the king. Judicial power is also shown to be a risky venture in which the king's authority both extends itself through and depends on the activities of those who represent and serve the law that the king, too, represents and serves. Its intrinsic risk is occluded, however, by the assumption of shared self-interest between master and servant; it works in the same mutually back-scratching way as do the local conspiracies.

In addition, judicial power mobilizes a strange logic of institutional representation. A servant who represents the king to the people gains authority by subjecting his own needs and desires to it, emptying himself into an incarnation of his office whereby he becomes a vessel for institutional power and receives in turn the obligation to be its hands, determine its character, and become its local representation. Pierre Bourdieu discusses this mutually enabling exchange by which an official, a servant, becomes both co-optee and controller of the authority he represents:

> Group made man, he personifies a fictitious person, which he lifts out of the state of a simple aggregate of separate individuals, enabling them to act and speak, through him, "like a single person." Conversely, he receives the right to speak and act in the name of the group, to "take himself for" the group he incarnates, to identify with the function to which "he gives his body and soul," thus giving a biological body to a constituted body. Status est magistratus; "l'Etat, c'est moi." Or, what amounts to the same thing, the world is my representation.[31]

Here the process of representing, say, the king's law, obliges an official to constitute it, embody it, shape it from a mass of statutes and precedents to an agency capable of work in the world. But the "fictitious person" that the official must generate in order to do this approximates past representations of that law and authority with an inevitable imprecision it can never acknowl-

---

[31] Bourdieu, *Language and Symbolic Power*, 105.

edge; the institution, in other words, changes imperceptibly and inevitably with each new representation. And further, the world is never *only* one official's representation, particularly when there are other officials and a directing head of the institution continually generating competing ones. There is a crucial elision, moreover, between the office and the person incarnating it, particularly when he has endowed it with his own agency, and consequently there is always a space where the subjective can bleed into the official and where the person of the servant or representative (supposedly abnegated) can come clandestinely to inhabit the law he represents. And significantly, these spaces for personal power within the law keep the system running by gratifying participation within it. Such spaces must be made to seem exceptional rather than structural, however, and must be displaced whenever they become visible. This is why impartiality—a performed submission to the law as a collective institution—is promised not only by the sheriff but also by the king.

Bourdieu's schema also underscores an institution's constant need for representation. Without a continual stream of servants willing to focus and embody it, the institution would disintegrate into an "aggregate of separate persons" with a corresponding reduction in authority and social persuasiveness: it would no longer seem larger than individuals; it would no longer be able to constitute itself as a tradition continuous through time and founded on the authority of antiquity; and it would no longer work to differentiate the status of those within it from those without. Ultimately, recruiting representatives/representers is crucial not only to the authority of institutions but also to their survival.

In the ballads, Little John's subversive services make three things clear. First, they show how eager the masters of legal institutions (themselves empowered representatives) are to have servants to represent them locally. The law is shown to be structurally involved in amassing systems of maintenance, recruiting servants, and distributing pardons, privy seals, and livery at the slightest signs of initiative or gratification. Second, they show how easily institutional desires can be manipulated by an enterprising servant whose subversive intentions are obscured by the impersonalizing fictions of the logic of representation. Third, they show how a servant, by manipulating those desires, can tease apart the logic of representation which imbricates the agendas of king and local official by affiliating both to an institution larger than themselves. A prototypical bad servant, Little John uses his position to profiteer happily and unrepentantly because he refuses to accept the representational logic that makes servants local incarnations of their master's authority.

Yet Little John does not simply accentuate the weaknesses of the chains of representation linking centralizing legal institutions with social peripheries; he also proposes an alternative, an economy not of self-aggrandizing institutions but of obstreperous individuals. This alternative emerges in his first exchange with Robin Hood in *Robin Hood and the Monk*. Robin Hood is determined to go into Nottingham to hear a mass and disregards Much's anxious advice to take twelve well-armed outlaws with him. Instead he selects John alone as his special servant:

"Of all my mery men," seid Robyn,
"Be my feith I wil non have,
But Litull John shall beyre my bow,
Til that me list to drawe."
"Thou shall beyre thin own," seide Litull Jon,
"Maister, and I wyl bere myne,
And we well shete a peny," seid Litull Jon,
"Under the grene wode lyne."
(35–42)

Here John refuses to be the bearer of Robin's regalia, pointing out that he has a bow of his own to carry, and that if Robin will just carry his, they can have a wager and see who can win more at shooting. Robin immediately ups the ante by betting three pennies for every one that John shoots for, reclaiming at least a financial mastery. But in the resulting contest John wins "of his maister / Five shillings to hose and shone" (49–50), a staggering profit that not only demonstrates that Robin was having a very bad shooting day but also subverts the logic of livery and maintenance: John is not given "hose and shoon" in exchange for subordinating his skills and services to his master's desire; he keeps those skills for himself and wins enough from his master in equal contest to pay for his own upkeep. Robin then proves himself a sore loser by calling John a liar and striking him. At this, the self-reliant servant gets angry, draws his sword, and leaves Robin's service with a threat:

"Were thou not my maister," seid Litull John,
"Thou shuldis by hit ful sore;
Get the a man wher thou wille
For thou getis me no more."
(59–62)

The ballad relates the consequences of Robin's abuse of power: he is captured in Nottingham and eventually rescued only by John himself, whose faithfulness to past loyalties ("He was my maister" [199]) is more exemplary than most others' to present ones. The rest of the ballad shows how John cannily works the role of authoritative representative to his own ends by pretending to fulfill the desires of king and sheriff. With Much he kills the monk who was instrumental in Robin's capture and steals the letters from the sheriff to the king telling of the capture. He then carries the letters to the king in the monk's place. The king welcomes him and, exuberant at Robin Hood's capture, rewards Little John and Much with £20, makes them yeomen of the crown, and gives John the royal privy seal to take to the sheriff (a "grith"

[341], or security, that protects the bearer as well as its recipient). John, thus made the king's representative, brings the seal to the sheriff, who asks him about the monk. John tempts the sheriff's ambitions when he informs him that the king was so happy to get the news of Robin Hood's capture that he made the monk abbot of Westminster. The sheriff is overjoyed, gives John his best wine, and beds him down in his own house. John gets up in the night and goes down to the jail, where he terrifies the jailer with news of Robin's escape. The moment the jailer comes out, John pins him to the wall with his sword, steals his keys to adopt another servant's disguise ("'Now wil I be jayler,' seid Little John," [279]), and breaks Robin out. He does not hesitate to rub Robin's face in the lesson about the invidious nature of leadership John has been trying to teach him:

> "I have done the a gode turne for an ill,
> Quit me whan thou may. . . .
> I have brought the under the grene-wode lyne;
> Fare wel, and have gode day."
> (305–6, 309–10)

John, pointedly, does not seek a reward for loyalty from Robin. He has not forgotten that he has left Robin's service, and he is prepared to leave again—immediately. Robin's response shows that he is trying, however unsuccessfully, to absorb John's lesson:

> "Nay, be my trouth," seid Robyn
> "So shall hit never be;
> I make the maister," seid Robyn
> "Of alle my men and me."
> (311–14)

This willingness to give up command, however laudable, is not quite what John is after. John's critique of mastery and representation requires not the reversal of roles within the system but its complete abolishment:

> "Nay, be my trouth," seid Litull John,
> "So shalle hit never be;
> But let me be a felow," seid Litull John.
> "No noder kepe I be."
> (315–18)

By refusing mastery and choosing fellowship—the ever-negotiated bonds between equals over the traditional bonds of affiliation and representation between master and servant—John lifts both himself and Robin Hood out of the system he has shown to be so devastatingly permeable and self-serving. The intensity of his criticism is accentuated twice more in the ballad: first, in its depicting the outlaws' immediate return to the plenitude of the green-wood, where we leave them feasting; and second, in its lingering over the fates of the beguiled sheriff and king.

These scenes reveal the dark side of the system of representative affiliation. Like the unraveled provincial conspiracies, its motivations emerge most clearly when it is thwarted. But the increased intimacy implicit in the systemic logic of institutional representation makes its devolution even more nightmarish. The provincial conspiracies were fantasies of economic control, and their punishment is the exposure of their impoverishment. The logic of representation between master and retainer demands the death (or at least abnegation) of the person to serve the institution, the emergence of personal shortcoming in a representative therefore risks actual death as punishment. The sheriff wakes to find Robin gone and sends out a desperate promise of reward for anyone who turns him in again—he mobilizes, that is, the same power system of magisterial endowment that had failed Robin. But the chain of command has been eroded by John at every level. The sheriff realizes that his own relationship with the king has been irretrievably damaged.

> "For I dar never," seid the scheref,
> "Cum before oure kyng;
> For if I do, I wot serten
> For sothe he wil me heng."
> (295–98)

The sheriff's misgivings would have been well founded had not the king also been befuddled. The king's musings on his own helplessness to punish the sheriff are fascinating:

> "Litul John has begyled us both,
> And that full wel I se;
> Or ellis the schereff of Notyngham
> Hye hongut shulde he be."
> (335–38)

Filled with amazement at how thoroughly he has been taken in, the king spends two stanzas marveling at his own blindness. This realization shatters the king's presuppositions about his superiority and mocks the logic of hierarchical representation itself, as if the smaller faults of the king's servants have been multiplied in him. The sheriff simply lost the prisoner, but it was the king who paid the outlaw and invested him with his own authority:

> "I made hem yemen of the crowne,
> And gaf hem fee with my hond;
> I gave hem grith," seid oure kyng,

"Thorowout all mery Inglond."
"I gaf theym grith," then seid oure kyng:
"I say, so mot I the,
For sothe soch a yeman as he is one
In all Inglond ar not thre."
(339–46)

There is probably more than a shade of relief in that last couplet, but Little John emerges in the king's speech as an exemplary yeoman, someone to be admired as well as feared. The next stanza intensifies this feeling of admiration into a kind of envy:

"He is trew to his maister," seid oure kyng;
"I sey, be swete Seynt John,
He lovys better Robyn Hode
Then he dose us ychon."
(347–50)

Here, Little John is linked interestingly to Saint John, his namesake, traditionally the disciple whom Christ loved and who loved him the most in return. Loyalty and troth thus become not only personalized but also sanctified in a circuit of affection from which the king feels excluded. Before relegating the matter to the limbo of the diplomatically unmentionable, the king highlights the obligation with which such personal loyalty enjoins its recipient, reversing the status of master as giver and servant as gifted and inverting the top-down solicitation of gratitude as social control:

"Robyn Hode is ever bond to hym,
Bothe in strete and stalle;
Speke no more of this mater," seid oure kyng,
"But John has bygyled us alle."
(351–54)

John has also dramatized what he preached for king, sheriff, and Robin alike: the social power implicit in an individual who knowingly and cannily refuses the costly bargains offered by the economy of master and retainer, exploiting the need for representation of institutions. He emerges from the end of the ballad as absolutely preeminent.

The critique of power implicit in John's lesson in *Robin Hood and the Monk* thus goes even beyond the social agendas of the 1381 rebels, who reportedly wished to retain the king but equalize the ranks of everyone under him. And it is not a peaceful, easy, or utopian critique. No one is innocent who takes the part of master or servant, whether Robin Hood, the sheriff, or the king. John's judgment of the logic of representation dictates that masters and servants be bound in mutual responsibility for the abuses of power they enact. This harsh recognition perhaps explains, though it does not render less troubling, John's roadside slaughter of both of the sheriff's messengers, the monk and his young servant. Instead of relying on representation, John's lesson tries to articulate a system of social relations based not on bondage but on trust without bondage, on personal affection rather than institutional representation, drawing its principles from an interiority based on a history of personal interaction—a fellowship. And while his critique may be utopian in this trajectory, it is unflinchingly direct in its social implications. John "beguiles us all" because he knows and can play on the desires and fears that animate the links between center and periphery, legal institution and representative, master and servant. When pushed too far, however, he is also prepared to dispense with the whole system.[32]

In the *Gest*, John plays a similar game but with a less radical trajectory. He is again invited into the sheriff's service and seduces his cook with promises of a better service out in the forest. In other words, he upsets the sheriff's maintenance system by proposing a competing one but does not try to overset the institution of maintenance itself. Yet even this minor threat has unnerving implications: John's offer to the cook at the beginning of the *Gest* is a dress rehearsal for Robin Hood's offer to the king himself at the ballad's end. In Fitt 7, the king and the outlaw actually reverse roles in an episode that illustrates, with some irony, how much kings can learn from outlaws.

The role reversal begins when the sheriff of Nottingham comes in person to warn the king that the outlaw has grown beyond his power to control. Robin Hood has set up his own alternate seigneury with resounding success:

"He wyll avowe that he hath done,
To mayntene the outlawes stronge;
He wyll be lorde, and set you at nought,
In all the northe londe."
(1293–96)

---

[32] At the end of a very useful essay on the dramatic Robin Hood of the Renaissance plays, Peter Stallybrass codifies a range of ways in which orthodoxy can be critiqued by (or deploy) heterodoxy and vice versa: (1) orthodoxy can produce heterodoxy as a form of licensed misrule; (2) it can exclude and demonize it; (3) heterodoxy can negotiate, reveal, fracture, or contest the workings of orthodoxy or, more profoundly, its principles; and (4) most radically, heterodoxy can "interrogate the boundaries between Doxa and Opinion" and become the means for questioning deep-laid assumptions about the structures of everyday life. I would argue that most of the Robin Hood ballads work within the space of the last two uses, but that *Robin Hood and the Monk* is the most radical, given the force of the king's and Robin Hood's assumptions about leadership and their reluctance or inability to learn what John is trying to demonstrate. See Peter Stallybrass, " 'Drunk with the Cup of Liberty': Robin Hood, the Carnivalesque, and the Rhetoric of Violence in Early Modern England," in *The Violence of Representation: Literature and the History of Violence*, ed. Nancy Armstrong and Leonard Tennenhouse (New York: Routledge, 1989), 45–74, esp. 70.

In response to this terrifying vision (which, in the fifteenth century, barons like the Percys and the Nevilles—to say nothing of the house of York—came close to realizing), the king, frustrated beyond endurance by the inability of his legal representatives to capture the outlaw, comes to Nottingham himself. He is appalled at the scope of Robin Hood's poaching on his hunting rights: there are almost no royal stags left. After six months of hunting the outlaw, the king is no closer to his quarry. It takes the advice of one of his foresters to alter his tactics; with Robin-like acumen, the forester urges him to dress up as a monk, Robin's favorite victim. By disguising himself the king already is beginning to think like the outlaw and proves amazingly effective by doing so. He has barely gone a mile into the forest when, with comic punctuality, Robin Hood turns up to administer his usual truth test: if a victim declares honestly how much money he is carrying, he will usually get at least half of it back (unless he has very little, in which case it will be doubled or tripled). The king passes the test and is treated to an evening of royal entertainment, which fills him with envy: "His men are more at his byddynge / Then my men be at myn"(1563–64). To emphasize the point, the king is served with his own poached venison and enjoys a contest demonstrating the outlaws' shooting prowess. Here on his home ground Robin Hood misses his mark and submits himself to the king/monk's admonitory buffet, which is delivered with such force that he looks at his "guest" with new interest, as a lord eyeing a potential servitor. It is at this point that the king is recognized; all the outlaws kneel down and ask his pardon and are reincorporated back into the king's rule. Yet even after this, the king persists in playing the part of Robin's servant, begging and acquiring suits of green livery—a clear attempt to appropriate by affiliation the outlaw's mana. This tactic backfires the following day when they return to Nottingham in a sea of green mantles and terrified onlookers believe that Robin Hood has killed the king.

The king has the last laugh, however. Like *Robin Hood and the Monk*, the *Gest* naturalizes the power of Robin Hood's alternate society by linking it indissolubly to the forest. Once Robin Hood returns to serve the king, he suffers the same anxieties of maintenance that beset his former oppressor, seeing his own followers slip away until "by than the yere was all agone / He had no man but twayne" (1737–38). Recidivism is inevitable. His triumphant return to Yorkshire (under the cover of a pilgrimage to a Barnesdale chapel of Mary Magdalene) is as overt a paean to unregenerate masculine mastery as Peter Pan's crowing, and even more effective:

Robyn slewe a full grete harte,
His horne than gan he blow,
That all the outlawes of that forest
That horne coud they know.
(1785–88)

And, magically, the men appear:

> And gadred them togyder,
> In a lytell throwe;
> Seven score of wyght yonge men
> Came redy on a rowe
> And fayre dyde of theyr hodes,
> And set them on theyre kne:
> "Welcome," they sayd, "our mayster,
> Under this grene wode tre."
> (1789–96)

We should be grateful that kings do not have it so easy.

Both *Robin Hood and the Monk* and the *Gest*, then, implicate in their critiques the king as the ruler of the realm and the highest representative of the law. They show him to be motivated by fears—of competition, abandonment, disorder, and impotence—similar to those that drive his provincial representatives, but because they strike at his status as representative of a higher institution, the stakes are significantly greater. They differ in the extent of their critique: the *Gest* plays on the fears of uncontrollable social competition and is structured by Robin's investigation of authoritative figures from local to monarchical all the way up the social ladder; *Robin Hood and the Monk* levels a more fundamental critique of the assumptions underlying institutions of representation and maintenance. The ballads also differ on their proposals for the bandits' social alternatives: the *Gest* naturalizes Robin Hood's leadership by associating it with a performative masculinity that gains strength from its rebellious iconoclasm and distance from society; *Robin Hood and the Monk* tries to imagine a society formed by the constant play of obligation between powerful individuals who are bonded by affections that are all the stronger and more binding for being unuttered and unwitnessed, outside the usual economies of oath and self-interest that bind servant to master. Both ballads agree, however, that yeomen and commoners can prove themselves at least as honorable and principled as sheriffs and kings, and they underline this lesson in a way that reveals an unprecedented field of play for their social agency.

In this monarchical critique, these ballads set local self-determination against centralized authority in one final and quite concrete way. They situate Robin Hood's threat as imaginatively "northern": "He wyll be lorde, and set you at nought, / In all the northe londe." Nottingham is the gateway to the north, and the apparently older location of Robin's base of operations is Barnesdale in south Yorkshire. By making Robin Hood a northerner, the ballads put into play the fourteenth-and fifteenth-century stereotypes that southerners attached to the north. These stereotypes alienated the north, de-differentiated its many varied counties, amalgamated their diverse regional histories, and fantasized it as lawless, violent, and backward, making it a medieval equivalent of the American Wild West, a place of projected nostalgia and danger. This imagining of the north actually makes sense of the divergent enticements Robin Hood ballads could offer for different audiences throughout England: "southerners" could both indulge in and displace the appeals of lawlessness or their nostalgia for a simpler past; provincials and northerners could reinforce their sense of regional autonomy and resistance to monarchical bureaucracy. All of these are, of course, imagined constructions; that the north was nothing of the sort is persuasively argued by A. J. Pollard for the fifteenth century.[33] Frank Musgrove also cautions against amalgamating the different counties he covers in his study on the north, even as imputes to them a larger than regional cultural force.[34]

But the ballads' northerly affiliation evokes particularly fraught tensions between royal and local administration of the law, especially during the political decentralizations of the fifteenth century, when the north appeared to be slipping from monarchical control. Monarchical influence, already geographically attenuated in Yorkshire, was stretched even thinner after the episodic reconsolidations of Henry IV, and Henry V. Under Henry VI, monarchical influence was almost superseded by the local pull of powerful baronial families. Of course, many outriding provinces more than a day's journey from London forged distinctive regional identities (and the north itself comprises very different regions). Nevertheless, the fifteenth-century growth of northern power was extraordinary; the north became a region largely independent of and rivaling the south. South Yorkshire in particular (whose towns the early ballads name) achieved a cultural and political preeminence that during the mid-fifteenth century (the presumed date of the *Gest*)[35] actually succeeded in overshadowing London and the south. Therefore, it seems arguable to link this regional renaissance to the *Gest*'s imaginative landscape as it obliges a monarch (even a Yorkist one, if Stephen Knight is correct, and the Edward of the *Gest* is Edward IV) to journey to the northern peripheries of his realm to meet a poacher whose authority ends by exceeding his own.[36]

It is here, I believe, that the Robin Hood written ballads speak to their fifteenth-century audiences as eloquently as to their fourteenth-century ones. The circulation of mid-century manuscripts attests to their currency, despite the fact that literary works and chronicles written as early as the late fourteenth century refer to Robin Hood stories. The mid-to late fifteenth century was a time of particularly strong retrenchment of local authority in the

[33] See A. J. Pollard, "The Characteristics of the Fifteenth-Century North," in *Government, Religion, and Society in Northern England, 1000–1700* (Phoenix Mill: Sutton Publishing, 1997), 131–43.

[34] Frank Musgrove, *The North of England: A History from Roman Times to the Present* (Oxford: Basil Blackwell, 1990), 10–14.

[35] Knight, *Robin Hood: A Complete Study*, 44–97.

[36] Musgrove reads the Yorkist monarchy itself as reversing southern centrality—a version of northern colonialist domination over the south which led to a period of unparalleled cultural and political preeminence (*The North*, 158–70).

north, when slackening monarchical control allowed local authorities of different estates—the gentry, the clergy, and the barony—to build coalitions with one another, pass ordinances, and experiment with novel enforcement strategies such as fines. They augmented their affinities by distributing livery at home, and used their burgeoning local influence to gain leverage at the royal court. The early Robin Hood ballads highlight both the costs and the opportunities of such retrenchments. As they recount the successful exploits of the bandits, they reach several crucial conclusions about the way social and legal authority is evolving: first, that resistance is possible; second, that the networks are more permeable and self-conflicted than they appear; and third, that individual initiative even on the part of the "middling" folk can be very well rewarded.

It is this third conclusion that links the bandits most interestingly to the opportunistic officials whom they are contesting. It also provides for fifteenth-century audiences points of identification with the outlaws, ranging from commons through the yeomanry to clergy, to the gentry themselves. Finally, it is the source of the major controversies that have marked the ballads' critical history as scholars strive to place Robin Hood firmly at some social level: to make him either a revolutionary peasant hero or a pleasantly distanced fantasy for the gentry.[37] I am less concerned with pinning Robin Hood down than commenting on the consequences of his slipperiness—the creation of a literary tradition that accommodates a range of responses: calls for legal and social reform, entertainment, carnivalesque and institutionally supportive violence (as when parish groups raised money for church repair by staging Robin Hood fight plays in the sixteenth century), and genuinely revolutionary social interrogation. The socially invasive mimicry that is such an important resistance strategy for the outlaws—their capacity both to parody and to pronounce authoritatively upon kingship, gamesmanship, chivalry, patient poverty, and representative service—would seem to open up the ballads to a plurality of audiences. It also presages both the subsequent gentrification of their hero in the Renaissance plays and the genuinely radical gender politics of Peacock's eighteenth-century *Maid Marian*. The late medieval Robin Hood ballads delight in fantasies of self-sufficiency without isolation, homosociality without predation, and continuance without institutional ossifi-

[37] The great debate on this topic raged between Hilton, Keen, and Holt in the pages of *Past and Present* from the late 1950s through the 1960s. It turned on the elusive meaning of the term "yeoman" in the ballads and ranged over possible date of origin, milieu, and audiences of the ballads' performances. Hilton argued for a peasant audience, as did Maurice Keen in *The Outlaws of Medieval Legend* (London: Routledge, 1961), while Holt argued for an audience among gentry household functionaries. See Rodney Hilton, "The Origins of Robin Hood," *Past and Present* 16 (1958): 30–44; J. C. Holt, "The Origins and Audience of the Ballads of Robin Hood," *Past and Present* 18 (1960): 89–110; Maurice Keen, "Robin Hood—Peasant or Gentleman?" *Past and Present* 19 (1961): 7–15; and J. C. Holt, "Robin Hood: Some Comments," *Past and Present* 19 (1961): 16–18. See also the later conclusions reached by Peter Coss, "Aspects of Cultural Diffusion in Medieval England: The Early Romances, Local Society, and Robin Hood," *Past and Present* 108 (1985): 35–79.

cation. And while the appeal of such a greenwood world has continued to invite nostalgic, mythic, realist, & ironic re-creation of all sorts, at least some of its ideological stakes first become visible within the shifting and embattled late medieval socio-legal landscape to which the ballads hold up a mocking mirror.

2 Land, Lepers, and the Law in *The Testament of Cresseid*

Jana Mathews

M**uch** of the fifteenth century was, for Scotland, a period of agricultural crisis and depression. Burgh records speak of the exhaustion of marginal lands and overworked soils, the exploding peasant population and lack of feudal tenures, the sporadic pestilence and famines incurred by flood, drought, and topographical pollution, and the legal conflict between two powerful and contrasting sets of interests: landowner and tenant, overlord and laborer.[1] It is upon this terrain of agrarian waste and socioeconomic ruin that Robert Henryson lays out his most controversial work. *The Testament of Cresseid* opens with a poetic representation of a medieval farmer's worst nightmare: early in the planting season, showers of hail and blasts of wind descend from the north, freezing the ground and destroying any immature seedlings planted there:

> Ane doolie [dismal] sessoun to ane cairfull dyte [poem]
> Suld correspond and be equiualent:
> Richt sa it wes quhen I began to wryte
> This tragedie; the wedder richt feruent,

I am grateful to Ralph Hanna, Sally Mapstone, Marjorie McIntosh, Elizabeth Robertson, James Simpson, and the editors of this collection for their helpful comments on this essay. I wish to thank Bruce Holsinger, under whom I have had the privilege to study, for his support and assistance in the writing process.

[1] The court registers of Dunfermline, the burgh that Henryson is believed to have lived in for most of his life, contain numerous accounts of agricultural disasters. See Ebenezer Henderson, *The Annals of Dunfermline and Vicinity, 1069–1878* (Glasgow: John Tweed, 1929), 150–82. See also Sir J. D. Marwick, ed., *Extracts from the Records of the Burgh of Edinburgh, 1403–1528* (Edinburgh, 1833), 71–72.

Quhen Aries, in middis of the Lent,
Schouris of haill [gart (began)] fra the north discend,
That scantlie [hardly] fra the cauld I micht defend.
ʒit neuertheles within myne oratur [oratory]
I stude, quhen Titan had his bemis bricht
Withdrawin doun and sylit [concealed] vnder cure [cover],
And fair Venus, the bewtie of the nicht,
Vprais and set vnto the west full richt
Hir goldin face, in oppositioun
Of God Phebus, direct discending doun.

Throw out the glas hir bemis [beams] brast [burst] sa fair
That I micht se on euerie syde me by;
The northin wind had purifyit the air
And sched the mistie cloudis fra the sky;
The froist freisit, the blastis bitterly
Fra Pole Artick come quhisling loud and schill,
And causit me remufe [remove] aganis my will.
(1–21)[2]

The immediate "tragedie" in the first stanza is the "feruent" or harsh weather, and with the storm's descent comes the expectation of imminent material loss.[3] The narrator's self-conscious insertion of himself into the sequence—as a figure who is forced to move inside "aganis [his] will"—demonstrates that he is not a detached chronicler of the climatologically induced destruction, but is a literary figure who is metaphorically part of the agricultural discourse he describes. Although the text explicitly situates the narrator inside the "oratur," and away from the elements, he is anxiously gazing outside "throw out the glas" (15). The narrator, in essence, looks into a mirror, and thus at himself. What he sees—a ruined landscape—is a reflected image of his own decayed and aging flesh. Each reference to the deterioration of the land in the opening stanzas is matched by a parallel description of the disfigurement of a concordant region of the narrator's body: the "feruent" (bitter or sickly) storm is like the narrator's "grene" (bitter) and "faidit hart" (24); the freezing wind that blasts sprouting plants is analogous to the "greit cald" (27) that deadens sexual virility; and the "froist freisit" (19) is associated with old blood that "kendillis nocht sa sone as in ʒoutheid [youth]" (30).[4]

This opening sequence, so rich in agricultural imagery, seems narratively

---

[2] Robert Henryson, *The Testament of Cresseid*, ed. Denton Fox (London: Nelson, 1968). All subsequent citations are to this edition and will be given in the text.

[3] Walter Scheps reads the *Testament* through the lens of Caledonian climatology, comparing Chaucer's use of weather patterns with Henryson's ("A Climatological Reading of Henryson's *Testament of Cresseid*," *Studies in Scottish Literature* 15 [1980]: 80–87). Included in his essay is a discussion of the Scottish planting season. See also Alasdair A. MacDonald, "Fervent Weather: A Difficulty in Robert Henryson's *Testament of Cresseid*," *Scottish Studies* 4 (1984): 271–80.

[4] *Dictionary of Old Scots Tongue*, s.v. "fervent" 3; *Middle English Dictionary*, s.v. "grene" 3a.

and thematically removed from the main body of the poem. At the end of the introductory monologue, the narrator, frustrated by his losses, leaves his post at the window and sets out to continue Chaucer's epic story of *Troilus and Criseyde*. Whereas most of the recent criticism of the *Testament* has focused on its relationship with its famous English exemplar, I find that Henryson's poem illuminates a new and complex exchange between fifteenth-century legal discourse and literary language in the Scottish vernacular, demanding that we view its debts to Chaucer through the lens of legal innovation and characterization.[5] Henryson's version of the legend chronicles the demise of the heroine, who, after engaging in an illicit affair with Diomeid, is summoned to appear before a fictional council comprising eight planetary deities. In a hasty trial, the gods find her guilty of the crime of blasphemy and punish her with leprosy. What is so striking about the *Testament* in legal terms is the profoundly altered status of Criseyde/Cresseid herself. Chaucer's powerful widow, who was endowed with enormous authority in *Troilus and Criseyde*, has become a leper, a disenfranchised juridical body devoid of legal agency.[6] As we shall see, Henryson's heroine cannot be completely understood unless we examine the poem's complex legal refiguration of literary character, a revision that I explore here in terms of the poem's literary and political relation to contemporaneous ideologies regarding the law of personhood.

Medieval conceptions of personhood contained various social, religious, and political dimensions, including the idea that an individual was most appropriately defined through his relationship to a superior authority (such as God, a baronial lord, or a king). Situating itself within this tradition, the narrator's monologue links the *Testament*'s interpretation of identity construction to agricultural tenure, a practice largely governed in medieval Scotland by aristocratic overlords and legal courts. The introduction depicts the forceful conflation of the human body with the land as a juridical act that promotes the blending of identities, a process that inevitably destroys the discernible boundaries between human and territory and renders these bodies indistinguishable. In an era of labor crisis and agricultural ruin, the destruction of land necessarily generates a parallel destruction of the identities of laborers who work on it.

I argue that through its deployment of agricultural terminology, legislation, and formulas, *The Testament of Cresseid* stages a literary intervention into the contemporary juridical debate in Scotland regarding the definition of

[5] The classic study of the relationship between Chaucer and Henryson is Marshall Stearns's chapter in *Robert Henryson* (New York: Columbia University Press, 1949), 48–69. More recent studies include David Benson, "Critic and Poet: What Lydgate and Henryson did to Chaucer's *Troilus and Criseyde*," *Modern Language Quarterly* 53 (1992): 23–40; and Robert Kindrick, "Henryson's 'Uther Quair' Again: A Possible Candidate and the Nature of the Tradition," *Chaucer Review* 33 (1988): 190–220.

[6] John Finlay discusses the roles of women in Scottish courts in "Women and Legal Representation in Early Sixteenth-Century Scotland," in *Women in Scotland, 1100–1750*, ed. Elizabeth Ewan and Maureen M. Meikle (East Linton: Tuckwell, 1999), 165–75.

legal personhood. Specifically, the body of Cresseid—which is mapped in the poem as both a physical entity and a material territory—serves as a vehicle through which Henryson can explore the law of sasine (i.e., "seisin," possession of freehold) and its dictation and eradication of the identity of the indentured tenant. Further, an examination of fifteenth-century leper statutes, seignorial accounts, and tenement disputes illuminates the poet's representation of the legally devalued subject as part of a larger discourse of exclusion, a discourse reserved in medieval Scotland for the discussion of beggars and lepers.

Before we turn to the *Testament* itself, it will be necessary to examine in some detail the poet's literary and professional connection to the legal practice of agricultural tenure, a system that was nearly extinguished in England by the fifteenth century but had not yet reached its most complete and logical development in Scotland.[7] As we shall see, Henryson's literary representation of aristocratic abuse corresponds to actual "legal dramas" played out in Scottish burghs and recorded in local registries.[8] Yet as much as Henryson's poems function as legal allegories, they are also participants in legal revisionism. Indeed, Henryson's own life records reveal that the poet's personal loyalties were charged with an ambivalence that infiltrates his texts and deeply informs his secular approach to literary character.

Henryson and the Law of Land

Like his literary alter ego in *The Testament of Cresseid*, Robert Henryson was deeply connected to his native land.[9] After earning a law degree from Glasgow College in 1462, he returned to his native burgh of Dunfermline, where he served as head schoolmaster, presumably until his death around 1499.[10]

---

[7] I. F. Grant, *The Social and Economic Development of Scotland before 1603* (Edinburgh: Oliver and Boyd Publishers, 1930), 200. See also C. D'Ollvier Farran, *The Principles of Scots and English Land Law* (Edinburgh: W. Green & Son, 1958), 17–28.

[8] I agree with R. J. Lyall's claim that Henryson's *Fables* are not merely allegories but reflections of contemporary local practices ("Politics and Poetry in Fifteenth-Century and Sixteenth-Century Scotland," *Scottish Literary Journal* 3 [1976]: 5–29).

[9] For details of Henryson's life, I am indebted to Denton Fox's biographical summary in *The Poems of Robert Henryson* (Oxford: Clarendon Press, 1981), xiii–xxv.

[10] "Anno Domini etc. [M.cccc.] xij die decimo mensis Septembris Incorporatus fuit venerabilis vir Magister Robertus Henrisone in Artibus Licentiatus et Decretis Bachalarius" (*Munimenta alme universitatis Glasguensis*, ed. C. Innes, Maitland Club, no. 72 [Glasgow, 1954], 7:69). The date of Henryson's death is still a much-contested subject. In 1968 Denton Fox placed the poet's death "before 1505." The content of a minor poem attributed to Henryson—"Ane Prayer for the Pest"—suggests a slightly earlier date, around 1499. The poem probably refers to the plague that struck Edinburgh in 1499 and killed many of its citizens. The likelihood that Henryson did not live long after the plague (owing either to illness, old age, or both) is suggested in a passage of the text in which Henryson includes himself among the diseased who seek mercy from God:

Superne lucerne, guberne this pestilens,
Preserue and serue that we nocht sterf thairin,
Declyne that pyne be thy devyne prudens,

Cartulary records from Dunfermline Abbey indicate that he also served as the church's official notary public, a legal office sanctioned by the pope in the early fifteenth century and held almost exclusively by lawyers extensively trained in canon and civil law. Historically, notaries were responsible for drafting, recording, and authenticating provincial legislation, episcopal and capitular acts, testaments, and various land transactions including sasines, annual rents, reversions, leases, and wadsets (mortgages).[11] Henryson's detailed knowledge of agricultural legality is reflected in three surviving charters drafted and signed "Maister Robertus Henrison, notarius publicus" from 1477 and 1478.[12] All deal with the lands of Spittalfields, near Inverkeithing, that were granted by the Abbot of Dunfermline to George de Lothreisk and Patrick Barone, burgess of Edinburgh, and to Margaret, his spouse.

It is safe to assume that Henryson was equally fluent in the language and usage of other documents of land law, given the explicit references to the writ in *The Sheep and the Dog*; the brief in *The Tale of the Wolf and the Lamb*, and the assize (session of a court charged with the deliberation of civil actions) in *The Preaching of the Swallow*. These earlier works present a rich catalog of Henryson's consistent thematic investment in the unstable relationship between the emergent and constantly oscillating land laws and the rights of the Scottish laboring class. For example, in *The Tale of the Fox, the Wolf, and the Husbandman*, Henryson describes in great detail the many difficulties that beset tenant farmers, including outdated and ineffective farm implements, oxen that "waxit mair reulie," and intolerant and demanding landlords.[13] The *moralitas* to *The Sheep and the Dog* illustrates the partiality of Scottish civil courts. The Sheep, a poor husbandman, is attacked by the Wolf, who presides over the assizes of the itinerant Justice-Ayres:

> This volf I likkin to ane schiref [sheriff] stout
> Quhilk byis [buys] ane forfalt [forfeiture] at the kingis hand,
> And hes with him ane cursit assyis about,
> And dytis [indicts] all the pure [poor] men vp on land . . .
> (1265–68)

> For trewth, haif rewth, lat nocht our slewth ws twyn;
> Our syte, full tyte, wer we contryt, wald blin;
> Dissiuir did nevir, quha euir the besocht
> But grace, with space, for to arrace fra sin;
> Lat nocht be tint that thow sa deir hes bocht!

Cited in Fox, *The Poems of Robert Henryson*, lines 65–72.

[11] David Walker, *A Legal History of Scotland* (Edinburgh: W. Green Publishing, 1990), 2:276. For a detailed discussion of the function and usage of notarial instruments in fifteenth-century Scotland, see also Hector MacQueen, *Common Law and Feudal Society in Medieval Scotland* (Edinburgh: Edinburgh University Press, 1993), 94–97.

[12] *Registrum de Dunfermelyn* (Edinburgh: Bannatyne Club), MS fol. 63a, 63b, 64a. See also Henderson, 176.

[13] Cited in Fox, *The Poems of Robert Henryson*, 2252. All subsequent citations of Henryson's fables are from this edition and will be given in the text.

The Wolf, who purchases fines from the Crown, uses them to indict impoverished peasants and unlawfully exact payment from them. These literary details correspond to contemporaneous legal statutes which indicate that the Justice-Ayres were notoriously corrupt.[14]

Perhaps the most striking example of aristocratic abuse and tenant subordination in Henryson's works appears in one of his later fables, *The Tale of the Wolf and the Lamb*. In the culminating *moralitas*, Henryson uses beast allegory to illuminate the ways in which laboring husbandmen are mistreated by lords who are "peruerteris of the lawis" (2715):

> The thrid wolf ar men of heritage,
> As lordis that hes land be Goddis lane [loan],
> And settis to the mailleris [tenants] ane village,
> And for ane tyme gressome [annual rent] payit and tane;
> Syne vexis him, or half his terme be gane,
> With pykit [picked] querrellis for to mak him fane [want]
> To flit or pay his gressome new agane. (2742–48)

Cunning wolves, who represent the landed gentry, illegally seize the property and land of unsuspecting lambs—"maill men" (2708) and "laboureris" (2708)—and use misleading "termis" (2716) and contracts to trick their tenants into working without pay and abandoning their rented pasturage on the pretext of a quarrel. The passage's specific reference to the landlord's stealing of a tenant's "gressome," or annual rent, is probably a topical allusion to the five anti-eviction laws passed by parliament in the second half of the fifteenth century. Although the statutes were surely intended to alleviate tenant burden, their number and repetition testify to their ineffectiveness.[15]

While the beast fables illuminate the social and legal injustices inherent in the Scottish seignorial system, their flatness lies in their inability to imagine any solutions to the socio-legal problems they discuss, as well as in their failure to conceive of a legal order that opposes (or at least challenges) that in which they are situated. An obscure record included among *The Acts of the*

---

[14] Stearns, *Robert Henryson*, 31.

[15] In 1429, King James mandated that barons could not remove "coloni" or "husbandi" from their lands if leases were still valid. See *The Acts of the Parliaments of Scotland, 1127 to 1707. Printed by the Command of His Majesty King George the Fourth in pursuance of an address to the House of Commons of Great Britain*, ed. T. Thomson and C. Innes, 2 vols. (Edinburgh, 1844), 17; hereafter *APS* with volume and page number. The parliament of James II ordered that lords could not evict their leased tenants if the land legally changed hands. The act, passed in 1449, reads: "It is ordained, for the safety and favour of the poor people that labour the ground, that they, and all others that have not taken or shall take lands in times to come from Lords, and have times and years thereof, that, suppose the Lords sell or alienate these lands, the Takers shall remain with their tacks unto the ische [*sic*] of their times, into whosoever hands these lands come, for such male [rent] as they took them for before" (*APS*, 2:35). Identical statutes were passed in 1469 and 1491 (*APS*, 2:96, 2:225). For more information, see Grant, *Social and Economic Development*, 244–64.

Lord Auditors of Causes and Complaints may explain Henryson's persistently ambivalent exploration of feudal abuse. The document, dated March 23, 1481, refers to a charge filed by a group of "Trekware" (Traquair) tenants, including a "Robert Henrisone," on charges that their landlords, identified as George, David, and Margaret Murray, wrongfully demanded double mail-rents:

> In the actiouns and causes presewit be george burns James henrisone, Johne Mudy Robert henrisone marione myddilmaist / Adam wilsone Johne hog Robert Mark will pacok James of burns / laurence wod / Wilȝaim henrisone / et Katrine blenkes tennandes of the landes of trekware on ta parte aganis James erle of buchane and margarate of murray george of murray et dauid murray on þe top parte anent [sic] the takin of doubill malis of the saide landes of trekware / The saide tenandes beand present be thar procuratores et the saide lord erle beand personaly present / and the said margarete of murray et dauid murray being peremptorly summond et oft tymes callit et not operit / The lordes Auditores decretes et deliueris that the saides margarate george et dauid has done wrang in the takin vp of the malis of the saide landes / and ordanis thaim to Restor et geif agane to the saide tennandes same ekle of the malis as thai haue takin vp of the saide landes of the termes of thre ȝeres bigain et part thai haue nane Intrometting þer with in tyme to cum bot [sic] that thai be frely broikit et joisit [sic] be þe saide lord erle efter the forme of his infeftment schewin et producit before the saide lordes et ordanis letres to be writin In dew forme herapon.[16]

The Lord Auditors ruled that the Murrays did "wrang" in demanding excess rent from their tenants and ordered the landlords to return the money to their subjects. The topical evidence contained in the document relating to date and location is compelling, given what we know about Henryson's life.[17] The historical details relating to the poet's alleged victimization are fascinating, but what is perhaps more important to our understanding of Henryson's

[16] *Burns v. Buchane*, in *Acta dominorum auditorum: The Acts of the Lord Auditors of Causes and Complaints, 1466–1494* (London: House of Commons, 1807), 96; hereafter *ADA* with participating parties and page references.

[17] It must be noted that local documents record a number of individuals bearing the name Robert "Henrisone" or Robert "Henderson" living in the general region of Edinburgh, which of course casts doubt on the ability of scholars or historians to link specific historical documents decisively to the poet. Fifteenth-century Trekware (Trakware, Traquair) was approximately twenty-five miles south of Dunfermline and eighteen miles south of Edinburgh. Historical records place Henryson in Glasgow in 1462 and in Dunfermline in 1477–78. Where the poet resided in the years before, in between, and after these dates is unknown. Given his acclimation toward centers of industry, politics, and law, it is entirely possible that he lived for some time in Traquair. The burgh was a favorite hunting and fishing retreat for James I, II, and III and the castle there was a popular meeting place for the king and his vassals. Sir James Stewart, the Black Knight of Lorn and husband to Queen Joan, the widow of James I, was granted the lands by royal charter in 1439. James of Buchane, Stewart's son, was knighted in 1469 and legitimated twenty years later. For more information, see Peter Maxwell Stuart's pamphlet *Traquair House Guidebook* (Peebleshire, Scotland: Jarrold, 1986), 22.

participation in the Scottish seignorial system is something that is not explicitly stated in the document: the conditions of his tenure. Henryson's education and profession automatically excluded him from the ranks of abject tenancy, and it is likely that he was, in fact, quite wealthy. Thus, while Henryson was legally subject to his baronial landlord—as all tenants regardless of social rank or wealth were—the circumstances of his tenure were vastly more pleasant than those of the subjugated characters depicted in the fables. Henryson's role within his community was thus extremely paradoxical: at the same time that he was championing the rights of the peasant population in his poems, he was, in his professional capacity as a lawyer, creating laws that would be used to subvert their legal rights and alienate them as legal subjects. What is peculiar about Henryson's ambivalence toward peasants—his belief that they should be empowered but also repressed—is that the attitude is naturalized. In other words, such legal contradiction, rather than obstructing Henryson's vision of the world, serves as a lens through which he can view his community—and the competing ideologies fighting for control within it—in a richer way.

Land Law and a Leper

The Testament of Cresseid (late 1480s–early 1490s) marks Henryson's poetic movement from fable to cultural and natural myth. Cresseid is introduced in the poem as "the flour and A per se" (78).[18] The botanical personification is repeated six times throughout the poem, which describes the heroine in varying stages of anatomical progression (budding, blooming, wilting). Here, Henryson is clearly playing on a trope common to courtly love poet-

---

[18] By depicting Cresseid this way, Henryson immediately graphs floral imagery onto Chaucer's more literate comparison in *Troilus and Criseyde*: "Right as our firste lettre is now an A, / In beaute first so stood she makeles" (*The Riverside Chaucer*, ed. Larry Benson [Boston: Houghton Mifflin, 1987], 1.171). Feminist critics have also discussed the female body in terms of these images. Annette Kolodny contends that bodily transgression promotes the simultaneous fracturing and blending of identities, a process that inevitably destroys the discernible boundaries between human geographic territory but at the same time motivates what she calls a "pastoral impulse," the innate legal and psychological desire to create a compromised identity—one that is definable—through the image of the gendered land (*The Lay of the Land: Metaphor as Experience and History in American: Life and Letters* [Chapel Hill: University of North Carolina Press, 1975], 26). For Peter Stallybrass, the conflation of flesh and field is both a literary construction as well as a social reality. The married woman in particular not only becomes a legal discourse in that her legal identity is suspended but also is ideologically configured as "the fenced-in enclosure of the landlord, her father, or husband" ("Patriarchal Territories: The Body Enclosed," in *Rewriting the Renaissance: The Discourses of Sexual Difference in Early Modern Europe*, ed. Margaret Ferguson, Maureen Quilligan, and Nancy Vickers [Chicago: University of Chicago Press, 1986], 123–42). Mikhail Bakhtin identifies the female body as a "locus of class conflict" in which the battle between the haves and the have-nots is topographically mapped onto physical features. The inevitable consequence is a distorted cartographic image—a map symbolizing the self that is recognizable as neither human nor agrarian (*Rabelais and His World*, trans. Helene Iswolsky [Cambridge: MIT Press, 1968], 26–27).

ics in which the female body is depicted as a product of human cultivation.[19] The text extends the personification of the garden to include the mimetic processes of agricultural production and sexual reproduction. Casting herself as farmable fauna, Cresseid tells Venus, "The seid of lufe was sawin in my face / And ay grew grene throw ʒour supplie and grace" (137–38). Cresseid functions as both a mappable space and a cultivable geographic body, yet the image also identifies Troilus as the appropriate and authorized planter of the field. It is with Venus' grace and Troilus' body that Cresseid becomes sexually fertile and develops into a desired and valuable marriageable commodity. The fetus or the "seid of lufe," however, does not properly gestate in the belly, but is sown in the face. It is this improperly planted seed, which we learn later is Diomeid's, that Cresseid laments "with froist is slane / And I fra luifferis left, and all forlane" (139–40). The striking contrast between (re)productive and destructive seeds seems to draw a tight interpretive boundary that the rest of the text ostensibly sustains: Troilus is the authorized lover and can father legitimate offspring, while Diomeid's unsanctioned love must always be abortive. What is most provocative about the analogy, however, is its implicit, generalized anxiety regarding the authority over and ownership of bodies. The paradigm that is introduced and naturalized is one in which the success and failure of respective sexual unions is determined not by the participating bodies but through an external authority (in this case Venus).

Just as Cresseid is relegated to a passive role in regard to her own sexual economy, the *Testament* implies that sovereignty over her agricultural body is equally out of reach. The topic of arable land could not be discussed in fifteenth-century Scotland without reference to the notion of ownership, and the identity of the tenant could not be discussed without mention of his master. In his thirteenth-century treatise on English law, Bracton describes the feudal villein under the power of his lord as civilly "dead."[20] And as Elizabeth Fowler has noted, civil death marks the descent into selflessness, a space

---

[19] There are also historically specific reasons why Henryson likely represented Cresseid in the manner he did. Chaucer employs the metaphor sparingly, instead resurrecting archaic forms of descriptive comparisons heavily influenced by classical mythology and continental courtly tradition. Thus, Chaucer's notable absence of agricultural terminology afforded Henryson the freedom to explore the issue of bodily duality on the figure of Cresseid without concern for any historical impediment or residual literary influence related to his famous predecessor. In addition, Henryson's "agriculturalizing" of traditional court motifs reflects the pervasive atmosphere of political and economic instability of late fifteenth-century Scotland. In an era four times without a king and with no centralized government, the popularity of the court and its culture was rapidly dwindling. See Louise Fradenburg, *City, Marriage, Tournament: Arts of Rule in Late Medieval Scotland* (Madison: University of Wisconsin Press, 1991), 35–46; and William Ferguson, *The Identity of the Scottish Nation* (Edinburgh: Edinburgh University Press, 1998), 36–75.

[20] "Est etiam mors civilis in servo in servitute sub potestate domini constituto" (*De legibus et consuetudinibus Angliae*, trans. Samuel E. Thorne [Cambridge: Belknap Press of Harvard University Press, 1968], 421b). Also cited in Sir Frederick Pollock and Frederic William Maitland, *The History of English Law before the time of Edward I* (Cambridge: Cambridge University Press, 1899), 1:433.

where characters are controlled by others.[21] Just as the field tended by the peasant farmer is subject to the peripheral but omnipotent authority of the feudal lord, so the boundaries of Cresseid's body / land are tightly secured within the narrative and legal jurisdiction of the planetary deities.[22] At the beginning of the narrative, Cresseid accuses the gods of having broken their promise to keep her forever attractive to men: "ȝe gaue me anis ane deuine responsaill [reply] / That I suld be the flour of luif in Troy" (127–28). In the courtroom, Cupid replies that he has fulfilled his end of the bargain—"The quhilk *throw me* was sum tyme flour of lufe" (279, emphasis added)—but the heroine, having blasphemed the gods, has not. Cresseid's failure to adhere to her contract enables the gods to assume control over her body, thereby consigning her to the role of a legal subject.

The nature of the gods and their authorial attitude toward their subject is made strikingly clear in what Jill Mann dubs "the planetary sequence." Building on John MacQueen's classic interpretation of the deities as physical manifestations of the indifferent and involuntary "natural processes of time and change, growth and decay," Mann argues that the planetary gods are legal instruments by which man comes to internalize his position in a world "whose laws are enacted through him and yet irrespective of him."[23] Despite this, the gods are not exactly practitioners of an abstract, cosmic law. Nor do they serve as "perceptive moral arbiters."[24] An obscure reference to Mercury's role in the courtroom suggests that they can be read as representatives of a juridical authority: "Thus quhen thay gadderit war, thir goddes seuin [seven], / Mercurius thay cheisit [chose] with ane assent / To be foirspeikar [chief speaker] in the parliament" (264–66).

It is not surprising that Henryson assigns Mercury the title of "foirspeikar," given the character's traditional representation within mythological convention as a lawyer or civil advocate. The deity's connection to secular legal procedure makes it tempting to read the "parliament" that he oversees not as a generic "meeting" or "assembly" but as a specific juridical congregation and metaphorical governing body of law. Indeed, the structural format of the trial that the gods conduct reflects some of the legal procedures associated with a

---

[21] Elizabeth Fowler, "Civil Death and the Maiden: Agency and the Conditions of Contract in *Piers Plowman*," *Speculum* 70 (1995): 768.

[22] The narrator, himself a character, is equally confined within the text. His plea to Saturn later in the text—"O cruell Saturne, fraward and angrie . . . / Withdraw thy sentence and be gracious" (323, 327)—demonstrates his own level of subjectivity and, thus, inability to intervene on his heroine's behalf.

[23] Jill Mann, "The Planetary Gods in Chaucer and Henryson," in *Chaucer Traditions: Studies in Honour of Derek Brewer*, ed. Ruth Morse and Barry Windeatt (Cambridge: Cambridge University Press, 1990), 96; John MacQueen, *Robert Henryson: A Study of the Major Narrative Poems* (Oxford: Clarendon Press, 1967), 70.

[24] Lee Patterson, "Christian and Pagan in the *The Testament of Cresseid*," *Philological Quarterly* 52 (1973): 700. For an alternative reading of the dream sequence in the poem, see Ralph Hanna III, "Cresseid's Dream and Henryson's *Testament*," in *Chaucer and Middle English Studies in Honour of Rossell Hope Robbins*, ed. Beryl Rowland (London: Allen and Unwin, 1974), 288–97.

specific fifteenth-century parliamentary judicial committee with which Henryson would have been familiar: the Lord Auditors.[25] This appointed tribunal, composed of representatives from the three estates, met in Edinburgh between parliamentary sessions and functioned as an adjunct juridical body that heard and ruled on overflow cases assigned to the lower courts (assize, church, burgh). The court exercised the appellate jurisdiction of parliament, which was limited to civil causes. Within this genre of law, however, fell a wide range of crimes and offenses, including borowgang or suretyship, broken marriage contracts, spuilize (theft), and unpaid mailrents.[26]

The most common grounds for action of wrong tried in these courts—and those crimes in which Henryson surely was most fluently versed—were claims of varying degrees of damages to land and feudal tacks, including (but not limited to) molestation, wrongful occupation, and unlawful manuring.[27] Henryson complicates his depiction of the fictional parliament by overlaying this overtly juridical image with a patina of mythological and literary tropes. The poem positions the gods in their traditional mythological elements and endows each with complementary characteristics: Saturn's face, for example, is "fro[ns]it" (155) because he represents a cold humor, while Jupiter's primeval apparel evokes images of pastoral tribunals of love. Similarly, Mars, the god of war, is dressed in armor and carries his conventional battle implements at his side, and Phebus, the god of sapience, is appropriately accompanied by four Ovidian horses. Yet it is precisely by securing the deities within literary convention that the poet can reconceive these images in terms of contemporary legal theory and practice. The clothing worn by the gods and the instruments that they bear clearly identify them as mythological figures, but they also refer to a peculiarity of the Scottish court system: a 1455 parliamentary statute mandated that all parliamentary committee members color-code themselves according to social rank "under the pains of a ten pound fine."[28] Nobles were ordered to wear red mantles; burgesses, blue; and the clergy, their black ecclesiastic robes. It seems that Henryson interpolates these social markers into his poem and uses them to link the deities to the three estates. Mercury is "cled in ane skarlot goun" (250) and matching red hood (244).

---

[25] For my discussion of the structure and composition of the Lord Auditors, I am indebted to David Walker's research in *A Legal History of Scotland*, Vol. 2, 309–21.

[26] For a complete listing of the types of charges brought before the court, see the appendix in *ADA*, 1466–94.

[27] The members of the council represented the three estates and were chosen for their practical experience with land law (as landlords) or their specialist knowledge of particular statutes or legislative areas. Between 1478 and 1485, a total of fifty-four men sat as Lord Auditors of causes and complaints for a total of eighty-seven days spread over twelve sessions of parliament; twenty-two were ecclesiastics, fourteen were nobles (two earls and twelve barons), and eighteen were burgesses. Although the exact number of members per council is unknown, it is likely that the court's composition was similar to that of parallel committees—such as the Lords of Session and Lords of Council—which typically contained nine members. For more information, see Walker, *A Legal History of Scotland*, 2:318–19, and *APS*, 2:36, c. 10.

[28] *APS*, 2:43, cc. 11–12.

Mars carries a bloody sword at his side and his face is described as a "reid visage" that "grislie glowrand ene" (191). Saturn, representing a burgess, appears in court with a bluish pallor, and out of his nose run watery "meldrop[s]" (158). The black clerical robes are worn by Venus (221) and Cynthia (255). Significantly, an ecclesiastical image appears on the breast of the latter: a churl, trying to reach heaven, "micht clim na nar" (263) because he has broken the law by stealing a bunch of thorns.

By oscillating throughout the "parliament" sequence between mytho-literary tradition and imposed juridical convention, Henryson is able to redefine courtly and mythological behavior as legal procedure. As a governing body, the gods claim "power of all thing generabill" (148); that is, they declare omnipotent authority over the supernatural world. This trait, however, is matched only by their self-proclaimed ability to "reull and steir" (149). The puns on the legal terms "rule" and "steer" and the verbs meaning "to chart or map" (on a plot of land) and "to direct or arrange a farm implement or animal" (such as a steer) allow Henryson to conflate the notions of governance and plowing.[29] The implications of the compounded allusion are clear: the gods' jurisdiction encompasses both the agricultural and legal realms.

In the fictionalized courtroom scene, the planetary sequence appears where an informed reader would expect the traditional elements of the fifteenth-century Scottish trial to be—including the testimonials of the litigant, defendant, and witnesses. While the deletion of Cresseid's voice only substantiates what we already know—that she is a legal subject—the insertion of the planetary caricatures in this narrative frame suggests that the descriptive sequence represents an important part of the trial proceedings. The portraits of the deities seem to function as testimonies in their own right, both substantiating the gods' authority to accuse and judge and determining the guilt or innocence of a defendant without participating in the laborious hoop-jumping associated with fifteenth-century juridical procedure. At the same time, the caricatures reveal a horrifying reality of the poetic legal system: the gods are endowed with legal authority but do not use this power to enact earthly forms of justice. The gods' appearance and behavior echo, but do not exactly imitate, common law procedure, and this highlights the terrible recognition that the literary "parliament" evokes the moral objective of temporal law only to defeat it. Thus, the various legal implements and instruments that the gods attach to their clothing or carry at their sides are not material tokens of legal authority, but suggest that earthly law too is inherently ambiguous and mutable.

Just as Henryson relies on literary devices to redefine the function of the deities in the poem, he uses contemporary legal theory to draw a striking parallel between the procedures and protocol of the fictional court and that of its secular counterpart. In doing so, he illustrates the courts' similar ideological agendas of subordination while exposing the gods' intentions as decidedly

[29] *Middle English Dictionary*, s.v. "reule" 9a; "steiren" 1a.

more severe. After listening to the testimonies of the litigant, defendant, and appropriate witnesses, the Lord Auditors typically retired to a private chamber to consider the evidence and determine a verdict. Nearly all of the judgments recorded in the casebooks of the Lord Auditors between 1466 and 1494 adhered to a prescribed four-point formula aimed at ensuring the validity of the document and definitiveness of the ruling. After a brief summary of the charges filed—which included identification of the legal parties involved and a description of the land in dispute—the document moved to the verdict, and from there to a description of the punishment to be meted out to the guilty party. Consider the following case, filed March 20, 1478:

> In þe actions et causes presewit be thomas Anderson burges of coupir agains alexander of lawthres of that Ilk anenet [*sic*] þe soume of 1 mark [sic] clamit be þe said thomas to be aucht to him be þe said alexander be his obligations because of þe alienation maid be the said alexander of the landes of the Spittailfelds et certain vþer landes otrar þe tenores [sic] of the said obligation as was allegit / Baith the saide partijs being present be ther procuatores / And ther Richtes Resones et allegacons in þe said mater at lenth herd sene et vnderstandin the lordes Auditores decretes et deliueris that the said alexander sall otent et pay to the said thomas the said somes of 1 mark [sic] efter þe forme of hes obligationes maid to him þeruppon / Becaus it was clerly prevyt befor þe said lordes that he analijt [*sic*] þe said landes of Spittalefeld et certane vþer landes otrar þe tennor [sic] of þe sam yn And ordanis letres tobe writtin to distreȝe him his landes et gudes herefor.[30]

The court ruled that Alexander was in default in his payment of "obligations" to his landlord, Thomas Anderson, and ordered him to pay the specified sum of money or face the permanent forfeiture of his "gudes."

This case is fascinating for a number of reasons, one of which concerns its staging within a region with which Henryson was intimately connected. The poet was serving as notary public when this case was filed; in fact, one of the surviving charters signed by Henryson—which also deals with Spittalfield— was dated the same month and year. The ownership, holding, and maintenance of the lands of Spittalfield were clearly topics of heated debate in Dunfermline in the 1470s. As the legal practitioner responsible for producing the legal transactions regarding these lands, Henryson may have dealt directly with the conflict between Thomas Anderson and his tenant Alexander. Perhaps the dispute central to this case inspired the poet to include a reference to the region in the *Testament*. After Cresseid is diagnosed with leprosy, her father commits her to the local leper hospital, which the narrator calls "the spittaill hous" (391). In the 1920s, Ebenezer Henderson asserted that this was a topical allusion to St. Leonard's Hospital, a leprosarium outside Dunfermline.[31] Given the poet's professional involvement in the burgh's juridical

---

[30] *ADA, Anderson v. Lawthres,* 83.
[31] Henderson, *The Annals of Dunfermline and Vicinity,* 170.

and legislative arenas, the "spittaill hous" could also be a reference to the courtroom of Henry Spittal, the chief advocate of Dunfermline's assize courts in 1488–89.[32] Although the assize courts were compositionally different from the Lord Auditors (assize courts consisted of non–parliament members), they heard and ruled on the same types of land dispute cases. Assizers were notoriously corrupt and were often suspected of illegal collusion. If the literary "spittaill hous" is a representation of Spittal's legal house, then it is not a locus of safety and security but a site of partiality and privilege. Cresseid's chances of finding redemption as a leper in the "spittaill hous" are just as remote as Alexander's odds of emerging as the victor in a dispute with his overlord regarding the lands of Spittalfield.

A key element of the judgment is the formulaic phrase acknowledging that both Anderson's and Alexander's testimony had been "seen, heard, and understood" by the auditors. By linking sensory perception to a cognitive process, the document exposes a basic ideological principle of Scottish land law: legal understanding comes primarily through firsthand sensory experiences with the law.[33] Those who testify in court participate in this process, and therefore are "understood." By logical extension, legal parties who are absent are excluded from judicial comprehension, and therefore cannot be accurately registered into the legal memory of the court.

The phrase thus denotes a specific fifteenth-century legal problem—that of juridical identification and representation. The casebooks of the Lord Auditors between 1470 and 1490 reveal that court absenteeism was largely limited to a legally marginalized population: indentured tenants. Over half of the cases filed in these two decades indicate that the tenant, who was almost always summoned to court by his landlord on charges of land abuse, was "peremptorly summond" and "oft tymes callit" but "not operit."[34] The notable absence of the tenant in juridical proceedings bore immediate consequences—he was found guilty by default—and points to larger ramifications that bear crucially on the legal fate of Cresseid in the *Testament*.

The sheer quantity of absentee defendants in one court system over such an extended period of time raises the suspicion that perhaps many of the accused were purposely denied a voice in court. Numerous complaints concurrently filed by tenants in the *Acta dominorum auditorum* dispute default court rulings on the grounds that they were summoned at a place where they had no residence, or that they were never summoned at all.[35] The court's silencing of the tenant—whether intentional or incidental—in effect validates the exis-

[32] Ibid., 169.

[33] For a discussion of the significance of physical tokens and material artifacts in the medieval Scottish legal system, see Walker, *A Legal History of Scotland*, 2:309–10.

[34] For examples of cases adhering to this format, see *ADA, Wemys v. Wemys and Malevil*, 101; *Carmichael v. Ramsay*, 103; *Spens v. Forster*, 119–20.

[35] *ADA, Ogilvy v. Ogilvy*, 5; *Ramsay v. Boyes*, 41. That the court did not know where the tenant lived is unlikely, given that the litigant was the tenant's landlord (and thus the defendant almost always lived on his lord's land). It seems more probable, then, that little if any effort was ex-

tence of the legally constructed hierarchy of the auditors and yet destabilizes this hierarchy by exposing its underlying ideology. The implicit threat to the authority of the court is, of course, speech. To acknowledge the presence and testimony of a litigant, defendant, and witness in an official legal context is to inscribe on these individuals a legal identity, to establish their claims as juridical authorities. The voices of all those present are not only seen and heard but understood; they are written down and registered as part of the legal memory of the court. To put it another way, not only do the words of courtroom speakers influence the outcome of the trial, but also their very words become law. By preventing the tenant from being seen, heard, and understood in court, the legal system denies him both a legal identity and, perhaps equally important, the right to challenge the law or create his own.

This distinct historical-legal phenomenon of late fifteenth-century Scotland manifests itself in the courtroom scene in the *Testament*, but with an important twist: the deities aim to prevent Cresseid from speaking both inside *and* outside the courtroom. Cupid convenes the court by ringing a silver bell. The same musical instrument also "rauischit" Cresseid "in spreit [spirit], intill ane dreame scho fell" (142–43). The heroine's descent into unconsciousness—a state in which she remains during the entire legal proceeding—marks her transformation from legal subject to legal nonentity. Although she is physically present, clearly Cresseid is not an active participant in the trial. There is no discussion of Cresseid's guilt, then, because her fate is determined before the court even assembles. Cupid's bell is less a symbol of the law than an instrument of destruction, calling the gods together not to dispense justice but to silence their subject and sentence her to death. The panel's conviction of Cresseid on the charge of blasphemy—instead of lechery as we would expect—is a legally important distinction because it identifies Cresseid's verbal insurrection against the gods, rather than the material loss of her body / land resulting from her infidelity, as the greater offense. Cresseid's "greit iniure" (290), as Cupid calls it, is an act of verbal violence that is potentially lethal, for misrepresenting the gods in speech—and undermining their fame and name—is the only way these immortal bodies can be harmed. When she "blaspheme the name / Of his awin god, outher in word [or] deid" (274–75), then, Cresseid participates in a "discourse of errancy," an insurgent language that challenges and violates the decorum of appropriate speech.[36] Through her blasphemous words, Cresseid attempts to regain self-control the only way she knows how: by illegally usurping the legal identity of her superiors and appropriating their juridical authority onto herself. Her speech, I would suggest, is a legal instrument analogous to Jupiter's sash: it is a material token that represents an aspect of the law. In this case, it symbolizes authoritative

---

pended by the juridical council to notify tenants of impending court dates or to summon them in ways in which they could respond (e.g., an illiterate farmer could not respond to a writ).

[36] Catherine Cox, "Froward Language and Wanton Play: The 'Commoun' Text of Henryson's *Testament of Cresseid*," *Studies in Scottish Literature* 29 (1996): 63.

possibility, the potential of being seen, heard, and understood inside and, by extension, outside a court of law. It is the threat of losing their own privileged rights of personhood to a legal inferior that motivates the gods' hasty and harsh judgment against her.

The "sentence" that is passed down on Cresseid differs in specific ways from the structural format of a temporal land dispute ruling, and these revisions enable Henryson to point to juridical failings in secular procedure and protocol without implicating his text as a participant in them. They also mark specific clauses and phrases as "legal gaps," juridical spaces that can be manipulated, revised, and later reconstituted. These legal spaces are critically important to Henryson's literary project, constituting the formative basis for his ideological rewriting of the law of personhood. The transition from the trial to the judgment phase of the fictionalized court is appropriately marked by the narrator's summary of Cresseid's offenses against the gods and the introduction of Saturn and Cynthia, the appointed deities who will deliver the judgment and assign the punishment:

> Than thus proceidit Saturne and the Mone
> Quhen thay the mater rypelie [thoroughly] had degest [digested]:
> For the dispyte [offense] to Cupide scho had done
> And to Venus, oppin and manifest,
> In all hir lyfe with pane [pain] to be opprest,
> And torment sair [sore] with seiknes incurabill,
> And to all louers be abhominabill.
> (302–8)

Despite the gods' anxious attempts to bypass juridical procedure and hasten the conclusion of the trial, this passage reveals that they unwittingly lapse into it. Cresseid's fate is given more than a cursory glance; it is deliberately and willfully ingested into the bodies of the gods, where it is figuratively absorbed, transformed, and digested. That the heroine's physical suffering becomes a food source for the gods testifies to the underlying weakness of the juridical body. If healthy and whole, legal subjects are potentially threatening, for they have the strength to act on their rebellious desires. In order to sustain itself and maintain its legal authority, the juridical body must debilitate its subjects. Only when its subjects are consumed is the immediate threat of insurrection removed.

The adjective used to describe the way in which legal subjects are metaphorically eaten alive—"rypelie"—serves as the terminological nexus by which Henryson connects the ostensibly disparate ideas of digestion and juridical procedure. The common definition of the term connotes images of mature or "ripe" foodstuff, yet it is perhaps more useful for our purposes to explore the significance of this term as a legal locution (defined by the *Middle English Dictionary* as "with thorough consideration of the facts and evidence at hand").[37] Although the word does not appear in the *Anderson v. Alexander* case, it is employed in numerous contemporary Lord Auditors' rulings to describe the manner in which the court contemplated the opposing testimonies. In a 1476 dispute between John, Lord Carlisle, and John of Maxwell concerning the latter's alleged illegal occupation of "the place of guvane hagges," the Lord Auditors "Ripely avisit decretes et deliueris that because the said Johne grantit in pertinence of thai[m] / that he had na clame nor Richt to the said place nor landes."[38] Cases filed later that year and in 1489 and 1493 conclude in similar ways: "The lordes auditoures Ripely avisit decretes et deliuevers"; "The lord auditores Ripply avist, decrettes et ordinis"; and "The lordes auditores Ripply avist apone the said exceptions."[39] By inserting this term into a legally charged narrative frame, Henryson makes a pointed criticism of the council of deities and their secular exemplars. Although each claims to engage in contemplative legal thought, both fail to provide evidence that they actually do so. The gods "degest" Cresseid—that is, they *consume* her—but do not *consider* her as anything other than an expendable object. This gesture to contemplate Cresseid is completely self-serving: the gods, like the auditors, can only view their subjects in terms of their use-value to themselves.

Once the formulary introductions are appropriately dispensed with, the narrative segues into the actual ruling, which is divided into two parts. Saturn, the "hiest planeit" (297) and "lawest of degre" (298), serves as the panel's mouthpiece and steps forward to deliver the judgment:

> This duleful [sorrowful] sentence Saturne tuik on hand,
> And passit doun quhair cairfull Cresseid lay,
> And on hir heid he laid ane frostie wand;
> Than lawfullie on this wyse can he say,
> 'Thy greit fairnes and all thy bewtie gay,
> Thy wantoun blude, and eik thy goldin hair,
> Heir I exclude fra the for euermair.
>
> 'I change thy mirth into melancholy,
> Quhilk is the mother of all pensiuenes;
> Thy moisture and thy heit in cald and dry;
> Thyne insolence, thy play and wantones,
> To greit diseis; thy pomp and thy riches
> In mortall neid; and greit penuritie
> Thow suffer sall, and as ane beggar die.'
> (309–22)

Saturn's sentence lists the consequences of the punishment in progressing degrees of severity: the heroine's temperament will sour, then her body will dis-

---

[37] *Middle English Dictionary*, s.v. "ripeli" 1a.
[38] *ADA, Carlisle v. Maxwell*, 50.
[39] *ADA, Mure v. McLellan*, 50; *Murray v. Buchane*, 134; *Crauford v. Peltegren*, 173.

integrate, and her material wealth will deplete. Finally, Cresseid "suffer sall, and as ane beggar die." That a reversion in social rank is marked as a worse fate than emotional and physical deterioration suggests that the passage's central concern is social rather than moral.[40] Cynthia's judgment echoes this sentiment:

'Thy cristall ene [eyes] mingit with blude I mak,
Thy voice sa cleir [clear] vnplesand hoir [rough] and hace [hoarse],
Thy lustie lyre [skin] ouirspred with spottis blak,
And lumpis haw appeirand in thy face:
Quhair thow cummis, ilk man sall fle the place.
This sall thow go begging fra hous to hous
With cop and clapper lyke ane lazarous [leper].'
(337–43)

By positioning the reference to beggary at the end of a list of agonizing corporeal punishments, the passage implies that the sores, welts, and lesions are not themselves the punishments but merely the means to a more horrific end. As a member of "ane rank beggair" (483), Cresseid is relegated to a social position not unlike that of the evicted or misplaced tenant. Homeless and hungry, she is consigned to wander "fra place to place, quhill cauld and hounger sair" (482).

In the *Testament*, the gods' anxiety registers a concern as serious as that of the secular landlord; as representatives of the law, they know that insurrection challenges the existing legal order and threatens to reverse the existing division of power. Nervous that their legal authority is about to be usurped by their own poetically constructed legal subject, they take it upon themselves to eliminate the threat of future insurgency. By "excluding" Cresseid from her body, they render her homeless. Nor do they stop here, for their designs extend far beyond making her "as ane beggar" (322). Indeed, the gods seek to reduce Cresseid to nothingness, eradicating the lingering physical markers of legal identity that she still bears.

The Law of Leprosy

While numerous crimes and offenses necessitated the legal forfeiture of property or sacrifice of life, only one circumstance in fifteenth-century Scotland allowed for the legal revocation of the rights of personhood: a diagnosis of leprosy.[41] By afflicting Cresseid with the mysterious disease—with the

---

[40] For essays that treat the gods' judgment as a catalyst for the heroine's moral growth, see Mairi Ann Cullen, "Cresseid Excused: A Re-reading of Henryson's *Testament of Cresseid*," *Studies in Scottish Literature* 20 (1985): 137–59; and John McNamara, "Divine Justice in Henryson's *Testament of Cresseid*," *Studies in Scottish Literature* 11 (1974): 99–107.

[41] Most individuals who were convicted of a felony forfeited their property, land, and moveable goods to the Crown and were executed. The mentally ill were committed to asylums and hospi-

"seiknes incurabill" (307), as Venus calls it—the planetary deities, in essence, sentence her to a death that is both corporeal and legal. In his influential study of medieval leprosy, Peter Richards describes the process of "exclusion," a practice instituted in Scotland in the late twelfth century and not fully abandoned until the nineteenth.[42] Soon after his diagnosis, the leper was led to the local church, where he was encouraged to participate in a final confession and then a "last Mass." During the ceremony he was often required to kneel beneath a black cloth that symbolized the descent into the grave. The priest then revoked the leper's legal rights: he was stripped of his possessions, birthright, and name and was forbidden to talk to non-lepers, appear in town, or touch anything outside the leper colony except with a stick or rod. Finally, in an act meant to represent the burial, the priest led the leper to the parish cemetery and shoveled dirt onto his feet, telling him that he was hereby, forever, and always "dead to the world."[43]

Clearly the symbolic burial of the leper parallels the actual disposal of his legal rights and identity. The assignment of the title "leper" legally negated all other preexisting identities—including that of tenant.[44] Without a discernible self—a body that society identifies as being endowed with human qualities—the leper ceases legally to exist. In this way Cresseid is not "lyke ane lazarous," a walking corpse, because even the dead still have the legal right to bequeath land and property as well as to name heirs through a will. Rather, she is a visible but unrecognizable (and thus unidentifiable) mass of bones and flesh. Her anonymity is clearly elucidated in the "half-recognition" scene, the passage in which a battle-weary Troilus rides by the begging lepers, one of whom is Cresseid, and is moved by her resemblance to his former lover.[45]

> Seing that companie, all with ane steuin [voice]
> Thay gaif ane cry, and schuik coppis gude speid [good speed],

---

tals; while the individual was institutionalized, the Crown held legal guardianship over his possessions and property. Upon the individual's release or death, all holdings were returned to him or his heirs (*Regiam Majestatem*, ed. Rt. Hon. Lord Cooper [Edinburgh: Skinner, 1947], 2, c. 40). With his diagnosis, however, the leper lost all of his legal rights. For more information, see Gerard Lee, *Leper Hospitals in Medieval Ireland* (Dublin: Four Courts Press, 1996), 1–72.

[42] Peter Richards, *The Medieval Leper and His Northern Heirs* (Cambridge: D. S. Brewer, 1977), 50–51. See also John Comrie, *History of Scottish Medicine* (London: Bailliere, Tindall and Cox, 1932), 193–202; and Christopher Daniell, *Death and Burial in Medieval England, 1066–1550* (New York: Routledge, 1997), app. 1, "Jews and Lepers."

[43] Sabine Volk-Birke reads this ceremony through the lens of religious redemption, arguing that the disease spiritually cleanses the body in preparation for divine redemption ("Sickness unto Death: Crime and Punishment in Henryson's *The Testament of Cresseid*," *Anglia* 113 [1995]: 163–83).

[44] By using leprosy as the agent responsible for Cresseid's loss of identity, Henryson is surely playing with the term's secondary use; according to the *Middle English Dictionary*, "leprous" (1b) not only referred to a gamut of flesh-eating diseases, but also was used by medieval alchemists and farmers to describe a diseased or corrupted element or plot of land.

[45] Thomas Craik, "The Substance and Structure of the *Testament of Cresseid*: A Hypothesis," in *Bards and Makars: Scottish Language and Literature: Medieval and Renaissance*, ed. Adam Aitken, Matthew McDiarmid, and Derick Thomson (Glasgow: University of Glasgow Press, 1977), 22.

'Worthie lordis, for Goddis lufe of heuin,
To vs lipper [lepers] part of ʒour almous deid!'
Than to thair cry nobill Troylus tuik heid,
Hauing pietie, neir by the place can pas
Quhair Cresseid sat, not witting [knowing] quhat scho was.
Than vpon him scho kest [cast] vp baith hir ene [eyes],
And with ane blenk it come into his thocht
That he sumtime hir face befoir had sene . . .
(491–500)

A primary reason why the hero does not fully recognize the heroine is that she is so severely disfigured. Although he can conjure a hazy image of Cresseid in his mind, he is unable—despite persistent attempts—to connect this image to the face that he sees before him.[46] Troilus' lapse of memory—what one critic has called "psychological delusion, a kind of absent-mindedness"— serves as the catalytic mechanism that actualizes the heroine's loss of identity.[47] Cresseid's nonexistence is no longer a theoretical possibility but a material reality. Because her post-leprosy body is not registered in legal memory as human, female, or lover, Troilus cannot identify her as such. When he passes her on the highway, he cannot distinguish the "place" where Cresseid sits from her actual body. Thus, he imagines not "quha" she is, but "quhat scho was": Cresseid is no longer legally a woman, but she once was. Now Troilus can only see Cresseid as a gap once filled with something that he "befoir had sene."

Cresseid's legal exclusion preoccupies the narrator throughout the *Testament*. Early in the poem Diomeid tires of Cresseid and sends her a "lybell of repudie" (74), or bill of divorce. As a result, the heroine is "excludit fra his companie" (75). By using the term "exclude" within this particular context, Henryson implies that the legal consequences of divorce are analogous to the destructive effects of leprosy. By exchanging Troilus' death (which occurs in Chaucer's version of the legend) for Diomeid's divorce, Henryson enacts a similar measure of legal death; for in the Middle Ages, a woman typically lost the legal rights of ownership over her property, land, and moveable goods upon her divorce.[48] Later in the poem, Saturn reiterates the link between legal and corporeal exclusionism. In his condemning speech against Cresseid he says, "Thy wantoun blude, and eik thy goldin hair / Heir I *exclude* fra the for euermair" (314–15, emphasis added). Here, the deity directly refers to the juridical process of exclusion, juxtaposing the physical effects of the disease— disintegrating blood and wilting hair—with their legal consequences. The

---

[46] Ibid.

[47] Jane Adamson, "The Curious Incident of Recognition in Henryson's *The Testament of Cresseid*," *Parergon* 27 (1980): 17.

[48] Felicity Riddy explores the discourse of exclusion that pervades the *Testament* in "'Abject odious': Feminine and Masculine in Henryson's *Testament of Cresseid*," in *The Long Fifteenth Century: Essays for Douglas Gray*, ed. Helen Cooper and Sally Mapstone (Oxford: Clarendon Press, 1997), 229–48.

eradication of a specific legal privilege—the right to one's namesake—is alluded to when Cresseid enters the leper colony. The narrator, explaining the reason behind her agonizing moans, says, "And still murning, scho was of nobill kin" (398). Similarly, the text depicts Cresseid's father as an ecclesiastical "father," the priest who performs this procedure. After being "excludit" (75) from Diomeid's presence, Cresseid rushes to the temple, where her father, Calchas, "wes keiper of the tempill as ane preist" (107). She immediately confesses her sins to him—"Fra Diomeid had gottin his desyre / He wox werie and wald of me no moir" (101–2)—and requests assistance. In accordance with official guidelines governing the law of exclusion, Calchas leads her to a private oratory, where is she is directed to ask for forgiveness from the gods. Knowing "weill that thair was na succour" (376) for his daughter, he waits for her to awaken from her dream and then delivers her to the leper hospital outside of town.

The most powerful interpolation of the process of exclusion in the poem occurs in Henryson's description of the lepers themselves. The *Testament* may be the only nonlegal text that adopts the exact terminology used in contemporary law for lepers. Medieval religious and literary references to lepers—including those in Wyclif's sermons, the Bible, and the *Ancrene Wisse*—use only generic terms such as "lepurs," "lepres," and "lepirs."[49] In calling a band of lepers "lipper folk" (526, 580), Henryson explicitly mimics fifteenth-century leper statutes that use the same phrase to describe the community they legally repress. A statute passed by James I in 1427 forbade lepers from entering the burgh on certain days and at specific times: Item That na lipper folk, nouther man nor woman, enter na cum in a burgh of the realme bot thrise in the oulk, that is to say, ilk Monounday, Wednejday and Friday, fra ten houris to twa eftrnoon and quhair fairis and mercattis fallis in thay dayis, that thay leif thair entrie in the burrowis, and gang on the morn to get thair leving.[50] A similar statute passed the same year further restricts lepers from religious spaces: "Item, That na lipper folk sit to thig, nather in kirk na in kirk ʒaird na uther place within the burrowis"; and a 1466 law concludes, "And thairfor na man sall tak on hand to herberie [harbor] lipper folk, under the pane of ane unlaw."[51] As part of the formulaic makeup of a leper statute, the phrase "lipper folk" is really nothing more than a legalistic formula, a linguistic construction so repetitively employed in such similar contexts that it loses its meaning. To the experienced legal reader, then—that is, Henryson's fifteenth-century audience—the physical referents of "lipper folk," the lepers themselves, are equally devoid of meaning. By interpolating this generic term into his text, along with similar constructions such as "lipper man" and "lipper woman," Henryson participates

---

[49] *Middle English Dictionary*, s.v. "lepre, 1,2,3," "leprous" 1a, and "lepur 1."

[50] *APS*, 2:16, c. 8.

[51] Ibid., *Leges Burgorum*, c. 62, cited in *The Practicks of Sir James Balfour of Pittendreich*, ed. Peter G. B. McNeil (Edinburgh: Stair Society, 1962), 1:131.

in a literary revisionism of juridical exclusion. His lepers, save Cresseid, are not inscribed with any identity outside their assigned title of "lipper folk." They are anonymous, faceless figures who wander through the narrative but have no significant impact on it.

Although the majority of the leper statutes enacted in fifteenth-century Scotland were designed to make the leper "invisible" by physically excluding him from public spaces, there is one peculiar statute (registered in the *Statutes of the Gild*) that seems to reverse the ideological mechanism of exclusion by deliberately drawing attention to the leprous body:

> Item, It is statute, that na lipper folk enter within the portis of the burgh: And gif ony happinis to enter, he sall incontinent to be cassin furth be the Serjand of the burgh: And gif ony lipper folk dois in the contrare of this our inhibitioun, and usis to enter within the burgh, the cleithing of the bodie sall be takin fra him and brint [burnt], and he beand nakit, sall be put furth of the burgh. It is in like wayis statute, that sum honest men of the burgh sall gader almons, to be gevin and distribute to all lipper folk in ony meit and convenient place without the burgh.[52]

Lepers who unlawfully entered the gates of the city (and refused to leave on command) were stripped of their clothing and "put furth of the burgh." Medieval conceptions of leprosy, which viewed even the clothing of lepers to be contaminants, undoubtedly deemed this behavior medically necessary to preserve the health of the masses. Yet the very act of public removal of clothing from a sick body also constitutes a grotesque spectacle, one that was, curiously enough, sanctioned by the law. For the viewing public, surely the most exciting parts of the naked leper body were not the organs that were now exposed but the parts of the body that were missing—those that had literally fallen off through the destructive machinations of the disease.

We must bear in mind that removing the medieval leper from his habit was surely no small feat. Henryson's representation of Cresseid's apparel, which includes "ane mantill and ane bawer hat / With cop and clapper" (386), is typical of medieval leper garb (the poet most likely found inspiration for his character's clothing in the attire worn by lepers who lived at St. Leonard's). A fourteenth-century marginal painting in the *Exeter Pontifical* provides a particularly complete description of the English leper's uniform, which is assumed to be similar to the Scot's: an ankle-length tunic made of coarse red-brown cloth with sleeves closed to the wrist, a russet cowl, and black cape.[53] The labored process of removing the clothing from the leper's body piece by piece served a specific ideological purpose: it imitated the slow, agonizing effects of the disease itself, which little by little ate away at flesh and tissue until

---

[52] *Statutes of the Gild*, c. 16, cited in McNeil, *Practicks of Sir James Balfour,* 131.
[53] British Library, MS Lansdown 451, f. 157.

it fell off the bone. As the public watches with horrified yet enraptured gazes as the leper is stripped and revealed for what he is, or at least what the spectators see him to be—a disfigured mass of bones and flesh—the juridical process of exclusion approaches full circle. The leper is excluded by the church, the law, and finally the community. All segments of the process are thus designed with a common goal: to dehumanize the leper in every way possible and emphasize that the diseased body is not the "other" but "another," something that is decidedly devoid of human attributes and thus undeserving of respect by the public or the law.

In the *Testament*, Cresseid is stripped of her metaphorical clothing—her social and legal coverings of respectability and value—through the dehumanizing effects of leprosy. Henryson does not shield this process from the reader's critical gaze but rather highlights the "spectacle" of the heroine's deteriorating body in the poem by cataloguing the various debilitating manifestations of the disease:

> 'My cleir voice and courtlie carrolling,
> Quhair I was wont with ladyis for to sing,
> Is rawk [harsh] as ruik [crow], full hiddeous, hoir [rough] and hace [hoarse];
> My plesand port, all vtheris precelling [excelling],
> Of lustines [delightfulness] I was hald maist conding [worthy]—
> Now is deformit the figour of my face;
> To luik on it na leid now lyking hes [no person now enjoys].
> Sowpit [wearied] in syte, I say with sair siching [sore sighing],
> Ludgeit [dwelling] amang the lipper leid [leper folk], "Allace!'"
> (443–51)

Cresseid's once melodious voice is now raspy; her beauty, once esteemed above all, is hideously "deformit," and her figure, once supple, has grossly decayed. By serving as the agent and voice who describes these disfigurements, Cresseid participates in (and even promotes) the very discourse that has reduced her to nothingness. Devaluing herself and acknowledging the permanence of her corporeal and legal losses, she surrenders the final component of her identity: the belief that she in fact has one.

At this point in the narrative, with Cresseid's body reduced to nothingness and her person devoid of a legal identity, we cannot imagine any fate for the heroine other than a gruesome and torturous death. In fact, courtly tradition demands it. We expect the end to come quickly, but it is curiously suspended for forty-one lines. In this narrative space Henryson fashions a legal text that is profoundly revisionary. The poem's documentary conclusion of the legal narrative that has preceded it disputes the modes of authority governing the law of personhood while actively refiguring Cresseid within it.

Where There's a Will, There's a Way

Having just concluded her Complaint, in which she laments the fallen state of her diseased body, Cresseid secludes herself in the leprosarium and "with paper scho sat doun / And on this maneir maid hir testament" (575–76). At first glance, Cresseid's inscriptions seem innocuous. Molded into what she calls "hir testament," they seem to reflect her *voluntas*, her last will. Cresseid, however, should rightly be prohibited from having a "will" (in both senses of the term). As we remember, it is her unrestrained *voluntas* that gets her into trouble with the gods in the first place. Unable (or unwilling) to control her blasphemous speech, she is afflicted by the deities with a punishment designed to prevent her from participating in any legal procedure—including the drafting of a valid testament. By relegating Cresseid to the space of the legally dead, the law seemingly thwarts any possibilities of future rebellion. According to *Black's Law Dictionary*, a legal persona is dependent on a network of social relations: "Persona est homo cum statu quodam consideratus."[54] In a study of the modern identity, Charles Taylor similarly suggests that "a self exists only within 'webs of interlocution.' . . . [T]he full definition of someone's identity usually involves . . . some reference to a defining community."[55] Having been stripped of her points of social and legal reference, Cresseid is ostensibly "selfless."

Yet the medieval law of exclusion contains a loophole that presented a potential opportunity for the legal effects of leprosy to be reversed. In erasing a subject from legal memory, the law simultaneously released him from the constraints of legal subjectivity. While the leper is not included in the law, then, he is technically not governed by it either. This legal gap allows Cresseid to exist outside the law—to carve a legal space for herself in the narrative that is completely divorced from the feudal court system and set within her own prescribed (and self-controlled) boundaries.

It is into this space that Cresseid inserts her twelve-line testament. The contents of her will clearly delineate her "will" (*voluntas*) regarding the interment of her corpse and dispersal of her goods:

"Heir I beteiche [bequeath] my corps and carioun
With wormis and with taidis [toads] to be rent;
My cop and clapper, and myne ornament,

---

[54] "A person is a man considered with reference to a certain status." See Henry Campbell Black, with Joseph Nolan and M. J. Connolly, *Black's Law Dictionary: Definitions of the Terms and Phrases of American and English Jurisprudence, Ancient and Modern* (St. Paul, Minn.: West Publishing, 1979), 1029.

[55] Charles Taylor, *Sources of the Self: The Making of Modern Identity* (Cambridge: Cambridge University Press, 1989), 36.

And all my gold the lipper folk sall haue,
Quhen I am deid, to burie me in graue.

'This royall ring, set with this rubie reid,
Quhilk Troylus in drowrie [love token] to me send,
To him agane I leif it quhen I am deid,
To make my cairfull deid vnto him kend [known].
Thus I conclude schortlie and mak ane end:
My spreit I leif to Diane, quhair scho dwellis,
To walk with hir in waist [uninhabited] woddis and wellis.
(577–88)

As Julia Boffey has noted, Cresseid's testament conforms to the four-point formula characteristic of most fifteenth-century wills.[56] What is peculiar about the heroine's testament is not the way in which property is bequeathed, however, but the discourse of self-exclusion that underlies it. She begins by disposing of her carcass, which is to be buried "in graue." This hackneyed phrase evokes the medieval tradition of bequeathing one's body to the particular church or religious institution that will dispose of it. As a pagan and leper, Cresseid is excluded from this ritual and therefore must dedicate her "corps" to an unconsecrated piece of land—one that is appropriately filled with "wormis" and "taidis." The text's revision of religious tradition is enlarged in the heroine's dedication of her soul. By leaving her spirit to Diana, the mythological goddess of the hunt, Cresseid consigns herself to spend eternity in the "woddis and wellis," a marginalized space well outside the courtly garden and cultivated field with which she is familiar. The use of the phrase "to be rent" within this legal context is also interesting, as it generates inevitable comparisons to two disparate elements of medieval testamentary convention. Taken in its verbal form (as it appears here), the phrase functions as a metaphor for earthly burial. By requesting that her body be "rent," or shredded, by animals and insects, Cresseid acknowledges herself a participant in the organic processes of decay and decomposition. At the same time, however, this phrase evokes the Christian tradition in which a testator likens himself to a husbandman who "rents" his body from the Lord God during his mortal tenure and returns it to him upon his death. Cresseid's leprous body, of course—which does not legally exist—cannot be given to an ecclesiastical lord or a temporal one because it is not recognized as property. It is precisely

---

[56] Julia Boffey, "Lydgate, Henryson, and the Literary Testament," *Modern Language Quarterly* 53 (1992): 41–56. Traditionally, testators began their wills with a formulary statement in which they dedicated their spirit to God and their bodies to the parish church where they were christened or blessed. Next came the bequests of material items, namely, land and moveable goods such as furniture, jewelry, clothing, and religious books. The will typically concluded with a formulary statement attesting that the testator was sound in mind and body, ensuring that his *voluntas* was consistent with the content of the will he transcribed. For more information on the structural format of the medieval British will, see Michael Sheehan, *The Will in Medieval England* (Toronto: Pontifical Institute of Medieval Studies, 1963), 163–230.

through her marginalized position within the law and the church structure—the ownership of her body is ambiguous—that she is able to claim her corpse for herself.

Within this bequeathal sequence emerges a striking paradox: Cresseid claims the wasted body as her own only "to obliterate all physical traces of her existence."[57] By burying her body and distributing her goods, Cresseid seems to thrust herself further into the realm of anonymity. Yet perhaps this is precisely the point: for in anonymity, she is a cipher, an empty space inscribed with nothing yet obligated to no one.

By documenting her *voluntas*—and having it carried out after her death—Cresseid turns the law of personhood inside out. She manipulates established law in order to create a new law that in turn enables her to inscribe on herself an identity that no one can repress or eradicate. By including Cresseid's testament within its narrative body, the *Testament* literally writes her into its own poetic will (the narrative after all is a "testament"). Not only does Cresseid participate in authorized legal discourse, but also her illegal will (in both senses of the word) becomes a validated part of this discourse.

The heroine's reemergence as a legal person is consolidated through her reinsertion into legal memory. Immediately after Cresseid's death, an anonymous leper man delivers word of her demise to Troilus:

> Quhen he had hard hir greit infirmitie
> Hir legacie and lamentatioun,
> And how scho endit in sic pouertie,
> He swelt [fainted] for wo and fell doun in ane swoun;
> For greit sorrow his hart to brist [burst] was boun [ready];
> Siching full sadlie, said, 'I can no moir;
> Scho was vntrew and wo is me thairfoir.'
> (596–602)

Where once Cresseid is a "blenk" in Troilus' mind, now she is a "legacie," an indelible textual imprint in his memory. Troilus transfers this mental image of his lost love into a physical text, inscribing her story on a marble tombstone. The words carved into the stone—along with the heroine's name—constitute a "ressoun," an explanation for the text. "Lo, fair ladyis," he writes, "Cresseid of Troy [the] toun, / Sumtyme countit the flour of womanheid / Vnder this stane, lait lipper, lyis deid' (607–9). Troilus' words indicate that Cresseid's corpse is not bequeathed to the fair ladies of Troy and, by extension, to the reader, as an exemplum. Cresseid's written "legacy," by contrast, emphatically is.

In her Complaint, Cresseid tells the audience "in ʒour mynd ane mirrour mak of me" (457). Henryson's poetic mirror seems to cast forth an image of

---

[57] Boffey, "Lydgate, Henryson, and the Literary Testament," 53.

hope and restoration. Cresseid, once crippled, is now whole; where once she was invisible, now she can be "seen"—and, by implication, "heard" and "understood"—in both literal and legal senses. Yet if the *Testament of Cresseid* has transformed the legal status of Chaucer's Criseyde beyond recognition, it has also highlighted the author's culpability in the heroine's fate. Henryson keeps his character alive long enough for her to obtain a legal identity, but destroys her before she can exercise her new rights. Thus, the heroine's subjective will is ultimately subordinate to Henryson's own *voluntas*, his desire to express—however implicitly—that Cresseid's words are always his words, and his words are law.

3 The Literature of 1388 and the Politics of Pity in Gower's *Confessio amantis*

ANDREW GALLOWAY

Although Gower spent much of his life writing about law, in the sense of ethical and natural law, only as he neared the end of his literary career—possibly already lapsing into the blindness that stopped his writing in 1401—did he write directly about the state trials of 1388, 1397, and 1399, in which Richard and the nobility had waged open war. The issues behind these trials strained tranquillity throughout Richard's reign; the clashes themselves display how the recurring crises of his reign were typically couched in terms of law and generated further conflicts by their legal weaponry.[1] Indeed, the trial of 1388, along with its aftermath, was arguably the defining event of political culture in the early 1390s, when Gower was producing and revising the *Confessio amantis*, although he never mentions the event there. In contrast to the silence in that acclaimed poem, Gower's short, pro-Henrician Latin poem, the *Cronica tripertita*, completed after Richard's death in 1400, recounts each of those momentous proceedings when parliament served as a legal battlefield between Richard and the higher nobility. It, like most of Gower's topical works, stands decidedly low in modern estimation, not rescued even by its Dantesque division into the "human" endeavors of 1388 (when a group of Richard's uncles and others tried, convicted, and executed

---

[1] Gower's blindness began during the first year of Henry IV's reign (September 30, 1399–September 29, 1400) and largely stopped his writing by the following year. See the three successive versions of his short poem explaining this progression, "Henrici quarti primus," "Henrici Regis annus," and "Quidquid homo scribat," and note his late dedicatory letter of the *Vox clamantis*, all printed (with the versions of the short poem in reverse order) in *The Complete Works of John Gower: The Latin Works*, ed. G.C. Macaulay (Oxford: Clarendon Press, 1902), 365–66, 1–2. All citations of Gower's Latin works, with references by book and line number, are from this edition; unless otherwise noted, all translations are mine.

for treason many of Richard's closest supporters), the "infernal" endeavors of 1397 (when Richard retaliated by convicting the attacking lords as traitors), and the "divine" endeavors of 1399 (when England saw its first parliamentary deposition, an event Gower describes in terms of nothing less than evangelical law, when "the proud" Richard was cast down and "the humble" Henry exalted).[2]

I will go to no great lengths to redeem the *Cronica tripertita* as a literary masterpiece. I propose, however, that the state trials it describes and the literature they occasioned—along with a particular ethical category that Gower's *Cronica* displays—had considerable importance in Gower's overall literary production. In this essay, I first show how the 1388 parliamentary trial generated a spate of narratives with notable satirical or pathetic power, whose narrative strategies and intensity derive, it seems, as much from the trial's legal irregularities as its political import. Though historical in form, generally anonymous, and often extant only in the forms imposed by monastic chronicles, they may be considered a literary corpus, to which Gower's *Cronica tripertita* was a belated and not undistinguished addition.

The essay then offers a more speculative claim reaching beyond explicit responses to 1388: that some issues producing and further generated by that first parliamentary trial explain the central concerns and dramatic intensity of the *Confessio amantis* too, versions of which were released in what is often described as the politically quiet years of the early 1390s. Although only Gower's *Cronica tripertita* is directly classifiable with the literature of 1388, I argue that this parliamentary trial in particular, the Merciless Parliament, along with Richard's actions that led to it and his responses (even before his own parliamentary retaliation in 1397 and still later his deposition, granted a show trial in parliament in 1399) brought to focus an ethical issue that Gower emphasizes and explores throughout both the *Cronica* and the *Confessio*: the menacing and unreliable nature of pity as a political and legal instrument. The question of just how we might theorize Gower's exploration of pity in the *Confessio* as an unnamed trace or oblique assessment of 1388 and its political and cultural aftermath must await that demonstration.

The Merciless Parliament

The parliament of February–May 1388 was in some constitutional and legal terms unprecedented, partly because of the attacking nobility's savage

---

[2] In John H. Fisher's phrase, it is a "mere exemplum or addendum" to the larger ethical unity of his sequence of long poems (*John Gower: Moral Philosopher and Friend of Chaucer* [London: Methuen Press, 1965], 115). For a different view of Gower's achievement in the *Confessio*, which removes it from the spirit of the other works, see Winthrop Wetherbee, "John Gower," in *The Cambridge History of Medieval English Literature*, ed. David Wallace (Cambridge: Cambridge University Press, 1999), 589–609. Wetherbee's important essay still dismisses the *Cronica* as mere propaganda.

peremptoriness, partly because of the novel ingenuity of its strategies for out-maneuvering the king's legal position. The events of this parliament might best be understood as a baronial effort to control the young king's and his officials' considerable expenditures and taxations and, worst of all from the gentry's perspective, the king's recent efforts to hold baronial property and lives ransom in a newly emphasized threat of charges of treason. During the course of the parliament, a group of powerful nobles (especially Richard's uncles, Gloucester, Arundel, and Warwick, joined by Henry Bolingbroke and Thomas Mowbray) used the novel tactic of preemptively "appealing" the king's closest friends for treason, on the grounds that they were "accroaching royal power and disenfranchizing the king of his sovereignty." Thus the lords did not (yet) assail Richard for acting too autocratically, but instead attacked his favored associates on the grounds that they were acting like kings.[3] In the short term, the appellant lords were dramatically successful. They used for trial evidence nothing more than the rough-and-ready principle of common opinion: gauntlets fell like snow in parliament before the king when one of the accused, Nicholas Brembre, asked (in vain, it turned out) to wage trial by battle, as the tract writer Thomas Favent declares; most other sources mention the general shouting of guilt, and the sometimes awkward efforts to round up people who could agree that the accused were "notorious." Yet the appellant lords succeeded in condemning those present to death, refusing by the "law of parliament" (a notion first mentioned here) to allow the accused any legal counsel, detailed consideration of the appeals, or reply beyond a plea. They added to these procedures the still less precedented tactic of condemning in absentia even those accused who had fled, and stripped them of all their personal property except for what was already entailed to their heirs.[4] Those unable to escape suffered more. The London mayor Nicholas Brembre and the former chief justice Robert Tresilian were drawn and hanged; Richard's aging tutor Simon Burley was spared such dishonor and torture by being simply decapitated; and, among others less prominent, the minor clerk Thomas Usk, who himself had appealed of treason Brembre's enemy John of Northampton, was with painstaking elaborateness dispatched as well (his ex-

---

[3] *Rotuli Parliamentorum, ut et Petitiones . . . Tempore Ricardi R. II* (London: House of Lords, 1783), 3:230; henceforth *Rot. parl.* The legal charge of "accroachment" has similarities to a cruder complaint from a source in Henry Knighton's chronicle about the behavior of justices of the king's peace in the provinces, that they were known as "second kings." See *Knighton's Chronicle, 1337–1396*, ed. and trans. G. H. Martin (Oxford: Clarendon Press, 1995), 444–45; henceforth Knighton. This source, apparently a provincial complaint about the disruption caused by the Merciless Parliament, is discussed later in the text.

[4] *Historia sive Narracio de Modo et Forma Mirabilis Parliamento apud Westmonasterium anno Domini Millesimo CCCLXXXVI . . . per Thomam Favent Clericum Indictata*, ed. May McKisack, Camden Miscellany 14 (London: Camden Society, 1926), 16 (par. 18); henceforth Favent, citing by page in McKisack, and by paragraph number of my English translation in the appendix to this volume. On the novel procedures, see Anthony Musson and W. M. Ormrod, *The Evolution of English Justice: Law, Politics, and Society in the Fourteenth Century* (Basingstoke: Macmillan, 1999), 108–9. For the financial penalties, see Knighton, 432–33, 498–99, 502–3; and C. D. Ross, "Forfeiture for Treason in the Reign of Richard II," *English Historical Review* 71 (1956): 560–75.

ecution alone represents the full tradition of death for treason: he was drawn, hanged, then taken down and beheaded in no fewer than thirty strokes, whether still alive or not is unclear).[5]

To accomplish all this in the four months of this parliament, in which at least some regular business was conducted, and with the king usually present (as was required for medieval parliament to have authority, unlike the parliament convened in 1326 to condemn Edward II), legal procedure had to be made as well as found.[6] The claim of "accroachment" was not covered by the 1352 Statute of Treason, whose details were formulated, it has been argued, to protect subjects from the king's unlimited appropriations of property in treason cases (if so, there is some irony in how the Lords Appellant also exceeded the 1352 statute both in the charge and the severe financial punishments of the condemned).[7]

But the novelty was less in the charge or the venue—parliament, after all, had been the scene of state trials since Edward I's reign[8]—than the legal instrument. An "appeal," that is, a personal and written accusation rather than a simple oral deposition, if used in common law, required the accused to be present; only in civil law could conviction by default occur.[9] But in 1388 most of the accused were not present, having hidden or fled in advance of the Lords Appellant. This situation seems to explain why, when Richard challenged the procedure, the judges at the parliament at first declared that the appeal fell between "what either one law or the other requires," thus displaying, as Anthony Tuck argues, some independent loyalty to professional ethics, since Walter Clopton, who had just replaced Robert Tresilian as chief justice, was one of Gloucester's retainers.[10] The lords' stentorian reply to this initial procedural challenge is given in the Parliament's Rolls, in an assertion of parliamentary legal preeminence that anticipates some parliamentary claims during the seventeenth-century Civil War.[11]

[5] For Usk's end, see L. C. Hector and Barbara Harvey, eds. and trans., *The Westminster Chronicle, 1381–1394* (Oxford: Clarendon Press, 1982), 314–15; henceforth *West. Chron.* On methods of execution for treason, see J. G. Bellamy, *The Law of Treason in England in the Later Middle Ages* (Cambridge: Cambridge University Press, 1970), 12–14, 21–26.

[6] On the parliament condemning Edward II, see M. H. Keen, *England in the Later Middle Ages* (1973; reprint, London: Routledge, 1997), 97–101; Michael Prestwich, *The Three Edwards: War and State in England, 1272–1377* (1980; reprint, London: Routledge, 1993), 98–99.

[7] See Bellamy, *Law of Treason*, 65–90.

[8] Ibid., 23–58.

[9] Alan Rogers, "Parliamentary Appeals of Treason in the Reign of Richard II," *American Journal of Legal History* 8 (1964): 108.

[10] *Rot. parl.*, 3:236; Anthony Tuck, *Richard II and the English Nobility* (New York: St. Martin's, 1974), 122. Modern interpretations of why Clopton briefly upheld Richard's challenge to the "Appeal" differ in emphases and details; some conjecture is necessary to understand Clopton's remark. See Nigel Saul, *Richard II* (New Haven: Yale University Press, 1997), 192, and Keen, *England in the Later Middle Ages*, 281–83.

[11] For the seventeenth century, see Christopher Hill, *The Century of Revolution, 1603–1714* (London: Norton, 1982), esp. 50–51; see also Conrad Russell, *The Crisis of Parliaments: English History, 1509–1660* (London: Oxford University Press, 1971), 329–41, esp. 334.

Whereupon the said lords of parliament . . . were agreed in declaring that in so high a crime as is set forth in this Appeal . . . the trial will not be carried out anywhere else than parliament, nor by any other law than the law and procedure of parliament. And that it pertains to the lords of parliament . . . by ancient custom to be the judges in such a case, and to judge such cases with the king's assent. . . . And that their intention is not to carry out such a high case as this Appeal is . . . in any other lower court or place in the realm, which courts and places are nothing but executors of ancient laws and customs of the realm and of ordinances and statutes of parliament.[12]

As Nigel Saul points out, this vague claim to "ancient custom" and "the law and procedure of parliament" ("Ley et Cours du Parlement") left the lords free to invent the rules as they went along.[13] Indeed, by common law procedures, never before used in parliamentary trials, they denied Nicholas Brembre the right to legal counsel or response beyond a reply of "guilty" or "not guilty"; but following *civil* law they denied Brembre the right to prove innocence by battle, because according to that law such battle was allowable only when there were no witnesses. (He and some of the other accused sought to frustrate the novel procedures by refusing to plea [*West. Chron.*, 318–19].) The charge against Brembre even shifted during the course of his trial from treason to mere knowledge of treason.[14] Denying the plaintiffs a hearing was a particularly notorious aspect of the trial; in 1397, when John of Gaunt was interrogating Arundel, Gaunt is said to have remarked that Arundel was being tried by the law of England, "not by your law, for by that law you would be denied a hearing."[15] The reference to "your law" is clearly to that of 1388.

In fact, the lords' use of an "appeal" of treason may have been overdetermined in several ways. Impeachment, the means of parliamentary control of a king's expenditures and actions which the Good Parliament's indictments of Edward III's associates had created in 1376, had never been used for treason; impeachment for treason was used apparently for the first time in the Merciless Parliament along with the "appeal" (but the accounts are inconsistent, and at any rate impeachment was only an ancillary instrument).[16] Interest in impeachment as a primary legal instrument in state trials had probably been

[12] "Sur quoy les ditz Seigneurs du Parlement . . . de lour commune acorde estoit declare, Qe en si haute Crime come est pretendu en cest Appell . . . la Cause ne serra aillours deduc q'en Parlement, ne par autre Ley qe Ley et Cours du Parlement, Et q'il appertient as Seigneurs du Parlement . . . d'aucien Custume du Parlement, d'estre Juges en tieux cas, et de tieux cas ajugger par assent du Roi. . . . Et auxint lour entent n'est pas de reuler ou govener si haute Cause come cest Appell est . . . en ascunt Court ou Place plus bas deinz mesme le Roialme; queux Courtes et Places ne son qe Executours d'auciens Leys et Custumes du Roialme et Ordinances et Establisementz de Parlement" (*Rot. parl.*, 3:236).

[13] Saul, *Richard II*, 192.

[14] See Rogers, "Parliamentary Appeals," 113–17.

[15] From the continuation of the *Eulogium* chronicle, 3:374; quoted and translated by Rogers, "Parliamentary Appeals," 116.

[16] See *West. Chron.*, xlii, 280–81, 28–87.

dampened when, in the first sally of open conflict between Richard and the higher lords in 1386, the Commons had impeached his chancellor Michael de la Pole for financial corruption and abuse of his office, and Richard had responded with his notorious set of "questions to the judges" regarding such procedures (the "questions" were listed in 1399 as one of the reasons for deposing Richard).[17] The judges, a group secretly assembled in 1387 from the highest judicial positions, had replied to Richard's tendentious queries as any king might have wished. Regarding parliament's right to impeach his chancellor, its power to impose a supervisory council over the king's expenditures and ignore his dissolution of that parliament, even its legitimacy in having presented the Ordinances against Edward II in 1311, they declared that not only were these expressions of parliamentary power not valid, but also those who had instigated them had indeed violated the king's prerogative (the question Richard asked them to rule on) and thus were guilty of treason.[18] The answers, somehow leaked to the Lords Appellant, offered no radical departure in legal theory but established a specific legal threat against any further parliamentary use of impeachment against Richard's associates. Since the judges were condemned in the Merciless Parliament for these answers, as Alan Rogers has argued, impeachment must still have been considered a viable instrument, one the lords could have used.[19] Nonetheless, the lords could better maintain a guise of adhering to the king's law by turning to an instrument more commonly used (though never before in parliament) to lodge charges of treason.

It is possible that the choice of "appealing" associates and supporters of the king for treason was suggested in another way, from its recent use by one of Richard's minor supporters, Thomas Usk. Usk figures surprisingly prominently in the charges of the Merciless Parliament. The London author of the *Testament of Love*, sometime legal scrivener, and obsequious fan of Chaucer, Usk had in 1384 lodged an "Appeal" against the London mayor John of Northampton and his three supporters, William Essex, John More, and Richard Northbury. Although he wrote his "Appeal" in London before the coroner, Usk delivered it orally before the king and council at Reading. Summarizing Usk's oral presentation, the Westminster chronicler states that these were charges of treason. Northampton was almost immediately convicted, his life spared only at the queen's intercession, and Nicholas Brembre, Richard's longtime financial supporter, was able to return to office as London's mayor (seizing the office "with strong honde" and threatening opponents by carrying "grete quantitee of Armure to the Guyldehall," as the London Mercers' Guild complained at the 1388 parliament [*Rot. parl.*, 3:225]). Richard's desire

[17] Article 2 of "The Record and Process of the Renunciation of King Richard the Second," *Rot. parl.*, 3:415–53; translated in Chris Given-Wilson, *Chronicles of the Revolution, 1397–1400* (Manchester: Manchester University Press, 1993), 173.

[18] *West. Chron.*, 196–202 and references there.

[19] Rogers, "Parliamentary Appeals," 104.

to advance the useful Brembre may partly explain Richard's encouragement of Usk's "Appeal," or at least the animus with which the appellant lords regarded it.[20] Northampton was present before the king and council when Usk appealed him on July 20, 1384; but the others Usk's "Appeal" mentions, Essex, More, and Northbury, were arrested only a month later, when (as the *Westminster Chronicle* records) the king ordered that officials should "proceed judicially against [More, Northbury, and Essex] whom public accusation and popular scandal charged with flagrant crimes and outrages."[21] They were therefore in effect appealed (though not summarily convicted like Northampton) in absentia. Upon their arrest, Robert Tresilian—then chief justice, whom the Lords Appellant would later in turn appeal and execute— declared that since they had already been appealed and indicted for treason, if they were condemned to death for their crimes, they would have all their property, movable and immovable, confiscated. They confessed, begged mercy, and were condemned to drawing and hanging. At that point, Michael de la Pole, the king's chancellor, "joined the gathering" and declared that "since they voluntarily submitted to the king's grace [*gratia*], the king, of his special grace, grants them their lives," though "they shall be kept during his pleasure in places of safety until, if it seems expedient, he thinks fit to show them increased grace."[22]

I shall focus in due course on such lofty casualness in the king's and his agents' interposing of an unpredictably expansive or contracting *gratia*. A more pertinent point for the moment is that the Lords Appellant's use of an appeal for treason (and, moreover, against defendants who were, at first at least, absentee and nearly convicted by simple notoriety) had some precedence in the king's and his supporters' legal endeavors. It is not, to be sure, a strong precedent, but some evidence suggests it was known to the Lords Appellant. Sometime between January 20 and mid-February 1388, quite possibly before the parliamentary trial began February 3, the chief justice presiding over the Merciless Parliament, Walter Clopton, Gloucester's retainer, who on January 1, 1388, had replaced Tresilian as chief justice of the King's Bench, ordered the gathering of documents dealing with Northampton's case of 1384, including what Paul Strohm identifies as a Latin summary of Usk's

---

[20] *West. Chron.*, 90–96; on Usk generally, see Paul Strohm, "Politics and Poetics: Usk and Chaucer in the 1380s," in *Literary Practice and Social Change in Britain, 1380–1530*, ed. Lee Patterson (Berkeley: University of California Press, 1990), 83–112; on Brembre's assistance to Richard, see Saul, *Richard II*, 184.

[21] "Ad procedendum juridice contra predictos super tam notoriis criminibus et excessibus publice appellatos ac eciam notorie diffamatos" (*West. Chron.*, 94–95).

[22] "Mox dominus Michael de Poole cancellarious domini regis concionem intravit, et . . . dixit: 'Licet isti propter scelera commissa mortem subire celeriter debuissent, tamen quia regie gracie se ultro dederunt rex concedit eis vitam tantum de sua gracia speciali; nichilominus tamen vult quod usque ad beneplacitum suum in locis securis interim custodiantur donec, si videatur expedire, eis graciam facere duxerit ampliorem'" (*West. Chron.*, 96–97; *gratia* is translated throughout as "grace" to avoid the many synonyms that Hector and Harvey use).

"Appeal," among a group of King's Bench memoranda.[23] The collecting of these documents may, as Strohm speculates, have been part of an effort to redeem Northampton after the fact; but the timing suggested by other evidence from the Close Rolls makes the parliament of 1388 a more likely occasion for collecting these texts. On January 12, 1388, orders were issued to the abbot of Reading to send a certain collection of King's Bench memoranda directly to the Lords Appellant—obviously in preparation for the parliament scheduled in early February. Orders for other documents went out a week later to various courts at Westminster on behalf of the Appellants; but the January 12 orders to supply the Appellants with King's Bench memoranda from Reading Abbey, where Usk had orally presented his "Appeal" before the king, suggest that Usk's case might well have been pondered for its evidence against the king, and for its possibilities of legal precedence.[24]

Since the debate about the nature and legitimacy of an appeal in the Merciless Parliament took place at the opening of parliament on February 3, it is even possible that the lords, with the help of Gloucester's man, Chief Justice Clopton, had set a trap for Richard. Their florid speech on the "law and procedure of parliament" shows that they were entirely ready for such a challenge, indeed, ready for Clopton's rather peculiar ruling that their "Appeal" fell between common and civil law. For by claiming an undefined "law and procedure of parliament," they could indeed stand as they henceforth did between "both laws," drawing from whichever legal procedure they wanted to ensure the execution or destruction of their opponents. It seems possible that they had available the precedence of Usk's "Appeal," subpoenaed from Reading Abbey, should evidence be needed to convince the other members of parliament of the kinds of precedent that law in such unusual contexts allowed.

Usk's brutal execution bespeaks his importance, at least in symbolic terms, in the whole proceeding, small fry though he was.[25] He was picked out in the lords' "Appeal" for having confected "false indictments and attainders" of the king's enemies after he was made under-sheriff of Middlesex (the post that the king had given him as reward for his own "Appeal"), a charge for which I have not found any corroborating evidence, unless it refers to Usk's "Appeal" itself.[26] At any rate, Usk's place in the lords' "Appeal" seems strategic in several ways. Legal irregularity is best defended by accusing the other side of greater

[23] See Paul Strohm, "The Textual Vicissitudes of Usk's 'Appeal,'" in *Hochon's Arrow: The Social Imagination of Fourteenth-Century Texts* (Princeton: Princeton University Press, 1992), esp. 156; Strohm does not suggest the connection I propose. The summary is PRO KB27/507/40a–43b.
[24] *Calendar of Close Rolls Preserved in the Public Record Office: Richard II, Volume 3, 1385–1389* (London: H.M. Stationery Office, 1921), 387, 394; see May McKisack, *The Fourteenth Century, 1307–1399* (Oxford: Oxford University Press, 1991), 455–56, for other kinds of documents the Lords Appellant might have been seeking.
[25] I discuss some other aspects of Usk's circumstances and perspective in "Private Selves and the Intellectual Marketplace in Late Fourteenth-Century England: The Case of the Two Usks," *New Literary History* 28 (1997): 291–318.
[26] *Rot. parl.*, 3:234; *West. Chron.*, 258–59; Favent 19 (par. 22).

irregularity. Although it seems cruel to add this historical burden to all the errors of political judgment Usk made on his own behalf, his legal creativity and insistence on destroying his former employer Northampton and his associates may have been a small starting point for a rapidly opening rupture of tradition in legal proceedings. His tactic may have contributed to the strategems of the Merciless Parliament, including his own execution, thence all the way to Richard's reprisal in 1397, when Richard in turn "appealed" the Lords Appellant for treason, executing Arundel, apparently assassinating Gloucester, exiling others, and confiscating the properties of all the Lords Appellant and their families—actions that led directly to the articles of deposition in parliament against Richard himself two years later.

Usk concludes his 1384 English "Appeal" with a plea for "grace & . . . mercy" from the king, assuring him that he is "euer as verrey repentant as I kan" for his own part in Northampton's regime.[27] As it turned out, the most dangerous outcome possible both for him and for Richard was that Usk received such royal "mercy" in abundance. For as with many forms of "mercy" in the period, it meant not only that its beneficiary was immediately advanced, but also that his enemies were savagely attacked. In this case it was an early skirmish in what would rapidly develop nearly into civil war.

The Literature of 1388 and Gower's *Cronica tripertita*

The Long Parliament of 1640–53, with its civil and religious war between parliamentarians and royalists, produced a myriad of pamphlets, printed speeches, and scurrilous verses in English—including, in 1642, a loose and tendentiously parliamentarian translation of Thomas Favent's treatise with a list (lengthened in the second printing) "of many memorable Matters done by Parliaments, in this Kingdom of England." Likewise the Merciless Parliament of 1388, with its own rupture of traditional legal procedures and dislocations of legal authority, produced a fertile field for satiric, polemical, and even quasi-epic Latin historical works.[28] Satire and polemic are the inevitable genres in such a case; epic, or mock epic, a logical result of events possessing both public legal ceremony and historically momentous deaths. Latin too was inevitable, given the administrative circles whose members were most likely to discuss and think about the events, and given their likely desire to keep the controversies from setting off any more widely popular rebellions, as writings in English might easily have done.

But these generic distinctions are crude tools of analysis. All the writings

---

[27] Usk's "Appeal" is printed in R. Allen Shoaf, ed., *Thomas Usk: The Testament of Love* (Kalamazoo, Mich.: Medieval Institute Publications, 1998), 423–29; here at 429, l. 193.

[28] See Russell, *Crisis of Parliaments*, 336, 347. The translation of Favent is available in *The Harleian Miscellany: A Collection of Scarce, Curious, and Entertaining Pamphlets and Tracts* (London: White and Cochrane et al., 1811), 7:256–71.

about 1388 possess some degree of pathos and epic dimension; all also point to a sudden vacuum of political faith in which ethics that might go unstated in earlier times suddenly need to be stated, or at least satirically implied. A certain depletion of trust in the body politic and in tradition as such probably attends every circumstance in which rulers and governing peers become so relentlessly bent on conflict, and so willing to cite "ancient custom" in the interest of inventing new legal weapons. Such a depletion of trust must be even more complete when rulers and their governing peers draw on wide resources of learning and lay literacy. Expanding secular uses of learning may ultimately be a more fundamental culprit than an Usk, or a Gloucester or Richard, in the disruption of traditional legal and political procedures, and in the use of law for political ends. The Lords Appellant, for example, were said to have paused at Newmarket Heath during law sessions when they were on their way first to meet the king, "laying hold" of a cluster of judges and lawyers, "remarking that in the difficult enterprise on which they had now embarked it would be useful to have such experts constantly within call" ("detinentes eos . . . dixerunt illos in tam arduo negocio jam incepto tales peritos utile habere semper presentes" [*West. Chron.*, 220–21]). Within a year or two of the parliament, moreover, Richard commissioned and received an elegant manuscript containing a remarkable selection of fourteenth-century English statutes. Interestingly enough, the compilation features those statutes and ordinances that most *threatened* royal prerogative, dating from the reigns of Edward I and Edward II. It included, for example, the Ordinances of 1311, which restrained Edward II and concerning whose treasonous nature Richard had, among other things, questioned the judges in 1387. Clearly, such a compilation would allow for careful study of royal authority, and calculated deployment of the ethics or principles that upheld it, but it would do so inversely, as it were: from the position of one wishing to construct in rebuttal a very conscious assertion of a "traditional" royalist position.[29]

Such legal calculation by a layman—in this case the king—in confecting traditional authority is no anomaly in this period. Richard Firth Green has written on the hollowing out throughout the fourteenth century of folk law's principles of reconciliation—"treuth" in the sense of "loyalty, obedience, interpersonal reconciliation and harmony," its traditional range of meanings—by textual, learned king's law, which valued "treuth" in the new sense of this word of "veracity," a sense and a new legal context that Green aptly identifies not as encouraging reconciliation but as producing new weapons to fight with.[30] The sometimes wildly satiric, sometimes somberly ironic or epic writ-

[29] Saul, *Richard II*, 237; the volume is St. John's College, Cambridge, MS A 7. Saul's comment on the volume as a "manifesto for the reassertion of royal power" elides its challengingly antiroyalist contents. But I believe that Saul is right about the intentions the volume represents.

[30] Richard Firth Green, *A Crisis of Truth: Literature and Law in Ricardian England* (Philadelphia: University of Pennsylvania Press, 1999). On legally confected traditions in fourteenth-century England generally, see also my "Making History Legal: *Piers Plowman* and the Rebels of Fourteenth-Century England," in *William Langland's Piers Plowman: A Book of Essays*, ed. Kathleen Hewett-Smith (New York: Routledge, 2001), 7–39.

ings about the trial of 1388 are the direct products of this world of legalistic "treuth," of increasingly legalistic political conflict, and of a fascination with the ethics of power rather than of reconciliation.

The longest, most detailed, and most "epic" account of the Merciless Parliament is in the Monk of Westminster's chronicle, from which much of the verifiable information about 1388 presented have has necessarily come. This chronicle demonstrably incorporates several accounts, one from a source sympathetic to the Appellants, another in French "after the manner of those employed in the king's service about the court of Westminster" which is also generally but not entirely sympathetic to the Appellants, and which is closely paralleled by the official parliamentary roll and a collection of materials in Westminster archives.[31] These two accounts are fitted together with a narrative of the opening and final stages of the parliament probably based on the chronicler's own or a proxy's attendance, an account marked by praise for the king trying to uphold the church's privileges when the right of sanctuary in Westminster Cathedral is claimed by Tresilian, by pathos at the executions of the condemned, and by dry scorn for those who managed to escape. Here, in his own portions, political partisanship disappears into a more general somberness, an ironic view of petty arguments when suffering is at stake, and an outrage that these struggles could threaten the ancient right of sanctuary of the church—the last involving an intricate defense that further displays the legalistic temper of the period.

In terms of secular party politics, the most partisan portion of the Westminster Monk's account is the first pro-Appellant treatise he incorporated. This section is epic in the sense of being a carefully unfolding paean to and justification of the lords' actions while they try to save themselves and the kingdom (as the lords are quoted as telling the king) "from treachery lurking unseen and the snares that spell death" (*a laqueis mortiferis*: see, e.g., Psalm 17:6).[32] Much of this account sets forth, by way of eloquent speeches, the lords' wise realization that they should persecute Richard's close friend, the opportunistic duke of Ireland, Robert de Vere, rather than the king himself, for whom their loyalty was unabated (*West. Chron.*, 216–19). The main action of this narrative lies in the purportedly diligent efforts by the Lords Appellant to keep the accused in secure places pending parliamentary judgment, and the king's and others' increasingly devious strategems permitting the accused to escape. Thus de Vere disguises himself as a groom to see the king, who allows him to depart overseas; later, the king declares ignorance of which persons he was supposed to detain (224–57). The main legal irregularity of the 1388 "Appeals" and their prosecution—the absence of most of the accused—is therefore here justified in advance of the parliament itself. The narrative

---

[31] "Secundum modum curialium apud Westmonasterium in obsequio domini regis famulancium Gallico sermone conscriptus" (*West. Chron.*, 278–80; the sources are analyzed at xlviii–xliv).

[32] "A cecis insidiis et a laqueis mortiferis" (*West. Chron.*, 210–11; the section occupies 208–34). Compare Favent's final sentence, 24 (par. 27 and note), and the discussion of Favent later in this essay.

implies this justification through the course of the lords' diligent pursuit of the accused, punctuated by their own noble speeches regarding their concern for honor, due form, and proper royal governance. The lords, for instance, are said to pause at the London Guildhall to explain to the mayor "under what legal forms" they were proceeding; and in the midst of their pursuit they consider how to pare down the king's household at Westminster, whose excesses appear more egregious at every turn. They discover, for example, that his buttery contains over one hundred officials (226–29).

The Monk's own probably original account, while the most confused, is also the most ridden with pathos, all the more evident beneath the dry tone in which he presents the jousting of clumsy legal strategies. Brembre, forced like all the accused to answer briefly "yes" or "no" to the articles, wanted to settle the matter by battle, but he was denied this option because "witnesses deposed to the truth of the charges," a view supported by how the Commons "kept on crying out that all those charges were true" ("acclamabant omnia fore vera que sibi fuerunt objecta" [308–9]). Abruptly changing focus before this question of witnesses is settled, the narrative describes how Tresilian is found in the sanctuary of Westminster Cathedral, then dragged from there by the "fell clutches" ("funestis manibus") of Gloucester. When he demands right of sanctuary and refuses to answer the charges because "the proceedings against him were founded in error," he is told that "by due process" ("per debitum processum") judgment had already been pronounced against him; and he is at once drawn and hanged (311–12). Meanwhile representatives from London crafts had been brought in to pronounce on the charges against the former mayor Brembre, whose case had been held over awaiting some corroboration of the charges; but "after spending some time in needless chatter these people at length returned home with nothing accomplished" ("qui circa verba superflua vacantes demum sine effectu ad propria redierunt"). So London officials are brought in, including the present mayor, who express their "personal belief" ("super credulitate eorum") that Brembre was indeed aware of the treasons, a different charge than the original one, that he had himself committed treason. Whereupon he too is promptly drawn to the gallows, "devoutly recit[ing] the Placebo and Dirige with the friars along the way and ask[ing] pardon of everyone; and thus, with great contrition, [he] brought his life to an end." His piety and contrition "moved almost all the bystanders to tears," the Monk observes ("devote Placebo et Dirige et ab omnibus veniam postulavit: sicque cum ingenti contricione vitam finivit. Ejus revera contricio et devocio cunctos pene astantes ad lacrimas provocabant" [314–15]).

Usk's clumsy execution, already mentioned, is given its most detailed and dryly factual description in the *Westminster Chronicle*. Burley's conviction and death as described there are even more awkwardly managed. He is said to be inconsistent in answering the charges, accepting some while denying others. So Gloucester demands Burley's death, and Richard and other lords, who "were eager to save lord Simon's life" ("zelabant pro vita domini Simonis"), try to gain for him a second chance to answer the charges, while Gloucester's associate Sir John Cobham (as the Westminster Monk alone notes) comments that the aged Burley had been a sick man at the time of the first questioning and should be treated more indulgently. This, however, is denied: "by parliamentary process" ("per processum parliamenti"), his hands are tied and he is beheaded, though spared drawing and hanging (330–31). A series of others are jailed and exiled, ending the proceedings in a tatter of small tragedies. Although the Monk has justified the Lords Appellant generally, the secular political world he portrays lacks any sense of inherent order and justice.

The Monk's ideals of better order lie elsewhere, in the traditions of the church. Here he expresses his only fervent partisanship. For this purpose he uses liturgical phrasing, and heavily emphasizes any liturgical moments (as in the recitations of the psalms while the condemned are drawn to their deaths) to frame his narrative with ecclesiastical authority. He does so dramatically in his conclusion. He (like Favent, who will be discussed later on) describes the ceremonial conclusion to the parliament, where a mass and sermon are presented while the king sits before a book and cross on a small altar table and renews his coronation oath. Like the official parliamentary rolls, the Monk's account here closes by mentioning Richard's general pardon for all those who rose with or against the Lords Appellant and a general threat to all who violate the provisions of the parliament (*West. Chron.*, 342–43; cf. *Rot. parl.*, 3:250). But the Monk adds a meaningful further detail to his scene of the presentation of universal pardon (a detail indeed written at the bottom of his manuscript leaf and marked for insertion, suggesting it came to him or was composed after the rest of the narrative): after the king has reaffirmed his coronation oath, the bishops of the land, "assembled under a single stole, immediately fulminated sentence of excommunication against those who should thereafter dare to break their oath or to rouse the king's anger against the lords or use false insinuations to excite him" ("sub una stola coadunati sentenciam excommunicacionis fulminabant in illos qui hujusmodi sacramentum in posterum presumpserint violare seu regem contra dominos concitare aut ipsum eorum falsis suggestionibus provocare"). Thus, while the scene ends with the king's universal pardon, it also ends with a warning from the higher spiritual authorities of the church about the dangers of inciting the king's anger over what the lords had done, and thus a warning about the ease with which he could in fact break the terms of the universal pardon. Favent also closes with the warning of excommunication for those who would weaken the parliament's agreements, but he makes no mention of concern for the king's residual feelings or unstable pardon (24 [par. 27]).

In retrospect, this concern looks precisely toward 1397, when, as the fourth article of the 1399 deposition states,

> although the king pardoned the duke of Gloucester and the earls of Arundel and Warwick and all their supporters, in full parliament and with its assent, and for many years behaved towards them in peaceful and benevolent fashion, yet he

continued to bear hatred in his heart towards them, so that when an opportunity came he ordered the seizure of the duke of Gloucester, his own uncle . . . and caused him, without response or any legal process, to be secretly suffocated, strangled, and barbarously and cruelly murdered. The earl of Arundel, although he pleaded both a charter of general pardon and a charter of pardon which had been granted to him, and requested that justice be done to him, he wickedly ordered to be decapitated.[33]

The accusation is that Richard gave universal pardon but was, in a personal sense that violated his official dispensation, unpardoning and unmerciful. Within his generally ecclesiastical framework of concerns and loyalties, the Monk of Westminster perceives this point already in 1388, and thus ends his narrative with an assertion about the unreliability of the royal dispensation of mercy and pardon.

The same emotional and legal characterization inheres in the name traditionally given to the parliament of 1388. The sole extant source for this name is from the chronicle of Henry Knighton, canon of an Augustinian priory in Leicester. Knighton's house was part of the Lancastrian holdings; he generally praises John of Gaunt, the father of Henry Bolingbroke, who joined the Appellants, as *pius dux* (echoing Virgil's formula for Aeneas). In general, Knighton's narrative offers splicings of accounts of heroic efforts by the Appellants to overcome the favorites' "many deceits practiced upon the king and the kingdom" ("multis falsitatibus regi et regno per eos factis" [Knighton, 453]). But Knighton is also our source for the information that "it is called the parliament without mercy nor did it provide mercy to anyone without the consent of the lords" ("uocatur parliamentum istud 'parliamentum sine misericordia' nec alicui misericordiam faceret sine consensu dominorum" [Knighton, 414]). The rubricator of Knighton's manuscript at a later point entitles it "the parliament that worked wonders" ("Parliamentum apud Westmonasterium operans mira" [Knighton, 430]); but this name is more commonly used by others (including Knighton in his own text) for the parliament of 1386 which impeached Michael de la Pole. Given his generally pro-Appellant posture and sources, and his evidently reliable contact with wider sources than many chronicles, Knighton seems indeed to be capturing a common if rather anti-Appellant name for the parliament.

The pro-Appellant tendency is so strong in Knighton that anything appearing critical of the Appellants in his narrative deserves special authority. In Knighton's account, the king's supporters ("evil counselors") are called "predators" and are shown fleeing in disguise before the Appellants can bring them to trial. In Knighton these disguises are elaborated to absurdity, part of the tradition that thus implicitly excuses the Lords Appellant for convicting them in absentia. Alexander Neville, archbishop of York, drops his luggage and scurries north disguised as a simple priest; de Vere pretends he is a

---

[33] Given-Wilson, *Chronicles of the Revolution*, 173–74.

Cheshire archer; Michael de la Pole shaves his head and beard and dresses as a Flemish poulterer, selling chickens from a basket. Yet at the ensuing battle at Radcot Bridge, de Vere flees over the Thames "with wonderful daring" ("mirabili ausu"), and the Lords Appellant in fury overwhelm the remaining crowd of soldiers, "shamelessly stripp[ing] and spoil[ing] them of everything down to their skins" ("nudauerunt . . . usque ad uerecundiam nuditatem inuerecunde spoliauerunt"), although they leave them alive except for those who "drowned through their own folly" ("propria stulticia . . . submersos fuisse" [422–24]).

But just as Knighton is our sole source for the name "the parliament without mercy," so Knighton alone includes in his pastiche of social disorder framed and occasioned by the 1388 parliament a long complaint from provincial communities to the king concerning the disruption in the whole kingdom that the length of the Merciless Parliament and rebelliousness of the attacks on the king have occasioned (442–51). It is one of the few preserved examples of the literature of 1388 that is not generally pro-Appellant (a characterization that includes the official rolls of parliament). The document included in Knighton's chronicle seems not to take its origins from the civil servants and London writers who generated so much of this body of writings, but rather from the provincial gentry. It mainly complains about the corruption of the king's law when reaching into provincial courts, and it turns to the legal struggles between the king's favorites and the Appellants in blurred statements presenting a confusion of attacks by and against members of the king's council, to which "le peple" (as if as uninterested in the details of court party politics as the writers) can think of no response except anarchy:

> And therefore on the coasts in divers parts of your kingdom the poor commons' houses have been burned, their villages and persons held to ransom, their ships altogether destroyed, and the land left empty and bare of all manner of wealth, so that you have not the power to defend your land or to maintain your royal estate, to the great grief and distress of all your wise counsellors, for the people who rise know no other remedy, except to arrest those manipulators of your council who call the great men of your council traitors to you and your kingdom, like those who know neither right nor reason.[34]

And while thus criticizing courtly party politics *tout court* and the king's law, it elaborates a larger problem in the king's governance—the corrupt granting of pardons:

[34] "Eins ount estez sur lez costiers du miere en diuers parties de uostre roialme lez maysones de lez pouers comines arsez, lez uillagez et lez personez raunsones, et la naue tote outrement destruytz, et la terre tote uoyde de pourer de tote maner de tresoure, qe uous nauez dont uous poiez uostre terre defendre ne uostre estate reale tenere, a graunt doloure et poissance de toux uous sagez, pur le peple qe se leua ne saueyt altre chose faire forsque aretter gouernours de uostre counsayle, appellantz lez pliis graundez de uostre consayle traytours a uous et a la roialme come gentz qe bien ne sauoient ne resone" (Knighton, 444–45). I have at points rendered the translation of this document more literal.

And beyond that, your great judges of laws of your land do not do at all times and to all persons equal execution according to what your laws ordain, being inclined to excuse offences upon orders made under the privy seal or the great seal, against your good laws, or at the prayers of other lords whose retainers they are, wherefore they are not able to perform their duty to which they have been sworn, and that utterly to the destruction of your poor commons if it be not soon redressed.[35]

The complaint about the legal corruption resulting from maintenance was amplified in a formal petition from the Commons in the second parliament of 1388, at Cambridge, and partly answered by a statute there against mainte-nance (a statute hypocritically offered by Richard, who had a vast group of personal retainers but who evidently wanted to mobilize sentiment against the higher nobility who had attacked him).[36] But the provincial complaint Knighton copies stresses the abuse of pardons "by command of the privy seal or the great seal, against your good laws." This complaint is reiterated in a statute of 1390, in which the king is enjoined "not to grant lightly charters of pardon . . . for murder, the death of a man killed by attack, assault, or malice aforethought, treason, or rape of a woman." The same complaint about royal pardons—though, perhaps significantly, lacking complaints about pardon for treason—appears again in the "Advice of the Lords," a parliamentary docu-ment uncertainly dated between 1386 and 1392.[37]

Thus Knighton includes in his narrative both a definition of the parliament of 1388 as merciless and a collective voice of "le peple" complaining about the king's and his officers' corrupt dispensations of legal pardon, both matters of special dispensation long central to medieval law but emerging prominently as points of discussion in 1388 and later.[38] He concludes, however, with yet more vicious satire on the king's associates as they are convicted and executed. In Knighton, Tresilian is found not in sanctuary at Westminster Abbey but hiding in an apothecary's house near Westminster "so that he could watch the

[35] "Et outre ceo uoz graundez iuggez dez lez loyes de uostre terre nient fessauntz en touz temps ne as touz personez egale execucion solonc lez uoz loyez ordeignes, einz sount enclynes deschuere loffence dez maundementz par priue seale, oue per graunt seale, encontre uoz bonez loyes, et lez priers dez altres seignurs oue queuz ils sount de retenuz, qils ne fount parfaire lour deuoyre a queles ils fount iurrez, tout outrement en destruction de uostre dit pouer comine sil ne soit pluis hastyment redresse" (Knighton, 444–45).

[36] *West. Chron.*, 358–59; Knighton, 510–11; Musson and Ormrod, *Evolution of English Justice*, 110.

[37] *Statutes of the Realm* (Record Commission, 1810–28), 2:68–69; *Proceedings and Ordinances of the Privy Council*, ed. Harris Nicolas (Record Commission, 1834–37), 1:86; reprint, S. B. Chrimes and A. L. Brown, *Select Documents of English Constitutional History, 1307–1485* (London: Adam and Charles Black, 1961), 155 and 161. An example of such a pardon, ironically from 1390, the very year Richard was warned against giving them out, is printed in M. Dominica Legge, *Anglo-Norman Letters and Petitions*, Anglo-Norman Texts 3 (Oxford: Basil Blackwell, 1941), letter 120, 175–76.

[38] For treatment of the earlier history of the king's pardon, see Naomi D. Hurnard, *The King's Pardon for Homicide before A.D. 1307* (Oxford: Oxford University Press, 1969). I return to Rich-ard's pardons later.

lords and magnates of the realm going in and out of parliament, and discover what was going on in parliament, for he had been a calculating man all his life."[39] When discovered, Tresilian had "dressed himself as a poor and feeble man, in a rough, torn, shabby tunic, and had put on a false beard, long and full, of the kind called a 'Parisian beard,'" which so completely concealed him that only his voice was recognizable. But "this time his caution turned out to be the height of stupidity," for he was betrayed by his servant.[40] All of this pre-empts the question whether it was legitimate to violate the sanctuary of Westminster by hauling him into parliament; since Tresilian lurks in a nearby apothecary's house, the issue of sanctuary does not come up.

Knighton's accounts of the other executions are similarly rounded off with satisfying ironic aptness. Brembre was said to have set up "at the height of his power as mayor" ("in sua plenaria potestate maioratus") a public block and axe to chop off the heads of those who rose against him in the city. These enemies numbered 8,500, Knighton claims, although Knighton does not say whether Brembre actually beheaded them all in his putative reign of terror. The claim seems to sharpen and inflate astronomically the account found in the Mercers' earlier parliamentary complaint concerning Brembre's reelection of 1384, where, according to the Mercers' Guild, Brembre stated publicly that "xx or xxx of us were worthy to be drawen and hanged" (*Rot. parl.*, 3:225). Knighton further declares that Brembre wanted to make himself duke of Troy, since London used to be called the second Troy and Brembre wanted to rename it that; but he was killed on the same chopping block he had established (Knighton, 500–501). In Knighton, Brembre's absurd social and historical pretensions, and his murderous plans for thousands of Londoners, clearly add to the justness of his execution, and the justness of a parliament without mercy.

Chroniclers are invaluable as collecting points for Latin and English political writings and satire circulating widely, the kind of "news" which is otherwise generally lost. For example, the brief surviving tract that Thomas Favent independently wrote on the parliament possesses many large and some small parallels to the Westminster Monk's and Knighton's narratives, but with a shifting affiliation to their distinctive details.[41] In most of his unique touches and in overall tone, Favent is even more wickedly satirical than Knighton. While the Appellants arrive in parliament first to present their charges, the accused—Neville, de Vere, the earl of Suffolk, Tresilian, and Brembre—huddle in the dark nooks and crannies of Westminster, like "Adam and Eve [hid-

---

[39] "Ut sic uideret dominos et magnates regni intrantes ad parliamentum et egredientes, et exploraret quid ageretur in parliamento, quia in tota uita sua semper cautulose egerat" (Knighton, 498–99).

[40] "Fingens se pauperem debilem, in tunica hispida et dilacerata et debili, feceratque sibi barban prolixam et longam artificiose, quam barban 'barbam Parisiensem' uocabant . . . iam cautela eius uertitur in summam stulticiam" (Knighton, 498–99).

[41] See the translation in the appendix to this volume.

ing] from God": both an exegetical and perhaps a sexual satire of their intimacy as co-conspirators ("velut Adam et Eua a Deo primitus" [Favent, 10 (par. 10)]). Tresilian is finally caught (as in Knighton) after hiding on the rooftops in a ridiculous disguise, here one that Gloucester's soldier sees through (rather than, as in Knighton, Tresilian's own servant betraying him [Favent, 17 (par. 19)]). In Favent it is revealed that Tresilian at his execution had strange amulets and magical symbols sewn inside his robe, which he claimed would keep him from dying; as an aggressive response, he is stripped and hanged nude (18 [par. 19]). The only detail that suggests pathos for the royal supporters on trial appears as a brief second thought at one of the chief points of judicial irregularity in the proceedings: when it is proposed that those absent be tried, Richard is suddenly struck by a "charitable conscience" to remember that it is best to be "mindful of the end of every labor," so he delays judgment to see if any further witnesses will appear (16 [par. 16]). Favent's next statements suggest that considerable opportunity has been allowed for this before John Devereux, who happens to be acting in the king's place that day, "finally" ("tandem") declares their guilt and pronounces sentence (16 [par. 17]).

The ethical and legal problems of the 1388 parliament are smoothly evaded by Favent's fluent, satirical narrative. He favors ironic Christian allusion, though this does not always keep his moral clear: he evokes Lenten penance in his description of the opening of the parliament—a season that is "ydoneum et acceptabile" to punish delinquents (14 [par. 15]); he persistently calls the favorites "pseudodomini," an obvious trope on *pseudoprophetae*, the false prophets of Apocalypse; yet he offers Tresilian's execution as a parody of the Crucifixion, with Tresilian ascending to Tyburn as if climbing Calvary, and presumably the stripping of his magical symbols like the dividing of Jesus' clothing (18 [par. 19]). Favent ends his narrative, moreover, with a quotation of psalmic language about the "snares of death" that, intriguingly, echoes similar allusions appearing twice in the Westminster narrative, once in the lords' speech; since *laqueus* can also mean "noose," as elsewhere in Favent, there is a distinct possibility of quasi-religious satire here too (24 [par. 27 and notes]). The mocking of religious imagery and language as well as his human targets is as striking here as in Chaucer's *Merchant's Tale*; it is just one sign of many of the popular support the Appellants garnered, or, better, the intense satirical energy that the challenge of legal and political authority unleashed. Indeed, Favent's aggressive eagerness for "news" about the events expresses itself in his regret that Tresilian would not confess publicly at any of the several pauses provided for this during his torture of being drawn before hanging (the procedure that Favent elsewhere remarks drenched the streets with the flesh of the condemned ("vicos carne inundantes"[19 (par. 22)]). Favent can only assure his readers that he has done his best to find out what Tresilian said on the gallows to his discreet confessors (18 [par. 19]). Favent even goes out of his way to anticipate and dispute any sense of legal impropriety in the preceeding. When Brembre wishes to consult before entering a plea, then demands a judicial combat, Favent notes that the lords' willingness to take him up on this and fight proves they are not inflexibly tied to the law (not, of course, that he explains why the law would deny Brembre a hearing or which law is in question). Favent then implies that Brembre is denied the battle or delay only because the Mercers happen to arrive to deliver uncoerced testimony about Brembre's various extortions and injuries; and by this vague accusation, Favent suggests, Brembre is conclusively and finally undone ("tunc stetit Brembre confuse tantum" [16–17 (par. 18)]).

Favent as narrator is merciless indeed, especially at the outset; yet his detailed attention to each of the executions and the torments these involve cumulatively dulls any sense of righteous justice in such bloodshed. Against his display of such horrors, his repeated mentions of the clergy who rise and depart when a "judgment of blood" ("iudicium sanguinis") is about to occur suggests a certain displaced repugnance, also perhaps registered in his mention of the frantic kisses of Tresilian's daughters and the dead faint of Tresilian's wife as his drawing and hanging is begun (18 [par. 19])—though this is immediately followed by the grotesque comedy of Tresilian's death. Yet Favent declares the executions ceased when the parliament finally itself began to feel revulsion at continuing "the horrible torments of this kind, of the death of fellow Christians" ("huiusmodi horribilia tormenta mortis suorum Christianorum" [22 (par. 25)]), and this sense of satiation well describes the gradually flagging satire in the narrative itself. Favent's final statement, already mentioned, using a psalmic phrase about freedom from the lethal "snare" or "noose," may be read as a complex and uneasy reflection on the preceding hangings, and the mere possibility of such a pun in a prayer is perhaps the clearest sign of the stress that his pitiless and satiric outlook has exacted: "Now let England, rejoicing, exult in Christ, since by his scars, and by our filthy, bitter remains, the snare [noose] is thoroughly destroyed, and we are free, thanks to God" ("Jam gaudens exultet Anglia Christo cum suis sicatricibus et squalorosis reliquiis nostris amariis laqueus contritus est penitus et nos liberati sumus; Deo gratiarum acciones" [24 (par. 27)]).

Gower's account in the *Cronica tripertita*, though completed the furthest in time from any of these others, most resembles the tone of the Westminster chronicler, writing from the perspective closest to the events. For Gower's poem is not a satire in the jaunty sense of Favent or the elaborate narrative cunning of Knighton; it proceeds through its 1,075 lines, and the section on 1388 through its mere 215 lines, with epic somberness. Gower opens the description of 1388 with a historical perspective from political prophecy: the date appears in a verbal riddle like those used in John Ergome's *Vaticinium* and other satiric prophecies of the period, and the narrative intertwines direct description of key moments in the conflict (e.g., Richard's questions to the judges, those "long-time traitors" [line 23]) with beast allegory like that found in Geoffrey of Monmouth's vague political allegory in the tradition of the prophecies of Merlin in the *Historia regum Britanniae*.[42] Here, the Swan, the Horse and the Bear are the three main Appellants—Gloucester, Arundel, and Warwick. Gower also mentions the presence of Mowbray, earl of Nottingham (as "crowned wings," Nottingham's heraldic emblem), and he emphasizes the importance from the beginning of the presence of Henry Bolingbroke, earl of Derby ("he who carried an 'S'"—the badge that produced the linked 'S's, livery symbol of the House of Lancaster): he is a "young, noble, and righteous" addition to their faithful band, sent "as if from Heaven" ("Qui gerit S . . . Nobilis ille quidem probus et iuuenis fuit idem, / Sic quasi de celis interfuit" [1.53–54]). Finally, he notes that Henry Percy, the "northern moon" (because earl of Northumberland), "was on this occasion not in the struggle but joins the company in mind" ("Hac sub fortuna presens aquilonica luna / Non fuit ad sortem, sequitur set mente cohortem" [1.55–56]). The "traitors" whom they vanquish or exile have explicitly unstable allegorical identities: de Vere is the Boar (*Aper*, "wild boar" [e.g., 1.65], but compare Latin *verres*, French *verrat*, "tame boar; male breeding pig," whence de Vere's punning heraldic badge of a boar's head), but when he flees he is "turned into a hare, losing all honor" ("sic Aper in leporem mutatus perdit honorem" [1.95]). Other traitors' names occasion ironic wordplay based on English puns: the puns are possibly deliberately strained as part of the castigation. Alexander Neville is "predo cleri Noua villa Macedo"—"new ville Macedon [i.e., Alexander of], robber of clergy" (1.103). Michael de la Pole is "de puteo Michaelis": "Michael of the ditch-pool" (1.109).

Completing his work from the distance of 1400, Gower predictably presents a thematic history, the themes of which are justice, piousness, and pity, versus corruption, impiousness, and lack of pity. In fact, the theme of *pietas* versus *impietas* dominates the *Cronica*. The word *pietas* is invariably translated by Gower in the *Confessio amantis* (as the Latin glosses show) as "pity" rather than "piousness" or "dutiful respect," the classical and earlier medieval Latin senses; and throughout the *Cronica*—as normal for late medieval Latin—*pietas* carries the primary sense of "pity" (e.g., "rex pietosus . . . mite prolongat tempora vite" ["the pitying king (Henry) compassionately prolonged the span of (Richard's) life"] [3.388–89]).[43] But in both languages, *pite / pietas* also involves "piety" as a minor secondary sense (in neither language at this date is a separate word or sense "piety" available; it is found in English only in the late fifteenth century, when in Humanist Latin *pietas* regains the classical sense). In the *Cronica*, the secondary sense "piety" is clear from the frequent

---

[42] Ergome's *Vaticinium* is again an important fourteenth-century parallel; on this work, see A. G. Rigg, *A History of Anglo-Latin Literature, 1066–1422* (Cambridge: Cambridge University Press, 1992), 265–68. On Bower's heraldic allegory, see also Frank Grady's remarks in this volume.

[43] For comment on late medieval Latin *pietas* and Middle English *pity* and *piete*, all of which denoted "pity" primarily and "piety" secondarily, see *Oxford English Dictionary*, s.v. "pity" *sb*; see also *Middle English Dictionary*, s.v. "pite."

association of *pietas* with *pius*: "Sic pius in Cristo pietatem sentit in isto" ("Thus the one pious to Christ receives pity for himself"), as Gower says of Henry Bolingbroke (3.428). Although, as this shows, *pius* essentially means "pious" (for which no English equivalent yet existed), it too becomes imbued in the *Cronica* with "pitying."

The layering of "pity" with "piousness" allows *pietas* in the *Cronica* to define both compassion and pious adherence to justice, at times almost regaining the classical sense. Thus Richard is the epitome of a lack of pity and righteousness: "Sic malus ipse malis adhesit, eisque sodalis / Efficitur, tota regis pietate remota." ("Thus an evil one attached evil ones to himself and made himself their ally, with the king's pity/pious fairness having entirely departed" [1.19–20]). King Henry, in contrast, at the end is seen as "the pitying [or pious] king," *rex pietosus, rex pius*, because at that point he does not execute all of his enemies (3.382–93). As a marginal gloss at the end of the *Cronica* summarizes, "Note here according to the common saying concerning the pitiousness of the most serene king Henry, and the unpitiousness by which the most cruel Richard, while he was able, tyrannically vexed the kingdom."[44]

Once the theme of "pity" has been so emphatically struck—and facile and easily applied as these dichotomies seem, they gain in power as they are repeated—we are sensitized to the ethic as we read Gower's small epic. And it seems to propel the work along, though not toward the simplistic ends of the most extreme pro-Appellant accounts. The "bold nobles" find the king seated at Westminster, where he recognizes from the faces of those who will be future great nobility that they (and he: the Latin is ambiguous) would be without laughter ("proceresque futuros / Vidit, et ex visu cognouit se sine risu" [1.123–24]). They wish to pluck vice from his side, and "a way is found, by which they would establish a parliament, so that they might purge the kingdom and repair the state of the realm" ("Est iter inuentum, statuunt quo parliamentum, / Vt sic purgarent regnique statum repararent" [1.129–30]). They thus represent the return of *pietas* in the sense of pious justice, even though this involves severe "purging." The accused are judged instantly by "os commune locutum" ("the common spoken word" [1.132]), a reference to the peremptory shouting for conviction at the parliament which most contemporary accounts emphasize. Here, however, the phrase justifies the irregular use of sheer notoriety by invoking the trope of "universal consensus," a trope that Gower elsewhere heavily if (given his simultaneous claims to special authority) paradoxically exploits.[45]

From here the account gets more somber still. Indeed, Gower stands far from the facile partisan satires of 1388, even supplying in his descriptions of

---

[44] "Nota hic secundum commune dictum de pietate serenissimi regis Henrici, necnon de impietate qua crudelissimus Ricardus regnum, dum potuit, tirannice vexauit" (3.462–68 marg.).

[45] For comments on Gower's paradoxical use of that trope in his other Latin writings, see my essay "Gower in His Most Learned Role and the Peasants' Revolt of 1381," *Mediaevalia* 16 (1993 for 1990): 329–47.

the royal favorites' deaths something of the pity that he blames the king for lacking. Simon Burley's beheading is described briefly enough, but more lines follow that emphasize his age, the queen's tears, his own falling head:

> Corruit in fata gladii vestis stragulata;
> Stat quia non recta, magis est culpanda senecta:
> Lacrima Regine dum poscit opem medicine,
> Obrutus amittit caput et sua funera mittit.
> (1.140–43)

(The striped garment fell to the fate of the sword. It is clear that when old age is not righteous, it is more to be blamed. Even while the queen's tear begged for medicinal help, he, overwhelmed, lost his head, and sent forth his destruction.)

In fact each of the deaths goes on a few lines too long for rousing propaganda, evoking reasons to pity these figures, at least for their fates and their executions, if not their bad luck at being scapegoats for the king's crimes and the Appellants' revenge. Of Brembre he states:

> Hunc quasi consortem dilexit rex, quia sortem
> Consilii cepit, quo mortem fine recepit:
> Furcis pendebat, quem primo terra trahebat,
> Ictum sic ensis non sentit Londoniensis.
> (1.156–59)

(Him the king loved like a consort, because he had accepted the decision of the council, for which he finally received his death: he whom the earth earlier had carried was suspended from the gallows: thus the Londoner did not feel the sword's blow.)

The narrative point of view places us partly in the perspective of what he feels by stressing what his body, now a thing, does not feel. Tresilian, a particularly absurd figure in all the other accounts except the Monk of Westminster's, is granted some dignity:

> Hic scelus instigat proceres, quos sepe fatigat,
> Vnde fatigatus tandem perit hic sceleratus:
> Crimine prestante super hoc quod fecerat ante,
> Ad furcas tractus fit ibi pendendo subactus.
> (1.164–67)

(This scoundrel stirred up the great men, whom he often wearied, whence, himself wearied, at length—criminous one—he perished. By a crime outstripping what he had done earlier, he was dragged to the gallows where he was overcome by hanging.)

Gower summarizes, "Pendula sors tristis morientibus accidit istis, / In manibus quorum pendebant iura virorum" ("A sad, dangling fate came to those dying ones, in whose hands had hung the laws of men" [168–69]). Although he continues to work such verbal ironies, Gower never stoops to Favent's aggressive satire or Knighton's grotesque means of finding poetic justice in the deaths (such as Brembre's dying on the beheading block he constructed for his 8,500 London enemies, or Tresilian undone by his prying curiosity about the proceedings of the parliamentary trial). Rather, Gower's view of the Ricardian party is governed by an almost Virgilian sense of the victims of history, the secular writer's correlative to the Monk of Westminster's ecclesiastic epic with its ultimately ironic and cautionary view of the secular power struggle.

Pity in the *Cronica* is thus at once a posture of justice, sorrow, and piety, and its affective sense is a strong feature of the narrator's own perspective when he describes the first, "human" endeavor of 1388. But "pity" shifts in the course of the narrative from this affective narrative mode to a principle of enlightened if severe royal policy. The pious pity that Henry is allowed to claim at the end—"probus Henricus, pietatis semper amicus" ("upright Henry, always the friend of pity" [3.452])—stands for an ideal of humility in the face of divine judgment, thus allowing Henry to be among those carrying out the "common cry" for justice by executing the traitors of 1388 (where, indeed, his participation as "heaven-sent" assistance is more emphasized than in other accounts of 1388). While showing his "pity" in sparing Richard from death, Henry is praised at the close for his species of pious pity that is just to the realm, "pitying" in a sense that generates good policy, including the lifting of onerous obligations, relief of taxes, and the preservation of great men's inheritances for their heirs—all the benefits of the purge that, in retrospect, 1388 can be seen to have accomplished:

O quam pensando mores variosque notando,
Si bene scrutetur, R. ab H. distare videtur!
Clarus sermone, tenebrosus et intus agone,
R. pacem fingit, dum mortis federa stringit:
Duplex cautelis fuit R., pius H. que fidelis;
R. pestem mittit, mortem pius H. que remittit;
R. seruitutem statuit, pius H. que salutem;
R. plebem taxat, taxas pius H. que relaxat;
R. proceres odit et eorum predia rodit,
H. fouet, heredesque suas restaurat in edes;
R. regnum vastat vindex et in omnibus astat,
Mulset terrorem pius H., que reducit amorem.
(3.462–77)

(Oh, to one considering and observing their different characters, how far does R., once well considered, seem to stand from H.! Clear in speech, inwardly murky and in conflict, R. pretends peace, while he weaves bonds of death: R. was doubly deceptive, H. pious/pitying and faithful; R. sent plague, pious/pitying H. redeemed death; R. established slavery, pious/pitying H. salvation; R. taxed the humble people, pious/pitying H. loosened the taxes. R. hated the higher nobility and gnawed their treasures; H. cherished them and restored their heirs to their halls. R. devastated the kingdom and stood as a conqueror against all; pious/pitying H. quieted the terror and brought back love.)

Pious pity now covers a large ground of royal policy. Springing at first from the author's own perspective, the ethic has expanded to fill all of the needs of a damaged kingdom. At the end it is an extension of Henry's power, rather than his or anyone's sympathy. So reconstituted, violent purgation has been redeemed as an act of mercy, a species of compassionate justice. A parliament without mercy has been made into a parliament embodying *pietas*. The narrator's pity at the deaths in 1388 is assuaged and transmuted in the only way possible for viewing the outcome with relief and celebration: by revealing the higher plan of true pity in purging and reforming the entire body politic, for which the "human" tragedies turn out to be the necessary first step.

The *Confessio amantis* and the Politics of Pity

Something like this position on "pite" as a form of affective sympathy commuted by purgation into justice can be seen developing in the *Confessio amantis*, but as a complex and dialectical process, with far greater extremes both in exposing mere compassion as too indulgent and in extolling severe vengeance as the form of true "pite." Indeed, the movement toward defining true "pite" as just punishment emerges as the overall "argument" of Gower's most important and elusive work, but that point also includes the price that the individual subject pays for this transformation.

The parallel here to the movement of pity in the *Cronica*, which I will try to substantiate later on, does not in itself imply that Gower in the *Confessio* was already assessing the actions or digesting the legality and ethics of the Merciless Parliament. But the *Confessio*'s silence about 1388 does not rule out this possibility. For many reasons, overt reference to the event would necessarily be repressed from the *Confessio*, versions of which began to appear soon after the parliament (and we may assume that since the earliest dedication of the *Confessio* is dated 1390, some of the work may have been under Gower's hand from the time of the Merciless Parliament). Gower's position as a Latin writer, addressing clerics and administrators, the primary group that wrote, read, and discussed national history, contemporary and past, allowed him to produce topical poetry; witness his account of the rebellion of 1381 in book 1 of the *Vox clamantis* (apparently dedicated at some late point to Archbishop Thomas Arundel, brother of the appellant lord and persecuted by Richard).

His position as a vernacular poet was different. Vernacular poetry of the late fourteenth century inherited and sustained an ethos of standing mute in the face of contemporary or topical claims, even when they are obvious. To take a small instance, in the *Confessio*, Gower warns in English of the consequences of the Schism, "At Avynoun thexperience / Therof hath yove an evidence" (Prol. 330), but only in his nearby Latin gloss does he name names: "videlicet tempore Roberti Gibbonensis, qui nomen Clementis sibi sortitus est, tunc antipape" ("that is, in the time of Robert Gibbon, who took for himself the name Clement, then the antipope"[Prol. 200 marg.]).[46]

It seems highly unlikely, to say the least, that only in 1400 did Gower suddenly read and begin collecting the extensive and detailed materials about 1388 that he used for the *Cronica*. Given the severe proclamations after the event about not rousing the king's anger, and given the certainty that such anger was there to be roused, he would have had much to lose by writing about it, perhaps even speaking or thinking too directly about it in the 1390s, even in Latin. Nonetheless, showing that Gower's *Confessio* moves fitfully toward the articulation of ethical and legal senses of "pity" found in the *Cronica*, where it includes "purging" corruption and carrying out legal punishment, is to suggest that the *Confessio* too may be placed among the literature of 1388, indeed, that in some respects it offers a deep meditation on the ethical and legal problems of that event.

It is actually evidence for rather than against this proposal that on the very theme of "pity," Gower differs drastically in his overt assessment of Richard in the *Confessio* and the *Cronica*. For there is no question that if the Richard of the *Chronica* is said to be full of *impietas*, the *Confessio* calls him the very embodiment of "pite" (8.2992*).[47] But there are hints even in the "Ricardian" prologue and epilogue of the *Confessio*, internally dated 1390, that things are not so simple, both with this king and, more fundamentally, with this ethic so heavily stressed as a legal and social contract. It is probably coincidence that, just as Favent asserts throughout his account, in a repetitive drumming theme, that one should "be mindful of the end of every work"—he even has Richard think this at a legally critical moment of the trial, as noted earlier—so Gower, in his "Ricardian" prologue, remarks after receiving his commission from the king, "in proverbe I have herd seye / That who that wel his werk begynneth / The rather a good ende he wynneth" (Prol. 86–87*). Coincidence or no, of course, this might still be taken as a subtle warning to and about Richard, rather than as concerning Gower's own literary labors. But more weight should be given to how the Richard whom Gower presents in the prologue to the *Confessio* (as opposed to what he says about the king in the

---

[46] I cite, by book and line number, from G. C. Macaulay's edition of *The English Works of John Gower*, 2 vols. (London: Oxford University Press, 1900).

[47] Following Macaulay's lineation, passages that Gower revised and are printed by Macaulay as parallel texts are cited with asterisks.

epilogue) is not exactly pitying; he "bad me doo my besynesse / That to his hihe worthinesse / Som newe thing I scholde boke" (49–51*). We are perhaps overhearing a conversation between the king and Gower, rendered in indirect discourse, in which Richard describes himself as "his hihe worthiness": not the self-image that Gower states emphatically in book 7 of the *Confessio* a king should emphasize. "Pite is the foundement / Of every kinges regiment, / If it be medled with justice," as he says throughout book 7 (4197–99). Indeed, Nigel Saul has shown that Richard, from beginning to end of the 1390s, demanded imperial, indeed divine, epithets—in large part, Saul suggests, in order to overemphasize the royal authority that 1388 fundamentally undermined. As the St. Alban's chronicler declares, each of his favorites found "strange and flattering words hardly suitable for mere mortals . . . extend[ing] his arms and supplicat[ing] with his hands, as if praying to him, entreating his high, excellent and most praiseworthy majesty that he might deign to concede these or those things. And the young king . . . delighted in these words."[48]

If Richard through the 1390s would demand quasi-divine epithets, Gower, while articulating these, could nonetheless strive to redefine them. God, "the hihe mageste," showed pity through the Incarnation (7.3108); so too should the king in his "hihe worthiness":

> Forthi the lond mai wel be glad,
> Whos king with good conseil is lad,
> Which set him unto rihtwisnesse,
> So that his hihe worthinesse
> Betwen the reddour and Pite
> Doth mercy forth with equite.
> A king is holden overal
> To Pite, bot in special
> To hem wher he is most beholde;
> They scholde his Pite most beholde
> That ben the Lieges of his lond.
> (7.4167–77)

Vastly exceeding any of the brief comments on mercy in the tradition of mirrors for princes, royal pity in Gower is proffered, even before the *Cronica tripertita*, as the crucial social and legal contract between the asymmetrical powers of a monarchial system. Here it seems to mean simply compassion for the weak, but the obvious social implication, that pity is an expression of power, is spelled out more clearly elsewhere. In the Ricardian epilogue, Gower affirms that Richard's person reveals

---

[48] Nigel Saul, "Richard II and the Vocabulary of Kingship," *English Historical Review* 110 (1995): 861–63.

What is a king to be wel thewed,
Touchinge of pite namely,
For he yit nevere unpitously
Ayein the liges of his lond,
For no defaute which he fond,
Thurgh cruelty vengaunce soghte.
(8.2992–97*)

But this is virtue exemplified simply by a temporary lack, *so far* ("yit"), of vi-
ciousness; his pity is cruelty held in abeyance. In short, the rub in the emphasis on royal pity is that it is predicated on a suspension of cruelty. As such, it is
an expression of power, good or evil, and it therefore demands a careful if tenuous distinction between its good and bad forms.

Nor was Gower alone in revealing this menacing connection between pity
and power in the 1390s. In 1392, Richard Maidstone in his eulogistic report
of King Richard's "reconciliation" with the city of London, after the king had
severely punished it monetarily and legally in early 1392 for having refused to
give him enough money, described the city's presentation of a tablet to the
king naming his virtues, among which prominently figures pity (*pietas*: following Gower, medieval Latin conventions, and the obvious contextual
senses, I again translate *pietas* as "pity," and *pius* as "pious"). Here again pity is
a sign of violence held back:

Sed super haec pietas, compassio veraque cordis,
Dignificans animum, vos probat esse probum.
Spes etenim populi potior fit, et ad pietatem
Qua datur his venia, regis et ira cadit.
Significant satis hoc tabulae quas cernitis istae,
Quas regi pia plebs obtulit ecce pio.[49]

(But above all pity, and the compassion of a true heart, dignifying the soul,
proves you to be worthy. For the hope of the people grows stronger, because
even the king's wrath lapses into pity, by which pardon is given to these. These
tablets, which you see—behold!—the pious people bringing to the pious king,
represent this sufficiently.)

This sounds like a more obsequious version of Gower's "Ricardian" epilogue
to the *Confessio amantis*—or Gower's passage a more skeptical version of this.
But both writers articulate royal pity as a contingent solution for a dangerous
threat, and in so doing redefine pity as a direct expression of power.

Richard clearly gloried in this kind of pity, the arbitrary gestures of grace
proffered through and as sheer power. Throughout the 1380s and 1390s, as

[49] Thomas Wright, ed., *Political Poems and Songs Relating to English History . . . from the Accession
of Edw. III to That of Ric. III*, Rolls Series (London: Longman et al., 1859), 1:295.

already noted in passing, Richard was prone to be excessive rather than re-
strictive in his use of that fixture of medieval legal equity, the royal pardon:
after 1377, 1382, 1388, and 1398 he issued novel general pardons, covering
felony and treason that anyone had committed (except murder and certain
other felonies) during those moments of widespread unrest, apart from
specifically named exceptions, who would feel or already had felt his wrath.[50]
Such general pardons bound the nation in a contingent, textual relation to
the ruler's merciful dispensation—a kind of proto-constitutionalism, but
based on a presumption of monarchial absolutism. The terror these pardons
induced can be glimpsed by the assertion of the Commons in parliament in
1382 that the price of obtaining one from Chancery had driven some of the
poor into hiding and outlawry (*Rot. parl.*, 3:139). Some ten thousand are extant from Richard's reign.[51] Just as he was inclined in 1397 to issue charters
for those condemned of treason with the exact properties to be confiscated
left blank, subject to his later will (*carte blanche*), so he was inclined to use general pardons as a social contract contingent on his pity; one recalls the "yit" in
Gower's contorted logic in the "Ricardian" epilogue referring to the king's
lack of *un*pitying action.

As Gower, Richard Maidstone, and the Monk of Westminster (in his final
comments on 1388, quoted earlier) all show, the danger of this unpredictable
basis for a social contract loomed well before the parliament of 1397, when
Richard enacted retribution against the Lords Appellant, and when Arundel
made a scene because he claimed he had been granted a general pardon covering his actions in 1388.[52] Richard's pity and pardon could appear as rapidly
and unpredictably as they had vanished; indeed, that seems part of Richard's
point. Pardons so used sent a "message" of royal power behind their pity, and
sometimes did so with unnerving wit. Indeed, the legal groundwork (or excuse) for Richard's counterattack in the 1397 parliament emerged from his indicting and then, in a bizarrely ironic manner, pardoning a clerk of parliament. In early 1397 Thomas Haxey, as clerk of parliament, had carried from
the Commons a petition requesting the king (as often before) to reform the
vast expenditures of his household, which, this petition stated, included too
many bishops and ladies. Richard seized the occasion to declare treasonous
any effort to control the king's household—thus establishing the grounds for
the king's retaliation against the Lords Appellant later that year. Haxey, the
minor clerk, nearly had to play the Usk, though this time in the service of the
king's, not the lords', legal precedence: he was himself condemned for treason. But he was then entirely pardoned by the king, "at the request," the
Close Rolls state, "of the bishops and numerous ladies in the king's house-

[50] See Musson and Ormrod, *Evolution of English Justice*, 82, 87, 99–100, 108.
[51] Ibid., 82.
[52] See the account in the *Vita Ricardi Secundi*, trans. Given-Wilson, *Chronicles of the Revolution*,
58–59.

hold."[53] Whether extemporaneous or carefully planned, the king's ironic explanation for his pity appears highly staged, and fraught with aggressive assertions of power, as well as clear evidence of how readily the language of legal attack could be reversed into the language of pity and pardon, and vice versa.

These lineaments of legal and political power in pity may explain the odd pressures shaping the ethic in the narratives of the *Confessio* and in Gower's overall writing, possibly even moving his loyalties away from Richard at an early date. But since the ethic's association with power had partly created the problem, his increasing emphases on the ethic did not offer simple solutions for the political and legal culture he inhabited. On the one hand, Gower's concern with pity as a principal element of the social contract of monarchy exponentially increases in the last decade of his life. It is mostly lacking in the earlier French and Latin works; its expansion in the course of his writing the *Confessio* can be charted with the added stories in the section on pity in book 7; finally, in 1400 the theme of pity nearly overtakes the narrative of "In Praise of Peace," written for Henry IV, turning the short poem midway (from line 330) into little else but a praise of pity. It may be no coincidence that, along with his Lancastrian insignia of 'S's, Pite was one of the three presiding personified virtues carved on Gower's tomb.[54] Yet, on the other hand, although much of his increasing emphasis seeks to articulate the social contract of royal pity, the *Confessio* also displays an equally vigorous effort to disparage and crush "pite" used as an oppressive instrument in the service of corruption, all the while advancing a sense of true "pite" as including, indeed mainly being, justice, vengeance, even extreme violence. Gower's project becomes the difficult one of distinguishing good and bad pity when both are palpable instruments of power; the unstable closeness of the categories is revealed by the frequent reliance on irony and satire, where what is upheld can disappear so readily in the elusive implications of what is condemned.

In demoting and quashing false "pite" in the *Confessio*, Gower is inclined both to produce claims for or scenes of pathos and demands for pity, often specifically legal ones, and also to undercut them, often very aggressively. Indeed, the strongest zeal for violence and cruelty I can detect in this pacifist's writings appears in these instances of punishing those species of pity that imply duplicity and self-serving power. Elaborate gestures or evocations of pity are revealed as hollow, inauthentic, or somehow inadequate in numerous tales, where they are savagely exposed or crushed—crushed both by the outcomes and by Gower's adroit ironies and juxtapositions. Condemnation of

[53] A. K. McHardy, "Haxey's Case, 1397: The Petition and Its Presenter Reconsidered," in *The Age of Richard II*, ed. James L. Gillespie (New York: St. Martin's Press, 1997), 93–114.

[54] For Berthelette's description from 1532, see Macaulay, *Latin Works*, xxii. John Stow notes that Pite's features with those of the other figures were destroyed in the Reformation. See ibid.; Fisher, *John Gower*, 37–38.

lovers with "fals pitous lokynge" are obvious enough castigations of the false form of the ethic (1.680), although the pervasive, self-deluded pity of the Lover himself will require fuller consideration later. Legal judgments in which pity is decisively and brutally rejected are more pertinent, and are indeed pervasive.

Some of these I can note only in passing. In the story of Mundus and Paulina, where Mundus, with the help of the temple priests, has pretended to be a god to seduce the chaste and gullible pagan Paulina, the priests' effort to throw all blame on the duke, who masterminded the seduction, elicits a lengthy and energetic repetition on how "thilke excusement was non" (1.1022, 1029), capped by their rapid execution. The duke himself is spared, but only barely, an emphasis perhaps on the justness of executing accessories while sparing leaders (which has echoes of the convictions in 1388). In "The Trump of Death" (1.2021–253), a king has honored poor, aged pilgrims because he sees an image of his own death in their faces, and he punishes his brother, who has criticized him for such attention to beggars, by sending to his brother's door the notification of certain death, the trumpet. Gower has greatly elaborated from his source (*Barlaam and Josaphat*) the moment when the king's brother's wife and children appeal to the king to rescind his execution order; it becomes a poignant scene of the queen's desperate appeal for pity, comparable to the descriptions of Queen Anne pleading for Simon Burley's life in 1388, which Gower briefly mentions in the *Cronicon*:

> Tho casten thei that he and sche
> Forth with here children on the morwe,
> As thei that were full of sorwe,
> Al naked bot of smok and scherte,
> To tendre with the kynges herte . . .
> Ther was no wiht, if he hem syge,
> Fro water mihte kepe his yhe
> For sorwe which thei maden tho . . .
> And alle at ones doun thei falle,
> If eny pite may be founde.
> (2168–203)

As Masayoshi Ito shrewdly observes, Gower wants the reader to realize that the humiliating and publicly moving appeal for pity by the king's brother's family is hollow, because the king's brother lacked real pity and humility when he scorned the ancient pilgrims.[55] To this I may add how well this scene recasts *true* "pity" (and thus perhaps anxiously revisits the deaths of Burley and the others) as a species of rigorous justice. In the tale, the king's pity

---

[55] Masayoshi Ito, "Gower's Use of *Vita Barlaam et Josaphat* in *Confessio amantis*," *Studies in English Literature* English number (Tokyo, 1979): 3–18.

emerges not as sheer compassion but as a moral lesson, when the king ultimately "with hise wordes wise / His brother tawht and al foryive" (2252–53).

It bears repeating that, even though "false" pity is exposed as self-serving
and duplicitous—that is, as a means for enhancing one's power—"true" pity is
also elaborated as a form of power (as when the king in "The Trump of
Death" uses his absolute power to "teach" his brother). The difference is in
the implicit claim for the *purpose* behind such pity. But rather than try to
argue for a specific set of conditions that make for "good" or "bad" pity in the
work, it is more pertinent to step back and note the similarity, and the reasons
for the difficulty of distinguishing them. As Nietzsche, theorist of *ressentiment*, might note, pity always carries some implication of power. In Gower's
works and Ricardian culture, however, pity is distinctively and specifically su-
percharged with an implication of power, and with an accompanying effort to
destroy what are perceived as the false uses of pity by opponents. This implication appears as a problem in the *Confessio* in ways that do not appear in the
later *Cronica*, in the sense that the former explores greater extremes of these
views. I take this problematic connection of pity and violence in the *Confessio*
as the signs of a fuller, less tidily resolved exploration of the legal, political,
and ethical social contract that pity as an instrument of power establishes.
And if this is an exploration of the issues and events of 1388 and Richard's responses at a level below any acknowledgment in the narrative, it is not clear
that it was or needs to be considered as entirely visible to Gower himself.

In fact, however, the connection between pity and vengeance is often explicit both in the stories and as a point of discussion between the narrator and
Genius, and it climaxes with the Lover's own trial at the poem's end. Thus in
the story of the secret lovers Pyramus and Thisbe, Pyramus fanatically has
not allowed any mercy for himself when he thinks his planned night meeting
with Thisbe has led to her being killed by the lion: "I am cause of this felonie,
/ So it is resoun that I die" (3.1431–32). In narrative recompense for his severe rejection of pity, Thisbe, safely hiding in a cave, experiences an overwhelming access of pity for him and for all whose hearts the gods have "sette"
so fruitlessly "afyre": "With many a wofull pitous lok / Hire yhe alwei among
sche caste / Upon hir love" (3.1458–60). Yet this pity leads her, as she subsides
in a series of listing dips then a slide below waves of sorrow, to kill herself:

> Hire love in armes sche embraseth,
> Hire oghne deth and so pourchaseth
> That now sche wepte and nou sche kiste,
> Til ate laste, er sche it wiste,
> So gret a sorwe is to hire falle,
> Which overgoth hire wittes alle.
> As sche which mihte it noght asterte,
> The swerdes point ayein hire herte

Sche sette, and fell doun therupon.
(3.1483–91)

This is pity used as a vehicle of judgment, but in perverted and tragic form ("Which overgoth hire wittes alle"). Emphasizing that such a disastrously misconceived form of pity has led to the tragedy, the Lover, in mimetic rather than analytic response to the tale, wildly indulges in self-pity, which turns instantly into desire for vengeance against his own beloved, who will not requite his love. He compares Thisbe's feckless address to Pyramus' dead body with his own efforts to persuade his beloved, a ludicrously self-obsessed interpretation which nonetheless shrewdly registers how a destructive form of pity has been the chief issue in the tale. He has just as much luck as Thisbe in getting through to his lover because of standoffishness (Daunger), which "Mai wel be cleped sanz pite" (3.1550). Indeed, he adds—continuing to imply a cross-gendered identification of himself and Thisbe, and his beloved and Pyramus—if he died from such lack of pity, his beloved might well be convicted for murder. He then marshals the sort of legal case which might in that event be brought, displaying increasing resentment of the crime his lady would have committed, inflaming his proleptic desire to punish her:

Me thenkth sche mihte noght be qwyt
That sche ne were an homicide:
And if it scholde so betide,
As god forbiede it scholde be,
Be double weie it is pite.
For I, which al my will and witt
Have yove and served evere yit,
And thanne I scholde in such a wise
In rewardinge of my service
Be ded, me thenkth it were a rowthe.
(3.1588–97)

Because of his own way of sympathizing with and pitying Thisbe, his petulant demand for pity turns into a capital case against the woman who does not pity him enough. The merging of pity with desire for judicial violence here appears openly as a form of *ressentiment*, of bitter impotence. As such, it explicitly shows how pity is a species of power or desire for power, a connection that both the "true" and "false" kinds of pity cannot avoid, even in a ludicrously hypothetical criminal trial.

The stories specifically on "pity" in book 7—the book presenting the proper "policy" for kings—still more directly present this connection between pity and violence or vengeance, and not even in the elusive mode of irony and self-irony. "The Jew and the Pagan," a tale found in only some copies of the *Confessio* (including two of those that replace the dedication to Richard with the one "for Engelondes sake" and add a dedication to Henry

Derby in the epilogue),[56] presents a likely candidate for contemplating pity in relation to the nature of upholding a code of law. In it, the traveling Pagan, whose "lawe which I use" is "To loven alle men aliche, / The povere bothe and ek the riche" (7.3223–26*), helps the traveling Jew, whose "lawe" is "to noman be felawe" unless that other is himself a Jew (3239–40*). The Jew convinces the Pagan that, to be true to his law, the Pagan should give the Jew his ass to ride on; but (of course) the Jew in being true to *his* "lawe of Juerie," that is, of cheating all those who are not Jews, cheats the Pagan and rides away (3285–97*).

The tale might provide a point about the confining nature of any law so literally adhered to; instead, Gower's elaboration of what follows in the story explains how, at some stage of his thinking at least, he can present such an anti-Judaic, violent tale as an instance of "pity" as "policy," that is, as a species of good kingship. Robbed of his ass, the Pagan prays to his God for vengeance and "mercy," using language in this tale that intriguingly evokes "appeal." Although this, one of Gower's very rare uses of the word, is in a different sense from "lay a charge," the results of the story efface that distinction, contextually pulling the use of "appele" here into precisely the sense of 1388:

> "Unto thi dom, lord, I appele;
> Behold and deme mi querele,
> With humble herte I thee beseche;
> The mercy bothe and ek the wreche
> I sette al in thi juggement."
> (3305–9*)

At once he comes upon the bloody corpse of the Jew, killed by a lion, and his own ass safe nearby. The moral brings this result into the theme of pity overtly, and also emphases how pity in this kind of "appeal" is best expressed through vengeance and castigating power:

> Lo, thus a man mai knowe at ende,
> How the pitous pite deserveth.
> For what man that to pite serveth,
> As Aristotle it berth witnesse,
> God schal hise foomen so represse,
> That thei schul ay stonde under foote.
> (3330–35*)

The same point appears in the final tale of the *Confessio*, the tale of Apollonius, and again, more pointedly, in the Lover's own final fate. The plot of the

---

[56] The "Stafford" and Wollaton Hall manuscripts, described in Macauley, *English Works*, 1:clii, cvi.

tale of Apollonius becomes in Gower's hands a vehicle for scenes emphasizing the connection between power and pity, where unjustly used pity is the object of savage retribution, and justly used pity the vehicle of enormous power. To summarize briefly: the hero tries to woo the daughter caught in an incestuous relation with her father, only to lose her at sea and be led back to her by their daughter Thais, whose own fate involves capture, attempted rape, and long exile. As Gower presents it, the tale features pity as power in numerous ways. One notable instance is when Thais, sold by the pirates to work in a brothel, renders all of her customers impotent with pity by her mournful complaints:

> Ech after other ten or tuelve
> Of yonge men to hire in wente;
> Bot such a grace god hire sente,
> That for the sorwe which sche made
> Was non of hem which pouer hade
> To don hire eny vileinie.
> (8.1426–31)

Another is when Gower makes the center of the tale an archetypally hollow gesture of public pity—pity as an abuse of power. I say "center of the tale" because this scene, significantly elaborated from its source, constitutes the justification for the violent vengeance that later climaxes the tale. The scene is a delicately rendered public display of mourning by Dionise and her husband, with whom Apollonius has first left his daughter, after they have tried to murder her in jealousy (and believe they have succeeded, since pirates took her away). The presentation of Dionise's and her husband's false evocations of pity is characteristic of Gower's brilliantly pointed elaboration of his sources for his own purposes. His late classical source presents a terse, impersonal, and formal epitaph that the genuinely mourning townspeople compose: "Dii manes: cives Tarsi Tarsiae virgini beneficiis Tyrii Apollonii ex aere collato fecerunt" ("To the spirits of the dead: the citizens of Tarsus erected this monument by subscription to the maiden Tarsia because of the benefactions of Apollonius of Tyre").[57] In Gower, this moment is replaced with an eloquently plangent epitaph that the falsely mourning, murderous couple themselves have fashioned:

> "O yee that this beholde,
> Lo, hier lith sche, the which was holde
> The faireste and the flour of alle,
> Whos name Thaisis men calle.
> The king of Tyr Appolinus
> Hire fader was: now lith sche thus.

---

[57] From the edition and translation of the *Historia* in Elizabeth Archibald, *Apollonius of Tyre: Medieval and Renaissance Themes and Variations* (Cambridge: D. S. Brewer, 1991), 148–49.

Fourtiene yer sche was of Age,
Whan deth hir tok to his viage."
(8.1533–40)

The epitaph's multiple superficial claims on the reader's pity are so many ways to increase the reader's resentment against "false" pity as the primary tool of the evilly despotic. But *good* pity retains its connection with power too. Gower's presentation of the story's resolution emphasizes the king of Miletene's pity on Apollonius, which leads him to send Thais to comfort him, ultimately resulting in their reunion as father and daughter.

With the presentation of pity as a function of power in a good purpose, the ever-present shadow of this connection—pity as an instrument of corrupt legal power—must be purged all the more fully. The slaughter of Dionise and her husband, as those who have connected pity with public power for nefarious ends, performs this thematic purgation or clarification, an exaggerated destruction of "bad" pity to seek some stable base for the otherwise tenuous position of "good" pity that similarly bespeaks power. It seems sheer cathartic pleasure on the part of the narrator to put to death those who have so manipulated pity. Indeed, the punishment is called a form of "mercy":

Atteint thei were be the lawe
And diemed forto honge and drawe,
And brent and with the wynd toblowe,
That al the world it myhte knowe:
And upon this condicion
The dom in execucion
Was put anon withoute faile.
And every man hath gret mervaile,
Which herde tellen of this chance,
And thonketh goddes pourveance,
Which doth mercy forth with justice.
Slain is the moerdrer and moerdrice
Thurgh verray trowthe of rihtwisnesse,
And thurgh mercy sauf is simplesse
Of hire whom mercy preserveth;
Thus hath he wel that wel deserveth.
(8.1947–62)

They receive the death reserved for traitors. Like the use of "appele" in "The Jew and the Pagan," this and other features of the account would speak to the issues of 1388 for those readers of Gower's poem who were also among the clerical, administrative, and noble readers of the voluminous literature about that event produced during and just after it.

The position of this last tale of the *Confessio* suggests that something fundamental in the poem's larger themes has been restated or resolved. In the context of the other tales noted earlier, one may conjecture that the tale's ideological achievement here is to establish a sharp distinction between "mercy" instantiating just expressions of power, even execution, and displays of pity serving corrupt or perverse kinds of power. But Gower does not stop there. Although the end of the *Confessio*'s last tale has already accomplished an ideological remaking of pity like that which will later govern the portrayal of 1388 in the *Cronica*, Gower continues on in his final passages of the poem, putting more pressure on the ideological formulation that true pity is identical with extreme judicial punishment. His subplot displaying the Lover's state of mind has, throughout the poem, been used to point up feckless self-pity; after the final tale of Apollonius, this development culminates in an absurd "bille" of supplication requesting a requitement for a love that, given the narrator's real age and impotence, has no possibility for realization. As pity has just been emptied out of the scene of the executions of the false manipulators of pity in the tale of Apollonius, so it now wholly evaporates from the presentation of the aged and feckless Lover.

While softened by a claim as "mere illusion," however—an amorous and literary error from which John Gower will awaken—the poem's final events, taken literally, are horrifying in how they bring to bear on the Lover himself the new ideological formulation that the poem has generated: of pity as vengeance and violence as pity. After the narrator is revealed as, in effect, a traitor to the cause of Love, all the "court" raises a deafening shout that Venus pity him—"sche . . . myhte noght forsake / So gret a clamour as was there, / Let Pite come into her Ere" (8.2730–32). But the result of such common cry for "Pite" is that the Lover is subject to what amounts to a judicial punishment of castration, effectively if crudely carried out by the blind, "groping" Cupid:

> This blinde god which mai noght se,
> Hath groped til that he me fond;
> And as he pitte forth his hond
> Upon my body, wher I lay,
> Me thoghte a fyri Lancegay,
> Which whilom thurgh myn herte he caste,
> He pulleth oute, and also faste
> As this was do, Cupide nam
> His weie.
> (8.2794–802)

Here is the climax but also the unassimilated residue of the *Confessio*'s themes, in a moment rife with echoes of the parliamentary trial of 1388—especially the general clamor of parliament ("we hauet hym, we hauet hym," as Favent reports they shout when Tresilian is brought in [17 (par. 19)], or the general roar condemning Brembre [16 (par. 18)], the "os commune locutum" that Gower himself will mention in the *Cronica*), a clamor that leads, as the use of mere notoriety led in that parliament, to a violent judicial punishment. But at the close of the *Confessio*, more directly and chillingly than in the *Cronica*, it is explicitly "pity" that mobilizes this punishment. Read as the agent of judicial punishment, carried out in 1388 style, pity here has become utterly merciless, a legal instrument of absolute power over individual subjects of a dictatorial parliament, however loudly the ethic's legitimacy is proclaimed by efforts to denounce and purge a putatively false and corrupt mirroring ethic.

It is speculation, of course, to claim that this complex development of pity as vengeance and violence in the *Confessio* responded to the issues and procedures of the "parliament without mercy" and the social contract of arbitrary royal pity which the parliament paradoxically helped exacerbate in the early 1390s. Yet I think it worthwhile to try to theorize the connection as if it did securely obtain; for bringing the *Confessio* into the ambit of the literature of 1388 allows new appreciation of the legal and political import in the ethical issues it negotiates. This view also opens for consideration a more continuous horizon of all of Gower's literary works, early and late, and along with those, the remarkable Latin writings generated by the events around him. They may all be seen as part of one continuous cultural problem and one interwoven assessment of legal and political ethics.

One way to theorize this hypothetical connection further would be to emphasize how the *Confessio* would therefore be speaking to several circles of readers, one a general learned audience accustomed to ethical instruction and ethical satire, another the specific civil servants, clerics, and nobility at the royal court who were closely involved in the parliamentary proceedings that had begun in 1386 with the impeachment of Michael de la Pole, and developed into further legal complexity and political consideration with 1388 and the years following. This suggestion of deliberate multiple addresses to multiple audiences, the most select being a readership adept in Latin, would certainly fit the form of the work, of English verse with Latin verse and extensive marginalia.

Another, not incompatible way to theorize this connection would take wider account of the problems of the vision of pity as an instrument of legal power in the *Confessio*. In this wider view, the economy of pity in the *Confessio amantis* would, to use a notion originated by Kenneth Burke, be a symbolic resolution to the intractable problems of pity in the historical context, though one that could not in the nature of its terms achieve harmony.[58] Once pity is reinterpreted as an instrument of legal vengeance, any violence can present itself as really a form of true pity: in turn, any such reinterpretation can stand revealed as mere rationalization, as ideological argument, as false pity, demanding violent justice and merciful purgation.

Either approach to the *Confessio*'s presentation of pity, in fact, would imply

---

[58] Kenneth Burke, *The Philosophy of Literary Form* (Berkeley: University of California Press, 1973), e.g., 5–6; see also the essays in *Language as Symbolic Action: Essays on Life, Literature, and Method* (Berkeley: University of California Press, 1966).

some of the coming dangers. For, like much of the political culture in the 1390s, Gower showed pity to be a menacing instrument of political and legal power, yet he continued to amplify his claims for the ethic, as the only imaginable resolution of the king's claims to autocratic power. Whereas "early" Gower was evidently in some measure a pro-Ricardian writer, the efforts by "mid-" and "late" Gower to emphasize royal pity continually led him to set forth the implied menace in it, and thus to produce narratives that have more in common with the merciless outlook of the Lords Appellant seeking to deflate Richard's power than with Richard's own interests. Yet in turn this also led him to further emphases on pity as an instrument of oppressive legal and political power in any hands, indeed, a lethal ethic when advanced to the level of legal instrument and social contract.

The king's building responses to 1388, which exploded in 1397, when (after granting Haxey his strange pardon) Richard reversed the judgments of the Merciless Parliament with a mercilessness of his own, were thus in some ways predictable from Gower's treatments of the ethic in the *Confessio*. In the escalating duel of constitutional and parliamentary law, and under the constant threat that the king's use of "general pardons" established, one could only wait for the king to retaliate still more severely. In fact, Richard never matched the Lords Appellant in actual bloodshed, though he was more shrewd in his efforts to destroy their families' wealth.[59] But charged as it became with enormous political and legal power, pity was a threat as well as a binding social ethic. Gower articulated both, and tried, in a dynamic dialectic and brilliant if ultimately impossible venture, to disentangle them.

Decades ago, T. F. T. Plucknett observed that the ascendingly disruptive and violent series of state trials in Richard's reign "seem to be all of them variations—one might say Enigma Variations—upon an undisclosed theme which still eludes us."[60] Although it would be rash to suggest what any one "theme" in this developing tension was, I think that the literature of 1388, and the renunciation and hyperextension of the legal and political uses of pity in other writings of the period, help us partly thematize the long, ascending legal and political trauma surrounding Richard in his last decade. It would be even rasher to declare that this is what makes the complex narrative developments of the *Confessio amantis* possible; but if only to reopen discussion of Gower, in tandem with some of his historian contemporaries, as a topical writer of genius, and of the discourse of medieval ethics as a focal point of socially immediate legal and political arguments and energies, this seems a useful claim to make.

[59] See Ross, "Forfeiture for Treason," 574–75.
[60] T. F. T. Plucknett, "State Trials under Richard II," *Transactions of the Royal Historical Society*, 5th ser., 2 (1952): 159.

4   Palamon's Appeal of Treason in the *Knight's Tale*

RICHARD FIRTH GREEN

Most readers will be familiar with Palamon and Arcite's first sight of Emelye in the *Knight's Tale* and the childish squabble it provokes. What may be less readily recognized is that this scene marks one of Chaucer's more striking departures from his model, Boccaccio's *Teseida*, where the young cousins Palaemon and Arcites, far from engaging in mutual recrimination, are happy to agree that the figure they see walking in the garden is Venus and to conclude that the arrows Cupid has loosed off through their prison window must have struck both alike. Each is equally happy to acknowledge the depths of the other's torment, and, far from quibbling over an unattainable *amour lointain*, sensibly does his best to console the other. True, Chaucer has imported some of their animosity from a later scene in Boccaccio (the combat in the grove), but even there the Italian offers nothing to compare with Palamon's fierce denunciation of his cousin:

"It nere," quod he, "to thee no greet honour,
For to be fals, ne for to be traitour
To me, that am thy cosyn and thy brother
Ysworn ful depe, and ech of us til oother."
(1129–32)[1]

Why has Chaucer chosen to rewrite his source here? Certainly not in the interests of compression, his usual way with the *Teseida*; nor can he be shown

[1] All Chaucer quotations are taken from *The Riverside Chaucer*, ed. Larry D. Benson, 3rd ed. (Boston: Houghton Mifflin, 1987).

to be medievalizing Boccaccio (as C.S. Lewis claims was his habit with *Il Filostrato*),[2] at least not in any straightforward manner; still less does this scene flatten out the distinction between the two cousins (another tendency that has been noted in his rewriting of the *Teseida*). If anything, his version here points up an apparent distinction between a dreamy, romantic Palamon—"I noot wher she be womman or goddesse, / But Venus is it soothly as I geese" (1101–2)—and a more down-to-earth Arcite: "myn is love as to a creature" (1159). And why, more to the point here, has he chosen to give their dispute an unmistakably juridical cast?

It is quite clear that when Palamon levels the weighty charge of *treason* (i.e., *fidei laesio*, or breach of promise) against Arcite, he means by this that he regards his cousin as having broken the terms of their contract as brothers-in-arms: "But that thou sholdest trewely forthren me / In every cas, as I shal forthren thee— / This was thin ooth and myn also certeyn" (1136–38). In 1962 Maurice Keen showed that brotherhood-in-arms, long assumed to be the exclusive province of romance heroes like Amys and Amiloun, Eger and Grime, or, as here, Palamon and Arcite, might in fact be a perfectly mundane contractual arrangement between professional soldiers, essentially a form of insurance policy designed to double their chances of collecting on the spoils of battle or halve their risk of having to pay out crippling ransoms.[3] A year later, K.B. McFarlane, apparently independently, published a copy of just such an agreement made by two English squires, Nicholas Molyneux and John Winter, and drawn up on July 12, 1421, in Harfleur: "Wishing to augment the love and fraternity already growing between them," they engaged themselves as sworn brothers-in-arms, "loyal one to the other without any dissimulation or fraud," and if either were taken prisoner by the king's enemies—"which God forbid"—the other was bound to do all that was possible to secure his liberation, provided that the ransom demanded for him did not exceed £1,000; should both be taken prisoner at the same time, one was to remain as hostage while the other went to obtain the ransom money for both). Molyneux and Winter's indenture does not make any explicit mention of an obligation to further one's brother-in-arms' fortunes in love (though interestingly both Amys and Grime seem to assume that this is part of the deal), but it does specify that if one of them should be sent home, he was to use their common stock "to seek out and purchase the most profitable manors [*heritages*] that he is able to find for the profit of them both, or of the survivor, or for their heirs."[4] Anyone familiar with the *Paston Letters* will recognize that acquiring manors might well mean making a suitable match, and John Paston II's experiences suggest how important friends and intermediaries might prove to be in such a venture. It is not, then, a great stretch to imagine that a

[2] C.S. Lewis, "What Chaucer Really Did to *Il Filostrato*," *Essays and Studies* 17 (1932): 56–75.

[3] Maurice Keen, "Brotherhood in Arms," *History* 47 (1962): 1–17.

[4] K.B. McFarlane, "A Business Partnership in War and Administration, 1421–1445," *English Historical Review* 78 (1963): 309–10.

knight might expect his brother-in-arms to assist him in making an appropriate marriage.

To Palamon's accusation of *treason*, Arcite replies in an explicitly juridical manner. He enters, as it were, two pleas, one special and the other general; both are what the common lawyers of Chaucer's day would have called demurrers (that is to say, denials that the law applies to the case at issue). The first is his equivocal claim:

> "Thow shalt," quod he, "be rather fals than I;
> And thou art fals, I telle thee outrely,
> For paramour I loved hire first er thow.
> What wiltow seyen? Thou woost nat yet now
> Wheither she be womman or goddesse!
> Thyn is affeccioun of hoolynesse,
> And myn is love as to a creature."
> (1153–59)

This verbal quibble, though it is not without its parallels in modern Anglo-American law, is likely to seem so blatant to modern readers that they will have difficulty regarding it as a seriously intended legal defense; yet such equivocation was rampant in medieval English courts. From a multitude of possible examples, here is one from 1286, when the prior of Barnwell in Cambridgeshire sued one of his tenants, Henry Tuillet, for building a wall that prevented his bailiff from gaining access to the property and thus collecting the rent. The jury found against him on the grounds that "Henry has not enclosed that tenement with that wall. For they say, that William, Henry's father, enclosed that tenement."[5] This seems to have been literally true in the sense that the father had paid for the building of a wall on his son's estate, but equivocal in the sense that it implied the tenement had already been walled when the son took seisin of it. If the prior had not been so incensed by this equivocation that he threatened to swear out a jury of attaint to convict the original panel, we should have known nothing of the matter, and the record of the jury's decision would have looked like a simple finding of fact. It is at least arguable that the elaborate formalism of common law pleading, designed presumably to counter just such equivocation, had had the effect of making it worse by Chaucer's day.

Arcite's second demurrer is the general one (medieval pleaders normally worked from the specific to the general for the obvious reason that to lose on a general exception would automatically invalidate any special exceptions they might have up their sleeves) that love lies outside the jurisdiction of human law. Interestingly, he introduces it with the legal tag: "I pose that thou

[5] M. T. Clanchy, "A Medieval Realist: Interpreting the Rules of Barnwell Priory, Cambridge," in *Perspectives in Jurisprudence*, ed. Elspeth Atwooll (Glasgow: University of Glasgow Press, 1977), 189.

lovedest hire herebiforn" (i.e., "even were I to grant that you had a prior claim on her . . ."). The verb *pose*, rare in Chaucer, is known in English before the Ricardian period from only a single legal text,[6] but is a common word in the law French of fourteenth-century yearbooks, with the sense of "to grant for the sake of argument, to postulate."[7] It does not seem to have been noticed that the text which Arcite quotes in support of his position, "who shal yeve a lovere any lawe?" is a variant of the legal maxim *necessitas non habet legem*, which Langland renders as "nede haþ no lawe,"[8] and which was used as a defense by those driven to steal the bare necessities of life: food, drink, and clothing.[9] Langland's point that in dire necessity the law of nature is to be regarded as a higher law than human, or positive, law is recast, not without irony, by Chaucer to apply to love:

> Love is a gretter lawe, by my pan,
> Than may be yeve to any erthely man,
> And therfore positive lawe and swich decree
> Is broken alday for love in ech degree.
> (1165–68)

And there, circumstances dictate, Arcite is forced to rest his case until the chance meeting in the grove offers him the opportunity to "darreyne" (1609) it by battle.

Darreyne, we should note, is also a specifically legal term,[10] and all four of its occurrences in Chaucer are restricted to the *Knight's Tale*: it is used a few lines later, when the knights are preparing for their combat in the grove (1631–32), and again when Theseus is giving instructions for the great tournament ("Everich of you shal brynge an hundred knyghtes / . . . Al redy to darreyne hire by bataille" [1851–53]); its final appearance is shortly before the tournament itself (2097). It might, of course, be reasonably objected that this final battle between the two Thebans is nothing like the single combat required of a formal judicial duel; it is in fact much more like a *mêlée*, a mock pitched battle, staged for entertainment. Chaucer has, however, modified his source in the direction of such a duel by focusing our attention on the struggle between the two knights themselves (together with their two principal champions) rather than on the general fighting that forms a backdrop to it,

---

[6] See *The Middle English Dictionary*, s.v. "posen" 1a and 1b. I owe this point to W. F. Bolton, who discussed *pose* as a term of art in a paper delivered at a meeting of the New Chaucer Society in Vancouver in 1988.

[7] See *The Anglo-Norman Dictionary*, s.v. "poser."

[8] William Langland, *Piers Plowman: The B Version*, ed. George Kane and E. Talbot Donaldson (London: Athlone Press, 1975), 20:10.

[9] For a full discussion, see "Fogassa's Case," in Edmund Plowden's *Commentaries* (London, 1571), ff. 1a–20b.

[10] See J. H. Baker, *A Manual of Law French*, 2nd ed. (Aldershot: Scholar Press, 1990), s.v. "deraigner" 1, "to vindicate by proof."

and, unconventional as it is in many of its details, the great tournament in part 4 clearly functions in the tale as a *judicium Dei*, that is to say, a trial by battle. Theseus's last-minute decree may have the effect of turning it into a harmless *hastiludium*, but the fact remains that the parties had at one point been prepared to fight to the death to prove the justice of their cause.

It is here, I believe, that we should look for an answer to the question with which I began: Why does Chaucer turn the affable discussion of Boccaccio's two young Thebans into an acrimonious and legalistic wrangle? The answer I am proposing is that Chaucer found in Boccaccio's story an ideal vehicle for exploring not merely the complex social interplay of violence and order, or even the paradoxical dependence of individual security on political force (themes that have been stressed by a number of critics of the poem), but also a quite specific legal process that brings such themes into particularly sharp focus: trial by battle. As I hope to show, the role of trial by battle was far from being a merely academic issue at the time he came to write the poem. Put simply, the quarrel between Palamon and Arcite has been deliberately framed in explicitly legal terms in order to provide the central conflict of the *Knight's Tale* with the appearance of a judicial or quasi-judicial casus belli, and nothing conveys Chaucer's view of the shabbiness of such a process more strongly than the fact that the litigant who finally wins the case is the one who loses the *judicium Dei*. In the *Teseida*, Arcites had formally married Emilia before he died (in other words, the judgment of battle had been made to justify, however fleetingly, Arcites' claim), and the suppression of this significant detail, I suggest, is one of the most telling of the alterations Chaucer makes to Boccaccio.

When Richard II came to the throne, the scope of formal trial by battle under the English common law was severely restricted, and the chances that those belonging to the knightly class would be called upon to defend themselves in such an arena were in practice very remote, at least away from the wilder border regions.[11] Indeed, it was getting on for a hundred years since anyone in southern England could have witnessed a civil trial by battle (and even then it would have been one fought by champions).[12] In 1375, however, an event occurred that was to bring the moribund process back to life in a dramatic and, for many, a deeply disturbing manner. In that year an English captain called Thomas Katrington had surrendered to the French the important Norman fortress of St. Sauveur, which had once belonged to the great soldier Sir John Chandos; on his return home, Katrington found himself appealed of treason in parliament by a knight called Sir John Annesley and chal-

---

[11] For an interesting account of trial by battle as "a popular aspect of march law" on the Scottish border right down to the end of the fifteenth century, see Cynthia J. Neville, *Violence, Custom, and Law: The Anglo-Scottish Border Lands in the Later Middle Ages* (Edinburgh: Edinburgh University Press, 1998), 76–77.

[12] See M.J. Russell, "Trial by Battle Procedure in Writs of Right and Criminal Appeals," *Tijdschrift voor Rechtgeschiedenis* 53 (1983b): 123–34.

lenged to defend himself in battle.[13] Annesley's motives were far from disinterested, for he was related by marriage to Chandos and had himself a propriatary interest in the lost French fortress. It took four years for the case to come to trial, in part because Katrington had some powerful friends at court (including John of Gaunt), but also because there were sound legal objections to such a procedure: "Those who feared to be overthrown on a similar charge opposed it strongly," writes Walsingham, "but at length after pressure had been applied to the judges and important knights of the shire it was decided that it was quite legitimate in an overseas case such as the present one (which had not arisen within the boundaries of the kingdom), for someone to wage battle," as long as the contest was supervised by the Constable of England and the Earl Marshal, that is to say, as long as the case was heard before the civilian Court of Chivalry.[14]

The battle itself, which took place at Westminster on June 7, 1380, was a great novelty and attracted hordes of spectators from London (more than turned up to watch Richard II's coronation, says Walsingham dryly). The lists that were built to accommodate them were large and impressive—it seemed as though they had been built to last forever, Walsingham says—and it is tempting to imagine that Chaucer may have been thinking of them when he came to write of the ones built by Theseus in Athens. Indeed, if the *Knight's Tale* was written in the early 1380s, it is hard to believe that he could not have done so.[15] Proceedings were supervised by the king himself, and by two of his uncles, John of Gaunt and Thomas of Woodstock; Woodstock was Constable, but Gaunt's role is unclear since the office of Earl Marshal at this time was actually held by Thomas Mowbray. Predictably, perhaps, the contest itself turned out to be a bloody and discreditable brawl and ended with Annesley, the smaller of the two men, pinned to the earth by the body of his exhausted and insensible opponent. It was a situation that set the judges something of a problem. Eventually, Katrington was dragged off but proved to be in no condition to continue the battle; he probably saved the executioner some trouble by dying of his wounds the next morning.[16]

If that were all there was to it, the bizarre case of *Annesley v. Katrington* would barely merit more than a footnote; but as so often in legal matters, once a procedural precedent had been set, it was to have unforeseen consequences. On the surface, *Annesley v. Katrington* looks to have very little in common with the quarrel between Palamon and Arcite. True, Palamon, like Annesley, accuses his opponent of treason, both during their initial quarrel in

[13] See John Bellamy, "Sir John de Annesley and the Chandos Inheritance," *Nottingham Medieval Studies* 10 (1966): 94–105.

[14] Thomas Walsingham, *Historia Anglicana*, ed. Thomas Riley, 2 vols., Rolls Series (London, 1863–64), 1:431.

[15] Helen Cooper has written that "on all counts a date in the early 1380s is likely" (*Oxford Guides to Chaucer: The Canterbury Tales* [Oxford: Oxford University Press, 1989], 61).

[16] Walsingham, *Historia Anglicana*, 1:433–34.

prison and later when he stumbles on Arcite sighing in the grove ("Arcite, false traytour wikke, / Now artow hent" [1580–81]). But treason here means the betrayal of their contract as brothers-in-arms, not the surrender of an important fortress to the king's enemies. Yet, as we have seen, Annesley was no public-spirited agent of the Crown; he was pursuing a private vendetta against a man whose actions he believed had cost him a valuable estate in France. Property disputes were the meat and drink of the common law courts, but two centuries of legal refinement had made the barriers to using battle as a way of resolving them so difficult to surmount that the process had fallen into disuse. Now here was a new process entirely outside the common law (the Court of Chivalry, like Admiralty, was governed by the rules of civil procedure)[17] which offered the vigorous and the belligerent a fast and attractive means of settling their differences with their neighbors. There can be no doubt that this represents a dramatic extension of the court's traditional jurisdiction; as G. D. Squibb notes, "by the last quarter of the fourteenth century the Court was dealing with litigation which had no apparent connexion with war,"[18] or, in Anthony Tuck's words, "in the 1370s and 1980s . . . the Court of Chivalry extended its jurisdiction to cover offences committed within the realm which were properly triable at common law: it heard cases of debt, breach of contract, trespass, and homicide."[19]

Three times in the first dozen years of Richard II's reign, parliamentary petitioners attempted to restrict the scope of this new and potentially coercive action, and it is clear that what lay behind these attempts was the fear that appeals of treason were becoming, as Keen and Mark Warner put it, "a cover for the pursuit of more private quarrels."[20] Indeed, it may well have been the constructive extension of treason to include allegations of breach of faith, like the one Palamon accuses Arcite of, which had allowed the court to expand its scope in the first place.[21] In 1384, "because many pleas falling within the jurisdiction of the Common Law have been taken before the [Court of] the Constable and the Marshal to the great damage and disquiet of the Commons," parliament petitioned that "this court should deal with what concerns it and in the way in which it was employed in the time of your noble ancestors."[22] The concluding clause implies that the problem was of recent origin (having arisen only since the beginning of the new reign in 1377), but as early

---

[17] See M. H. Keen, "Treason Trials under the Law of Arms," *Transactions of the Royal Historical Society*, 5th ser., 12 (1962): 85–103.

[18] G. D. Squibb, *The High Court of Chivalry: A Study of the Civil Law in England* (Oxford: Clarendon Press, 1959), 17.

[19] Anthony Tuck, *Richard II and the English Nobility* (London: Edward Arnold, 1973), 146.

[20] M. H. Keen and Mark Warner, eds., "*Morley vs. Montagu* (1399): A Case in the Court of Chivalry," *Camden Miscellany* 34, Camden Society, 5th ser., 10 (Cambridge, 1997), 147–95.

[21] See, generally, Sir William Holdsworth, *A History of English Law*, vol. 1, 7th ed. (London: Methuen, and Sweet & Maxwell, 1956), 574.

[22] *Rotuli Parliamentorum, ut et Petitiones . . . Tempore Ricardi R. II* (London: House of Lords, 1783), 3:202; hereafter *Rot. parl.*

as 1379 the Commons had petitioned that the Constable and Marshal should be precluded from hearing appeals of treasons and felonies that were alleged to have been committed within the realm, lest "all the people of the realm, of whatsoever condition, might thus be impeached and destroyed by the false contriving [*compassement*] of their enemies."[23] One of the cases that the 1384 petitioners may have had in mind was *Earl of Salisbury v. Montagu* (1383), a case *de fide laesa* concerning the withholding of an indenture.[24] The 1384 act was plainly ineffectual, however, for there were at least three cases in the following years that evaded its strictures: *Etton v. Merton* (1385) concerns forgery, prevarication, and breach of pact; *Tottenas v. Mareschal* (1386) concerns debt; and *Asthorpe v. Dynham* (1389) concerns nonpayment of an annuity and was again based on an allegation of breach of faith (*causa fidei lesione*).[25] In 1389 parliament tried again, and this time the petition was far more specific: it complained that the court of the Constable and the Marshal "has attracted to itself [cases concerning] contracts, covenants, trespasses, debts, detinues and other actions pleadable at Common Law to the great prejudice of the king and his courts and to the great grievance of the people." It restricted the jurisdiction of the Court of Chivalry primarily to what we should now call martial law and to certain civil actions arising overseas, and provided those wrongly accused before the court with the right of appeal to the king's council.[26] This statute was evidently more effective than the first, for in the fifteenth century the court appears to have restricted itself mainly to military matters.

Cases such as *Annesley v. Katrington* which actually came to a trial of arms seem to have been very rare in Chaucer's lifetime, but the threat of battle was clearly one of the most disturbing aspects of the new action. Although battle would not have been awarded where the appellee was able to produce conclusive evidence in his own defense, for anyone lacking such evidence the Court of Chivalry offered far less procedural protection than the common law courts. Lest the squabble between Palamon and Arcite be thought far too slight a thing to be considered in such a context, we might note that at least one case heard by the Court of Chivalry in Chaucer's lifetime concerned a woman, and that it was one of the few that did actually come to a trial of arms (and with fatal consequences). In *Vilenos v. Walsh* (1384), the appellant was acting against a man who had insulted (*oppresserat*) his wife;[27] interestingly, Walsingham remarks of this case that though the charge was treason, "effectualiter tamen, non erat proditor" ("still, he was not in actual fact a traitor").[28] In any case, from one point of view the very insignificance of Palamon and

---

[23] Ibid., 3:65.
[24] See Squibb, *High Court of Chivalry*, 18 n. 3.
[25] See ibid., 18 nn. 2–4.
[26] *Rot. parl.*, 3:265.
[27] See Keen and Warner, "*Morley vs. Montagu*," 152.
[28] Walsingham, *Historia Anglicana*, 2:118.

Arcite's dispute is precisely the point. The solemn rituals of trial by battle, once reserved for the oldest and weightiest of common law actions, those initiated on a Writ of Right, a measured process that might take years, even generations, to reach its awful conclusion, were now being invoked for things like the withholding of an indenture or the nonpayment of an annuity. If strong and healthy young knights were offered a legal pretext for threatening battle in such cases, where might it all end? A dispute over a marriage contract would surely not be beyond the bounds of possibility. The violent quarrel of the two Thebans, then, raises a very serious legal issue and one that must have seemed especially critical in the early 1380s. The public concern that led parliament to try to rein in the newly extended jurisdiction of the Court of Chivalry in 1379, and again in 1384 and 1389, is something that might without too much distortion be compared to the debate over gun control or capital punishment in our own day.

There is a further intriguing dimension to this question. A legal system that is prepared to contemplate men fighting to the death on so slim a pretext as a disputed contract is one that provides but minimal protection against the incursions of anarchy—and anarchy, as many critics have pointed out, lurks darkly in the wings of the *Knight's Tale*. For some, such as Charles Muscatine, the occasional irruptions of chaos and disorder into the poem offer little more than a thematic counterpoint to its central concern with the nature of the noble life.[29] But for others, they lie much closer to the heart of its meaning. Writing shortly after Muscatine's elegant exposition, Elizabeth Salter was already drawing our attention to the presence of two narrative voices in the tale, "one pressing home the 'derknesse' of the story, the other anxious to evade responsibility for it,"[30] and such critical sensitivity to narratorial ambivalence has survived into the more historicist accounts of recent decades. Whether we are being asked to focus on the ordering principles of social hierarchy, or courtly chivalry, or Ricardian polity, or medieval jurisprudence, a recognition of disruptive forces that are entailed by such structures is rarely far away—evoked either explicitly in the poem's "harsh actualities" and "moral incoherence," or implicitly in its "internal secrets" and "missing stories."[31] I hope that my reading of this one particular element in the legal fabric of the *Knight's Tale* will be seen as consonant with such historicist readings. If Chaucer is indeed manipulating the procedures that give shape to the dis-

---

[29] Charles Muscatine, *Chaucer and the French Tradition: A Study in Style and Meaning* (Berkeley: University of California Press, 1960), 175–90.

[30] Elizabeth Salter, *Chaucer: The Knight's Tale and the Clerk's Tale* (London: Edward Arnold, 1962), 23–24.

[31] These phrases can be found in Paul Strohm, *Social Chaucer* (Cambridge: Harvard University Press, 1989), 133; Lee Patterson, *Chaucer and the Subject of History* (London: Routledge, 1991), 229; David Wallace, *Chaucerian Polity: Absolutist Lineages and Associational Forms in England and Italy* (Stanford: Stanford University Press, 1997), 119; and Elizabeth Fowler, "Chaucer's Hard Cases," in *Medieval Crime and Social Control*, ed. Barbara Hanawalt and David Wallace (Minneapolis: University of Minnesota Press, 1999), 136.

pute between Palamon and Arcite in order to reflect on the threatened reemergence of trial by battle under the expanding jurisdiction of the Court of Chivalry, it is only natural that he should have made the figure of Theseus the focus for his concerns: when people could no longer rely on the measured processes of customary law for protection against violent extortion, it must have seemed as if all that stood between them and the exercise of arbitrary justice was the inscrutable will of their sovereign.

As the embodiment of justice, then, Theseus is properly an ambiguous figure in the *Knight's Tale*, and if Chaucer was using him to express concerns for the future of the rule of law under an autocratic young king, events were sadly to confirm his worst fears. Throughout most of Richard's reign, the Court of Chivalry was in the hands of his opponents (Thomas of Woodstock, the Constable, and Thomas Mowbray, the Marshal, were both Lords Appellant), but in 1397 he finally wrested control of it away from them, and their offices passed to two of the hated *duketti*: Richard's cousin Edward of Rutland, duke of Aumale, and his nephew Thomas Holland, duke of Surrey. As Tuck has shown, the power conferred on the new Constable and Marshal to punish traitors "at discretion according to their deserts" was widely regarded as a serious threat to the traditional legal rights of Richard's subjects.[32] One of the articles of his deposition claims that, in breach of Magna Carta, he had made use of the court of the Constable and Marshal to intimidate those of his subjects who might be tempted to criticize him, publicly or in private: "in which court the accused were allowed no other reply than to plead not guilty and then given no chance to justify or defend themselves except by their bodies, even though their accusers and appellants were strong, healthy young men, and the accused old and feeble, handicapped and infirm."[33] Without too much exaggeration, it might be claimed that had he lived longer, Richard's use of the Court of Chivalry as a prerogative court might well have become as notorious as Wolsey's use of Star Chamber.

[32] Tuck, *Richard II and the English Nobility*, 197–98.
[33] *Rot. parl.*, 3:420.

5 Language on Trial

Performing the Law in the N-Town Trial Play

EMMA LIPTON

Many accounts of medieval justice, following Michel Foucault and Elaine Scarry, have emphasized the theatrical nature of medieval punishment.[1] Perhaps because studies of medieval drama have also devoted considerable attention to the subject of bodily spectacle, this theatrical paradigm of justice in late medieval England has appealed to drama critics, who have seen a correlation between the spectacles of drama and justice.[2] Here, however, I

[1] See Michel Foucault, *Discipline and Punish: The Birth of the Prison*, trans. Alan Sheridan (Harmondsworth: Penguin, 1979); and Elaine Scarry, *The Body in Pain: The Making and Unmaking of a World* (New York: Oxford University Press, 1985). On the theatricality of medieval justice, see Richard van Dülmen, *Theatre of Horror: Crime and Punishment in Early Modern Germany*, trans. Elisabeth Neu (Oxford: Polity Press, 1990); Esther Cohen, *The Crossroads of Justice: Law and Culture in Medieval France* (New York: E. J. Brill, 1993), esp. 146–201, and "'To Die a Criminal for the Public Good': The Execution Ritual in Late Medieval Paris," in *Law, Custom, and the Social Fabric in Medieval Europe* (Kalamazoo: Medieval Institute Publications, 1990), 285–304. For a bibliography on crime in medieval England, see John Bellamy, *Crime and Public Order in England in the Later Middle Ages* (London: Routledge and Kegan Paul, 1973), 205–11. Many accounts have considered the image of Christ in relation to medieval attitudes to punishment and pain. Some examples include Mitchell B. Merback, *The Thief, the Cross, and the Wheel: Pain and the Spectacle of Punishment in Medieval and Renaissance Europe* (Chicago: University of Chicago Press, 1999); and Maureen Flynn, "The Spectacle of Suffering in Spanish Streets," in *City and Spectacle in Medieval Europe*, ed. Barbara A. Hanawalt and Kathryn L. Reyerson (Minneapolis: University of Minnesota Press, 1994), 153–68.

[2] Representative accounts centering on the spectacle of Christ's body include Peter Travis, "The Social Body of the Dramatic Christ in Medieval England," *Early Drama to 1600*, Acta 13 (1985): 17–36; Sarah Beckwith, "Ritual, Church, and Theatre: Medieval Dramas of the Sacramental Body," in *Culture and History, 1350–1600*, ed. David Aers (Detroit: Wayne State University Press, 1992), 65–89; and, especially relevant to my concerns here, Theresa Coletti, "Purity and Danger: The Paradox of Mary's Body and the En-gendering of the Infancy Narrative in the English Mystery Cycles," in *Feminist Approaches to the Body in Medieval Literature*, ed. Linda Lomperis and Sarah Stanbury (Philadelphia: University of Pennsylvania Press, 1993), 65–95. Among

emphasize a different connection between medieval justice and medieval drama than the disciplined body, namely, a shared interest in the representational, social, and political work of language.[3] My focus is on the late fifteenth-century East Anglian N-Town play, *The Trial of Mary and Joseph*, which recounts the apocryphal trial of the holy couple for adultery.[4] This scene appears in other late medieval East Anglian stories of the Virgin such as the *Stanzaic Life of St. Anne* and John Lydgate's *Life of Our Lady*; curiously, however, only the N-Town play sets the scene in a contemporary court.[5] As several critics have observed, the play alludes to a number of recognizable contemporary and archaic technical legal procedures such as the accusation by public rumor, defamation, compurgation, the oath, and the ordeal.[6] Yet the sheer number and assortment of legal procedures entertained in the play suggests that its main concern is not the faithful representation of legal procedures but rather, as I will argue, the linguistic basis of medieval legal practice. By invoking a variety of legal categories used in contemporary medieval

---

others, Seth Lerer has applied these paradigms to the *Croxton Play of the Sacrament* in "'Representyd in yower syght': The Culture of Spectatorship in Late-Fifteenth-Century England," in *Bodies and Disciplines: Intersections of Literature and History in Fifteenth-Century England*, ed. Barbara A. Hanawalt and David Wallace (Minneapolis: University of Minnesota Press, 1996), 29–62.

[3] For an account of the relationship between medieval legal language and drama emphasizing the history of rhetoric, see Jody Enders, *Rhetoric and the Origins of Medieval Drama* (Ithaca: Cornell University Press, 1992).

[4] A date of 1468 written on the manuscript gives a terminus ad quem for the cycle, but the play may have been performed or written down earlier. Critics disagree on the exact provenance of the cycle, but modern dialectologists have established the language of the plays as East Anglian. The emphasis in the cycle on the life of the Virgin Mary may be explained by the integration of a separate Mary play into an earlier cycle. This particular play, however, is believed to be a pageant from the original cycle and not part of the Mary play. For a discussion of the complex textual history of the cycle, see Stephen Spector, ed., *The N-Town Play: Cotton MS Vespasian D. 8*, EETS OS 11 (Oxford: Oxford University Press, 1991), 1: xiii–lv and 2: 537–43; Peter Meredith, ed., *The Mary Play from the N-Town Manuscript* (New York: Longman, 1987), 1–23; and Alan J. Fletcher, "The N-Town Plays," in *The Cambridge Companion to Medieval English Theatre*, ed. Richard Beadle (Cambridge: Cambridge University Press, 1994), 163–88. All citations to the N-Town play will be from the Spector edition and will be included in the text.

[5] On the rarity of the subject matter of the trial of Mary and Joseph, see Rosemary Woolf, *English Mystery Plays* (Berkeley: University of California Press, 1966), 174–77. For some texts that include the episode, see *The Middle English Stanzaic Versions of the Life of Saint Anne*, ed. Roscoe E. Parker, EETS OS 174 (London: Oxford University Press, 1928), 21–23; and *A Critical Edition of John Lydgate's Life of Our Lady*, ed. Joseph A. Lauritis, Ralph A. Klinefelter, and Vernon Gallagher (Pittsburgh: Duquesne University Press, 1961), 406–23. This edition of Lydgate includes a useful edition of the apocryphal source for the episode. As Theresa Coletti observes in "The Paradox of Mary's Body" (93 n. 54), the Holkham Picture Book includes backbiting Jews who provoke the Troubles scene, but not the trial itself (*The Anglo-Norman Text of the Holkam Bible Picture Book*, ed. F. P. Pickering [Oxford: Basil Blackwell, 1971], 20).

[6] For discussions of the legal content of this N-Town play, see Lynn Squires, "Law and Disorder in *Ludus Conventriae*," in *The Drama of the Middle Ages*, ed. Clifford Davidson, C. J. Gianakaris, and John H. Stroupe (New York: AMS Press, 1982), 272–85; Theresa Coletti, "The Paradox of Mary's Body"; Alison M. Hunt, "Maculating Mary: The Detractors of the N-Town Cycle's 'Trial of Joseph and Mary,'" *Philological Quarterly* 73 (1994): 11–29; and Cindy L. Carlson, "Mary's Obedience and Power in *The Trial of Mary and Joseph*," *Comparative Drama* 29 (1995): 348–62.

courts for assessing the relationship between a given utterance and the guilt or innocence of a given party, the play demonstrates that the critical assessment of language was crucial to medieval legal procedure.

More specifically, the N-Town play investigates the linguistic distinctions made in medieval trials by presenting a wide variety of legal procedures for addressing adultery and defamation, the most important being the practice of prosecution on the basis of public voice. The play shows that public voice cannot always be adequately distinguished from rumor and reveals that the difficulties of this legal method lie in its approach to language, through which public voice acquires judicial sovereignty by detaching itself both from evidence and from an ethical assessment of an individual speaker. The play ultimately advocates not, as we might expect, a hierarchical solution requiring the intervention of church authorities, but a sacramental model for legal language based on a nostalgic reworking of the legal procedure of the ordeal. Furthermore, in staging the relationship between language and action in the medieval courtroom, the play calls attention to the applicability of legal language to the dramatic setting. In other words, *The Trial of Mary and Joseph* does not simply act out the procedures of the medieval courtroom, but reveals how its own drama is informed by legal rituals such as the trial, and by sacerdotal rituals, such as the mass, which is invoked in Mary's ordeal performed at the end of the play. While there has been considerable discussion by scholars of medieval drama of the similarities and tensions between the drama and the ritual performance of the ceremony of the sacrament of the mass, this play invites us to reconsider the relationship between late medieval dramatic performance and the social and ecclesiastical rituals of the fifteenth-century court trial.[7]

The Power of Legal Language

The Trial of Mary and Joseph depicts a range of legal procedures recognizable to a fifteenth-century audience and seeks to capitalize on that recognition by refashioning its audience as both theatergoers and court witnesses. In the opening line of the play, Den the Summoner addresses the audience directly and summons them to court: "I warne ȝow here all abowte / þat I somown ȝow, all þe rowte!" (5–6), and a few lines later, "Fast com away . . . The courte xal be þis day!" (29, 33). To be sure, many medieval plays often began with some kind of summons, as they were often performed in the street, but the *The Trial of Mary and Joseph* immediately associates the dramatic tech-

---

[7] Some influential accounts of the mass as drama include Richard Axton, *European Drama of the Early Middle Ages* (London: Hutchinson, 1974), esp. 61–74; O. B. Hardison, *Christian Rite and Christian Drama in the Middle Ages: Essays in the Origin and Early History of Modern Drama* (Baltimore: Johns Hopkins University Press, 1965), esp. 35–79; Karl Young, *The Drama of the Medieval Church*, vol. 1 (Oxford: Clarendon Press, 1933); and Beckwith, "Ritual, Church, and Theatre."

nique with the summons to court.[8] Notably the Summoner lists a cross-section of the urban community, ranging from "Thom Tynkere" to "Miles þe Myllere" and "Bette þe bakere," a cross-section that corresponds to the people who would have been called to serve as witnesses in sexual cases tried in the lower ecclesiastical courts of medieval England. By identifying the people by trade, the summons further recalls the urban audience who would have witnessed the dramas in late medieval towns, as well as the guild members who were responsible for both financing and acting in the plays, thereby underlining the continuity between the drama of the contemporary urban courtroom and the fiction of the play itself. By simultaneously enlisting the audience for trial and play, the Summoner encourages viewers to consider the porous boundaries between drama and social life and the ways in which the law can function as a dramatic ritual that, while not fictional, can shape the roles people play in society.

The parallelism between the drama and the court in the Summoner's speech further reveals the institutional context behind the linguistic performance, making the audience immediately self-conscious about the relationship between action and linguistic authority within social structures. For example, with the phrase "I somown ʒow," the Summoner models the institutional basis of the performativity of legal language. Then at the end of his initial speech listing the people who are to come to court, the Summoner asserts that the court shall come into being, summing up the function of his speech: "The courte xal be þis day!" (33). The Summoner's summons may thus be said to be performative in the sense that J.L. Austin made famous when he defined the performative as the kind of speech in which "the issuing of the utterance is the performing of the action."[9] But in contrast to Austin's

---

[8] There has been considerable scholarly controversy and discussion of the staging of the N-Town plays. Most scholars believe that they were performed outdoors either as processional pageants or with some variation on place-and-scaffold production. Discussion of performance is complicated by the fact that many of the plays have staging characteristics different from those preceding or following them and also by the possibility that portions of the cycle may have been performed separately. For an overview of the vast body of scholarship on this subject, see Spector, *The N-Town Play*, 2:544–49. For the opening lines of plays as a way to grab the audience's attention on a noisy street, see Meg Twycross, "The Theatricality of Medieval English Plays," in *The Cambridge Companion to English Theatre*, ed. Richard Beadle (Cambridge: Cambridge University Press, 1994), 55. Alternatively, Spector suggests that in these lines, the Summoner may be taking a collection or preparing the audience for one later in the play (2:468).

[9] J. L. Austin, *How to Do Things with Words* (Cambridge: Harvard University Press, 1962), 6. Austin famously said that performative utterances are "in a peculiar way hollow or void if said by an actor on the stage"(22), and yet a growing number of critics have seen Austin's work as especially useful not only to studying theatricality but also, specifically, to studying the relationship between the performativity of social life and the stage. For a useful introduction to and overview of this material, see Andrew Parker and Eve Kosofsky Sedgwick, eds., *Performativity and Performance* (New York: Routledge, 1995), esp. 56–75. On the application of Austin's theory to the drama, see especially W.B. Worthen, "Drama, Performativity, and Performance," *Publications of the Modern Language Association* 113.5 (1998): 1093–1107.

purely formalist sense of the operation of performative language, the N-Town trial play carefully defines the performativity of Den's utterance, not as an inherent property of language, but rather as based in the institutional authority of the legal system. The Summoner begins his speech with the invocation of the authority of the highest official of ecclesiastical court, the Bishop: "Avoyd, serys, and lete my lorde þe buschop come / And syt in þe courte, þe lawes for to doo" (1–2). Thus it is the authority of the law that grants him the title of Summoner and allows for his words to be actions. Similarly, it is his role as a performer in the play that requires the audience to follow his bidding. As Pierre Bourdieu has argued in his sociological revision of Austin, the "specific efficacy" of performative utterances "stems from the fact that they seem to possess *in themselves* the source of a power which in reality resides in the institutional conditions of their production and reception."[10] In this case, the Summoner's role and his support by the institution of the court system makes his command effective, and indeed the Summoner's legal function, summarized in his title, is the ability to translate the language of the court book into action: "Tho þat ben in my book—þe court ȝe must com too!" (4). In short, the play hails the audience into being by appropriating the institutional force of a kind of performative legal language that does not require the language to be descriptive, that is, to be true.[11] The very beginning of the play thus calls attention to the ways in which legal language expresses the power of the court to make things happen simply through the authority the legal institution bestows on its language.

But the Summoner's initial speech sets in motion a more intricate analysis of the relationship between linguistic authority and action by invoking the context of the commissary court, the lower court that heard the majority of cases in the church courts. After the Summoner has called the court into being in the beginning of the play, two disreputable characters named Backbiter ("Bakbytere") and Raise-Slander ("Reysesclaundyr") accuse Mary publicly in open court of breaking her vow of chastity, claiming that they have seen Mary and speculating about how she might have become pregnant. Although the figure of the Backbiter is familiar from sermons and confessional manuals, this scene does not invoke the penitential context, but instead resembles the dramatic manner in which proceedings would have been conducted, in commissary court, where people were accused in open voice, an

[10] Pierre Bourdieu, *Language and Symbolic Power*, ed. John B. Thompson, trans. Gino Raymond and Matthew Adamson (Cambridge: Harvard University Press, 1991), 111.

[11] As a kind of ritual drama, the play alerts the audience to the larger ideological construction of the roles that may otherwise seem the function of a person's individual subjectivity. I am influenced here by Althusser's description of the way ideology interpellates individuals as subjects. He includes both the law and the church as key examples of ideological state apparatuses. See Louis Althusser, "Ideology and Ideological State Apparatuses (Notes towards an Investigation)," in *Lenin and Philosophy and Other Essays*, trans. Ben Brewster (New York: Monthly Review Press, 1971), 127–86.

abbreviated oral procedure.[12] Thus it could be said that the commissary court had a dramatic format in that it required a retelling or reenactment of the crime in court. This kind of trial was indeed a public display, but one that was entirely linguistic and not perpetrated on the body of the defendant. As in the N-Town trial play, the commissary court did not use lawyers to represent the litigants, and so the judge's conscience or assessment played heavily in the outcome of the trial. There probably would not have been a bishop in commissary court, as there is in this play, but his presence in the play emphasizes the key role of the judge in these proceedings. The Bishop, while reluctant to pursue the charges against the holy couple, uses his own discretion and evidently feels compelled to take these accusations seriously, since he has the Summoner bring Mary and Joseph to court to be questioned and compurgated.

Not only does the N-Town play reproduce the general framework of the commissary court, but also it depicts the procedure by which people could be accused by public rumor in the courts of medieval England.[13] Following the speech of the Summoner, the opening dialogue of the play shows how the charges against Mary and Joseph originate in gossip between her two accusers. One character asks the other, "canst þu owth telle / Of any newe thynge þat wrought was late?" (66–67), and the other reports having seen Mary conspiciously pregnant: "here wombe doth swelle / And is as gret as þinne or myne!" (80–1). Based on these observations, they speculate that she must have broken her and Joseph's recent public vows of chastity and possibly committed adultery as well, either with Joseph or some other "fresch ʒonge galaunt" (87). Neither of Mary's accusers has actually seen her in an adulterous act or has any firsthand knowledge of the crime, but that would not have prevented them from prosecuting her in the courts of late medieval England if the accusation was made by public voice or rumor. In the commissary court it was possible to proceed against a suspect with a bad reputation (*mala fama*) with no other accuser than the public voice (*publica vox*). Richard M. Wunderli suggests that the result of this structure was a problematic lack of proper distinction between well-intentioned public regulation and the gossip and ill

---

[12] Backbiting is often used to represent the sin of envy (see, for example, John Mirk, *Instructions for Parish Priests*, ed. Edward Peacock, EETS OS 31 [London: Kegan Paul, 1868], 35; and Chaucer's "Parson's Tale," in *The Riverside Chaucer*, ed. Larry D. Benson [Boston: Houghton Mifflin, 1987], 303) but also the vice of gluttony (see, for example, *Jacob's Well*, ed. Arthur Brandeis, EETS OS 15 [London: Kegan Paul, Trench and Trubner, 1900], pt. 1, 150–51; and *Three Middle English Sermons from the Worcester Chapter Manuscript F. 10*, ed. D.M. Grisdale [Kendal: Titus Wilson for the School of English Language at Leeds, 1934], 35–40). Open voice was used in the commisary court, as opposed to the consistatory court, where each step was written down. For the procedures of the commissary court, see Richard M. Wunderli, *London Church Courts and Society on the Eve of the Reformation* (Cambridge: Medieval Academy of America, 1981), 31–62. On the organization and procedure of the courts, see Ralph Houlbrooke, *Church Courts and the People during the English Reformation, 1520–1570* (Oxford: Oxford University Press, 1979), 21–54.

[13] For an analysis of the relevance of this procedure to the N-Town play, see Hunt, "Maculating Mary."

will of neighbors: "Private squabbles, malicious gossip, and legitimate charges alike found their way to ward and parish officials, where the accusations were shaped and hardened by legal rules into specific charges."[14] In other words, no one had to be certain of a suspect's guilt, but most members of the community, especially influential persons, had to believe that the suspect had committed the crime. Typically two well-respected male leaders of the community would have brought the rumor to the attention of the bishop, who then prosecuted the case "from the office."[15] This is the procedure followed by Bakbytere and Reysesclaundyr in the N-Town play, who are perversions of the system in which the leaders of the community acted as churchwardens and jurors. Although their names clearly suggest that they are not respectable citizens, the two fulfill the numerical requirement required by the procedure of accusation by public rumor.

This exchange between Mary's detractors further highlights the limitations of prosecution by public rumor by suggesting a parallel between this legal procedure and the literary genre of the fabliau. The detractors accuse Mary of lying by comparing her story to a well-known misogynist lai, "The Snow Drop," about a woman who becomes pregnant while her merchant husband is away, and swears she has been impregnated by swallowing a snowflake.[16] One detractor unknowingly parodies the Incarnation when he mockingly compares Mary's claim that she is innocent of breaking her vow of chastity to this fabliau:

In feyth, I suppose þat þis woman slepte
Withowtyn all coverte whyll þat it dede snowe;
And a flake þerof into hyre mowthe crepte,
And þerof þe chylde in hyre wombe doth growe.
(306–9)

In "The Snow Drop," the description of the wife's actions is unambiguously incriminating and clearly ascribes her pregnancy to her adulterous acts with a young lover:

And Love, which can't be hid from sight,
got both of them in such a stir
that soon he came to lie with her.
Their labors, though, were not in vain:

14 Wunderli, *London Church Courts*, 33.
15 Ibid., 32–33.
16 For a twelfth-century Latin version of this lai from the Cambridge Songs, see F. J. E. Raby, *A History of Secular Latin Poetry in the Middle Ages* (Oxford: Clarendon Press, 1934), 1:295–97, 2:34. For a later medieval French version, see "The Snow Drop," in Robert L. Harrison, *Gallic Salt: Eighteen Fabliaux Translated from the Old French* (Berkeley: University of California Press, 1974), 380–89. For commentary on "The Snow-Child" and the N-Town play, see Woolf, *English Mystery Plays*, 176.

the wife got pregnant by her swain
and had his son; thus matters ran.[17]

The detractors believe that they have uncovered a similarly clear-cut lie, a fabliau tale in which the old man Joseph is betrayed by his young lusty wife, Mary, and a younger man. One speculates that "Sum fresch ʒonge galaunt she lovyth wel more / þhat his leggys to here hath leyd!" (87–88), while the other asserts:

> That olde cokolde was evyl begylyd
> To þat fresche wench whan he was wedde.
> Now muste he faderyn anothyr mannys chylde,
> And with his swynke he xal be fedde.
> (98–101)

Thus the detractors' version of events makes the story of the Incarnation into a standard *senex amans* fabliau plot.

The detractors invoke a further parallel between the trial of Mary and the fabliau form's preoccupation with justice. In "The Snow Drop," for example, the merchant retaliates for his wife's infidelity by taking her illegitimate son with him on a trip and selling him to another merchant in exchange for seed. When the wife asks after the whereabouts of her beloved son, the merchant reports that he was out with the boy on a summer's day at noon and that

> the sun, so fiery, hot and bright,
> cast down on us its burning rays—
> it cost us dearly, did that blaze,
> because your son began to thaw
> beneath the solar heat.[18]

His response invokes the wife's lie about the circumstances of his conception, framing his deed as retaliatory. Indeed, the last lines of the fabliau present this response as justice served for her twin crimes of adultery and lying:

> Her lord avenged himself in full
> for the dirty trick she'd tried to pull
> by word and deed on him . . .
> her sins had got her in this mess.
> We get precisely what we're due,
> and she'll just have to drink her brew.[19]

---

[17] Harrison, *Gallic Salt*, 380–81. On lying and the fabliau, see Carl Lindahl, *Earnest Games* (Bloomington: Indiana University Press, 1987), 124–55.
[18] Harrison, *Gallic Salt*, 389.
[19] Ibid.

Clearly the detractors expect that bringing Mary to trial will yield a similar economy of justice in which the punishment fits the crime of her alleged carnality and lies.

The N-Town play, however, neatly inverts the expectations of its characters, the conventions of the fabliau, and its corresponding model of justice. When Mary refuses to represent the loquacious and lustful wife and tell her detractors the fabliau tale they desire, they accuse her of lying and insist that her body speaks for itself: "þu art with chylde we se in syght; / To us þi wombe þe doth accuse!" (302–4). Here they invoke another stereotypical element of fabliaux: the association of a woman's speech with her body, and specifically with her sexuality. Generally this serves as a means of condemning her speech as lies and her body as overly carnal; the body is both the impetus for dissembling and, paradoxically, the source of literal truth that belies the claims of its owner.[20] The detractors' assertions are undermined, however, by the fact that the truth of Mary's words is clear to the play's audience from the beginning, when she is identified as the Virgin Mary. The play overturns fabliau convention, moreover, by ascribing the values of carnal excess and bodily truth to the detractors themselves instead of Mary. For example, they harp excessively on Mary's appearance, calling her "fresch and fayr . . . to syght" and "a ȝonge damesel of bewté bryght, / And of schap so comely also" (91, 94–95). Their repeated references to her physical appearance suggest that they are indulging their own libidinous fantasies. When one detractor speculates that "such a mursel, as semyth me, / Wolde cause a ȝonge man to haue delyght" (92–94), he clearly imagines himself cast in the role of her young lover. Their misreading of the significance of Mary's body serves to associate their own lustful fictions with their wrongheaded tale of her adultery. Blind to her true nature, they take a literal and sexualized approach to representation. When the first detractor asserts, "þu art with chylde we se in syght" (302), he reads her body mimetically, believing that the truth resides in the appearance of Mary's body.[21]

This carnal fabliau model of speech is further linked to the language of rumor and with the legal procedure of accusation through public voice during the courtroom scene. The detractors come to court to recite a fabliau tale that centers on infidelity and explicit sexual details, a genre arguably familiar to the courts that routinely heard sexual cases. The first detractor's introduction of himself at the beginning of the scene directly associates fabliau with

---

[20] This association of women and carnality is familiar from Chaucer's Wife of Bath, who famously asserts, "My joly body schal a tale telle." A particularly colorful example is the fabliau "Du Chevalier qui fist les cons parler," in Harrison, *Gallic Salt*, 218–55. For a discussion of the association of speech with the female body in French fabliaux, see E. Jane Burns, *Bodytalk: When Women Speak in Old French Literature* (Philadelphia: University of Pennsylvania Press, 1993).

[21] On this scene's engagement with contemporary controversy over idolatry, see my "Performing Reform: Lay Piety and the Marriage of Mary and Joseph in the N-Town Cycle," *Studies in the Age of Chaucer* 23 (2001): 405–33.

the legal process: "To resye slaw[n]dyr is al my lay" (40), he says. While the most obvious meaning of "lay" in this context is "practice," the word is commonly used to characterize the genre of fabliau, and can also mean "law."[22] Thus, even in the pun of his first speech, this disreputable character has set the stage for the play's association of the law of public rumor with the literary genre of fabliau, which represents the self-generating of unfounded language.

The detractors' use of fabliau language and its association with the institution of public voice suggests a reciprocal model for legal language and literary genre and for social and literary institutions. Far from being only a literary conceit, the N-Town trial play's insinuation that fabliau and public rumor are institutionally linked is in fact consistent with recent findings that clerks or witnesses or both were influenced by literary forms in their creation and construction of written depositions, a theory confirmed even by a brief examination of medieval court records.[23] Furthermore, L. R. Poos has shown that women were more likely than men to be victims of rumor, corresponding to the gendering of the roles in fabliaux, where it is most often women who are associated with transgressive sexuality.[24] In the absence of better standards for differentiating between kinds of performative language, the courts of medieval England could, the N-Town play suggests, become simply an enactment of the fabliau.

That the characters Resyesclaundyr and Bakbytere are themselves personifications of speech-acts further critiques prosecutions by public voice by suggesting that the rumor alone acts as the prosecutor, disembodied from the intentions and actions of a human agent. Aside from raising suspicions about their integrity, the names of the two characters represent the simultaneously public and impersonal nature of these kinds of accusations, which did not require an individual eyewitness litigant. These personifications suggest that the ritual procedure of prosecution by public rumor is inevitably linked to—and even serves to produce—backbiting and the raising of slander.[25] The first

---

[22] See Spector, *The N-Town Play*, 2:602 for references to these uses of "lay" elsewhere in the N-Town cycle. Also see *Middle English Dictionary*, S.V. "lay" and "lei."

[23] A number of these cases are reprinted in Richard Helmholz, *Select Cases on Defamation to 1600*, Publications of the Selden Society, 101 (London: Selden Society, 1985). For the influence of literary forms on depositions, see Kathryn Gravdal, *Ravishing Maidens: Writing Rape in Medieval French Literature and Law* (Philadelphia: University of Pennsylvania Press, 1991), 122–40, 170–74; and for a study comparing the rhetorical crafting of pardon letters to literary texts, see Natalie Zemon Davis, *Fiction in the Archives: Pardon Tales and Their Tellers in Sixteenth-Century France* (Stanford: Stanford University Press, 1987). On law and narrative, see Peter Brooks and Paul Gewirtz, *Law's Stories: Narrative and Rhetoric in the Law* (New Haven: Yale University Press, 1996).

[24] L. R. Poos, "Sex, Lies, and the Church Courts of Pre-Reformation England," *Journal of Interdisciplinary History* 25.4 (1995): 585–607. Especially relevant is Poos's comment that "whore" is one of the most common epithets recorded for defamation cases (591).

[25] Victor Turner's influential theory holds that ritual does not simply represent or express a society's vision of itself, but actually creates that vision. For a discussion of this aspect of Turner's work and its relevance to medieval drama, see C. Clifford Flanigan, "Liminality, Carnival, and Social Structure: The Case of Late Medieval Biblical Drama," in *Victor Turner and the Construc-*

detractor boasts, for example, that, together with his brother Bakbytere, "More slawndyr we to xal arere / Within an howre thorweouth this town / Than evyr þer was þis thowsand ȝere" (46–48). In other words, he articulates a model of language detached from its referent, in which slander is presented as sui generis, a kind of language that itself generates more language. While not strictly performative in the Austinian sense, the detractors' words are inherently powerful because the act of pronouncing them within an institutional framework has the effect of causing Mary and Joseph to be hauled into court, despite the fact that they are detached from any description of or direct correspondence to provable events.[26] By representing the process of indictment by public rumor as a charge against the Virgin Mary, the play encourages the audience to think critically about this procedure; indeed, the very fact that the play is a retelling of a familiar biblical story crucially enables audiences to see this gap between rumor and evidence.

By staging this attempt by the detractors to turn biblical history into fabliau, the play shows how prosecution by public voice, while seemingly based on visible evidence such as Mary's pregnant body, can instead be based on the self-generating language of rumor and thus detached from any firsthand knowledge of the event described or the reliability of the accuser. That disreputable characters are given credence in the play suggests that there is no adequate system for assessing the validity of prosecutions by public voice, and, moreover, that the legal system offers insufficient protection against rumor and other falsely motivated accusations. The law of rumor has in essence broadened the institutional performativity of law so that it is no longer merely the Bishop and his authorized agent of law, the Summoner, whose language has inherent power to cause action, but the accusatory words of any speaker. In this way the play points to the larger cultural problem of how to regulate the public linguistic practices of the community, a problem common to law and drama alike.

The Language of Rumor and the Failure of the Law

The play shows a legal system aware of the problems of prosecution by public rumor but unable to control the power and purview of its language. In the play, the church hierarchy attempts to make use of the legal tools, such as the defamation laws and the practice of oath-taking, designed to regulate the language of rumor. The events of the play, however, such as the court's inability to distinguish the false oaths of the detractors from the true ones of the

---

tion of Cultural Criticism, ed. Kathleen Ashley (Bloomington: University of Indiana Press, 1990), 42–63.

[26] The utterances are not strictly performative in the Austinian sense because the words do not accomplish what they signify.

holy couple, suggest that these practices do not effectively protect people against false accusations.

After hearing the detractors' charges, for example, the Bishop accuses them of defamation, invoking the technical legal procedure by which people might defend themselves from false accusations by public rumor: "ʒe be acursyd so hire for to defame" (108). The stage directions likewise describe the Bishop as *audientes hanc defam[a]cionem*, referring to the technical name of the crime formalized by the Council of Oxford in 1222 which made it actionable in the church courts "maliciously [to] impute a crime to any person who is not of ill fame among good and serious men."[27] Defamation cases were the natural corollary of a system of justice that allowed suits to be brought on charges of bad reputation. The institutional response to accusations of public rumor was a countersuit for defamation, designed to restore to good reputation the person accused of having *mala fama*. The close association of these two kinds of trials is suggested by the fact that public rumor and defamation were both described as *diffamatio*, attesting to the ease with which the roles of plaintiff and defendant could be reversed in such suits.[28]

The punishment for defamation further attests to this disturbing reciprocity: since the effect of defamation was to damage the reputation of the defamed, a person convicted of defamation was required to apologize in public to the victim. According to the historian Richard Helmholz, the evident goal of this punishment was "the public humiliation of the defamer and the restoration, as far as possible, of the reputation of the person defamed."[29] Although technically trials by public voice and for defamation would have taken place on separate occasions, in fact a person who had successfully won a suit for defamation would have been unlikely to be sued successfully in the public voice. The words of the Bishop in the N-Town play suggest the close association of these two sorts of trials. While technically summoning Mary and Joseph to a trial by public voice, he instructs the Summoner to "Byd Joseph and his wyff be name / At þe coorte to appere þis day, / Here hem to pourge of here defame" (139–41), as if trial by public rumor might literally be simultaneously a trial for defamation. Like the trial by public rumor, the trial for defamation was indeed a public display, but one that, significantly, was entirely linguistic and not based on the display of justice on the body of the perpetrator.

In the case of trial for defamer, unlike a trial by public voice, the accusation or utterance of the speaker was evaluated not on its evidentiary value (i.e., whether or not it was provable) but by consideration of the motive of the speaker. In fact, it was possible for an utterance to be called defamation even

---

[27] Wunderli, *London Church Courts*, 64.

[28] *Diffamatio* was the word applied to the rumor in a suit prosecuted by the public voice (*publica vox*), and *diffimatus* the word applied to the defendant. The same word, *diffamatio*, was used in defamation cases. Ibid., 32.

[29] Helmholz, *Select Cases*, xl.

if the accusation was true.[30] Consequently, the law of defamation developed its own hermeneutic guidelines. According to Helmholz, the rules of defamation specified "that words were to be taken *in malem partem* when they were malicious and tended to harm the plaintiff."[31] We can see this logic at work in the Bishop's response to the detractors when he inquires: "Herke, ȝe felawys, why speke ȝe such schame / Of þat good virgyn, fyr Mayd Mary? / ȝe be acursyd so hire for to defame" (106–8). The Bishop's inquiry after the detractors' motives refers to the technical context of the defamation law, and yet this doubt is not sufficient for him to waive the trial. Under pressure from the detractors, who insist that the Bishop should summon Mary and see her pregnant body for himself, he instructs the Summoner to bring the couple to court, thus demonstrating that even someone as virtuous as the Virgin cannot be protected effectively against false public rumor by the legal mechanism of defamation laws, and that the threat of evaluation by the motive of the speaker is not enough to regulate the language of rumor.[32]

The Bishop's reluctance to prosecute Mary arises from his knowledge of her character, reflecting another criterion through which the medieval courts sought to regulate the power of the language of public rumor. He voices his doubt as to the detractors' assertions when he refers to Mary as "she þat is of lyff so good and holy" (109). The logic of evaluating an utterance according to the assessment of the ethical integrity of the accused resembles the linguistic logic behind compurgation, the procedure commonly used in trials by public voice in the commissary courts to protect the defendants from false accusations. By instructing the holy couple to arrive with witnesses, the Bishop evokes the trial practice whereby the accused defended himself or herself by taking a formal oath of innocence and by bringing compurgators, or oath-helpers, to swear to the trustworthiness of the oath. The play also follows the legal procedure for trial by public rumor when the Bishop suggests to the Summoner that he

> Byd Joseph and his wyff be name
> At þe coorte to appere þis day . . .
> If þei be clene withowtyn blame,
> Byd hem come hedyr and shew wyttnes
> (139–45).

---

[30] See Wunderli, *Church Courts*, 65; and Helmholz, *Select Cases*, xxx–xxxii. For a discussion of the implications of this aspect of defamation, see M. Lindsay Kaplan, *The Culture of Slander in Early Modern England* (Cambridge: Cambridge University Press, 1997), 15.

[31] Helmholz, *Select Cases*, xciv.

[32] The large percentage of defamation cases brought to the church courts—about one-third of the church court business—suggests that they were not an effective deterrent for rumor being used as public voice. See Wunderli, *Church Courts*, 63. In *The Culture of Slander*, Kaplan suggests that the rapid evolution of the slander laws in the early modern period indicated the recognition by legal authorities that existing laws were not effective in controlling slander (16).

As in the process of prosecution by public rumor, the defense rests not on the literal truth of what the accused person says but on the court's assessment of his or her ethical integrity and on the wider public reputation of the defendant.[33] Furthermore, the issue of reputation is emphasized by the repeated references to name and reputation, as when Mary says, "My name, I hope, is saff and sownde. / God to wyttnes, I am a mayd" (210–11). The procedure of compurgation is especially relevant to the dramatic performance of the N-Town play, in which the words spoken by the character of Mary on stage would have been judged in light of the audience's previous knowledge of this biblical character's virtue.[34]

One form that compurgation could take was oath-making, and the play demonstrates that the court is equally unsuccessful in using this legal tool as a means of distinguishing whether the detractors or the holy couple are telling the truth. In late medieval England, making an oath in God's name was, technically speaking, a kind of ordeal in which one invited God to participate directly in verifying the truth of one's utterance. Telling a lie in God's name would be dangerous, because God might intervene to demonstrate the falsity of one's assertions. According to Paul Hyams: "By the standard theory that *jurare est testem Deum invocare*, those swearing understood that God and the saints on whose relics the oath was made would be their witnesses, who could and would punish any perjury."[35] As Alison Hunt has shown, moreover, when Mary and Joseph act as their own witnesses in the play, their oaths reinject legal language with divinely sanctioned appeals to truth, and this, in turn, recalls the technical understanding of oath-making.[36] On the way to the court, Mary tells Joseph, "Almighty God xal be oure frende / Whan þe trewthe is tryed owth" (180). Here she literalizes God's participation in oath-making, and thus in compurgation, by suggesting that God will play the role of a compurgator in vouching for the ethical integrity of their character. She repeats the same gesture in front of the Bishop when she says: "God to wyttnes, I am a mayd. / Of fleschly lust and gostly wownde / In dede nere thought I nevyr asayd" (211–13). Here Mary uses God not just to vouch for her character but to speak to the facts of the matter, to validate both her public actions and her private thoughts. In effect, then, Mary and Joseph's oaths put God back in the process of vow-making, in contrast to their accusers, who continually make

[33] For compurgation, see R. H. Helmholz, "Crime, Compurgation, and the Courts of the Medieval Church," *Law and History Review* 1 (1983): 1–26, reprinted in *Canon Law and the Law of England* (London: Hambledon Press, 1984), 119–44; Helmholz's introduction to *Select Cases*, i–xxiv; and Charles Donahue, Jr., "Proof by Witnesses in the Church Courts of Medieval England: An Imperfect Reception of the Learned Law," in *On the Laws and Customs of England: Essays in Honor of Samuel E. Thorne*, ed. Morris S. Arnold et al. (Chapel Hill: University of North Carolina Press, 1981), 127–58.

[34] On the relevance of compurgation to the N-Town play, see Hunt, "Maculating Mary," 11, 17–18.

[35] Paul Hyams, "Trial by Ordeal," in *On the Laws and Customs of England*, ed. Morris S. Arnold et al. (Chapel Hill: University of North Carolina Press, 1981), 92–123.

[36] Hunt, "Maculating Mary," 16–17.

oaths (such as "be my trewth") as hollow and facile as the rest of their lies.[37] By putting oaths into the mouths of characters whose very names attest to their unreliability, the play further investigates not only the status of legal language but also the problem of interpretation that plagued the medieval courts.

The play suggests that if the law's approach to assessing language were effective, then Mary and Joseph's oaths would resolve the case, but they do not. Just as the threat of a countersuit for defamation is insufficient to stop the detractors, so too the process of compurgation is shown to be powerless to prevent the language of public rumor from being accepted as truth. Before Mary and Joseph are summoned, both the lawyers and the Bishop call attention to the language of the detractors. One of the lawyers says to them, for example: "ȝe be to besy of ȝoure langage! / I hope to God ȝow fals to preve" (130–31). Here he not only specifically characterizes their crime against the Virgin as linguistic but also reveals what is missing in their language, namely, the presence of any transcendental signifier or divine presence. Instead, as we have seen, the detractors' accusations are detached from any other referent but their own language. After the testimony of the holy couple, however, the Bishop appears to be taken in by the detractors' claims and begins to believe that it is Mary rather than her accusers who participates in the fabliau genre. He says to her, "Thu xalt not schape from vs ȝitt so; / Fyrst þu xalte tellyn us another lay" (230–31), apparently unable to distinguish the true oaths of the holy couple from the false oaths of the accusers. The fact that the church authorities cannot recognize which utterances have divine participation or content suggests that existing models of legal linguistic regulation are problematic, to say the least.

The Truth Test: A Dramatic Linguistic Model for the Law

Acknowledging that the methods of the court for controlling the power of rumor, such as the threat of a defamation suit or the process of compurgation, are not sufficient, and that the court is unable to properly assess the guilt or innocence of Mary and Joseph and later of their accusers, the Bishop intervenes to establish a truth test in the form of a potion, given to Joseph, Mary, and the detractors. After witnesses drink this potion, the truth of their words is supposed to show on their faces. This test harkens back to the ordeal, an archaic mode of legal adjudication by the late Middle Ages and one that would not have taken place in the commissary court when a person was accused by public voice. The truth test presents not an accurate reflection of contempo-

---

[37] On "truth" as a keyword in late medieval England, see Richard Firth Green, *A Crisis of Truth: Literature and Law in Ricardian England* (Philadelphia: University of Pennsylvania Press, 1999).

rary ecclesiastical court practice, but an alternative model of language as a solution to the problems and inadequacies of medieval legal practice.

The Bishop's explanation of the truth test shows that it addresses the inability of legal procedure to judge language effectively:

> Here is þe botel of Goddys vengeauns.
> This drynk xal be now þi purgacyon.
> þis [hath] suche vertu by Goddys ordenauns
> þat what man drynk of þis potacyon
> And goth serteyn in processyon
> Here in þis place þis awtere abowth,
> If he be gylty, sum maculacion
> Pleyn in his face xal shewe it owth.
> (234–41)

Through this test, the problem of linguistic truth will be solved, and it will be possible, as it has not been earlier in the play, to determine who is lying in the trial because the person's face will become the clear sign of guilt or innocence. This procedure, which will reground signs so they will finally correspond directly and firmly to the truth, thus advertises itself as opposite to the performative model of legal language introduced at the beginning of the play by the Summoner and echoed by Mary's detractors.

The test enacts a model of language in which God is literally a participant, recalling the anachronistic legal practice of the ordeal. Officially outlawed in 1215 by the Fourth Lateran Council, an ordeal was a mode of trial in which a suspect was subjected to a dangerous physical test and the result regarded as the immediate judgment of God.[38] The most common versions in England were being lowered into cold water or having one's hands burned with a red-hot iron; the survival or healing of the accused was seen as a sign of innocence. Although Mary and Joseph are not subject to physical danger, their test is similarly understood to enlist the direct intervention of God. Even though the ordeal would not have been used in a trial by public rumor, this procedure addresses similar issues because it was closely bound up with the defendant's reputation. Rather than having to endure the pain of the ordeal, a person with a better reputation or one who was supported by the community would simply have been asked to give an oath.[39]

In contrast to the traditional form of the ordeal the N-Town play's truth test is not so much a spectacle as a test of language that will confirm who is speaking truthfully. In fact, although the Bishop describes the truth test as one in which faces will show guilt, when Mary and Joseph circumnavigate the

---

[38] Hyams, "Trial by Ordeal," 92.

[39] The ordeal was reserved for prosecutions of people who had a bad reputation or those suspected of serious crime and was characteristically used in cases where there was a deep division within the community and so God's intervention was deemed especially necessary. Ibid., 98.

altar it is precisely the *absence* of visible sign that demonstrates their innocence. Joseph says:

> This drynk I take with meke entent.
> As I am gyltles, to God I pray:
> Lord, as þu art omnypotente,
> On me þu shewe þe trowth þis day.
> (250–53).

The linguistic emphasis of the N-Town version is clear in comparsion to the
versions of this episode in Lydgate's *Life of Our Lady* and in the Apocryphal
Bible, a source for the play. In the latter, for example, Joseph does not speak
at all; not his language but his appearance is emphasized: *Cum ergo bibisset se-
curus Joseph at girasset altare, nullum signum peccati apparuit in eo.*[40]

Similarly, when the detractors are forced by the Bishop to undergo the
same test, they are distinguished from the holy couple primarily by language.
Whereas Mary and Joseph stick to the same story, the detractors change
theirs. After drinking the potion, the first detractor exclaims:

> Out, out! Alas, what heylith my soulle?
> A, myn heed with fyre methynkyht is brent!
> Mercy, good Mary, I do me repent
> Of my cursyd and fals langage!
> (364–67)

The first portion of his speech recalls the pain associated with the traditional
ordeal by hot iron, but the only spectacle that ensues is possibly the actor's
use of gesture or facial expression; the change in his story identifies his crime
as linguistic.[41] In fact, the detractor's performance of the truth test produces a
similar change in the Bishop, who says:

> We all on knes fall here on grownd,
> þu, Goddys handemayd, prayng for grace.
> All cursyd language and schame onsownd,
> Good Mary, forȝeve us here in þis place.
> (370–73)

---

[40] "When therefore Joseph had drunk and had walked around the altar, no sign of sin appeared
in him." The relevant section of the text of the Apocrypha is reprinted in *John Lydgate's Life of
Our Lady*, 78–79.

[41] Notably, Lydgate's version does not give the same emphasis to language: "And al at onys, fell
dovne afore / This holy mayde, with humble Reuerence / And wold hir fete, haue kyssed ther
anone / Axyng mercy, of thayre grete offence / And she forgaf it, to hem euerycheone" (ibid.,
422).

Whether voiced by the detractors or by the Bishop, the limitations of the legal system that require Mary and Joseph to take the test are explicitly acknowledged as problems of language. Furthermore, the play depicts the miracle of the ordeal as a transformation of language, explicitly eschewing the elaborate spectacle that a staged ordeal might produce.

Even the Incarnation is expressed as a linguistic performance rather than a dramatic spectacle. During her perambulation, Mary says:

> God, as I nevyr knew of mannys maculacion,
> But evyr haue lyued in trew virginité,
> Send me þis day þi holy consolacyon
> þat all þis fayr people my clennes may se.
> (334–37)

Although Mary invokes the language of spectacle, the truth of her words is confirmed by the absence of visible sign. As the Bishop exclaims:

> þis woman with chylde is fayr and clene,
> Withowtyn fowle spotte or maculacion! . . .
> It shewyth opynly by here purgacyon
> Sche is clene mayde, bothe modyr and wyff!
> (348–53)

Unlike her detractors, moreover, Mary does not change her words after she has drunk the potion. Thus, although Mary is associated with the body by her detractors, it is her language rather than her body that proves the divine meaning even of her body itself. By contrast, in *The Life of Our Lady*, Lydgate describes the audience's rapturous gaze as Mary processes around the altar:

> And all the people, be gan to gasen faste
> If any signe, did in hir apere
> Outhir in colour, in contenaunce or chere
> But all for nought, playnely as I tolde
> The more on hir, they loken and byholde
> The more she was, to her sight fayre
> And lyche as phebus, in Ioly grene maye
> Whan he hathe chasede, the derke mysty eyre
> Shyneth more bright, the clere somers daye
> Whan þikke vapours, be dreven clene awaye.[42]

In this passage Lydgate's narrative voice dwells lovingly on the sight of Mary's face. In the N-Town play, however, this obsession with Mary's body has been associated with the detractors, who mistakenly equate the truth of Mary's

---

[42] Ibid., 420–21.

body with her mere physicality, while her body is also the sign of the higher truth of the Incarnation. Whereas the detractors have taken her body as the literal sign of her sinful carnality, in fact her body is both sign and embodiment of God and, consequently, a model for a higher form of representation in the play.[43]

In this way, Mary's performance of the truth test deliberately models a kind of language that is both the opposite of and the antidote to the false language of rumor. When the Bishop and her detractors beg her pardon, she responds, "Now God forȝeve ȝow all ȝowre trespace, / And also forȝeve ȝow all defamacyon / þat ȝe haue sayd, both more and lesse" (374–76). In this passage, the truth test is able to reverse the effects of the false language of public rumor, here referred to rightly as "defamacyon." The truth test is a model of representation opposed not only to rumor but also to the performativity of legal language more generally, because it specifically emphasizes the possibilities of language conveying sacramental force.[44] In medieval theology, a sacrament of the New Law effected what it signified; it was both a sign and cause of grace. Medieval theologians often quoted Saint Augustine's definition of a sacrament as "the sign of a sacred thing" or "the visible sign of invisible grace." A more precise definition of a sacrament was contested throughout much of the Middle Ages, but by the thirteenth century, the fuller definition of Peter Lombard had become more or less standard. As Lombard and others explained, a sacrament was a natural, not a conventional, sign, and bore a resemblance to the thing of which it was a sign.[45] Unlike the sacrament of the Eucharist, in which the wafer is a material sign of the sacrament, the truth test is a linguistic model of the sacrament. The truth test in the N-Town play specifically invites this comparison to the mass, since Mary refers to her body as a "tabernacle," invoking the frequent association of the Virgin's pregnant

[43] This use of Mary as the ideal speaker in the N-Town play is consistent with the role that Mary is often given in the Bible and in vernacular literature as a figure for someone who is quiet and says little, and thus she is a good representative in this play for the proper use of language. For example, in Lydgate's version, Mary's completion of the test is described as follows: "Al be that she, speke but wordes fewe / Withoutyn speche, shall the dede shewe" (Ibid., 78). As Edwin D. Craun observes in *Lies, Slander, and Obscenity in Medieval English Literature* (New York: Cambridge University Press, 1997), 52, the Virgin is often a figure for judicious speech, and she speaks only seven words in the Gospels.

[44] For a discussion of the anti-sacramentality of Austin's description of the performative utterance, see Timothy Gould, "The Unhappy Performative," in *Performativity and Performance*, ed. Andrew Parker and Eve Kosofsky Sedgwick (New York: Routledge, 1995), 21. Austin insists that in the performative the action is accomplished in the words themselves. As Gould notes, Austin insisted that the utterance does not refer to some inward, invisible act, for which the words would then be taken as the outward and visible—but still descriptive—sign. See Austin, *How to Do Things with Words*, 9.

[45] On the definition of a sacrament, see Seamus P. Heaney, *The Development of the Sacramentality of Marriage from Anselm of Laon to Thomas Aquinas* (Washington, D.C.: Catholic University of American Press, 1963), 50; *Hugh of Saint Victor on the Sacraments of the Christian Faith*, trans. Roy J. Deferrari (Cambridge: Medieval Academy of America, 1951), 154–55; and Elizabeth Rogers, *Peter Lombard and the Sacramental System* (Ph.D. diss., Columbia University, 1917; reprint Merrick: Richwood Pub. Co, 1976), 80, 122.

body with the Eucharist in late medieval painting.[46] Unlike the mass, in which the bishop or priest alone presides over the administration of the sacrament, in the truth test or the legal procedure of the ordeal, the words of an ordinary person can invoke God's participation and grace. Thus, the N-Town play promotes a model of representation that, while invoking the sacramental form of the Eucharist, also appropriates the more lay and communal standards of the medieval court.

Positioned between the law court and the mass, the N-Town play appropriates and adapts authoritative institutions of medieval representational practice to articulate its own place within the culture. The play distances itself from the self-generating language of rumor associated with the detractors throughout the play and with the legal procedure of prosecution by public voice. In contrast to public voice's fabliau-like focus on the body and a literal model of language, the play invokes the sacramental representation of the mass to show itself able to participate in signaling the invisible and the holy. But in contrast to the clerical domination over the ministration of the sacrament, and with it control over the representation of divine content, the drama makes sacramental representation part of the communal experience, staged by the guilds and confirmed by the lay community who constituted their audience. Fusing the communal logic of the court with the divine content of the mass, the N-Town trial play constructs drama itself as a site for the regulation of moral behavior.[47] By thus constructing the drama as a site for moral regulation, the N-Town play presents an alternative to the penitential tradition of depicting backbiting, and an alternative to the confessional model of individual regulation administered by clergy. Mixing courtroom and mass, the N-Town trial play works to promote the place of drama as one of the important rituals of late medieval life.

The N-Town play's staging of Mary and Joseph's trial makes its audience, and later critics, aware of the medieval court as a ritual, bound by a set of procedures that inscribe both participants and witnesses in conventional roles. The church authorities take up their adjudicatory role, while the community functions as accusers, defendants, and witnesses who participate in the determination of truth and justice. Surprisingly accurate in its depiction of many of the legal roles and technical procedures of the contemporary medieval court, the N-Town play also presents differences that highlight the limitations of

[46] Barbara G. Lane, *Altar and Altarpiece: Sacramental Themes in Netherlandish Painting* (New York: Harper and Row, 1984).

[47] My argument for the drama's bid for the lay regulation of moral behavior is consistent with Marjorie McIntosh's suggestion that in the fifteenth century, local courts encroached on the jurisdiction of the ecclesiastical courts and the higher secular courts by defining misconduct not in moral terms but as a disruption of community harmony. See Marjorie K. McIntosh, "Finding Language for Misconduct: Jurors in Fifteenth-Century Local Courts," in *Bodies and Disciplines: Intersections of Literature and History in Fifteenth-Century England* (Minneapolis: University of Minnesota Press, 1996), 87–122; and *Controlling Misbehavior in England, 1370–1600* (Cambridge: Cambridge University Press, 1998).

current legal practice and offer alternative practices. In this way, the play understands the court not as something fixed and unchangeable, but as suitable for revision and adaptation. Allowing the audience to see the similarities between court and drama, the play also encourages the audience to see the court as a socially determined ritual that could be altered to reflect the values and needs of the community. The play presents the practice of law as itself having a potential for reiteration with a difference in a way that can bring about larger cultural change. As Judith Butler remarks, "It is in the instabilities, the possibilities for rematerialization opened up by this process that mark one domain in which the force of the regulatory law can be turned against itself to spawn re-articulations that call into question the hegemonic force of that regulatory law."[48] In the N-Town trial play, the dramatic restaging of the law creates the possibility for imagining a law and a community life infused with sacramental force, a vision that ultimately both supports and challenges the traditional authorities and beliefs of late medieval England.

[48] Judith Butler, *Bodies That Matter: On the Discursive Limits of "Sex"* (New York: Routledge, 1993), 2. Although Butler discusses the performance of "sex" and the ways in which bodies never quite comply with regulatory norms, I have found her analysis of performance useful to the study of other forms of social performance.

6   "Acquiteth yow now"

Textual Contradiction and Legal Discourse in the
Man of Law's Introduction

Maura Nolan

Life I know is short, and law is long, very long, and we cannot study everything
at once; still, no good comes of refusing to see the truth, and the truth is that all
parts of our law are very closely related to each other, so closely that we can set
no logical limit to our labours.

F. W. Maitland

In termes hadde he caas and doomes alle
That from the tyme of kyng William were falle.
Therto he koude endite and make a thyng,
Ther koude no wight pynche at his writyng;
And every statut koude he pleyn by rote.

Chaucer, *General Prologue* to the *Canterbury Tales*

Chaucer's Man of Law would surely have agreed with Maitland's assessment of the relationship between human life and the life of the law, though
he does seem to have managed to "study everything at once," to have ingested
the entire tradition of English law and to have made himself something more
than the law's mere practitioner.[1] The Sergeant's remarkable capacity to speak
the law does not, however, provide him any advantage as a teller of tales. In the
Introduction to his tale, we find in the Man of Law a tentative and self-deprecating speaker, comparing himself unfavorably to Chaucer ("I kan right now

My thanks are due to Jill Mann, whose perceptive and thorough commentary greatly improved this essay. Thanks as well to Candace Barrington and Emily Steiner for their helpful responses and sensitive editing. Any errors or failings are, of course, my own.
[1] *The Frederic William Maitland Reader*, ed. V. T. Delany (New York: Oceana Publications,
1957), 157.

no thrifty tale seyn / That Chaucer . . . Hath seyd hem in swich Englissh as he kan" [46–49]) and refusing to compete in a poetic medium ("Though I come after hym with hawebake [baked hawthorn berries], / I speke in prose, and lat him rymes make" [95–96]).[2] But the implied contrast between the separate realms of the law and of poetry is immediately undermined when the Man of Law proceeds to tell a tale in verse. Nor is this contradiction the only moment of textual difficulty associated with the Man of Law; the Epilogue to the tale notoriously presents insoluble textual problems with major implications for the order and attribution of tales. I seek to explore the nexus of contradiction presented by the Man of Law, both as a legal speaker and as a textual phenomenon, arguing that the impossible demand for resolution presented to editors by the Introduction and Epilogue is structured by a legalistic relation between empirical fact—the textual difficulty, the legal evidence—and a transcendental abstraction, a final form for the *Canterbury Tales*, "the law." Furthermore, I argue that Chaucer himself recognized the tension between the concrete and the abstract in legal discourse, finding it both appropriable and threatening, both useful and dangerous. The Man of Law's Introduction thus stages a confrontation between the legal and the poetic which reveals the degree of Chaucer's investment in the latter as well as his need for the former.

What must first be addressed are the prior and incommensurable assumptions underlying the invocation—by scholars and by Chaucer—of the "law" as a category of analysis. The tension just described constitutes a divide that has been fundamental to the reconstruction of the legal past, a divide famously described by Maitland in his introduction to *The History of English Law*:

> It has been usual for writers commencing the exposition of any particular system of law to undertake, to a greater or less extent, philosophical discussion of the nature of laws in general, and definition of the most general notions of jurisprudence. We purposely refrain from any such undertaking. . . . The matter of legal science is not an ideal result of ethical or political analysis; it is the actual result of facts of human nature and history.
>
> Law, such as we know it in the conduct of life, is matter of fact; not a thing which can be seen or handled, but a thing perceived in many ways of practical experience. Commonly there is no difficulty in recognizing it by its accustomed signs and works. In the exceptional cases where difficulties are found, it is not known that metaphysical definition has ever been of much avail.[3]

---

[2] *The Riverside Chaucer*, ed. Larry D. Benson, 3rd ed. (Boston: Houghton Mifflin, 1987). All citations of Chaucer's works are from this edition and will be given in the text. For quotation from the *General Prologue*, see ll. 323–27.

[3] Sir Frederick Pollock and Frederick William Maitland, *The History of English Law before the Time of Edward I*, 2nd ed. (Cambridge: Cambridge University Press, 1968), xciii and xcv. Except for a chapter on Anglo-Saxon law, Maitland wrote the *History* in its entirety. For a brief account of his collaboration with Pollock, see Robert Brentano's chapter on Maitland in *Medieval Scholarship: Biographical Studies on the Formation of a Discipline*, vol. 1, ed. Helen Damico and Joseph B. Zadavil (New York: Garland, 1995), 131–52.

Maitland's distinction—the prior assumption he outlines here—between "fact" or "experience" and "philosophy," "ethics" or "metaphysics"—must be doubly situated, both as a response to specific bodies of historical evidence and as a delimiting frame within which succeeding legal historians have interpreted such evidence. In his 1968 introduction to the *History*, S. F. Milsom articulated what he called a "pious heresy," pointing out that Maitland "seems to have seen a society and its law whole and to have heard its disputes singly. The voices arguing he heard indeed in his sources; and all the materials made available since his death have confirmed that he heard aright. What is difficult to realize is the extent to which the picture as a whole must have been his own creation, the extent to which any picture of early legal development must remain uncertain."[4] The tension described here between the singular voices of the legal past and the historian's present need for a "picture as a whole" does not necessarily reflect, for Milsom, a failure on Maitland's part; it is rather an effect of the particular endeavor of legal history. As he states later in the introduction: "The legal historian plays a double part. As social historian he must observe the proportions allotted to things in the time of which he is writing. As historian of ideas he cannot forget what lay in the future, that this was to flourish and that was to fail; and he cannot avoid asking his records about matters that were of small concern to their makers."[5]

Milsom, like Maitland before him, understands the law to be a peculiar object of study, simultaneously a recorded practice and a governing abstraction, ascending out of the remotest feudal court, descending from the highest authority. This simultaneity appears in a number of guises, from Maitland's own distinction between "fact" and "metaphysics," to the scholastic division between positive and natural law, to more recent understandings of case and constitutional law. When "law" is invoked outside the context of legal history, however, it is precisely this foundational contradiction that must be jettisoned in order for "law" to serve an explanatory function. Thus literary critics, for the most part, deploy in their readings either the illuminating legal detail (the precise duties of a Sergeant of the Law) or the broadly applicable legal principle or homology (Bracton's civil law, Thomist natural law, the Lacanian law of the father).

Such uses of the law not only displace the tensions intrinsic to legal history, but also substitute their singular focus for a more productive notion of historicity itself, one constituted by the simultaneities of fact and abstraction, event and narrative, practice and ideology. What this substitution conceals—

---

[4] S. F. Milsom, introduction to *Pollock and Maitland, History of English Law*, xxv. Both in this introduction and elsewhere, Milsom has been one of the most important critics of Maitland's work. In particular, Milsom takes issue with the significance assigned by Maitland to the actions of Henry II and the work of Bracton, arguing that too great an emphasis on the legislative and the scholastic obscures the role of courts and individual jurists in the development of law. See S. F. Milsom, "'Pollock and Maitland': A Lawyer's Retrospect," *Proceedings of the British Academy* 89 (1996): 243–60, and "F. W. Maitland," *Proceedings of the British Academy* 66 (1982): 265–81.

[5] Milsom, introduction to *Pollock and Maitland, History of English Law*, xlix.

the genuine historical question or incongruity necessary to the literary text *in the first place*—can then be figured as a false problem, a textual difficulty to be bracketed and set aside as "indeterminate" or insoluble. In the case of the Man of Law, what has been set aside is a nexus of textual ambiguity that could, if considered, provide an index to the range of historical contradiction within which Chaucer produced the *Canterbury Tales*. As Ralph Hanna has argued, "We medievalists know comparatively little about the literary history of our period, and . . . nearly all we are going to discover will be from the bearers of texts, books themselves, which consequently we cannot afford to leave merely as errors already rejected."[6]

"This was a thrifty tale for the nones!"

The reaction of Chaucer's Host to the Man of Law's tale[7] has become one of the most controversial acts of literary criticism on record; not only its accuracy but its very existence has been challenged, defended, compromised over, and ignored. As part of the Man of Law's Epilogue, the Host's comment stands at the epicenter of what has been called "the greatest textual dilemma" in a work whose textual difficulty has produced a veritable industry of editing and commentary on editing.[8] The dilemma itself can be defined by a series of paradoxes produced by the same scholarly techniques it ultimately defies: the Epilogue is attested by a large number of manuscripts (thirty-five), but not by the two most authoritative, Ellesmere and Hengwrt; it contains the kind of interruption familiar to readers from the boisterous tale-telling of Fragment I, but the interrupter is variously identified as the Summoner (six manuscripts), the Squire (twenty-eight manuscripts), and the Shipman (one manuscript); this figure describes himself in terms unmistakably echoed in a later tale ("my joly body"), but the phrase seems to suggest a fourth possible speaker—a woman. Furthermore, the tale in which the locution is repeated belongs to the Shipman, the least attested of the three speakers.[9]

But the problem posed by the twenty-seven lines of the Epilogue extends far beyond these textual questions, perplexing as they are. For all modern ed-

[6] Ralph Hanna, *Pursuing History: Middle English Manuscripts and Their Texts* (Stanford: Stanford University Press, 1996), 81.

[7] Man of Law's Epilogue, l. 1165.

[8] Helen Cooper, *The Structure of the Canterbury Tales* (Athens: University of Georgia Press, 1983), 123–24. Although my sketch of the literature on the editing of the *Canterbury Tales* is far from exhaustive, I cite in particular those texts that provide the kind of detailed history this rich tradition deserves. For a broader survey of this history, see Paul Ruggiers, ed., *Editing Chaucer: The Great Tradition* (Norman, Okla.: Pilgrim Books, 1984).

[9] Larry Benson describes the problem fully in "The Order of the *Canterbury Tales*," *Studies in the Age of Chaucer* 3 (1981): 77–120, as does Helen Cooper in *Structure of the Canterbury Tales*; all of the manuscript evidence is of course derived from John Matthews Manly and Edith Rickert's edition, *The Text of the Canterbury Tales*, vols. 1 and 2 (Chicago: University of Chicago Press, 1940).

itors, the choice of how (or whether) to handle the Epilogue in an edition of the *Canterbury Tales* bears a significance far out of proportion to its length. Each of the individual difficulties I have outlined points to the broader question of tale order; each demands an editorial resolution that necessarily testifies to the editor's overall vision of Chaucer's poetic project. Whatever decision an editor makes, and however elaborate the justifications for it, the choice must ultimately be dictated either by a commitment to a reading of the *Canterbury Tales* or by an investment in a particular editorial method. As E. Talbot Donaldson observes: "We simply do not know anything about the condition of the manuscripts that Chaucer left or what happened between his death and the transcription of the earliest surviving manuscripts. Manuscripts are all we have to work with: little as they may tell us about antecedent conditions, they do tell us all we are ever likely to know about the text of Chaucer's poems."[10] There is no definitive manuscript evidence from which any decisive argument can be mounted for the placement of the Epilogue; its content— while interesting and perhaps significant—is hardly as crucial to the *Tales* as, say, the twenty-one lines in which the Host proposes the tale-telling game. Yet nearly all editions, including the current scholarly standard, the *Riverside*, as well as Donaldson's own, include it within the body of the *Tales* proper in its familiar place after the *Man of Law's Tale*.[11]

The stubborn persistence of the troublesome Epilogue testifies to the tantalizing appeal of a finished form for the *Tales*, an appeal produced partly by the enterprise of editing itself, as several critics have noted.[12] But the desire for completion is not merely a Victorian or modern invention; however jumbled or disordered the manuscripts, all contain gestures made by Chaucer toward the *idea*, if not the fact, of formal completion. To state the obvious, the *Tales* have a beginning which lays out a plan for the work; various speakers refer to that plan; a large proportion of tales are formally linked to others; the work has an ending, however unsatisfactory.[13] Furthermore, the earliest known readers of the *Tales*, the scribes who produced the inconclusive manuscript evidence, also seem to have been invested in a notion of completion: of

[10] E. Talbot Donaldson, "The Ordering of the Canterbury Tales," in *Essays in Honor of Francis Lee Utley*, ed. Jerome Mandel and Bruce A. Rosenberg (New Brunswick: Rutgers University Press, 1970), 199.

[11] The notable exception is that of N. F. Blake, whose edition, *"The Canterbury Tales" by Geoffrey Chaucer Edited from the Hengwrt Manuscript* (London: Edward Arnold, 1980), strongly defends the Hengwrt manuscript as the primary authority for the *Tales*.

[12] For a particularly polemical example that powerfully articulates the ideological underpinnings of any editing project, see Stephen Knight, "Textual Variants: Textual Variance," *Southern Review* 16 (1983): 44–55. See also Anne Hudson, "Middle English," in *Editing Medieval Texts: English, French, and Latin Written in England: Papers Given at the Twelfth Annual Conference on Editorial Problems*, ed. A. G. Rigg (New York: Garland, 1977), 34–57.

[13] Benson points out that "we have Chaucer's own word, in the Retraction, that, unfinished as *The Canterbury Tales* obviously was, he was finished with it" ("The Order of the *Canterbury Tales*," 80). This argument, of course, assumes the authenticity of the Retractions.

the eighty-two manuscripts containing at least some of the *Tales*, "fifty-five of them appear to have been intended as complete texts."[14]

Despite the insoluble nature of the problem posed by the Epilogue, then, it remains part of the Chaucer canon, not printed in the back of editions, but centrally located after the *Man of Law's Tale*. The publication of *The Riverside Chaucer* in 1987 effectively canonized F.N. Robinson's compromise, printing the text in brackets, adopting the reading "Shipman" in line 1179, and preserving the Ellesmere order. The primary critique of the Robinson-Benson solution, and of the edition as a whole, arose from a group of scholars, many associated with *The Variorum Chaucer*, who asserted the primacy of the Hengwrt manuscript as the earliest and best text of the *Tales*.[15] But the challenge mounted by this group has had little effect on the industry of Chaucer scholarship overall; most critics happily adopt the *Riverside* solution, preferring to perform interpretive work at a distance from the murk of manuscript evidence. Few scholars have been willing to assert with Donaldson that "Wife of Bath" is the proper reading of line 1179, despite the brilliant circumspection with which he proposed it: "Since the Wife of Bath is not now linked to anything preceding, the editor has adopted a bold (and controversial) suggestion that line 19 of the present passage originally read *Wif of Bathe*: this gives coherence to the chosen order, though it probably does not represent Chaucer's final intention—assuming he had one."[16]

As Donaldson's emendation reveals, the Epilogue represents a textual problem impossible to resolve on the basis of manuscript evidence alone. But it is not the only such problem in Fragment II. In the tale's Introduction, the Man of Law notoriously claims to "speke in prose, and lat him ymes make" (96) before telling a tale in rime royal. Some critics have attempted to show that "prose" might indeed mean verse, under certain conditions,[17] but most agree with Benson (and Robinson before him) that the error reflects an earlier version of the *Tales*, in which the Man of Law told the *Melibee*, and the Wife of Bath the *Shipman's Tale*.[18] Although this vestigial inconsistency has not—in contrast to the Epilogue—provided a flashpoint for editorial debate,

---

[14] *Riverside Chaucer*, textual notes, 1118.

[15] N.F. Blake has been foremost among these. See "The Relationship between the Hengwrt and Ellesmere Manuscripts of the 'Canterbury Tales,'" *Essays and Studies*, n.s. 32 (1979): 1–18; "The Chaucer Canon: Methodological Assumptions," *Neuphilologishe Mitteilungen* 90 (1989): 295–310; and "Geoffrey Chaucer: Textual Transmission and Editing," in *Crux and Controversy in Middle English Textual Criticism*, ed. A.J. Minnis and Charlotte Brewer (Cambridge: D.S. Brewer, 1992), 19–38. For a survey of the debate, see Dolores Frese, *An Ars Legendi for Chaucer's Canterbury Tales* (Gainesville: University of Florida Press, 1991).

[16] E.T. Donaldson, *Chaucer's Poetry: An Anthology for the Modern Reader* (Glenview, Ill.: Scott, Foresman and Company, 1958), 1074.

[17] See A.S.G. Edwards, "'I speke in prose': *Man of Law's Tale*, 96," *Neuphilologishe Mitteilungen* 92 (1991): 469–70; and Martin Stevens, "The Royal Stanza in Early English Literature," *Publications of the Modern Language Association* 94 (1979): 62–76.

[18] *Riverside Chaucer*, explanatory notes, 834; Benson, "The Order of the *Canterbury Tales*," 115.

both problems raise crucial questions about the very idea of a modern edition. The Epilogue presents the editor with an authentically Chaucerian text which temptingly offers final authorization to the overall vision of the *Tales* found in the Ellesmere manuscript, but which ultimately cannot make good on the promise of completion. By revealing Chaucer in a state of indecision—in the process of revision—the Introduction breaches the fictional divide between author and scribe on which editing once depended: authors have final intentions and complete works; scribes corrupt those works and misrepresent those intentions. As Derek Pearsall puts it, "scholars want an author to be represented as knowing what he is doing, or at least what he has done."[19]

The particular problems represented by the Man of Law's Introduction and Prologue have been taken up more generally in several discussions of Middle English textual editing. In part provoked by the 1975 publication of the Kane-Donaldson edition of the B-text of *Piers Plowman*, with its trenchant defense of editorial judgment and emendation, in part by *The Riverside Chaucer*, and in part by an expanded notion of what constitutes Middle English literature, critics have sought to reconcile the need for reliable editions with a historicist desire to do justice to the past. To cite an admittedly idiosyncratic selection, Lee Patterson's essay "The Logic of Textual Criticism and the Way of Genius: The Kane-Donaldson *Piers Plowman* in Historical Perspective," Ralph Hanna's *Pursuing History: Middle English Manuscripts and Their Texts*, and the collection edited by A. J. Minnis and Charlotte Brewer, *Crux and Controversy in Middle English Textual Criticism* have all, to varying extents, reformulated the practice of editing by addressing its foundational assumptions. All further attempt to bridge the gap between the worlds of editors and critics, taking seriously the claims of both and wholly the ambitions of neither.[20]

What is remarkable is that the insights—both theoretical and practical—represented by these interventions are almost nowhere to be found in recent critical work on the Man of Law. This phenomenon is partly caused by a focus on the *Tale* proper, with glancing attention (at best) to its frame; but it also reflects a more general reluctance within Chaucer studies of late to engage textual problems. Paradoxically, this reluctance derives from an original impulse to theorize the textual, to debunk the positivist foundationalism of textual editing by embracing the poststructural or psychoanalytic or New Historical: paradoxically, because in practice, what this turn has produced is a general silence in regard to manuscript inconsistencies and other forms of

[19] Derek Pearsall, "Authorial Revision in Some Late-Medieval English Texts," in Minnis and Brewer, *Crux and Controversy*, 39–48.

[20] In this list I largely exclude the Ellesmere-Hengwrt controversy, though it too partakes in these broader questions, setting what Anne Hudson has called an "eclectic" edition over against a "best text" version of the *Tales* ("The Variable Text," in Minnis and Brewer, *Crux and Controversy*, 49–60). See also Lee Patterson, *Negotiating the Past: The Historical Understanding of Medieval Literature* (Madison: University of Wisconsin Press, 1987), 77–113; and Hanna, *Pursuing History*.

textual contradiction, a silence that bespeaks, at some level, an atheoretical acceptance of texts and editions as given. But any exclusion of textual problems from serious consideration depends on an idea of history strangely alienated from the Real, a history in which contradiction comes to mean absence and to solicit silence; when the simple observation of indeterminacy stands in for analysis itself, the possibility of reading the indeterminate is foreclosed.

Thus the frame of Fragment II, with its endemic textual difficulty, has received correspondingly less critical attention than the *Tale*.[21] But for Chaucer, it was the frame that clearly held primacy of place. Despite the fact that it stands alone, without a prefatory link to the preceding tale, editors universally agree that Fragment II follows Fragment I. There is further consensus that the tale of Custance was not the Man of Law's original tale.[22] However significant the tale itself might be, then, its location was not as critical to the overall work as the placement of the Man of Law in the sequence of tellers; as Lee Sheridan Cox argues, Chaucer "became dissatisfied with the original tales, not the original sequence."[23] Charles Owen further suggests that "we have in the framework of the *Man of Law's Tale* unmistakable indications of reassignment of tales and of imperfect adaptation. . . . In the Man of Law's sequence, we are in touch with a very early stratum of the Canterbury material."[24] The priority of teller over tale is further suggested by the formality and complexity of the Introduction, as well as by the singular status of Fragment II; indeed, a number of critics have argued that the Man of Law's Introduction may have been intended as the introduction to the entire work:

The story-telling seems once to have begun with the introduction to the *Man of Law's Prologue* and *Tale*, when the Host notes the date and time of the day. It is ten o'clock on the eighteenth of April, as calculated by the angle of the sun with reference to the length of shadows and the latitude. No similarly precise indication of the time occurs again until before the very last tale, the Parson's, begun at four in the afternoon, as calculated by the length of Chaucer's own shadow. The two passages look as if they could be intended as a complementary pair, opening and closing the story-telling.[25]

[21] An exception to this claim is Elizabeth Scala's article, "Canacee and the Chaucer Canon: Incest and Other Unnarratables," *Chaucer Review* 30.1 (1995): 15–39. Scala's use of textual analysis to consider the relation of the *Man of Law's Tale* to the remainder of the work, and specifically to the *Squire's Tale*, provides an important insight into the workings of narrative in the *Tales*.

[22] See the *Riverside* notes for a summary of this position, 854.

[23] Lee Sheridan Cox, "A Question of Order in the *Canterbury Tales*," *Chaucer Review* 1.4 (1967): 228–52, 250.

[24] Charles Owen, "The *Canterbury Tales*: Beginnings (3) and Endings (2 + 1)," *Chaucer Yearbook* 1 (1992): 189–212, 195–96.

[25] Cooper, *Structure of the Canterbury Tales*, 63. See also Charles Owen, *Pilgrimage and Storytelling in the Canterbury Tales: The Dialectic of "Ernest" and "Game"* (Norman: University of Oklahoma Press, 1977), 25–30.

Whatever Chaucer "intended"—and here Donaldson's famous remark seems apposite—the manuscript evidence inevitably suggests a series of conclusions. First, the Man of Law stands as one of the linchpin tellers for the *Tales* as a whole; second, his importance can in part be measured by the amount of trouble—call it revision, error, or variation—produced by his telling; and third, the trouble does not emanate from his tale proper.

Critics have traditionally taken two approaches to the question of the Man of Law as tale-teller. The first considers the Man of Law categorically, as a lawyer, proceeding from the portrait in the *General Prologue* to historical evidence regarding the status of Sergeants of the Law in the fourteenth century.[26] The second, more literary model has typically sought to articulate what Marie Hamilton has called "the dramatic suitability" of tale to teller.[27] Attempts of the second sort work to establish some link between the law and the tale of Custance; for example, Carolyn Dinshaw argues that just as the law is a patriarchal discourse, so too does the tale participate in the patriarchal discourses of sexuality and sainthood.[28] But because of the disjunction between teller and tale, neither of these models can ultimately succeed; though the former has given us a great deal of information about the Man of Law's profession, and the latter some innovative and incisive readings of the tale, neither manages to account for the Man of Law's specific function in the project of the *Tales* as a whole.

As I will argue, the nexus of textual problems surrounding the Man of Law points to a set of more abstract considerations of the relation of poetic and legal discourse, considerations whose importance can be recognized only if and when the intractability of those textual problems is faced.

---

[26] Joseph Hornsby, *Chaucer and the Law* (Norman, Okla.: Pilgrim Books, 1988); idem, "A Sergeant of the Law, War and Wise," in *Chaucer's Pilgrims: An Historical Guide to the Pilgrims in the Canterbury Tales*, ed. Laura C. Lambdin and Robert T. Lambdin (Westport, Conn.: Greenwood Press, 1996), 116–34; Isobel McKenna, "The Making of a Fourteenth-Century Sergeant of the Lawe," *Revue de l'Université d'Ottawa* 45 (1975): 244–62; Karl P. Wentersdorf, "The Termes of Chaucer's Sergeant of the Law," *Studia Neophilologica* 53 (1981): 269–74; W. F. Bolton, "Pinchbeck and the Chaucer Circle in the Law Reports and Records of 11–13 Richard II," *Notes and Documents* 84.4 (1987): 401–7.

[27] Marie Hamilton, "The Dramatic Suitability of the 'Man of Law's Tale,'" in *Studies in Language and Literature: Essays in Honor of Margaret Schlauch*, ed. Mieczyslaw Brahmer, Julian Kryzanowski, and Stanislaw Helsztynski (Warsaw: Polish Scientific Publishers, 1966), 153–63. Other examples include Rodney Delasanta, "And of Great Reverence: Chaucer's Man of Law," *Chaucer Review* 5.4 (1970): 288–310; and Kevin Harty, "The Tale and Its Teller: The Case of Chaucer's Man of Law," *American Benedictine Review* 34 (1983): 361–71.

[28] Carolyn Dinshaw, "The Law of Man and Its 'Abhomynacions,'" *Exemplaria* 1.1 (1989): 117–48; see also David Lawton, *Chaucer's Narrators* (Cambridge: D. S. Brewer, 1985), 76–105; Joseph E. Grennen, "Chaucer's Man of Law and the Constancy of Justice," *Journal of English and Germanic Philology* (1985): 498–514; David Weisberg, "Telling Stories about Constance: Framing and Narrative Strategy in the *Canterbury Tales*," *Chaucer Review* 27.1 (1992): 45–64; and Patricia J. Eberle, "Crime and Justice in the Middle Ages: Cases from the *Canterbury Tales* of Geoffrey Chaucer," in *Rough Justice: Essays on Crime in Literature*, ed. H. L. Friedland (Toronto: University of Toronto Press, 1991), 19–51.

"Acquiteth yow now"

A reading of the Man of Law's Introduction suggests that Chaucer was confronting the double claims of legal discourse to pragmatic efficacy and abstract authority by staging a poetic negotiation of the relation between legal practice and some more absolute notion of "law." Immediately after fixing the date and time in an elaborate display of technological know-how, the Host turns to the Man of Law, couching his invitation to speak in a parodic set of legalisms:

> "Sire Man of Lawe," quod he, "so have ye blis,
> Telle us a tale anon, as forward is.
> Ye been submytted, thurgh youre free assent,
> To stonden in this cas at my juggement.
> Acquiteth yow now of youre biheeste;
> Thanne have ye do youre devoir atte leeste."
> (33–38)

The Host's summons lays claim to the specialized discourse of the law, abstracting its vocabulary from its epistemological foundation and subordinating its lexicon to an alternate making of meaning. But these legal terms also resonate within a poetic vocabulary specific to the *Canterbury Tales*, established by the Host in the *General Prologue* and modified by the Miller's interruption three tales previously. The game is proposed by the Host and characterized by the narrator using similarly legal terminology:

> "Ye goon to Caunterbury—God yow speede,
> The blisful martir quite yow youre meede!
> And wel I woot, as ye goon by the weye,
> Ye shapen yow to talen and to pleye;
> For trewely, confort ne myrthe is noon
> To ride by the weye doumb as a stoon;
> And therfore wol I maken yow disport,
> As I seyde erst, and doon yow som confort.
> And if yow liketh alle by oon assent
> *For to stonden at my juggement,*
> And for to werken as I shal yow seye . . ."
>
> Oure conseil was nat longe for to seche.
> Us thoughte it was noght worth to make it wys,
> And graunted hym withouten moore avys,
> And bad him seye his voirdit as hym leste . . .
>
> "And which of yow that bereth hym best of alle—
> That is to seyn, that telleth in this caas
> Tales of best sentence and moost solaas . . .
>
> And whoso wole my juggement withseye
> Shal paye al that we spenden by the weye.

And if ye vouche sauf that it be so,
Tel me anon, withouten wordes mo,
And I wol erly shape me therfore."
This thyng was graunted, and oure othes swore
With ful glad herte, and preyden hym also
That he wolde vouche sauf for to do so,
And that he wolde been oure governour,
And of oure tales juge and reportour,
And sette a soper at a certeyn pris,
And we wol reuled been at his devys
In heigh and lough; and thus by oon assent
We been acorded to his juggement.
(769–79, 784–87, 796–98, 805–18, emphasis added)[29]

The Host's imperative reminder to the Man of Law in the Introduction ("Ye been submytted, thurgh youre free assent, / To stonden in this cas at my juggement") precisely repeats the terms of the original agreement ("to stonden at my juggement"). But the legal vocabulary with which the agreement is defined and sealed does not itself produce tale-telling. Rather, the Host introduces the agreement as a means of structuring and controlling a behavior he identifies as natural to such groups of travelers: "And wel I woot, as ye goon by the weye / Ye shapen yow to talen and to pleye." Host and pilgrims thus figure for Chaucer two aspects of the creative process; the instinct "to talen and to pleye" must be ordered by "governour, juge and reportour."[30]

But as the Miller's interruption shows—and later editors would surely agree—ordering these tales will not be an easy task, not least because the Host himself does not seem entirely committed to his magisterial role as "governour, juge and reportour." Lee Patterson has argued that the Miller's reinterpretation of the Host's term "quiting," "allows into the tale-telling game the linguistic subversion that characterizes his own Tale," a reading of the disruptive potential of the Miller that brilliantly links the social and the discursive.[31] But the idea of "quiting" has in fact come from the Host. In turn-

[29] This passage contains a long list of additional terms with legal resonances. According to *The Middle English Dictionary*, "avys" came to refer (first appearance 1413) to legal advice (6d); "voirdit" was primarily a legal term (a); "vouche sauf" (2a and 2b) and "othes" (1b) indicate means of officially affirming pledges or promises.

[30] In an argument to which I cannot possibly do justice here, David Wallace insists on the importance of this passage to any understanding of the project of the *Tales*, holding that the construction of the "felaweshipe" of the pilgrimage, accomplished with a "lexicon of terms" from a variety of sources, is part of a broader historical and Chaucerian production of "associational forms" (*Chaucerian Polity: Absolutist Lineages and Associational Forms in England and Italy* [Stanford: Stanford University Press, 1997], 73).

[31] Lee Patterson, *Chaucer and the Subject of History* (Madison: University of Wisconsin Press, 1991), 244. The Host's request to the Monk introduces "quiting" as the principle that will order the game of tale-telling: "Now telleth ye, sir Monk, if that ye konne, / Somwhat to quite with the Knyghtes tale" (3118–19). The Miller famously takes up this term in his interruption: "I kan a noble tale for the nones, / With which I wol now quite the Knyghtes tale" (3126–27).

ing to the Monk with the injunction, "telleth ye . . . somwhat to quite with the Knyghtes tale" (Miller's Prologue, 3118–19), he refines the rules of the game. What the pilgrims agreed to do was to attempt to tell the tale of "*best* sentence and *moost* solaas," not to respond to the tales of other tellers. Furthermore, it is Harry Bailly who identifies the term "quite" as a particularly elastic one; he first uses it to characterize the goal of pilgrimage: "God yow speede, / The blisful martir *quite* yow youre meede!" The Miller may appropriate the word, but the Host serves as his model, both providing the form and suggesting the content.

Nor will it be the last time. In his invitation to the Man of Law, the Host commands him to "Acquiteth yow now of youre biheeste."[32] This pun on "acquit" and "quiting" functions according to a dual referentiality crucial to the *Tales*; it relies both on a general knowledge of a term's semantic range and on a specific recollection of the vocabulary of this game. In other words, it simultaneously puts into play two discursive systems, a poetic signification produced by the fictional world of pilgrimage and a legal lexicon rendered comprehensible only by reference to some external semiotic structure.

That external world has already been evoked for the reader by the Man of Law's portrait in the *General Prologue*, in which the Sergeant's professional activities are described in detail:

In termes hadde he caas and doomes alle
That from the tyme of kyng William were falle.
Therto he koude endite and make a thyng,
Ther koude no wight pynche at his writyng;
And every statut koude he pleyn by rote.
(323–27)

In an insightful reading of this passage, Anne Middleton argues that the use of the terms "endite" and "make" must be situated at precisely the same referential juncture between internal and external poetic worlds as "quiting":

In the *General Prologue* portrait of the Man of Law, Chaucer associates "making" and "enditing" as if they were similar skills: "Thereto he koude endite and make a thyng" (325). While both terms may refer to literary composition, the context—a list of the Man of Law's skills as a lawyer—introduces at least some ambiguity, suggesting that both may refer to the writing of legal instruments or documents: the making of a charge or accusation (OED s.v. indict[1]) or a proclamation (OED s.v. indict[2]); and the writing of a legal process, bringing a charge, pleading a cause, making a transaction (OED s.v. thing I. 2,3,4,5).[33]

[32] *The Middle English Dictionary*'s definitions of "acquit" and "quite" both include the meaning "to clear oneself of a charge" ("acquit" 4b; "quite" 4a and 4b); in both cases, the first recorded use of the terms in this way appears in the late fourteenth century (1390–1400).
[33] Anne Middleton, "Chaucer's New Men and the Good of Literature in the Canterbury Tales," in *Literature and Society: Selected Papers from the English Institute*, ed. Edward Said (Baltimore: Johns Hopkins University Press, 1980), 15–56, 54–55, n. 22.

This pun on a professional vocabulary is for Middleton the characteristic gesture of a subset of pilgrims she calls "new men," figures through whom Chaucer articulates a "theory of poetry" both secular and eloquent. The "new men" "'kidnap' terms, genres, and modes of idealization that traditionally support cultic values, whether those of a class or of a professed religion, into idealizing fictions of their own that shift the traditional uses for these terms and cultic objects."[34] For Middleton, it is this professional mode of being in the world that functions for Chaucer as a means to resolve an essential contradiction between "making," the "exercise of craftsmanship for the social pleasure and refreshment of others," and "poetrie," the high art of the past, "silent with respect to the present."[35] "Enditing" captures the best elements of both modes, offering "an art of celebrating the human world as if it mattered, and as if the act of celebration were itself virtuous."[36]

This definition of Chaucer's poetic practice is a specifically ethical one; Middleton asserts that the mode of appropriation she terms "kidnapping" functions in the *Canterbury Tales* as a kind of secular virtue. But as Jill Mann points out, to assert an ethic is not necessarily to affirm a principle:

> To say that the *General Prologue* is based on an ethic of this world is not to adopt the older critical position that Chaucer is unconcerned with morality. The adoption of this ethic at this particular point does not constitute a definitive attitude but a piece of observation—and the comic irony ensures that the reader does not identify with this ethic. Chaucer's inquiry is epistemological as well as moral. This is how the world operates, and as the world, it can operate no other way. The contrast with heavenly values is made at the end of the *Canterbury Tales*, as critics have noted, but it is made in such a way that it cannot affect the validity of the initial statement—the world can only operate by the world's values.[37]

Thus, the extrareferentiality of the puns on "quiting" and "enditing" must be understood in two stages, first as a mode or practice, and only secondarily in relation to any moral, ethical, or indeed political content. The special significance of the "kidnapping" of various discourses, then, lies not merely in its capacity to celebrate (or denigrate) but in its status as a distinctively Chaucerian formal procedure, part of a poetic, as Mann says, of the world.

---

[34] Ibid., 16.

[35] Ibid., 31, 33.

[36] Ibid., 24. In a different register, David Wallace also articulates this fundamental conflict in Chaucerian poetics, revealed for him in the contrast between Chaucer's "authorial signatures" in *Troilus and Criseyde* and in the *General Prologue*: "It assures us, clearly enough, that Chaucer brings to his writing ambitions of European magnitude. It also suggests, in substituting social predators for illustrious poets, that Chaucer harbors misgivings about the ethical value of such writing" (*Chaucerian Polity*, 81). Like Middleton, Wallace sees the Man of Law as a figure of compromise whose secular authority and discursive profession offer Chaucer an alter ego through which to define the social and literary meaning of his *poesis*. For both of these critics, the problem that Chaucer seeks to solve in the *Canterbury Tales* becomes, at least in the instance of the Man of Law, the relation of an ultimately secular notion of ethics to poetry.

[37] Jill Mann, *Chaucer and Medieval Estates Satire: The Literature of Social Classes and the General Prologue to the Canterbury Tales* (Cambridge: Cambridge University Press, 1973), 201.

Stopping short of ascribing a value-laden content to this poetic technique opens an interpretive space within which Chaucer's appropriation of particular vocabularies at specific junctures may be interrogated. Although the *Canterbury Tales* animate a variety of historical discourses and forms of thought—Fragment II alone contains gestures toward legal, theological, courtly, and mercantile ideologies and languages—it is the language of the law that is given primacy of place. Not only is the tale-telling game constituted in legal terms, but also the entrance into that game of the teller whose very identity is "of law" makes its own claim to foundational status. Whether or not (and most likely not) it is possible to demonstrate conclusively that the Man of Law's Introduction was intended as a beginning for the *Tales*, the independent status and consistent placement of Fragment II, as well as the Host's elaborate notation of the date and time, bespeak its fundamental importance to the project of the *Tales*. Furthermore, the Introduction dramatizes not only the simple poetic appropriation of legal discourse found in the *General Prologue*, but also the reciprocal attempt, and failure, of the law to speak poetry.

The Man of Law responds to the Host's legalisms with a commentary on contemporary poetry distinguished by its self-deprecating jocularity and squeamish moral delicacy:

> "I kan right now no thrifty tale seyn
> That Chaucer, thogh he kan but lewedly
> On metres and on rymyng craftily,
> Hath seyd hem in swich Englissh as he kan
> Of olde tyme, as knoweth many a man;
> And if he have noght seyd hem, leve brother,
> In o book, he hath seyd hem in another.
> For he hath toold of loveris up and doun
> Mo than Ovide made of mencioun
> In his Episteles, that been ful olde.
> What sholde I tellen hem, syn they been tolde?
>
> But certeinly no word ne writeth he
> Of thilke wikke ensample of Canacee . . .
>
> And therfore he, of ful avysement,
> Nolde nevere write in none of his sermons
> Of swiche unkynde abhomynacions,
> Ne I wol noon reherce, if that I may."
> (46–56, 77–78, 86–89)

Authority to speak, the Man of Law suggests to the Host, is not conferred simply by discursive appropriation; it must be legitimated according to a new standard of judgment: the morality of its content. But even as the Sergeant makes this assertion, he impeaches himself as a careless reader. Not only does he forget that Chaucer mentions Canacee in the Prologue to the *Legend of*

Good Women (F, 265; G, 219), but also in his proleptic description of his own tale, he mishandles the terms of poetic authority:

> "But of my tale how shal I doon this day?
> Me were looth be likned, doutelees,
> To Muses that men clepe Pierides—
> *Metamorphosios* woot what I mene;
> But nathelees I recche noght a bene
> Though I come after hym with hawebake.
> I speke in prose, and lat him rymes make."
> (90–96)

In attempting to display his poetic erudition by invoking a classical comparison, the Man of Law mistakes a story in the *Metamorphoses*—of King Pierus' ill-fated daughters, who lost a singing contest with the Muses—for Ovid's reference in the *Tristia* to the Muses as "Pierides." Even more damning is the fact that the Sergeant's choice of classical authority notoriously contains the kinds of tales he has vigorously condemned: the *Metamorphoses* contains a number of stories of incest among gods and humans. Moral judgement, then, takes second place to poetic skill; imitating the Chaucerian technique of borrowing legitimacy from the classical past, the Man of Law shows himself unable to monitor the content of his own verse.

But here obtrudes the textual difficulty. The Man of Law's assertion that he will "speke in prose" has a number of plausible explanations, most of which do not seriously challenge the comprehensibility of the *Tales* as a whole. Furthermore, it is possible to judge the plausibility of such explanations, based on factors such as manuscript testimony, historical comparison, and internal evidence. But posing a solution to a textual problem can only provide a starting point; merely noting that it seems most likely that the Man of Law's Introduction and *Tale* underwent substantial revision, and that the difficult line refers to an earlier stage in Chaucer's construction of the *Tales*, does not account for the problem that required revision *in the first place*. In a thematic sense, what brings the Introduction to an impasse is the question of skill, specifically the comparison of the Man of Law's skill to Chaucer's. As the line stands, it suggests the ultimate authority of poetry over law; the poet may depict the lawyer, but the lawyer cannot speak poetry. But at the same time, the Man of Law's definition of poetry explicitly limits "rymyng" to love poetry, the poetry of Chaucer's past, "He hath told of loveris up and doun," reinstantiating the philosophical division between "makyng" and "poetrie," "sentence" and "solaas," "rymyng" and "prose," which the *Canterbury Tales* sets out to dissolve. Paradoxically, the Man of Law's concession of defeat on one level constitutes a failure for Chaucer on another, suggesting that if the lawyer must speak in prose, then the law cannot be represented by poetry. It is this paradox that makes necessary the verse tale the Man of Law ultimately tells and that produces the textual impasse of the Introduction; having staged the subjection of law to poetry, Chaucer must insist on the capacity of poetry to represent even the imagination of a subject utterly constituted by the law.

The choice between verse and prose will reappear in the *Tale of Sir Thopas*, where Chaucer explicitly dramatizes the split. Here once again, the division is produced by lack of skill: Chaucer's "drasty speche" necessitates the same turn to prose suggested by the Man of Law—and, of course, the prose tale he tells was once the Man of Law's, the *Melibee*. This episode reenacts an old clash between frivolous romance and grave *sentence*, but that clash seems merely comic, the serious claims of courtly and theological discourses having been diffused throughout and contained by, the *Tales* as a whole.[38] What makes this version simple is the absence of the challenge posed by the law in Fragment II; this tale-teller carries with him no professional baggage, no discursive skills outside the world of poetry. The problem posed by the Man of Law, then, is not his ability or inability to "speke in verse"; it is that his language, the legal vocabulary appropriated with such ease by the Host and by Chaucer, makes the same kind of claim to secular authority as the vernacular poetic of the *Tales*.

For Chaucer, the discursive power of the law is both uniquely necessary and distinctly threatening. This contradiction must be understood both in relation to the historical conditions that make it possible and as a phenomenon particular to the poetic ambition of the *Canterbury Tales*. The susceptibility of legal discourse to Chaucerian usurpation, then, emerges from a specific context of historical development and political change. Richard Firth Green argues that the late fourteenth century constitutes a critical moment of transition in the history of English law, a moment at which "the increasing willingness to trust writing generated a corresponding crisis of authority, both intellectual and political."[39] For Green, the emergence of a centralized bureaucracy, along with the social upheaval of the Black Death, made demands on traditional systems of law that would produce "the dislocation caused by a powerful centralized authority employing a highly literate bureaucracy to enforce a common law still profoundly local and oral in its structural assumptions."[40] What this dislocation also engendered, however, was a discursive power dependent on its own capacity to generalize, to insist on its relevance in any particular instance of English secular life and to any member of English society.

---

[38] Lee Patterson, in "'What Man Artow?': Authorial Self-Definition in the *Tale of Sir Thopas* and the *Tale of Melibee*," *Studies in the Age of Chaucer* 11 (1989): 117–76, delineates the negotiation of Chaucerian identity in relation to these discourses, arguing that "neither tale represents a literary practice with which Chaucer can fully identify himself" (173), and finally that "the characteristic location of Chaucerian poetry is precisely the middle ground, the space between an atemporal beginning and a transcendent end" (174).

[39] Richard Firth Green, *A Crisis of Truth: Literature and Law in Ricardian England* (Philadelphia: University of Pennsylvania Press, 1999), 123.

[40] Ibid., 124.

As Green takes pains to point out, the late fourteenth century is, of course, merely a stopping place in the long development of centralized written law. The capacity of this law to fulfill its ambitions was limited, not only by the persistence of older forms but also by the competing claims of other discourses and structures to broad authority. Primary among these was the overwhelming reach of institutional church power, which had the additional advantage of a highly theorized notion of its own catholicity and a language—Latin—in which to express it. For a vernacular poet such as Chaucer, seeking to establish not only his own authority but also the authority of poetic and secular discourse itself, the language of the law could provide an essential vocabulary of legitimacy.

This legitimacy depended not on the executive power of the law to enforce its claims, but rather on its capacity for the interpellation of persons under its authority. When the Host chooses legal terms to bring order to what he defines as natural human behavior, "to talen and to pleye," he both asserts the broad applicability of those terms and assumes that their meaning will be generally understood. His reliance on this particular vocabulary implies that the most serious threat to the order he has imposed does not come from representatives of alternate structures of authority—the Knight, the Monk—or from figures who resist all authority—Miller, Reeve, Cook—but from that other practitioner of the law, the Sergeant. The construction in the *General Prologue* of a "compaignye" that cuts across traditional social boundaries requires an ordering principle neither aristocratic nor ecclesiastical, a vocabulary capable of describing a social relation in which knights and millers, monks and cooks, wives and nuns participate, at a discursive level at least, equally.[41] The law, with its fundamental claim to represent everyone (even outlaws are, after all, defined by the law) provides just such a vocabulary; everyone can be "endited" by poet or lawyer. But, as the ambivalence of the Man of Law's Introduction shows, Chaucer must also confront and attempt to subsume the legitimating force of the legal discourse he has found so useful.

The textual impasse persists. The Man of Law forever claims to speak in prose and tells a tale in verse. For Chaucer, too, legal discourse remains double-edged; appealingly elastic, threateningly pervasive, it perpetually confers authority and demands subjection. And for scholars, the danger lies both in glossing over that moment of textual contradiction and in substituting an easy homology for the historical tension it reveals. At a sufficiently distant realm of abstraction, law may as well be poetry, and vice versa. Such a collapse of categories can be resisted only counterintuitively, by maintaining that moment of contradiction, textual and thematic, which first produces the need for

[41] I am by no means suggesting here that medieval law served any kind of democratic or egalitarian function; indeed, the struggle I am depicting over the language of the law is precisely a struggle for power over the representation of others. The capacity of the law to "endite" is a very dangerous one.

interpretation. The Man of Law's Introduction stands at a particular historical juncture of law and literature, offering to Chaucer scholars the law as a productive means of historicist thinking, a way of deploying an abstraction while putting the historical detail to good use. Law in this instance maintains the tension between abstraction and particularity that is missing from both "positivism" and "theory." But as work on the Man of Law has shown, it is fatally easy to forget that tension while one is stuck in a morass of legal records or exhilarated by the plasticity of "the law." By turning to textual evidence, then, with its powerful resistance to abstracting modes of thought, I have sought to retain the capacity of "law" and "literature" to reveal the specific histories of conflict underlying the indeterminate and irresolute. Such a turn seeks as well an animating strain between modernity and the past, between the historical now and the historical then, which resists the tyranny of the part and refuses the false satisfaction of the whole.

7 Vernacular Legality

The English Jurisdictions of *The Owl and the Nightingale*

BRUCE HOLSINGER

> There are spiritual causes, in which a lay judge has neither cognizance nor (since he has no power of coercion) execution, cognizance of which belongs to ecclesiastical judges who govern and defend the priesthood; and secular causes, jurisdiction over which belongs to kings and princes who defend the realm, with which ecclesiastical judges must not meddle, since their rights or jurisdictions are limited and separate, except when sword ought to aid sword, for there is a great difference between the clerical estate and the realm.

> Henry Bracton, *De legibus et consuetudinibus angliae*

The confidence of Bracton's ground-clearing treatment of the division of legal jurisdictions in England belies the wider concern, expressed throughout the *De legibus*, that jurisdiction may not be as clearly definable as it appears. Historians of English law from F. W. Maitland's day to our own agree that the struggle over jurisdiction was a central preoccupation for insular legal culture in the first half of the thirteenth century, whose participants faced the task of sorting through 150 years of post-Conquest legal reform and ferment.[1] Bracton's treatise witnesses the theoretical and practical results of these transformations: it is here that the Latin *iurisdictio* enters the legal lexi-

For their generous and extensive comments on earlier versions of this essay, I thank Candace Barrington, Anna Brickhouse, Christopher Cannon, Jana Mathews, Elizabeth Robertson, and Emily Steiner.

[1] For Maitland's most extended treatment of jurisdiction, see the long chapter "Jurisdiction and the Communities of the Land," in Sir Frederick Pollock and Frederick William Maitland, *The History of English Law*, 2 vols. (Cambridge: Cambridge University Press, 1923), 1:527–688.

con on its widest scale yet, reflecting widespread debate over which institutions are to make and enforce which laws, as well as where, when, and how they are to do so. For Bracton and his revisers, jurisdiction is far more than a solely juridical problem, however. The medieval concern with legal jurisdiction was ipso facto a concern with numerous other aspects of social formation: royal power versus ecclesiastical privilege; the permeability of institutional borders (whether local or national); the administration of physical violence in the pursuit of justice; the role of coercion in the settlement of disputes; and the tenuous boundary between the sacred and the profane. For Maitland, jurisdiction by its nature constitutes "one of the main ties which keeps society together," as well as an ever-present source of conflict, anxiety, and explicit institutional conflict.[2]

As a contested juridical category and a constant source of written reflection, jurisdiction provides compelling social and historical models for rethinking the nature of the relationship between properly "legal" and "literary" forms of writing.[3] In an overview of legal writing in medieval England, Richard Firth Green observes that most scholarship on law and literature has proceeded down one of two paths, exploring either formal questions of legal discourse as a species of literature or representations of legal practices and procedures in literary texts. Jurisdiction is more naturally suited to what Green and others have identified as an emerging third area of investigation, the effort among scholars in the field to delineate literature and law as "parallel forms of discourse" that allow us to explore "how the lawyer's comparatively more formal analysis of mental or social processes can help us understand what the imaginative writer sometimes leaves unspoken or expresses only obliquely."[4] Surely, however, this will often work in reverse, and more antagonistically: the so-called imaginative writer may be able to expose logical or cognitive gaps unacknowledged or undertheorized within official legal culture and exploit them through the alternative medium of literary language. The *unofficial* literature of jurisdiction provides just such a window onto official legal discourse by employing jurisdiction as a literary mode of delineation, separation, and regulation.[5]

Perhaps no Middle English writing displays a more acute awareness of the problems and possibilities of jurisdictional discourse than *The Owl and the*

---

[2] Ibid., 527.

[3] For an inspiring example of such rethinking in American literary studies, see Christine Macdonald, "Judging Jurisdictions: Geography and Race in Slave Law and Literature of the 1830s," *American Literature* 71 (1999): 625–55.

[4] Richard Firth Green, "Medieval Literature and Law," in *The Cambridge History of Medieval English Literature*, ed. David Wallace (Cambridge: Cambridge University Press, 1999), 407.

[5] Green's magisterial study *A Crisis of Truth: Literature and Law in Ricardian England* (Philadelphia: University of Pennsylvania Press, 1999) explores the various discursive claims made on the status of "trouthe" by legal, literary, philosophical, and theological writers of the fourteenth century, claims that directly involve what might be called the jurisdictional prerogative of the institutions involved in the semantic contestations he treats.

Nightingale. As legal writers, judges, lawyers, parliaments, and kings worked to refine and elaborate practical jurisdiction through the thirteenth century, this linguistically innovative work engaged in a similarly "meta-legal" project, though with very distinct tools and motives. Rather than taking on the overt conflicts being addressed by Bracton and other legal writers, the anonymous poet of *The Owl and the Nightingale* struggles not with legal jurisdiction per se, but with the very notion of jurisdiction as a master category embracing numerous modes of social and institutional performance. In particular, I hope to show, the poem explores certain aspects of liturgy as a field of cultural production freighted with its own jurisdictional ambivalences. Liturgy and law converge into a vernacular poetics newly conscious of the performative dimensions of both disciplines; the musical vehicle of liturgical culture assumes a forensic authority that goes hand-in-hand with the juridical performance constituting the main narrative sequence of the poem. In this respect, even the making of literature itself comes under a kind of jurisdictional purview as the poem unfolds in an English vernacular that was experiencing an increasingly uneasy relation to the law.

In the first section of this essay I propose a heuristic model for exploring the relationship between law and vernacular literature in the Middle Ages, a model that I believe has particular relevance for the legal languages of a thirteenth-century work such as *The Owl and the Nightingale*. The second section provides a brief overview of jurisdictional disputes in English legal culture during the same century, suggesting that *The Owl and the Nightingale* was written and received in the midst of what can only be called a jurisdictional epoch. I then move to a reading of the poem's liturgical legalisms, arguing that the poet represents the constraints on liturgical performance in specifically jurisdictional terms. Having made a case for the poem's simultaneously legal and liturgical vernacular, I then consider these aspects of *The Owl and the Nightingale*'s legal imagination within the wider context of the musical culture of thirteenth-century England. As we shall see, the poem deploys an array of legal terminologies and procedures as a means of exploring what its writer saw as a liturgical problem, namely, what sorts of music belong where and when and with what results. At the same time, the poem invents its own vernacular musical lexicon—including English neologisms for particular liturgical genres—in order to expose the jurisdictional contestations that marked the recent legal history of the emerging nation. It will be worth remembering in this regard that the thirteenth century was a crucially jurisdictional one for post-Conquest English itself, a vernacular that was increasingly if hesitantly exploring its purview in the arenas of literature, law, liturgy, and many other public spheres. *The Owl and the Nightingale* can be read as an effort (an abortive one, perhaps) to participate in a burgeoning conversation regarding the nature and consequences of vernacular jurisdiction among those readers of English inhabiting the space the poem only once calls "Engelonde."

Vernacular Legality

In its inventive deployment of the English language to confront a complex and contemporaneous legal problematic, *The Owl and the Nightingale* provides us with an ideal example of what I would like to call "vernacular legality." For the purposes of this essay, vernacular legality will be defined as the self-conscious use of a medieval vernacular in order to explore a specialized realm of authoritative legal knowledge and practice whose documentary and discursive apparatus is confined primarily to Latin.[6] If the Middle Ages was "a time when knowledge of the law seems to have been the common property of poets," in John Alford's words,[7] vernacular legality constituted both a subgenre of legal writing in the vernacular as well as a strategy by which writers could manipulate and transform the law in the service of vernacular poetics. As Alford writes: "Legal expression aims for precision. This is the major reason for its conservatism. . . . It wants *certainty*. . . . Poets take the opposite point of view. Instead of adhering rigorously to the traditional uses of words, poets deliberately bend and stretch their meanings; far from trying to avoid the ambiguity of language, poets thrive on it."[8] Of course, as any good lawyer knows, while legal writing proper may *aim* for precision, the successful exploitation of its frequent ambiguity can be quite profitable. As an often deliberately ambiguous mode of expression, by contrast, literary language will always be a problematic and contested medium for writing about and intervening within matters of law.

A working notion of vernacular legality will allow us to address not only the ways in which vernacular writers recruit official legal vocabularies and institutions for their own purposes, but also, and perhaps more importantly, those means by which certain writers infuse the vernacular with a juridical and forensic authority that would otherwise be restricted to the agents of official legal culture.[9] By exploiting institutional and political differences be-

---

[6] Those abreast of recent developments in Middle English literary studies should recognize my debt here to the work of Nicholas Watson on "vernacular theology"; see especially "Censorship and Cultural Change in Late-Medieval England: Vernacular Theology, the Oxford Translation Debate, and Arundel's Constitutions of 1409," *Speculum* 70 (1995): 822–64. Watson's remarks on the analytical usefulness of the category "vernacular theology" could apply equally well to vernacular legality (I have substituted the word "legality" for Watson's "theology" and "legal" for "religious" in the following passage): "The word 'legality' focuses our attention on the specifically intellectual content of vernacular legal texts that are often treated with condescension (especially in relation to Latin texts), encouraging reflection on the kinds of legal information available to vernacular readers without obliging us to insist on the simplicity or crudity of that information: that is, the term is an attempt to distance scholarship from its habitual adherence to a clerical, Latinate perspective in its dealings with these texts" (823 n).

[7] John Alford, *"Piers Plowman": A Glossary of Legal Diction* (Cambridge: D. S. Brewer, 1988), ix.

[8] Ibid., xiii.

[9] It may help us resist the tendency, still somewhat common in the study of law and literature, to privilege the specialized knowledge of sanctioned legal institutions, procedures, and professionals over the supposedly "amateurish" literatures and authors that adapt or contest them. In

tween vernacular writers and legal practitioners, the medieval works I would include within the category of vernacular legality demonstrate that the law can be claimed as a powerful discursive weapon even by those possessing only a rudimentary knowledge of its technicalities and procedural intricacies. In fact, it may often be their very lack of such specialized knowledge that accords certain writers an authority to speak both with and against the law. In this sense, vernacular legality might best be understood as one of those modes of forensic discourse that the legal theorist Peter Goodrich has defined as "minor jurisprudences," "forms of legal knowledge that escape the phantom of a sovereign and unitary law" by constructing alternative juridical domains outside official legal culture. For Goodrich, the history of minor jurisprudence is a history "of lost critical and satirical traditions of jurisprudence, of alternative practices and competing forms of judgment which contemporary legal scholarship either forgets or ignores."[10]

A much-discussed passage from Chaucer's *Wife of Bath's Tale* illustrates the kind of alternative jurisprudence that vernacular legality might encompass. After an unnamed Arthurian knight rapes a "maide" walking along a river, he is brought before the king's court to face a presumably short trial and a clearly predetermined sentence. Just as the wheels of codified legal authority begin to spin, however, the Wife's narrative proposes a provisional form of jurisprudence that immediately displaces royal jurisdiction:

> dampned was this knyght for to be deed
> By cours of lawe, and sholde han lost his heed—
> Paraventure swich was the statut tho—
> But that the queene and other ladyes mo
> So longe preyeden the kyng of grace,
> Til he his lyf hym graunted in the place,

an influential essay originally published in the *Virginia Law Review*, for example, Richard Posner makes the caustic assertion that "if I want to know about the system of chancery in nineteenth-century England I do not go to *Bleak House*" ("Law and Literature: A Relation Reargued," in *Law and Literature: Text and Theory*, ed. Lenora Ledwon [New York: Garland, 1996], 64). The obvious response to Posner's claim (one that has been made by others) is that this depends very much on what one wants to know. If the scholar's concern is with procedural intricacies or the biographies of individual judges and litigants, Dickens may be of little help, it is true. But if we wish to understand the role of chancery in the English imagination, the manipulations of legal discourse in the service of a professional legal class, or the often crushing weight of the nineteenth-century English courts on family and person, the book is ideally suited to the task. A work such as *Bleak House* in fact embodies the spirit of vernacular legality in Victorian England; Dickens enlists the vernacular idiom of the nineteenth-century novel as a means of expressing in literary form the perils and consequences of legal privilege and exclusion. For a particularly brilliant response to Posner's assessment of the novel, see Dieter Paul Polloczek, "Aporias of Retribution and Questions of Responsibility: The Legacy of Incarceration in Dickens's *Bleak House*," chap. 4 of *Literature and Legal Discourse: Equity and Ethics from Sterne to Conrad* (Cambridge: Cambridge University Press, 1999), 124–202.

[10] Peter Goodrich, *Law in the Courts of Love: Literature and Other Minor Jurisprudences* (New York: Routledge, 1996), 2.

And yaf hym to the queene, al at hir wille,
To chese wheither she wolde hym save or spille.[11]

With the phrase "swich was the statut," the Wife is registering the legal embodiment of the "auctoritee" that she invokes in the first line of her Prologue.
By the time the knight returns from his quest, however, the Wife imagines
"The queene hirself sittynge as a justise" (1028). In the legalistic sections of
the poem, the system of royal justice (albeit displaced into the mists of the
Arthurian past) has given way to the queen's ad hoc court, in which the English vernacular serves as the legal medium of testimony, interrogation, sentencing, and, in the form of the *Tale* itself, transcription. The *Tale* thus defines
its own sphere of legal knowing by opposing a queenly jurisprudence to the
normative form of legal authority promulgated in and through "statut." One
of the points of the *Wife of Bath's Tale* (and, for that matter, of the medieval
"courts of love" more generally) is to suspend imaginatively the authority of
the royal courts in favor of a provisional, experimental, and fleeting form of
legal power—a power that here achieves much of its resonance from the ex-
periential vernacular of the Wife herself.[12] In this case, then, written "statut"
yields to ad hoc tribunal just as royal apparatus makes way for female jurisdiction.

Faced with such literary representations of minor jurisprudence, the historicizing law-and-literature scholar will naturally look outside the poem for
corresponding legal practices in the social realm in order to make sense of the
legal discourse within the text. As Theodore Ziolkowski argues in his sweep-
ing survey of Western literary representations of legal crises, as a means of
"locating each literary work within its own legal context," literary scholars
"need . . . enough understanding of legal history to provide in each case an
adequate and appropriate context for the literary work."[13] Yet the "legal context" of any legally minded literary work must include as well the legal world
internal and unique to the text itself. What I am suggesting, in other words, is
that many vernacular writings in medieval England *create their own legal cultures* that we will obscure if we privilege those writings that correspond most
closely to external legal norms. These fleeting legal domains have their distinctive rules, expectations, and personnel: they appoint women as judges,
overturn official statutes, and impose their own penalties. Part of the work

---

[11] *Wife of Bath's Tale*, 3.891–98, in *The Riverside Chaucer*, ed. Larry D. Benson, 3rd ed. (Boston:
Houghton Mifflin, 1987), 117–19; Chaucer citations hereafter given by line in text.

[12] See Goodrich, *Law in the Courts of Love*, 29–71. On "love-days" more generally as an alternative means of dispute settlement (with reference to the Chaucer passage as well as Langland's
Piers Plowman), see Michael T. Clanchy's important article "Law and Love in the Middle Ages,"
in *Disputes and Settlements: Law and Human Relations in the West*, ed. John Bossy (Cambridge:
Cambridge University Press, 1983), 47–67.

[13] Theodore Ziolkowski, *The Mirror of Justice: Literary Reflections of Legal Crises* (Princeton:
Princeton University Press, 1997), xi.

they do is to create and promulgate narratives in which official legal culture—that is, the sanctioned rules governing juridical life within the very social domain in which they are written—may have little or no say over the legal machinations the texts imagine in defining their own jurisdictions as they are transmitted and read.

We need to take these provisional legal cultures and their protocols just as seriously as we take any "actual" court, official procedure, or technical legal lexicon by accounting for the legal protocols established by and within the unique mode of literary production. This is not necessarily to argue for a "new formalism" in law-and-literature studies; I am not proposing that literary scholars abandon the rigorous study of legal history in favor of hermetic textual analysis. In fact, it is precisely the character of its official legal culture that makes thirteenth-century England ideally suited to an inquiry into the discursive, political, and literary implications of vernacular legality. For it was during this century that the legal profession proper—the subculture of attorneys, sergeants, pleaders, and so on—came into being as a recognizable and, by the second half of the century, explicitly regulated class of specialized laborers.[14] The changing structure and jurisdictions of national and local courts led in turn to an ever more complex litigation process, which required lengthy study of new legal technicalities and an increasing need for expert representation in what Alan Harding terms the "curious arts."[15] The English judiciary, too, underwent a rapid process of professionalization beginning in the reign of Henry II, picking up speed under Richard I, and culminating during the reign of John.[16] In many ways, the dawn of the thirteenth century can provide a unique historical answer to the question James Boyd White posed in the book that did much to initiate the critical study of law and literature: "What does it mean . . . to learn to think and speak like a lawyer?"[17]

The ramifications of these professionalizing developments for the historical relationship between legality and vernacularity cannot be exaggerated. The Icelandic sagas imagine the law as a kind of "spectator sport" in which the implied readership is constantly attuned to the legal procedures represented in the text.[18] In the Anglo-Saxon period legal language creates what Katherine O'Brien O'Keeffe has identified as a spectacular contin-

---

[14] On the origins and growth of the legal profession in England, see Jonathan Rose, *The Legal Profession in Medieval England: A History of Regulation*, published as *Syracuse Law Review* 48.1 (1998), and the many studies cited therein.

[15] Alan Harding, *The Law Courts of Medieval England* (London: George Allen and Unwin, 1973), 78.

[16] See Ralph V. Turner, *The English Judiciary in the Age of Glanvill and Bracton, c. 1176–1239* (Cambridge: Cambridge University Press, 1985), esp. chaps. 3 and 4.

[17] James B. White, *The Legal Imagination: Studies in the Nature of Legal Thought and Expression* (Boston: Little, Brown, 1973), xxxi.

[18] Ziolkowski, *The Mirror of Justice*, 56. For another perspective on this issue, see Henry Ordower, "Exploring the Literary Function of Law and Litigation in *Njal's Saga*," *Cardoza Studies in Law and Literature* 3 (1991): 41–61.

uum between juridical authority and the embodied subject in Old English literature.[19] Indeed, as Patrick Wormald has suggested, the surviving Old English law codes may constitute more "an index of governing mentalities" than evidence of the nature of pre-Conquest England as a *pays du droit écrit*.[20]

The thirteenth century witnesses an important shift in the relationship between law and vernacular writing. In England, this period represents a new burgeoning of vernacular legality, an era in which those who were excluded from legal schooling and specialization—a group by no means limited to laypersons but including monks, canons, nuns, secular clergy, friars, and many others—had often to define their own relationships with a newly specialized class of legal professionals. The rise of a discrete legal culture in the early thirteenth century anticipates in this respect the emergence of the larger administrative bureaucracy in the late fourteenth and early fifteenth centuries. As in Ricardian England—in which Green finds "a wider conflict between two legal orders," the folklaw and the king's law, preoccupying much of the period's legalistic literature—the decades after 1200 stage an extended conflict between an institutionalized legal apparatus and an increasingly marginalized legal vernacular.[21] Moreover, even as English was slowly losing its place and prestige as a legally viable tongue, the competing insular vernacular was branching off into so-called law French, a dialectically hybrid and hopelessly technical jargon used in the common law courts; by mid-century, law French cannot properly be termed "vernacular" in any meaningful way.[22] In all of these ways the thirteenth century forces the law beyond the reach of the nonspecialist; the result is a proliferation of new legalistic writing in the English vernacular existing alongside the documentary and legislative production of official legal culture, in relation to which this emergent writing is often brilliantly parasitic.

The elusive figure of Laȝamon presents an intriguing case in point. The translator-author of the English *Brut* identifies himself in the opening period of the poem as a priest with a living at Areley, happily performing the liturgy. In the first line, however, he has already named himself as "Laȝamon" or "Laweman" (the two extant manuscripts record the name differently). "Lawman," the authorial "man of law," invents a nom de plume that registers his

[19] Katherine O'Brien O'Keeffe, "Body and Law in Anglo-Saxon England," *Anglo-Saxon England* 27 (1998): 209–32.
[20] Patrick Wormald, *The Making of English Law: King Alfred to the Twelfth Century*, vol. 1 (Oxford: Blackwell, 1999), esp. 477–83.
[21] Green, *Crisis of Truth*, 166. On the circa 1400 bureaucracy and its scribal role in the promotion of vernacular literature, see Kathryn Kerby-Fulton and Steven Justice, "Langlandian Reading Circles and the Civil Service in London and Dublin, 1380–1427," *New Medieval Literatures* 1 (1997): 59–84.
[22] The best introduction to the nature and role of law French is J. H. Baker, "The Three Languages of the Common Law," *McGill Law Journal* 43 (1998): 7–24; see also Baker's introduction to his *Manual of Law French* (London: Avebury Publishing Company, 1979).

discursive affiliation with an as yet barely visible professional class of "law-men."[23] Whether or not Laȝamon was a judge with a local court under his ju-risdiction, to claim the status of a "lawman" in the early thirteenth century was inevitably to claim affiliation with an emergent professional workforce and a new form of legal knowing, speaking, and writing. As Christopher Can-non has put it, "The aim of Laȝamon's *name* is to make [his] poem's story, source, and style cohere."[24]

Although neither the author nor the narrator of *The Owl and the Nightin-gale* makes such an explicit nominal claim to institutional authority, the poem's sense of its own vernacular legality constitutes a compelling re-sponse to the consequences of such claims. Here we might pause to con-sider just a few examples of the poem's sophisticated and surprisingly self-conscious sense of its own participation in a thirteenth-century legal vernacularity. The poem both revives and invents a heterogeneous and amalgamated legal lexicon in order to claim its own literary jurisdiction, to define a sphere of minor jurisprudence in which legal discourse can be ac-commodated within the labile discursive and lexical field of an emergent vernacular poetics.

From the beginning the poem works to construct its own status as legal argument and its vernacular authority as legal discourse. Just before the Nightingale begins her side of the story, the narrator depicts her about to hold forth from the corner of a field: "þe Niȝtingale bigon þe speche / In one hurne of one breche."[25] The lawsuit, the legal "speche" that will in effect *become* the poem, is initiated in the corner of a fallow field. Rhyming "speche" and "breche," the couplet crafts an agricultural analogy that associ-ates the legal performance of the poem *tout court* with the physical labor of the farmer, who must begin to sow his crop in an arable but as yet unplanted field.

A passage much later in the poem amplifies this underlying agricultural metaphor by aligning it with a specific aspect of insular land law. The Nightingale is describing the range of options available to a desirous young woman, one of which is a church-sanctioned marriage that will erase the sin-fulness of premarital sex:

Heo mai hire guld atwende
A rihte weie þurþ chirche bende,
An mai eft habbe to make

[23] Laȝamon, *Brut*, ed. G. L. Brook and R. F. Leslie, EETS OS 250 and 277 (London: Oxford University Press, 1963).
[24] Christopher Cannon, "Laȝamon and the Laws of Men," *English Literary History* 67 (2000): 338.
[25] *The Owl and the Nightingale*, ll. 13–14, ed. Eric Gerald Stanley (London: Thomas Nelson and Sons, 1960). All subsequent references are to this edition and will be cited in the text.

Hire leofmon wiþute sake,
An go to him bi daies lihte
þat er stal to bi þeostre nihte.
(1427–32)

"She may escape her guilt the correct way through the bonds of the Church (i.e., matrimony), and may then have her lover as husband without *sake*, and go to him by the light of day who used to steal to her in the darkness of night." The term "sake" in line 1430 could be taken to refer to the general state of lacking cause for legal action or dispute (*Middle English Dictionary*, "sake" 1); Eric Stanley sensibly argues for an even weaker translation, "without blame."[26] Yet the logic of the passage and the erotic affiliations of its speaker make it more likely that the poet is playing on a specific legal usage of the term: "The right to the profits and fines from the adjudication of disputes arising within the bounds of a specified landholding" (*Middle English Dictionary*, "sake" 2). In other words, the term can denote the legal *jurisdiction* of an individual over a particular property dispute. The "breche" from the beginning of the poem—the legal "field" on which the poem is inscribed—has returned in the form of a challengeable right to profit from the legal harvest this field has produced. As she does elsewhere in the poem, the Nightingale here crafts a subtly underhanded argument *against* marriage as the exclusive locus of sexuality: the fornicating "maide" who chooses to take her lover to husband can do so only "wiþute sake," surrendering the right to claim legal profits or fines from land once she has subjected herself through matrimony to the legal authority of a husband.

This sort of passage (and there are many such in *The Owl and the Nightingale*) sheds intriguing light on the poem's more general stance toward England's legal past and the language in which this past endured in the author's historical moment. Raymond Williams's distinction between "archaic" and "residual" discourses is helpful here: archaic languages are those that are clearly visible as old, outmoded, even quaint; residual lexicons, by contrast, possess at least some prestige within a dominant culture, though they cannot be fully accounted for in that culture's terms.[27] The poem's use of "sake" here crystallizes this distinction, recalling as it does the ubiquitous Anglo-Saxon legal formula "sake and soke" (the king's thegns possessed the right of "sake and soke," or full jurisdiction, over their tenants).[28] Although the ancient term *sake* is the equivalent of the Latin *causa*, meaning "lawsuit" or "affair," the law-

---

[26] Ibid., 11.

[27] His most succinct discussion of these terms occurs in Raymond Williams, *Marxism and Literature* (Oxford: Oxford University Press, 1977), 121–27.

[28] See David Roffe's discussion in "From Thegnage to Barony: Sake and Soke, Title, and Tenants-in-Chief," *Anglo-Norman Studies* 12 (1990), 157–76.

men who compiled Domesday Book (1086) latinized the Anglo-Saxon *sake* as "saca." By the time *The Owl and the Nightingale* was written, the term could still be remembered and employed for its resonance as a marker of jurisdictional authority. While much of the poem's legal vocabulary may be inherited from an archaic past fully visible as old, then, the residual force of this vocabulary allows the poet to integrate this language within the fabric of the work's narrative, poetics, and rhetoric.

A similarly playful bilingualism is apparent in a passage that sets the work's legal lexicon against a competing source of institutional prestige for vernacular poetry. The Owl declares:

> ʒef eni mon schal rem abide
> Al ich hit wot ear hit itide.
> Ofte for mine muchele iwitte
> Wel sorimod & worþ ich sitte.
> (1215–18)

The first couplet translates thus: "If any man shall be pursued by the hue-and-cry, I know all about it before it happens." The "hue-and-cry" was the legal obligation on the part of every citizen to raise a clamor upon witnessing the commission of a felony (*Middle English Dictionary*, "rem" 1). Yet the passage directly follows the Owl's boasting about her extensive study in holy writ, the intellectual labor that has given her "insihte" and a prophetic lens into the future: "Ich con inoh in bokes lore, / An eke ich can of þe goddspelle / More þan ich nule þe telle" (1208–10); her book learning has even allowed her to plumb the mysteries of "þe tacninge," or the allegorical senses of the Bible. The passage is constructing an accusative pun on the philosophical sense of *res*, the "matter" of theology. The vernacular *rem* of legal obligation is the Latin *res* of theological prophecy, and "eni mon" may participate in the matter of the poem, itself a mode of juridical "speche" that embraces numerous aspects of legal usage.

I shall have more to say about the poem's English legality, which makes use of Latin, Anglo-Saxon, and even, as we shall see, French legal vocabularies in its simultaneously jurisdictional and poetic project. More broadly, I would propose, the creativity and humor evident in the legalities of *The Owl and the Nightingale* register the poem's quite powerful effort to claim a specific kind of jurisdiction for English poetry during a period in which the success and prestige of so-called Early Middle English as a literary language was hardly assured. In this sense, the poem is itself a profound argument for the jurisdictional viability—the *sake*—of a post-Conquest vernacular poetics, an argument that draws innovatively on other, extrapoetic modes and sites of performance in support of its discursive aims.

Writing Jurisdictions

The precise legal affiliations of *The Owl and the Nightingale* have long been a matter of debate, one that has given rise to a substantial law-and-literature bibliography in its own right. Janet Coleman notes in a 1987 article the enduring lack of the historical "key to this poem, a key that has thus far proved elusive to students of early English literature" and that she finds in twelfth-century debates over love and marriage in canon law.[29] Its exceptional erudition notwithstanding, Coleman's article should be seen as one in a long line of studies that suggest a distinctive legal context as the interpretive crux of the poem, as even a cursory glance at the titles of the many law-related articles written on the poem reveals.[30]

The sheer number of convincing yet diverging legal arguments about *The Owl and the Nightingale* illustrates the central point of the present essay. Taken collectively, these many (mostly excellent) studies suggest that the poem's overriding legal concern may be with any one of the following: canon law, secular law, natural law, marriage law, theoretical law, or procedural law; or rather, it may be with all of them at the same time; or rather, it may be with the conflicts, gaps, overlaps, and elisions *between* these systems and practices of law. The central legal concern of *The Owl and the Nightingale* is, in a word, jurisdiction. The poem's critical tradition elegantly recapitulates the poet's own concern to invent a vernacular poetics capable of registering the variety of legal practices, procedures, and authorities that have proliferated in England since the Conquest.

We get an initial sense of the poem's jurisdictional sensibility in a passage that interpolates the well-known courtly legend (told most famously by Marie de France in *Laüstic*) of a nightingale and the lady he comforts with his music. Here, the Owl accuses the Nightingale of using music to instruct the discontented wife in the art of sexuality—"An sunge boþe loʒe & buue, [both low and high] / An lerdest [instructs] hi to don shome / An vnriʒt of hire licome [body]" (1052–54)—and thus encouraging her through his art in her commission of adultery with a neighboring lord. In response, the Nightingale defends herself by relating the ultimate moral of the story, which in her version

---

[29] Janet Coleman, "The *Owl and the Nightingale* and Papal Theories of Marriage," *Journal of Ecclesiastical History* 38 (1987): 517–68.

[30] Monica Brzezinski Potkay, "Natural Law in the *Owl and the Nightingale*," *Chaucer Review* 28 (1994): 368–83; Michael A. Witt, "The *Owl and the Nightingale* and English Law Court Procedure of the Twelfth and Thirteenth Centuries," *Chaucer Review* 16 (1982): 282–92; Jay Schleusener, "*The Owl and the Nightingale*: A Matter of Judgment," *Modern Philology* 70 (1973): 185–89; Henry Barrett Hinckley, "The Date of *The Owl and the Nightingale*: Vivian's Legation," *Philological Quarterly* 12 (1933): 339–49; Coleman, "The *Owl and the Nightingale* and Papal Theories of Marriage"; and David Lampe, "Law as Order in *The Owl and the Nightingale*," *Acta* 7 (1980): 93–107.

concludes with a certain "king Henri" passing judgment on the lady's jealous
husband for his slaying of the nightingale:

> þat underyat [understood] þe king Henri—
> Iesus his soule do merci!—
> He let forbonne [banish] þene kniȝt,
> þat hadde idon so muchel unriȝt
> Ine so gode kinges londe:
> Vor riȝte niþe [malice] & for fule onde [ill will]
> Let þane lutle fuȝel [bird] nime
> An him fordeme [convicted] lif an lime.
> Hit was wrþsipe al mine kunne,
> Forþon þe kniȝt forles [abandoned] his wunne [struggle]
> An ȝaf for me an hundred punde.
> (1091–1101)

Critics have pointed to numerous parallels between this version of the
aventure and Marie's, but the juridical denouement is entirely absent from
Laüstic, which concludes with a strangely religious scene in which the wife's
lover encases the nightingale's body in a reliquary-like casket; "king Henri"
(or any other king, for that matter) goes unmentioned. In *The Owl and the
Nightingale*, by contrast, the adulterous dispute between the two knights is resolved through an explicit appeal to royal justice. The Nightingale places
herself in the midst of a local aristocratic conflict—"*Ich* hadde of hir milse an
ore"—yet carefully relates its resolution by means of a centralized and regal
judicial decision. The passage is symptomatic of the widening jurisdictional
embrace of the royal courts through the thirteenth century, perhaps especially the court *coram rege* embodied in the person of the king; seeking a resolution of a local narrative dispute, the poem nevertheless speaks to the increasing centralization of secular justice in the wake of the Angevin reforms.[31]
   Until relatively recently, the invocation in this passage of a deceased "king
Henri" was generally regarded as a reference to Henry II, whose death in
1189 provided scholars with both a terminus a quo for the composition of the
poem as well as a recent historical reference point for the poet; since Henry
III did not succeed to the throne until 1216, and the poem does not distinguish its own "king Henri" from any other, this reasoning went, *The Owl and
the Nightingale* must have been written sometime between 1189 and 1216.
Whereas some of the most authoritative studies of the poem continue to
argue for this traditional dating (the 1999 *Cambridge History of Medieval English Literature* twice places it "around 1200," confidently and without explanation),[32] Neil Ker, Neil Cartlidge, Alan Fletcher, and others have shown that

---

[31] On this process of centralization, see, among many others, the discussion by John Hudson,
The Formation of the English Common Law (New York: Longman, 1996), 221–24.
[32] David Wallace, "Introduction," and Thomas Hahn, "Early Middle English," in Wallace,
Cambridge History of Medieval English Literature, 5 and 77, respectively.

there remains no good reason other than convention to date the poem earlier than the middle or even the later decades of the thirteenth century.[33] It may not be too much to say, then, that *The Owl and the Nightingale* is a quintessentially thirteenth-century production, a poem crafted during an epoch in which English legal culture was preoccupied with defining the rule and role of jurisdiction.

An illuminating example of this thirteenth-century jurisdictional preoccupation is the making and preservation of Bracton's *De legibus et consuetudinibus angliae*. The manuscripts of the treatise bear traces of its entanglement in one of the more perplexing jurisdictional problems of the first half of the century, namely, the properly "English" character of English law. The treatise was initially compiled by Bracton during his years as a practicing judge in the 1240s and 1250s; it was this hands-on experience as a self-consciously English jurist that won the admiration and disdain of centuries of legal historians who disputed the national character of the treatise and its embodiment of what Maitland called "the Englishry of English law."[34] Yet the legal origins of the *De legibus* have been mired in a controversy dating as far back as the writings of John Selden in the seventeenth century, a controversy centering on the extent of Bracton's knowledge and use of Roman civil law in the composition of his treatise, which stages the most sophisticated encounter of its time between the substance of native English law and the legacy of Roman and continental jurisprudence. As Samuel Thorne has shown, the notorious *addiciones* and misplaced paragraphs in the surviving manuscripts of the *De legibus* are themselves a sign of the jurisdictional ambivalence of the treatise and its editorial history, a history littered with competing claims as to the properly "English" jurisdiction of the treatise itself.[35]

Bracton began compiling the *De legibus* in the decades following the first issue of Magna Carta (1215), and the legacy of Runnymede can be everywhere perceived in subsequent jurisdictional squabbles between the various English courts of the thirteenth century. J. C. Holt has gone so far as to identify a "crisis of jurisdiction" characterizing the legal climate in these years, one that came about despite (or perhaps because of) King John's early and sustained interest in matters of law.[36] The charter's seventeenth provision mandated that common pleas would cease following the king around the country but would instead be heard and resolved at Westminster. This demand, which resulted in a return to the bipartite royal court which had ob-

---

[33] N. R. Ker, *The Owl and the Nightingale: Facsimile of the Jesus and Cotton Manuscripts*, EETS OS 251 (London: Oxford University Press, 1963), ix; Neil Cartlidge, "The Date of the *Owl and the Nightingale*," *Medium Aevum* 65 (1996): 230–47; Alan Fletcher, "The Genesis of *The Owl and the Nightingale*: A New Hypothesis," *Chaucer Review* 34 (1999): 1–17.

[34] Pollock and Maitland, *History of English Law*, 1:188.

[35] See the editorial and reception history traced by Samuel Thorne in his introduction and in his essays, "Henry de Bracton, 1268–1968" and "The Text of Bracton's *De Legibus Angliae*," in *Essays in English Legal History* (London: Hambledon Press, 1985), 75–92 and 93–110.

[36] J. C. Holt, *Magna Carta* (Cambridge: Cambridge University Press, 1992), 179.

tained at the turn of the century, redressed a widespread perception that litigants were having to chase the itinerant king about the country in the pursuit of justice.[37] Clause eighteen was concerned explicitly with conflicts between central and local jurisdiction:

> Recognizances of novel disseisin, mort d'ancestor, and darrein presentment shall not be held elsewhere than in the court of the county in which they occur [*non capiantur nisi in suis comitatibus*], and in this manner: we, or if we are out of the realm our chief justiciar, shall send two justices through each country four times a year who, with four knights of each county chosen by the county, shall hold the said assizes in the county court [*in comitatu*] on the day and in the place of meeting of the county court.[38]

This concern with localizing such trials *in comitatu* was a sign of something much larger: a number of barons involved in the 1215 making of the charter worried (perhaps needlessly, though opinion is divided) about direct threats to the local jurisdictions of their seigneurial courts.[39] What does seem clear, at least for the early part of the century, is the extent to which local court officials—sheriffs, gaolers, and the like—sought to take financial advantage of the large number of excess cases that should have fallen under the exclusive jurisdiction of commissioned royal judges but often exceeded their capacity to manage.[40]

Even within the royal court system proper there transpired a great deal of self-reflection concerning the proper jurisdictional purview of the various courts directly under the king's control. George O. Sayles has called 1234 the "great year of legal reorganisation" in England, a year that saw the mandated closing of the London law schools and the first full-scale attempt to delineate the proper functions of the various civil courts. Sayles's paraphrase of the relevant legislation captures well the imperative flavor of this process of jurisdictional reordering:

> Let the "pleas of the crown" i.e. felonies and other criminal offences, continue to be investigated by means of local indictments and let them be adjudged locally and not centrally. Let the court at Westminster remain in existence as the "Common Bench" and have particular jurisdiction over real actions and personal actions of debt, detinue, covenant and account, in other words, the pleas that touched property rights and needed formal and unhurried procedure and could

---

[37] See Hudson, *Formation of the English Common Law*, 224.

[38] Edited and translated in Holt, *Magna Carta*, 456–57.

[39] Hudson, *Formation of the English Common Law*, 225. Such conflicts percolated down to the most local levels: clause 24 of Magna Carta prohibited sheriffs from trying crown pleas at shire courts, a common practice throughout the twelfth century; see Alan Harding, *Law Courts of Medieval England*, 73.

[40] Harding, *Law Courts of Medieval England*, 75.

be most conveniently heard in a sedentary court. Then let the king have a court of his own, the King's Bench, to accompany him as he traveled about the country with a special interest in his "private pleas."[41]

Though rarely leading to direct conflict, the "parallel jurisdiction" exercised by the Common Bench at Westminster and the (often) peripatetic King's Bench resulted in the unprecedented and—for many contemporaries—confusing coexistence of two central law courts duplicating each other's judicial labors.

Perhaps the truest jurisdictional crisis of the thirteenth century, however, concerned the proper relationship between secular law and ecclesiastical law. The two sprawling legal systems were constantly in tension during a century that began with a dispute between King John and Innocent III that resulted in a papal interdict upon England and the excommunication of its monarch.[42] Here again there were numerous areas of explicit jurisdictional conflict, ranging from the profound to the mundane. While the English church courts claimed the right to enforce contracts secured through an oath, for example, common law lawyers disagreed, arguing that such simple contracts were not enforceable against laypersons by the church.[43] Defamation became a particularly contentious area of struggle between secular and ecclesiastical courts in the latter part of the century; during the so-called *Scandalum magnatum* of 1275, the nobility sought to locate the jurisdiction of defamation cases—traditionally an ecclesiastical matter unless money was involved—in secular courts when "speakers of false words against great men" had the effect of causing "discord within the realm."[44] The matter of bastardy was open to constant jurisdictional contestation, involving as it did both secular law of land and inheritance and canonical definitions of marriage and legitimacy.[45]

---

[41] George O. Sayles, *The Court of King's Bench in Law and History*, Selden Society Lecture (London: Bernard Quaritch, 1959), 10.

[42] Although it would be wrong to see this as a struggle against the English church and its clergy per se, it was clearly part of a much wider Crown-church conflict that included issues such as taxation. See C. R. Cheney's essays, "King John and the Papal Interdict" and "King John's Reaction to the Interdict on England," collected in his *The Papacy and England, 12th–14th Centuries* (London: Variorum, 1982); the articles originally appeared in *Bulletin of the John Rylands Library* 31 (1948): 295–317 and *Transactions of the Royal Historical Society*, 4th ser., 31 (1949): 129–50. On the effects of John's earlier taxation of the clergy, see Cheney, "Levies on the English Clergy for the Poor and for the King, 1203," in his *The English Church and Its Laws, 12th–14th Centuries* (London: Variorum, 1982), which originally appeared in *English Historical Review* 96 (1981): 577–84.

[43] Richard Helmholz, *Canon Law and the Law of England* (London: Hambledon Press, 1987), 77–78; see also Pollock and Maitland, *History of English Law*, 2:201. The matter of coerced oaths was at the center of the church's initial condemnation of Magna Carta; see Cheney, "The Church and Magna Carta," collected in *The Papacy and England*, originally published in *Theology* 68 (1965): 266–72.

[44] Helmholz, *Select Cases on Defamation, to 1600* (London: Selden Society, 1985), xli ff.; the citation is from lxviii.

[45] Helmholz, *Canon Law and the Law of England*, 189.

So deep-seated was this ongoing jurisdictional struggle with the church that the secular courts invented their own peculiar mechanism for wrenching jurisdiction away from canon law courts. This was the Writ of Prohibition, a legal instrument designed to correct perceived jurisdictional overreaching by ecclesiastical judges. Its purpose, Richard Helmholz explains, was to "enforce, through the powerful self-interest of private litigants, the secular position on the proper jurisdictional boundaries between the courts of Church and State."[46] Bracton's description of the Writ of Prohibition describes the church's transgression of these boundaries as an almost treasonous usurpation ("iurisdictionem regis sibi usurpaverit"), in which a pleader is "made subject to another jurisdiction . . . against his will":

> When one is drawn in this way before an ecclesiastical judge [*iudice ecclesiastico*], who is unwilling to consider whether the jurisdiction is his but usurps the king's jurisdiction to himself, both offend, the judges who hold the plea and he who sues, [and thus], on the complaint of him who is thus drawn before one not his proper judge, let a writ of the lord king issue to the judges, forbidding them to proceed, and to him who sues, forbidding him to sue.[47]

Whereas older scholarship on the Writ of Prohibition maintained that its use in practice greatly favored the cause of secular justice, Helmholz has shown that the English church quickly became adept at formulating effective responses; indeed, "for every writ of prohibition or every threat of *praemunire* there was a counterbalancing sanction of excommunication to defend the Church's position."[48]

Of course, not all thirteenth-century jurisdictional discourse displays the contentiousness Helmholz finds in this particular area; it would be wrong to characterize the period simplistically as an era of crisis and confrontation between church and state, locality and nation, baron and king. There were numerous areas of law in which jurisdiction was clearly defined and only rarely a matter of debate, and the authority of certain courts over others was more often assumed as a matter of *ius* (right) than enforced as a matter of *lex* (law). Yet even in those areas in which jurisdiction seems to have been firmly settled, fierce disputes could often arise; in matters of marriage litigation, for example, conflicts between archdeacons, deans, canons, and bishops were by no means unusual. The thirteenth century was a period in which the episcopal courts began to wrest jurisdiction over marriage away from what one bishop's

[46] Ibid., 59.
[47] Henry Bracton, *De legibus et consuetidinibus Angliae (On the Laws and Customs of England)*, trans. Samuel E. Thorne (Cambridge: Belknap Press of Harvard University Press, 1968), fol. 402, 4:252–53.
[48] Helmholz, *Select Cases on Defamation*, 4.

partisan scorned as "simple priests or clerics having little or no experience in law" yet presiding as judges.[49]

Whatever the import of any particular legal issue, it seems clear that jurisdiction per se was one of the primary "meta-topics" of legal interest and anxiety throughout the thirteenth century. As I have already suggested, a recognition of the poet's deep awareness of jurisdiction as a contemporary legal problematic goes a long way toward explaining the variegated legal character of *The Owl and the Nightingale*. Yet I am emphatically *not* arguing that the poem's author was necessarily aware of the specific jurisdictional problems I have outlined; though he or she clearly had some level of familiarity with juridical protocols and terminology, we will continue to misconstrue the poem's unique legal imagination by aligning it with any specific contemporaneous legal procedure or institution. The poem will inevitably suffer by comparison; its failure to match up exactly with any given procedural practice will leave the impression that its knowledge of the law is confused, contradictory, and spotty, and that the poet was simply interpolating various legal tidbits for the purposes of humor, parody, or satire. The poem's modern editor, for example, argues that "the legal element seems incidental rather than central," a position he defends by repeating R. M. Wilson's observation that most of the legal vocabulary in the poem derives from Old English law rather than contemporaneous French.[50] Michael Witt similarly characterizes such terms as mere "legal trappings" that are "unessential," arguing that the poet "does not include within the debate legal elements which one might reasonably expect to find were he closely mirroring court procedure."[51] Yet this is precisely the point. In deploying an array of such familiar terms, the poem mines the legal vein of the mother tongue both to consolidate its own authority as a vernacular poem and, perhaps, to proclaim the right of its disputants to argue their cases in English.

Liturgical Jurisdictions

As I have already suggested, the legal lexicon of *The Owl and the Nightingale* is in need of a thorough reexamination, perhaps of the sort Alford has given us in his glossarial work on *Piers Plowman*.[52] I turn in the remainder of this essay to a particularly rich dimension of the poem's legality, one that reveals the culturally productive nature of law alongside another institutionally sanc-

---

[49] Richard Helmholz, *Marriage Litigation in Medieval England* (London: Cambridge University Press, 1974), 144; see the relevant discussions in Coleman, "The *Owl and the Nightingale* and Papal Theories of Marriage."
[50] See Stanley's introduction in *The Owl and the Nightingale*, 28.
[51] Witt, "The *Owl and the Nightingale* and English Law Court Procedure," 290, 287.
[52] Alford, *"Piers Plowman": A Glossary of Legal Diction*.

tioned and jurisdictionally regulated mode of discursive performance. Articulating one of her many disagreements with the Owl, the Nightingale echoes the opening lines of the poem by foregrounding the legal status of her poetic "tale":

> "Nay, nay," sede þe Niȝtingale,
> "þu shalt ihere an oþer tale.
> ȝet nis þos speche ibroȝt to dome.
> Ac bo wel stille & lust nu to me!
> Ich shal mid one bare worde
> Do þat þi speche wrþ forworþe."
> (543–48)

No, you will hear a counterplea ("an oþer tale"), the Nightingale protests, for our case is not yet brought to judgment ("dome"); with a "bare word" I will render your own legal speech "forworþe," that is, feeble or useless. Here the poet is translating from French (perhaps technical law French, perhaps simply Anglo-Norman) the term *nude parole*, denoting a plaintiff's statement that is unsupported by witnesses and thus obviates the need for the defendant's reply. The Nightingale is seeking to predetermine the rhetorical force of her next "speche," admitting its lack of external authority while suggesting that this very lack is what will lend it legal weight: it will be so powerful, so self-evident, and so indisputable that the Owl will be not only precluded from but incapable of responding. "*Dome*" here carries a symbolic legal weight that hardly needs addressing, resonating as it does with a long history of jurisdictional claims dating back to *Domesday Book*. When the Nightingale protests that her own "speche" has not yet been brought to "dome," and that "an oþere tale" must be heard by her rival before such a "dome" can take place, the poet is also making an implicit argument to his or her audience regarding the continuing viability of the longer "tale" and "speche" that *is* the poem— perhaps guarding against an unnecessarily harsh literary "dome" on this audience's part.

Just twenty lines later, however, the Owl parries with a bit of proverbial wisdom that inverts the legal logic of the Nightingale's *nude parole* by exposing it for what she believes it is: an insubstantial rhetorical performance with no more judicial integrity than a song:

> Alured sede, þat was wis—
> He miȝte wel, for soþ hit is:
> "Nis no man for is bare songe
> Lof [praised] ne wrþ [honored] noȝt suþe [very] longe;
> Vor þat is a forworþe man
> þat bute singe noȝt ne can."
> (569–574)

No man should be valued for his "bare songe" alone, the Owl contends; he is a useless man who can but sing. The Alfredian proverb reverses the specific legal imagery articulated by the Nightingale in the previous passage. The Owl has effectively deployed the Nightingale's own legalism against itself: if, for the Nightingale, *nude parole* renders her opponent's reply needless, for the Owl "bare songe," song without substance and as an act in and of itself, is inadequate as an argumentative strategy; the Nightingale's "bare word" is on its face "bare song," musical sonority with nothing underneath. The passage directly recalls a similar analogy from the opening of the poem: "& hure & hure of oþere[s] songe / Hi holde plaiding suþe stronge" (11–12). In this, the first explicit observation about the actual content of the birds' debate, the narrator casts "songe" itself as both the matter and the means of their legal "speche." The passage could be translated one of two ways: "they held especially fierce oral arguments *about* or *concerning* each other's song," or, alternatively, "they held especially fierce oral arguments *by means of* each other's song." Performances of song and legal pleading coalesce into a single musico-juridical spectacle, one in which the tenor and vehicle of the poem's central metaphorical strategy become indistinguishable.

Taken together, these passages begin to reveal the common ground between legal and musical utterance, "bare worde" and "bare songe," "plaiding" and "songe." They attest to the poem's wider attempt to mold the language of jurisdiction into a mode of vernacular legality capable of embracing seemingly distinct discursive formations: poetry, of course, but also the musical performance of the liturgy. Throughout *The Owl and the Nightingale*, liturgical and quasi-liturgical musics are subjected to a searching legal examination in which the institutional constraints of musical culture impose often strict limits on musical genres and performers.

Although the poem is clearly concerned with music's moral and ethical implications, the birds themselves seem equally obsessed with its jurisdiction: the controlling legal authority that determines where music should be performed, by whom, under what circumstances, at what times of the day and year, and so on. Legal and liturgical jurisdiction are often intimately conjoined; thus, when the Nightingale threatens the Owl with a religious curse— "God Almiȝti wrþe him wroþ, / An al þat werieþ linnene cloþ!" (1173–74)— the Owl responds by pointing out that the Nightingale has exceeded both her legal authority and her liturgical jurisdiction:

"Wat!" quaþ ho, "hartu ihoded,
Oþer þu kursest al unihoded?
For prestes wike, ich wat, þu dest;
Ich not ȝef þu were ȝaure prest,
Ich not ȝef þu canst masse singe:
Inoh þu canst of mansinge."
(1177–82)

The Nightingale's (apparent) lack of ordination—she is "unihoded"—denies her the canonical authority to "kurse" and engage in "mansinge" (excommunication) just as it prevents her from singing "masse."

Musical jurisdiction in the poem is as much a matter of physical location as it is a sign of institutional prerogative. Approximately midway through the poem, after cataloguing the moral and spiritual failings of her opponent's song, the Owl points to its severely restricted geographical reach:

> Al þat þu singst is of golnesse [lasciviousness],
> For nis on þe non holinesse;
> Ne wened [expected] na man for þi pipinge
> þat eni preost in chircce singe.
> ȝet I þe wulle an oder segge [opinion, statement],
> ȝif þu hit const ariht bilegge [interpret];
> Wi nultu singe an oder þeode [country]
> þar hit is muchele more neode?
> þu neauer ne singst in Irlonde,
> Ne þu ne cumest noȝt in Scotlonde.
> Hwi nultu fare to Noreweie,
> An singin men of Galeweie,
> þar beoð men þat lutel kunne
> Of songe þat is bineoðe þe sunne?
> (899–912)

Although the Owl's initial polemic against her opponent's song is a morally inflected one (she brands it as full of "golnesse," or lasciviousness), she soon begins to question this music's regional domain, wondering why the strains of the Nightingale's song do not reach into "oder þeode," or other lands: Ireland, Scotland, Norway, Galloway. That this is a specifically jurisdictional claim becomes clear when the passage is read alongside a description at the end of the poem concerning the judicial authority of Master Nicholas of Guildford, who is proposed as the best possible judge of the birds' debate. As the Wren claims, Nicholas

> . . . wuneþ [dwells] at Porteshom,
> At one tune [town] ine Dorsete,
> Bi þare see in ore utlete.
> þar he demeþ manie riȝte dom,
> An diht & writ mani wisdom,
> An þurh his muþe [mouth] & þurh his honde
> Hit is þe betere into Scotlonde.
> (1752–58)

Through his mouth and hand, that is, Nicholas exercises the sweepingly national power of his own legal jurisdiction, extending his judicial reach even as far north as Scotland—the second in the list of northern placenames evoked by the Owl against the musical jurisdiction of the Nightingale. This is a provocatively hyperbolic description of the power of a nonroyal judge, whether ecclesiastical or secular; rather than pointing out that no "real" judge other than the pope or the king could have wielded such influence in the thirteenth century, we would do better to consider the precise source of Nicholas's judicial authority and prestige.[53] According to the poem's disputants themselves, this authority derives primarily from the profundity of his musical knowledge.

Thus, after quelling the Owl's desire to settle the question through a violent trial by combat duel as the dispute gets under way, the Nightingale proposes that the birds take their musical dispute to Nicholas and allow him to determine through his musical "insiʒt" the outcome of their case:

> þo quaþ þe Hule [Owl], "Wu schal us seme,
> þat kunne & wille riʒt us deme?"
> "Ich wot wel," quaþ þe Niʒtingale,
> "Ne þaref þarof bo no tale:
> Maister Nichole of Guldeforde.
> He is wis an war of worde.
> He is of dome suþe gleu [skillful],
> & him is loþ eurich unþeu.
> He wot insiʒt in eche song,
> Wo singet wel, wo singet wronge;
> & he can schede [divide] vrom þe riʒte
> þat woʒe, þat þuster [darkness] from þe liʒte."
> (187–98)

Here Nicholas is singled out for the conventional judicial qualities of wisdom, truth, and circumspection, qualities that Bracton, for one, deems indispensable to any man who would preside on any bench. But Nicholas also "wot insiʒt in eche song," or "has profound insight into various kinds of song"; the poet defines his judicial knowledge precisely by means of his musical tastes, which will largely determine the overall content of the debate as the poem progresses.

Nor is Nicholas of Guildford the only "musical judge" proposed in the poem. Responding to one of the Owl's polemics against her musical lasciviousness, the Nightingale seems for a moment to take back her suggestion that Nicholas judge the debate, proposing instead that the birds take their case to the geographical center of canon law:

---

[53] Compare Stanley's translation of these lines: "And through what he says and what he writes things are the better as far as Scotland." If we take "dom" and "wisdom" as secondary antecedents of "Hit," however, the passage presents Nicholas's legal judgment as much more acute.

Ich warni men to here gode
þat hi bon bliþe on hore mode,
An bidde þat hi moten iseche
þan ilke song þat euer is eche,
Nu þu miȝt, Hule, sitte & clinge;
Heramong nis no chateringe;
Ich graunti þat we go to dome
Tofore þe sulfe þe Pope of Rome.
Ac abid, ȝete noþeles
þu shalt ihere an oþer þes.
Ne shaltu, for Engelonde,
At þisse worde me astonde.
Wi atuitestu me mine unstrengþe
An mine ungrete & mine unlengþe,
An seist þat ich nam noȝt strong
Vor ich nam noþer gret ne long?
(739–54)

It has been argued more than once that Nicholas is an official of the ecclesi-astical court, and that the proposal to "go to dome," or judgment, in Rome is thus evidence for the poem's primarily canonical legal framework.[54] Yet it seems to me that the passage is meant to signal a direct jurisdictional conflict between canon law and common law, between the sacred jurisdiction of the ecclesiastical courts and the earthly jurisdiction of the secular courts. Alexan-dra Barratt and others have pointed out that the poem recalls "elements of both canon- and common-law procedure,"[55] and as we have seen, the amalga-mated legal vocabulary throughout consists much more of Anglo-Saxonisms than it does of words drawn from either the French or Latin juridical lexi-cons.

It is surely no mistake that the sharp imperative break in this passage—"Ac abid, ȝet noþeles / þu shalt ihere an oþer þes. / Ne shaltu, for Engelonde, / At þisse worde me astonde"—is simultaneously a geographical break. The inter-jection directs both the reader's attention and the two disputants away from the "Pope of Rome" and toward their native "Engelonde," a word that ap-pears here for the first and only time in the poem. On one level, the break registers what Thomas Hahn has suggested are the overlooked nationalistic dimensions of *The Owl and the Nightingale*, its concern with its native affilia-tions as a vernacular production in an age of increasing national self-con-sciousness.[56] Yet I think the phrase also functions as a kind of poetic Writ of

---

[54] See in particular Coleman, "The *Owl and the Nightingale* and Papal Views on Marriage."

[55] Alexandra Barratt, "Flying in the Face of Tradition: A New View of *The Owl and the Nightin-gale*," *University of Toronto Quarterly* 56 (1987): 473.

[56] Hahn, "Early Middle English," 77; see also the comments in Thorlac Turville-Petre, *En-gland the Nation: Language, Literature, and National Identity, 1290–1340* (Oxford: Clarendon Press, 1996), 184–85.

Prohibition, as it were. Like the Writ, which sought to establish a secular jurisdiction by foreclosing the church's right to decide certain cases, the Nightingale's demand firmly roots the poem's own "case" in native soil. Even as the Nightingale appears to be proposing a legal appeal to the highest ecclesiastical authority, she herself demands that the disputants "abid" in "Engelonde," where the poem's own jurisdiction will remain up for grabs.

Liturgical Cultures and the Spirit of Regulation

The jurisdictional dispute at the heart of *The Owl and the Nightingale* never emerges as an explicit topic of debate. Nevertheless, while the avian squabbling over whose song is superior may seem far removed from the public jurisdictional crises obtaining in thirteenth-century legal culture, the liturgy and its music provide an ideally homologous discourse for exploring the nature of jurisdiction. We have already seen that many of the poem's most densely legalistic passages center on the musical proclivities of the two birds and even the musicality of proposed judges, so much so that music and law at certain moments seem almost indistinguishable.

This intermingling of musical and legal vocabularies might strike a twentieth-century audience as idiosyncratic (if not bizarre), but it was far from uncommon in medieval writings of vastly different periods and genres. As I have argued at length elsewhere, liturgy and legal performance were often imagined as analogous forms of public discourse and modes of enacted authority.[57] The title of a fourteenth-century Italian music treatise, *Ars cantus mensurabilis mensurata per modos iuris*, or *The Art of Mensurable Song Measured According to the Rules of Law*, announces its author's acknowledgment that musical performance can in fact be "measured" or regulated by law, a contention borne out in the treatise through repeated applications of legal formulae to musical phenomena. The Middle English poems *Piers Plowman*, *Mum and the Sothsegger*, and "De veritate et consciencia" all seem interested in the performative fallibility of legal pleaders and liturgical performers, both of which groups are susceptible to constant deviations from the norms and protocols of public utterance. Liturgy and law both embody divine authority while depending absolutely on the performative acts of human agents: men of law must enact the law just as clerics must enact the liturgy, and the earthly behaviors of both groups are a matter of constant anxiety and, in some cases, explicit regulation.

It should come as no surprise that *The Owl and the Nightingale*'s most searching treatment of jurisdiction takes the form of a sonorous conflict between what initially look like sacred and secular musics. The sober, plainchanting

---

[57] Bruce Holsinger, "Langland's Musical Reader: Liturgy, Law, and the Constraints of Performance," *Studies in the Age of Chaucer* 21 (1999): 99–141. The groundbreaking work on this analogy can be found in Jody Enders, *Rhetoric and the Origins of Medieval Drama* (Ithaca: Cornell University Press, 1992).

Owl seems to be contending with the desirous and ostensibly "secular" musical voice of the Nightingale, an assumption that has become practically a given in critical commentary on the role of music in the poem.[58] (Christopher Page, for example, hears the Owl's musicality sounding "the deepest notes of Christian spirituality," while the Nightingale is "a courtly creature" whose ebullient music has most in common with the songs of the troubadours and *trouvères*.)[59] Yet this supposedly strict divide between sacred and secular musics, between the "highly varied" music of the lyric and the "Gregorian" sobriety and uniformity of religious chant, was never as firm as its defenders supposed. Like that of law itself, the sacred and secular jurisdiction of liturgical music was regularly contested from the twelfth through the fourteenth centuries. The motet, for example, which exploded onto the musical scene in Paris in the late twelfth and early thirteenth centuries, blurs the boundaries between Latin and vernacular, liturgical and secular, and sacred and profane to such an extent that these boundaries themselves become practically meaningless in manuscript and performance.[60] From John of Salisbury's famous rant in the *Policraticus* against liturgical singers who attempt "to feminize all their spellbound little fans with the girlish way they render the notes and end the phrases," to Roger Bacon's complaint that liturgical chant has lapsed into a "shameless flaccidity" that "counterfeits in falsetto the sacred and manly harmony almost everywhere throughout the Church," to Pope John XXII's worry over a "dangerous element being introduced [into Latin liturgical music] by singing in the vernacular," ecclesiastical writers and lawmakers consistently worried that the liturgy was crossing boundaries between the sacred and the profane, the ecclesiastical and the secular, the masculine and the feminine.[61]

In *The Owl and the Nightingale*, this musical category confusion is registered in the perplexing musical affiliations of the two birds, neither of whom,

---

[58] In the words of R. L. Greene, "The question at issue is the struggle between the simpler type of music of the earlier Gregorian and pre-Gregorian music and the later type of highly varied secular music full of trills and runs such as was used by the troubadours" ("*The Owl and the Nightingale* and the 'Good Man from Rome,'" *English Language Notes* 4 [1966]: 3). The musicological context for Greene's observation is a sound one: the twelfth and thirteenth centuries were an age of intensive debate over the proper role of music in worship; fierce and often sexually charged polemics were launched from all sides condemning what various writers saw as the feminization, secularization, vernacularization, and overall moral corruption of the chant. Janet Coleman has gone so far as to align the Owl with the musical and liturgical conservatism of the twelfth-century Cistercians, arguing that she "is defending a briefer liturgy and one which replaced the Cluniac *laus perennis* with a much reduced hymnal" ("The *Owl and the Nightingale* and Papal Theories of Marriage," 550).

[59] Christopher Page, *The Owl and the Nightingale: Musical Life and Ideas in France, 1100–1300* (Berkeley: University of California Press, 1989), 3–4.

[60] See the study by Sylvia Huot, *Allegorical Play in the Old French Motet: The Sacred and the Profane in Thirteenth-Century Polyphony* (Stanford: Stanford University Press, 1997).

[61] Many of these passages have been discussed in a different context by William Dalglish, "The Origins of the Hocket," *Journal of the American Musicological Society* 31 (1978): 3–20. I have discussed these passages in detail in chapter 4 of *Music, Body, and Desire in Medieval Culture: Hildegard of Bingen to Chaucer* (Stanford: Stanford University Press, 2001).

as Barratt has pointed out, can be labeled as securely "sacred" or "secular."[62] Indeed, it is more accurate to say that the birds are deliberately confusing these musical categories even while pretending to uphold them. Just before making her momentary gesture toward ecclesiastical jurisdiction, the supposedly troubadour-like Nightingale locates her own musical labors squarely within liturgical culture, protesting that her musical facility extends well beyond singing "in sumere tide, / An bring[ing] blisse for & wide":

> Clerkes, munekes [monks] & kanunes [canons],
> þar boþ þos gode wicketunes,
> Ariseþ up to midelniȝte
> An singeþ of þe houene liȝte,
> An prostes upe londe singeþ
> Wane þe liȝt of daie springeþ.
> An ich hom helpe wat i mai:
> Ich singe mid hom niȝt & dai;
> An ho boþ alle for me þe gladdere
> An to þe songe boþ þe raddere.
> (729–38)

Clerks, monks, canons, secular clergy: the Nightingale's melodious labors are inextricable from the liturgical labors of various clerical cultures. The *opus Dei* demands singing "niȝt & dai" in a quotidian cycle of musical work, and the Nightingale—despite her tendency to sing outside privies and instigate adultery through her music—credits herself with energizing the liturgical *opus* of the English clergy.

Nor, conversely, is the Owl's musical jurisdiction limited to the cloister, as she makes clear while defending her preference for the winter season. During Christmastime, she claims, she aids "ech god man," regardless of social or ecclesiastical station, when he

> . . . his frond icnowe
> An blisse mid hom sume þrowe
> In his huse, at his borde,
> Mid faire speche & faire worde.
> & hure & hure to Cristes masse,
> þane riche & poure, more & lasse,
> Singeþ cundut niȝt & dai,
> Ich hom helpe what ich mai.
> (477–84)

---

[62] Barratt, "Flying in the Face of Tradition."

"Singeþ *cundut* night & day": as she voices this boastful paean to her own musical endurance, the Owl simultaneously coins the first recorded English usage of the word *cundut*, which translates the Latin *conductus*. This word, first employed specifically as a musical term in Latin sources in twelfth-century Aquitaine, refers to a musical genre that seems initially to have been intended as a processional chant perhaps accompanying the reader to the lectern, though its subsequent functions are far from clear.

The *conductus* first reached England on a wide scale in the first half of the thirteenth century, owing in part to the transmission of liturgical polyphony from the Cathedral of Notre Dame in Paris. Although literary scholars will be mostly unfamiliar with this history, musicologists have generally regarded the Notre Dame school as perhaps the most important engine of musical innovation in the later Middle Ages, giving rise as it did to the rhythmic modes and new polyphonic genres such as the motet. The legacy of Notre Dame to England is a confused one, however, and Nicky Losseff has suggested that much of what scholars have traditionally called the "Notre Dame *conductus*" repertory should actually be identified as the "northern European *conductus*" repertory—a distinction that has important bearing on specifically English contributions to the extant repertory.[63] The surviving *conductus* repertory in the British Isles begins with the so-called W¹ manuscript, Wolfenbüttel, Herzog-August-Bibliothek, MS Helmstadt 628, which was copied for the St. Andrews Cathedral priory in Scotland sometime after 1230 and represents one of the most important sources for the so-called *Magnus liber organum* first compiled in Paris. The manuscript represents both the influence of the Notre Dame school on liturgical polyphony in England and, as Losseff has argued, an indigenous polyphonic tradition emerging in the first half of the thirteenth century—the years when *The Owl and the Nightingale* was likely written.

W¹ contains dozens of *conductus* texts with their musical settings, providing intriguing thirteenth-century evidence of just the sort of composition the poet must have had in mind while penning the Owl's claim to "singeþ cundut." As Frank Lloyd Harrison showed long ago, one original liturgical function for the English *conductus* was as a substitute for the *Benedicamus Domino* in the Office on given feast days. In the course of the thirteenth century, however, the use of the *conductus* was extended to extraliturgical functions and even, Harrison notes, to thoroughly secular contexts and spaces.[64]

A brief look at two *conductus* texts from the ninth fascicle of W¹ will illustrate what musicologists agree is the bewildering range of thematic material treated in these songs. "Ex creata non creatus" celebrates the Virgin Birth, the stupefactions of Law and Reason that resulted when God became Man in the womb of the Virgin:

[63] Nicky Losseff, *The Best Concords: Polyphonic Music in Thirteenth-Century Britain* (New York: Garland, 1994), esp. 11–12.

[64] Frank Lloyd Harrison, *Music in Medieval Britain* (London: Routledge and Kegan Paul, 1958), 126.

Ex creata non creatus
Nasci nobis est dignatus
Qui pro nobis humanatus
Nate tulit esse natus,
Formam indutus huminis,
Sed salvo iure numinis,
Ut sic per partum virginis
Veteris posset criminis
Dilui reatus.

Not created from her created,
He is worthy to be born for us,
Who made human for us
Yielded to woman-born to be born,
Taking on the form of man,
Yet by the unshaken law of divine will,
That so by a virgin giving birth,
From ancient sins a sinner
Might be thoroughly cleansed.[65]

The poem explores the paradoxes of the Incarnation through the sorts of Neoplatonic oppositions between the human and the divine favored by twelfth- and thirteenth-century theologians. On the facing recto in W[1], however, was copied "Pange melos lacrimosum," an elegy commemorating the death by drowning of Emperor Frederick Barbarossa in 1190. The third stanza imparts a truly pagan flavor to the ruler's passing, offering analogies between the mourning of the empire and the personal sorrows of Athena and Mars at the loss of their human heroes:

Omnis tellus admiretur
Triste nubis pallium,
Sed sub nocte lamentetur
Rheni supercilium,
Omnis virtus fundat fletus,
Pallas plorat Nestorem,
Vatem plangat vatum cetus,
Lugeat Mars Hectorem.

Let the whole world wonder at
The sad cloak of night,
Yet 'neath cover of night be mourned
The cynosure of the Rhine;
Let all virtue shed tears:
Let Pallas bewail Nestor,

---

[65] "Ex creata non creatus," ll. 1–9, ed. and trans. Gordon Anderson, in *Notre Dame and Related Conductus* (Henryville, Ottowa: Institute of Medieval Music, 1982), 4:xv.

> Their prophet the company of prophets,
> And let Mars weep for Hector.[66]

Other *conductus* texts in the same gathering condemn the practices of usury and simony among the clergy, praise local saints and secular lords, or, as in "Ex creata," offer theological conundrums for devotional contemplation.

When the Owl claims to be helping Christmas celebrants "singeþ cundut niȝt & dai," then, she is invoking the musical genre whose own liturgical jurisdiction is perhaps the most obscure and contested in thirteenth-century England. Composed to mourn a drowned emperor or praise the Virgin Birth, collected in liturgical fascicles of *Benedicamus* substitutes, and sung in the dining halls of English aristocrats, the *conductus* represents the ideal liturgical (or better, perhaps, "paraliturgical") genre for exploring the problem of musical jurisdiction. The *conductus* itself was already pressuring liturgical boundaries in its first century of musical existence; the poet of *The Owl and the Nightingale* seems intent on featuring this jurisdictional ambivalence by making what may have been its first written appearance in the English vernacular the responsibility of the dour Owl, who performs a liturgical English even as she herself exposes the extraliturgical functions of a contested musical genre.

As the poem closes, the birds set out to take their case to Master Nicholas at Portisham, a small coastal village "Bi þare see" in Dorset. *The Owl and the Nightingale* concludes with its avian litigators perched on the boundaries of England, across the channel from the Norman territory the kingdom had lost after the turn of the century. Yet the poem directs its institutional gaze not outward to the Continent, but inward, at the new jurisdictional opportunities and dangers afforded by over a century of legal and liturgical change in the wake of the Norman Conquest. Forging its complex vision of music and law in the vernacular, indeed singing its own impressive case "for Engelonde," the poem insists on nothing less than legal and liturgical Englishness itself. The self-consciously insular law of the nation, the *legibus et consuetudinibus angliae* postulated in Bracton's title and elaborated in his treatise, here receives its first and surely its most unusual musical setting.

Jurisdiction is, by any measure, an unwieldy dimension of cultural practice, capable of encompassing an array of institutional and social disputes within the embrace of an overarching legal category. That legal jurisdiction provides a useful and illuminating lens on liturgical and literary discourse in *The Owl and the Nightingale* demonstrates the extraordinary malleability of the category itself. The poem adapts jurisdiction so seamlessly to its expressive needs that it leaves the modern student of law and literature wondering whether jurisdiction might be as naturally suited to liturgy as to the law.

We can begin to appreciate the ingenuity and even the expressive freedom

---

[66] "Pange melos lacrimosum," ll. 17–24, ibid., xvi.

of this work's legal vernacularity by juxtaposing it with subsequent confrontations between vernacular writing and legal jurisdiction. Later centuries in England, and in particular the Ricardian and Lancastrian periods, witness the construction of what I would suggest is a more explicitly regulatory relationship between the two domains. In a remarkable but rarely discussed passage near the beginning of Chaucer's *Friar's Tale*, the narrator pauses to defend the succeeding story as a direct affront to the juridical authority of the Summoner, who works as an official in the court of an overreaching archdeacon:

> For thogh this Somonour wood were as an hare,
> To telle his harlotrye I wol nat spare;
> For we been out of his correccioun.
> They han of us no jurisdiccioun,
> Ne nevere shullen, terme of alle hir lyves.
> (3.1327–31)

Notwithstanding its lighthearted invocation of the frame narrative's game of "quiting," the passage suggests fairly directly that the archdeacon's lack of ecclesiastical jurisdiction over friars in general is a primary motivation for the Friar's storytelling. Presumably, if the Summoner's archdeacon *did* in fact have jurisdiction over the fraternal orders, the Friar could *not* tell his story— or would not risk doing so under the threat of a legal summons to the court. The *Friar's Tale* thus presents itself as a lucky exception to the Summoner's jurisdictional authority: only a friar (or a prostitute: " 'Peter! So been wommen of the styves,' / Quod the Somonour, 'yput out of oure cure!' " [1332–33]) will be capable of eluding ecclesiastical censorship or sanction and successfully telling the tale that follows. The passage is a harbinger of the more direct threat to the vernacular expression of religiously controversial ideas realized shortly after the turn of the century.

Here, of course, I refer to the unprecedented prohibitions on religious expression entailed by Archbishop Thomas Arundel's Constitutions of 1409. As Nicholas Watson has shown in an influential study, this notorious piece of legislation had a drastic effect on the content and circulation of vernacular theological writings well into the middle of the fifteenth century.[67] Yet Arundel's Constitutions should also be understood in part as an exercise in literary jurisdiction. The language of approval, authorization, restriction, inspection, prohibition, and examination that predominates in many articles of the Constitutions makes it very clear that the legislation sought to expand the legal jurisdiction of the archbishop of Canterbury directly into new institutional and private domains. In terms of both its implicit aims and its apparent effects vis-à-vis vernacular religious writing in England, the legislation extended the authority of the church into areas of literary "making" over which the eccle-

---

[67] Watson, "Censorship and Cultural Change in Late-Medieval England."

siastical courts previously had had little or no direct say. The Constitutions were in effect a jurisdictional experiment with seemingly devastating results for insular literary production.

In this sense, the legislation speaks to what may be a less malleable relationship between vernacular literature and legal jurisdiction than that characterizing the thirteenth century. As other essays in this volume reveal (at least as I read them), English writing in the vernacular shows an increasing consciousness of the status of law as a discrete locus of executive and legislative power over the course of the thirteenth and fourteenth centuries. Thus, Emily Steiner shows that certain Lollard defendants consciously contest the jurisdictional privilege of written record in their documentary appropriations, while Maura Nolan suggests that Chaucer's awareness of the elasticity of legal discourse as it is appropriated into the vernacular is accompanied by a cautious stance toward the official jurisdiction of written law. *The Owl and the Nightingale*, by contrast, was written during an era when many forms of practical and institutional jurisdiction were either unsettled or directly contested *within* official legal culture—and thus perhaps more open to literary experimentation (or at least to experimentation of a different kind). The vernacular-legal relations traced in this collection are part of a process, in other words, one in which thirteenth-century texts played as crucial a role as the much later (and probably more familiar) writings treated in other chapters. In an age of simultaneous legal and literary innovation like the 1200s, the vernacular becomes a mode of legal engagement capable of transforming jurisdiction as a field of knowledge rather than simply reacting to its specified existence. Far from cowering in the face of jurisdictional overreaching by a paranoid church, parliament, or Crown, *The Owl and the Nightingale* seizes on jurisdiction as a creative opportunity for legal, literary, and musical invention. This is perhaps the poem's most remarkable contribution to the idea of the vernacular.[68]

[68] I refer here to the groundbreaking anthology edited by Ruth Evans et al., *The Idea of the Vernacular: An Anthology of Middle English Literary Theory, 1280–1520* (University Park: Pennsylvania State University Press, 1999), which offers a compelling vision of the forms of vernacular self-consciousness that immediately succeeded early Middle English writings such as *The Owl and the Nightingale*.

8 Inventing Legality

Documentary Culture and Lollard Preaching

EMILY STEINER

Just around 1350 a strange literary form appeared on the English scene: the fictive legal document, a lyric or prose tract in the form of a charter or last will and testament. Fictive documents are perhaps best described as apocryphal retellings of Christ's life through the tropes of affective piety, and as such they may seem at first to be conventional to the point of inconsequence. In the widely circulated poems called the *Long* and *Short Charters*, for example, Christ reads aloud a charter of heavenly bliss, which is bloodily inscribed upon his crucified body ("Wite ye þat are and schal be-tyde / þat Jhesu crist wiþ blodi syde / . . . Wiþ my chartre here present / I make nou a confirmament," etc.), and then further expands the charter motif to dramatize major gospel and post-Crucifixion events.[1] The Incarnation, for example, is the initial "sesyng" or formal occupation of heaven, the Crucifixion is the drawing up of the charter on Christ's flesh, the seals are the persons of the Trinity or the stages of penance, the Harrowing of Hell is the renegotiation of the devil's covenant, and the Eucharist is the indentured copy of the charter left in the priest's hands. The charter itself, the centerpiece of the poem, grants heaven in exchange for a rent of absolute penance (love of God and neighbor). The *Long* and *Short Charters*, surviving in over forty-five manuscripts, were copied continuously until the beginning of the sixteenth century, and, by the end of the fourteenth century, had generated a popular vernacular tract called the "Charter of Heaven," one of the fourteen religious

---

[1] Frederick J. Furnivall and Carl Horstmann, eds., *The Minor Poems of the Vernon Manuscript*, vol. 2 EETS OS 117 (London: K. Paul, Trench, Trübner & Co., 1892–1901), 644–45, ll. 93–97.

tracts compiled in *Pore Caitif*, and surviving in forty-seven out of fifty-six manuscripts containing full texts or extracts from the collection.[2]

This literary phenomenon is not entirely surprising, emerging as it did during a period in which justice was increasingly centered on the written record (conveyances of property, bonds of debt) and in which the royal bureaucracy and some personal bonds (wills, letters of retaining) were verging on vernacularization.[3] But we might further understand fictive documents not simply as a prescient moment in the history of the English language, but also as the point of intersection between what Nicholas Watson has so influentially called "vernacular theology," and what Bruce Holsinger calls in this volume "vernacular legality," the point at which the stuff of documentary culture (charters, seals, coffers) and its agents (grantors, notaries, witnesses) were being translated into the rhetoric and ideologies of popular piety.[4] To be sure, medievalists have long regarded legal documents as sites of Latinate bureaucratic corruption and as instruments of repression and insurrection, especially in regard to the events of 1381; influential studies by Susan Crane, Steven Justice, and Richard Firth Green have delineated, in very different ways, the contentious political and juridical space that documents occupied in late medieval England.[5] And in this sense, the fictive document might seem to be a deeply conservative literary genre, one that transmits religious or political orthodoxy by means of an oppressive textual apparatus. But, as the *Charters of Christ* literature suggests, documentary culture, when translated into the vernacular, provided an "intergeneric" framework that might be stretched to accommodate an astonishing variety of religious and political agendas. To this end, fictive documents reveal some important features of Lollard polemic as well. Namely, as I argue in this essay, late medieval preachers and polemicists used documents, both fictive and real, to challenge orthodox notions of textual authority and to produce an oppositional rhetoric. First, patently heterodox sermon writers borrowed the image of Christ's charter to contest the legitimacy of indulgences and letters of fraternity, and to describe what would come to be identified as a Lollard ideal of spiritual and textual community. Second, accused heretics on trial also invoked the rhetoric of legal documents

[2] Valerie Lagorio and Michael Sargent, "Bibliography: English Mystical Writings," in *A Manual of the Writings in Middle English, 1050–1500*, vol. 9 (New Haven: Connecticut Academy of Arts and Sciences, 1967), 3470–71.

[3] See Michael Clanchy, *From Memory to Written Record: England, 1066–1307*, 2nd ed. (Cambridge: Blackwell, 1993), 49–52, 200; and Richard Firth Green, *A Crisis of Truth: Literature and Law in Ricardian England* (Philadelphia: University of Pennsylvania Press, 1999), 38–39 and throughout.

[4] Nicholas Watson, "Censorship and Cultural Change in Late-Medieval England: Vernacular Theology, the Oxford Translation Debate, and Arundel's Constitutions of 1409," *Speculum* 70 (1995): 822–64.

[5] Susan Crane, "The Writing Lesson of 1381," in *Chaucer's England: Literature in Historical Context*, ed. Barbara Hanawalt (Minneapolis: University of Minnesota Press, 1992), 201–21; Steven Justice, *Writing and Rebellion: England in 1381* (Berkeley: University of California Press, 1994); Green, *Crisis of Truth*.

to redeem Lollard polemic from the trial documents of the institutional church. In short, legal documents came to represent for all sorts of medieval readers and writers, not simply the excesses of ecclesiastical bureaucracies and royal courts but the very relations of textuality. Or to put it another way, late medieval documentary culture offered a set of tropes to discuss the rhetorical, evidentiary, and foundational claims of official texts—tropes that in certain hands might be used to rewrite or reframe documentary culture itself.

Heterodox Polemics and Christ's Charter

The challenge of Lollardy was twofold: the redefinition of the Church as the community of the predestined elect, and the reorganization of spiritual community around an original text, Scripture, to the devaluation of other texts, practices, and authorities. Consequently, writers sympathetic to Lollard positions were often hostile to legal documents, particularly those issued by ecclesiastical bureaucracies, first, because such documents created "closed" and elitist spiritual communities, as opposed to the "open" community of the predestined elect; and second, because they usurped the authority of Christ and Scripture. For example, one of the most common, if not the most theologically relevant, objections to pardons and to letters of fraternity was that they were exclusive and thus uncharitable: by selling spiritual benefits for material gain, the clergy excluded the meritorious poor. The Lollard speaker in *Jack Upland*, for example, upbraids Friar Daw for withholding letters of fraternity from poor men: "Frere, what charite is þis . . . to suche riche men geve letters of fraternite confirmed by youre generall sele. . . . And yet a poore man, þat ye wite wel or supposen in certain to have no good of, ye ne geve him no such letters, þough he be a better man to god þan suche a riche man?"[6] Indulgences were also considered uncharitable because they were distributed with regard to singular rather than common profit. As one early Lollard writer complains, "þese pardouns bene not grauntid generally for fulfillyng of Goddis hestis and werkis of mercy to most nedy men, as Crist biddis, but for syngulere cause and syngulere place."[7] According to the "Sixteen Points of Lollard Belief," moreover, popes and bishops who issue pardons in return for money or service are subject to divine punishment, both because they exchange spiritual for material goods—an oft-repeated Lollard objection—and because the grantor assumes an exclusive power belonging to Christ alone. This last reason points to a more theologically significant objection to spiritual letters, namely, that they are not only uncharitable and singular but also superfluous and distracting. They purport to draw from the mer-

---

[6] *Jack Upland, Friar Daw's Reply, and Upland's Rejoinder*, ed. P. L. Heyworth (London: Oxford University Press, 1968), pt. 3., ll. 652–54.

[7] From "Octo in quibus seducuntur simplices Christiani," printed in *Select English Works of John Wyclif*, vol. 3, ed. Thomas Arnold (Oxford: Clarendon, 1871), 460.

188 | *Emily Steiner*

its of saints or of the fraternal orders, which have no bearing on salvation of the individual Christian. As one sermon-writer comments about fraternal letters, "ȝif men schewen þanne þese lettres oþur to God or his lawe, þei profiȝte nothing to hem, ne defenden hem aȝen God. And so þese lettres ben superflew, as ben þese ordres þat maken hem."[8] Finally, indulgences and letters of fraternity were criticized as newfangled documents lacking confirmation in Scripture, an objection derived from Wyclif's arguments for scriptural antiquity. Compared to Scripture, he pointed out, charters and indulgences are relatively recent texts and thus inherently false; consequently, such "new" texts should be upheld only if they are supported by the gospels.[9] According to the *Fasciculi zizaniorum*, for example, Wyclif argued that even if the Magna Carta itself promises to maintain the temporalities of the Church, this ordinance may be properly interpreted only in light of the gospels, which advocate clerical poverty.[10]

Contempt for ecclesiastical documents generated a wealth of antimaterialist rhetoric ridiculing their worthlessness and frailty. One Lollard writer, infuriated by the sale of pardons, fulminates that they are made up of a "litel leed not weiynge a pound, hengid with an hempryn thrid at a litil gobet of a calfskyn, peyntid with a fewe blake draugtis of enke."[11] Yet if some Lollards vilified the written record in order to discredit indulgences and emphasize the authority of Scripture, others seized on the image of Christ's charter to point up the weaknesses of indulgences and to describe heterodox ideas of spiritual and political community. We can see how heterodox writers might invoke Christ's charter ironically to talk about a charter that is not really a charter at all—a spiritual paradox of sorts. But the transfer of the image from orthodox to heterodox contexts was far from intuitive, and its unlikelihood suggests that the image appealed to Lollard-sympathetic writers for more compelling reasons than opportunities for antimaterialism. After all, the image of Christ's body as a bleeding charter nailed to the cross was strongly associated with an iconographical tradition antithetical to Lollard sensibilities. The *Long* and *Short Charters'* graphic instruments of torture, for example, and their description of the sealing wax and the bloody words carved into the parchment of Christ's flesh, recall images of the crucifix that were anathema to committed Lollards. The prose "Charter of Heaven" from *Pore Caitif*, for instance, tries to make Christ's charter more vivid to its readers by reminding them of these familiar images of the crucifix: "þe printe of þis seel is þe shap of oure lord ihesu crist hanginge for oure synne on þe cros as we moun se bi þe ymage of

---

[8] *English Wycliffite Sermons*, ed. Anne Hudson, vol. 1 (Oxford: Clarendon, 1983), 329.
[9] *The English Works of Wyclif*, ed. F. D. Matthews, EETS OS 41/74 (London: Trübner & Co., 1880), 287.
[10] *Fasciculi zizaniorum magistri Johannis Wyclif*, ed. W. W. Shirley, Rolls Series 5 (London: Longman, Brown Green, 1858), 4–5, 18–19.
[11] Anne Hudson, *The Premature Reformation: Wycliffite Texts and Lollard History* (New York: Clarendon Press, 1988), 300.

þe crucifix."[12] Notably, some Lollard versions of *Pore Caitif* omit this ostensibly repugnant sentence.[13]

Readers of the *Charters of Christ* also identified them with indulgences and relic worship. One fifteenth-century reader doctored his *Short Charter* into a pardon granting an indulgence of 26,030 years and 11 days. Another *Short Charter* was carved into a gravestone in Kent (ca. 1400), a practice usually reserved for indulgences, which were sometimes carved onto the tombstones of dignitaries (passersby who prayed for the dead earned a specified number of days off purgatory).[14] The image of Christ as a crucified charter also reminded readers of illustrations of the *arma christi* and of Christ as the Man of Sorrows, which were used to decorate indulgences and often served as substitutes for relic worship.[15] The fifteenth-century illustrator of British Library MS Add. 37049 likewise depicts the charter of Christ as a juxtaposition of the Man of Sorrows and the *arma christi*. In this graphic illustration, Christ gazes down sorrowfully at his midsection, which has been expanded into an unfurled parchment nailed to the cross. On the parchment are written the verses of the *Short Charter*, and, floating around the Cross, are the instruments of Christ's torture. Affixed to the stem of this cross is a pierced and bleeding heart, a Eucharistic image which simultaneously represents the seal of the charter.

In short, Christ's charter belonged to a literary and iconographic tradition that Lollards should find in extremely bad taste. But although one "mainstream" readership treated Christ's charter as an exaggerated pardon, another, "edgier" readership nevertheless recruited it as ammunition *against* indulgences and letters of fraternity; the ambiguity of Christ's charter lay, in other words, not in the language of its text but in its flexibility as a sign of absolute textual authority. More specifically, Christ's charter appealed to both orthodox and heterodox writers because it had come to signify a public letter available to all readers and listeners. Moreover, Lollards could accept the image of Christ's charter because it appeared to be a kind of foundational grant coequal with Christ's crucified body and with Scripture. As I have ar-

---

[12] Printed by M. C. Spalding in *The Middle English Charters of Christ* (Bryn Mawr: Bryn Mawr College Press, 1914), 102.

[13] See M. Teresa Brady, "Lollard Interpolation and Omissions in Manuscripts of the *Pore Caitif*," in *De Cella in Seculum: Religious and Secular Life and Devotion in Late Medieval England* (Cambridge: D. S. Brewer, 1988), 188.

[14] As Flora Lewis explains, "the public veneration of relics [was] paralleled by their private veneration, encouraged through [illustrated] grants of indulgences" ("Rewarding Devotion: Indulgences and the Promotion of Images," in *The Church and the Arts*, ed. Diana Wood [Oxford: Blackwell Publishers, 1992], 179–94). See also Nicholas Orme, "Indulgences in the Diocese of Exeter, 1100–1536," *Transactions of the Devonshire Association for the Advancement of Science, Literature, and Art* 120 (1988): 21.

[15] The York *Horae*, for example, contains a tiny versified pardon illustrated with the crown of thorns, the instruments of the Passion, and the crucifix, on the stem of which is a pierced heart oozing drops of blood. See *The Lay Folks' Catechism*, ed. T. F. Simmons and H. E. Nolloth, EETS OS 118 (London: Trübner & Co., 1901), 159 n. B.13.

gued elsewhere, charters and patents were used to represent Christ's body and word because they were nominally public texts directly addressed to a universal audience of readers and listeners, or at least could be regarded as such.[16] Fourteenth-century writers also imagined certain kinds of legal documents to be transhistorical and performative: they seemed to transmit the original voice of the grantor to future generations and continually implement his or her wishes.[17] This desire for documentary agency and immediacy is represented formulaically by official Latin salutations (typically, "Sciant presentes et futuri quod ego N. . . . dedi et concessi et hac presenti carta mea confirmaui . . . [Let all present and future know that I N. have given and granted and with this present charter of mine have confirmed . . .]"), but even more convincingly in the vernacular transformations of those formulas (as in the salutation to the *Charter of the Abbey of the Holy Ghost* [ca. 1380s]: "*Sciant presentes & futuri &c.* Wetiþ ye þat ben now here, & þei þat schulen comen after you, þat almighti god in trinite, fader & sone & holy gost, haþ gouen & graunted & wiþ his owne word confermed . . . etc."). In pious contexts, then, legal documents came to signify the original, continuous, and public proclamation of the contract of the Redemption. But whereas, for fourteenth-century writers, Christ's charter was largely a penitential strategy of making Christ's Word and Passion immediate to the laity, for later sermon writers with Lollard sympathies, it might represent a relationship between text and community diametrically opposed to that represented by ecclesiastical letters. For these writers, ecclesiastical letters constituted private and privileged communities organized by the pope and fraternal orders, but Christ's charter might serve as the foundational text for a spiritual brotherhood inclusive of all (saved) Christians, unmediated by institutional clergy and their texts, and authorized by the Crucifixion and the gospels.

Such a drastic appropriation of Christ's charter can be seen, for example, in an interpolation of *The Lay Folks' Catechism* (appearing in Lambeth Palace Library MS 408 and Douce 274), in which Christ's heavenly grant is opposed to indulgences and equated with the gospels.[18] What we take to be a copy of the original vernacular text, recorded in Archbishop Thoresby's register in 1357, was intended for the sacerdotal instruction of the laity and includes a lengthy exposition on the Ten Commandments. But whereas Thoresby's copy simply

---

[16] Emily Steiner, "A Charter for Poetry: *Piers Plowman* and Medieval Documentary Poetics" (Ph.D. diss., Yale University, 1999).

[17] *Yorkshire Writers: Richard Rolle of Hampole, an English Father of the Church and His Followers* (London: S. Sonnenschein & Co., 1895–6), 338–40.

[18] For a discussion of the manuscript tradition of *The Lay Folks' Catechism* and its interpolations, see Anne Hudson, "A New Look at *The Lay Folks' Catechism*," *Viator* 16 (1985): 241–58. As Hudson shows, the Lollard-sympathetic views of the Lambeth interpolator are often riddled with contradictions (for example, he does not omit Thoresby's injunction that any layperson who learns his catechism will enjoy an indulgence of forty days), and, moreover, no two interpolated manuscripts of the wildly variant *LFC* corpus are the same.

extols the virtues of the Ten Commandments, the interpolator finds an occasion to denounce pardons and temporalities. If you break the Ten Commandments and do not amend, he says, you will be "dampnyd in helle in body and sowle withouten ende," despite your impressive collection of a "þowsand bullys of pardoun, lettris of fraternite, and chauntres."[19] Conversely, if you fulfill the Ten Commandments, you will enjoy perpetual bliss in heaven, whether or not you have ever purchased a pardon. In short, concludes the interpolator, pardons and fraternal letters have no legal bearing on salvation. Heaven is a grant issued in the gospels and authorized by Christ's crucified body: "þe erytage of heuyn ys þyn be graunt of cristys gospel, aselyd with his precious blod þat may neuer be fals: for no creature in erthe ne in heuyn."[20]

It is certainly not necessary to insist on the Lollard affiliations of this interpolator to see that his statements about ecclesiastical documents might be controversial. Granted, his diatribe against indulgences is not so different from that of the dreamer in *Piers Plowman* who, after seeing Piers tear the Pardon, complains that, despite his own belief in the power of indulgences, he is astonished at how frequently rich men use them as an excuse to break the Ten Commandments ("but Dowel yow helpe, / I sette youre patentes and youre pardon at one pies hele!").[21] Significantly, however, in the case of the *Lay Folks' Catechism* interpolator, he has creatively reimagined the claims of documentary culture in order to express clearly heterodox positions; although he does not use the word "charter" to describe Christ's land grant of heaven, he clearly refers to a written document and to the *Charters of Christ* literature. The *Short Charter*, for example, also imagines Christ's charter to be sealed with his own blood: "To this chartre trewe and good / I have set my seal, myn herthe blood."[22] The passage from the *Lay Folks' Catechism* has distinct verbal echoes, moreover, in the "Charter of Heaven" from *Pore Caitif*. The *Lay Folks' Catechism* insists that Christ's charter is sealed with his blood and therefore is both legally incontestable and physically indestructible: it "may neuer be fals: for no creature in erthe ne in heuyn." Likewise, the "Charter of Heaven" confirms that Christ's charter is imperishable because it is inscribed on Christ's body: "þis scripture is oure lord Ihesu crist: chartre & bulle of oure eritage of heuene . . . þis chartre may not fiyr brenne ne watir drenche: neiþir þeef robbe neiþir ony creature distroie," and a few lines later, "alle þe creatures in heuene neiþir in erþe neiþir in helle moun not robbe it neiþir bireue it fro þe."[23] In short, the interpolator argues for the primacy of Scripture and against ecclesiastical documents by identifying a divine charter

---

[19] *The Lay Folks' Catechism*, 57, ll. 879–83.
[20] Ibid., ll. 888–91.
[21] *Piers Plowman: The B Version*, ed. George Kane and E. Talbot Donaldson (London: Athlone Press, 1975), ll. 194–95.
[22] Spalding, *Middle English Charters*, 98, ll. 27–28.
[23] Ibid., 102.

with Christ's crucified body, but notably, by doing so, he has also adapted the materialist discourse of fictive documents to articulate what would become distinctly Lollard concerns.

A second, more conspicuously heterodox sermon, compiled in an early fifteenth-century manuscript (Rawlinson C. 751) with the "Charter of Heaven," also uses Christ's charter to discredit other spiritual letters and, further, to posit a predestined community of believers. The preacher admonishes those who think that, by becoming lay brothers of a fraternal order "bi lettre and bi seel," they will partake of the good deeds performed by the brothers.[24] Rather, they should believe that those who will be saved are free partners of all good deeds performed from prelapsarian Eden to the Day of Judgment through the mercy of God and according to their deserts. They should steadfastly believe, moreover, in a universal brotherhood of the predestined constituted by Christ's charter, rather than in the exclusive brotherhood of fraternities founded by profane letters—a distinctly Lollard position:

> Alle we beþ breþeren of oo Fadir in heuene, and breþeren to oure Lord Jesus Crist, and into his broþerhede we beþ receyued bi þe worshipeful chartre of þe hooli Trinyte: Fadir, and Sone, and Hooli Goost. The chartre of þis breþerhede is þe blessid bodi þat hynge on a cros; writen wiþ þe worþi blood þat ran doun fro his herte, seelid wiþ þe precyous sacramente of þe auter in perpetuel mynde þerof. And þis blesside bretherhede schal abiden foreuere in blisse (whanne alle false faitouris schullen fare) wiþ hire Fadir.[25]

As in the case of the interpolated *Lay Folks' Catechism*, this passage links Christ's body on the cross to a divine charter and, by doing so, quite deliberately evokes the *Charters of Christ* tradition. Like the passage from the *Lay Folks' Catechism*, moreover, this one borrows Christ's charter to formulate an inclusive spiritual fellowship authenticated by Scripture and by the liberating terms of the Passion. Conversely, it uses Christ's charter to prove that the documents of the institutional church, pardons and letters of fraternity, represent new practices and exclusive communities lacking proper authorization.

The capacity of a divine charter to embody heterodox ideas of textual authority and textual community can be seen even more clearly in a third tract from the 1380s, "The Grete Sentence of Curs Expoued," which invokes Christ's charter to accuse the orthodox clergy of treason, to castigate clerics who have turned bureaucrats, and to demonstrate royal sovereignty over the temporal possessions of the Church. We have already seen that Lollards condemned pardons and fraternal letters as "singular," selfish or self-ruled acts. "The Grete Sentence" neatly turns singularity into sedition by creating an analogy between Christ's charter (Scripture) and the king's charter (Magna

---

[24] For a description, see Jeremy Griffith's introduction to Gloria Cigman, ed., *Lollard Sermons*, EETS OS 294 (Oxford: Oxford University Press, 1989), xxiv–xxv.
[25] *Lollard Sermons*, 113, ll. 266–84.

Carta). It begins by arguing that worldly clerks, "bi fals prechynge . . . bi sik-ernesse of letteris of fraternyte and synguler preieris," teach all men to be "rebel aȝenis þe kyng and lordis" and to destroy the "pees of þe kyng and his rewme."[26] It then compares the king's charter to Scripture and contrasts both to the "singular" and unauthorized claims of canon law. According to the Magna Carta, the king donates temporal goods to the church as alms, but some clerks deceive the king and malign his charter by styling themselves sovereign lords, as royal servants or possessioners. They are subsequently cursed every time the Magna Carta is proclaimed: "alle þe þat falsen þe kyn-gis chartre and assented þerto ben cursed solempnely of God and man, pup-pliched foure tymes in þe ȝeer." By analogy, they are even more cursed by "þe *chartre of alle kyngis*, þat is holy writt," in which God commands all priests to live "in honest povert and forsake seculer lordischip . . . as crist and his apos-tlis diden" (306, emphasis added). By impugning the Magna Carta, that is, the clergy necessarily impugn Christ's charter as well; together, the two charters make a case for royal sovereignty, but also for the primacy of royal docu-ments, as contrasted with the treasonous, newfangled, and self-interested texts of the institutional Church.

Getting the Last Word: The Lollard Heresy Trials

I have argued thus far that documentary culture provided heterodox ser-mon writers with a language to describe some of their most controversial ideas about private religions, indulgences, scriptural authority, and royal sov-ereignty. More surprisingly, perhaps, Lollards' appropriations of fictive docu-ments were paralleled by similar strategies in their encounters with episcopal officers. Like Lollard polemicists, Lollards on trial positioned themselves against documentary culture to contest orthodox ideas of textual authority. But whereas some sermon writers borrowed the image of Christ's charter to discredit indulgences and to formulate heterodox notions of spiritual and po-litical community, Margery Baxter and William Thorpe used documents—both fictive and real—to rescue Lollard polemic from the evidentiary lan-guage of written record and to rehabilitate a distinctly Lollard hermeneutic. For both Baxter and Thorpe, just as for the Lollard sermon writers, docu-mentary culture sets the terms for which a debate on textual authority may take place. What both the sermons and the trial records show, in other words, is that medieval documentary culture not only served as an easy target for all sorts of critiques of bureaucratic corruption and institutional oppression, but also provided its critics with rhetorical alternatives by which that criticism might be effectively deployed. Or to put it a different way, it was precisely in its role as a foundational text that the document became, by the turn of the

---

[26] Arnold, *Select English Works*, 298. Subsequent citations to this tract will be cited in the text.

fifteenth century, an indicator of a wide range of religious and political communities, most of which hinged in some way on the status of the written word.

Between 1428 and 1431 a notary named John Excestr copied the records of the Norwich heresy trials into a court-book or personal *dictamen*.[27] His book suggests that most of the trials likely consisted of a routine exchange of documents. The presiding bishop probably presented the defendant with a Latin deposition (perhaps read aloud in English) listing the defendant's heretical beliefs or practices. Witnesses would be called in, if necessary, to corroborate or expand on the document. The defendant would admit to statements as charged, formally retract them, and state his or her intention to submit to the correction of the Church under pain of burning. An official abjuration would then be drawn up in duplicate and sealed by the confessed heretic, who swore to keep his or her copy forever ("That other partie indented Y receyve undir the seel of office . . . to abide with me unto my lyves ende").[28] Nearly all of the abjurations were written in English ("in ydiomate Anglicano concepto") as well as Latin, and in the first person so that the defendant understood what he or she was retracting and might take legal responsibility for it.[29] Both the Latin certifications and English abjurations, however, are fairly standardized in form—the English idiom here is neither creative nor unruly—and generally efface idiosyncratic comments that may have cropped up during the trial. Most of the defendants, moreover, could read neither English nor Latin and were assigned proxies who read their abjurations aloud.[30]

The deposition of the Lollard hostess and household preacher Margery Baxter differs from the others in its idiomatic English expressions of Lollard doctrine, some of them seeming to have "seeped" unintentionally into the Latin record. For example, Baxter's friend Joan reported her to have said that when relics are worshipped, Lucifer enjoys on earth the honor that he lost after his fall, "*in adoracione* of stokkes and stones and ded mennes bones" (42). This phrase "stokkes and stones" recalls typical Lollard iconoclasm: one early Lollard writer asks about images, "What almes is it to peynte gayly dede

[27] Steven Justice, "Inquisition, Speech, and Writing: A Case from Late Medieval Norwich," in *Criticism and Dissent in the Middle Ages*, ed. Rita Copeland (Cambridge: Cambridge University Press, 1996), 239–322.

[28] Norman Tanner, ed., *Heresy Trials in the Diocese of Norwich, 1428–31*, Camden Miscellany 20, 4th ser. (London: Royal Historical Society, 1977), 187. Subsequent citations of the Norwich heresy trials are to this edition and will be cited in the text.

[29] Other Latin documents refer to the accused in the third person. The only exception to this rule is the case of the chaplain Robert Cavell, whose Latin abjuration is addressed in the first person, presumably because as a cleric he understood the Latin of his abjuration and was thus able to take legal responsibility for it: "Cuius scripti indentati unam partem idem Robertus Cavell in manibus suis tenens coram dicto patre legit publice" (ibid., 94).

[30] The following formula is typical: "Quem tenorem per magistrum Johannem Wylly, notarium publicum, tunc ibidem presentem, publice perlectum idem Willelmus asseruit se de verbo ad verbum totaliter audivisse et plenarie intellexisse. Et quia idem Willelmus Bate asseruit se fore laicum, ipsam abiuracionem legere nescientem propria in persona, ipse constituit prefatum magistrum Johannem Wylly organum vocis sue" (ibid., 159).

stones and roun stokkis wiþ such almes þat is pore mennus good and lyfelode," and disparages those pilgrims who "cleuen sadly strokande and kyssand þese olde stones and stokkis."[31] It is not clear why Excestr recorded these statements; it may be that the peculiar idiom testified to the speakers' heterodoxy or was too exciting to render into Latin, or, as Steven Justice has argued, the notary was merely bored.[32] Whatever his reasons, these statements disrupt the written record while also making visible the purpose of that record: to convert Lollard idiom into conventional—and punishable—English formulas.

This rhetorical challenge to documentary culture illuminates a more deliberate challenge that John Excestr did not see fit to relay in English. Baxter was reported to have said that even if she was convicted of heresy, she should not be burnt because she has had and still has ("habuit et habet") a charter of salvation in her womb ("unam cartam salvacionis in utero suo"[49]). If Baxter really made this strange pronouncement (and in a certain sense, of course, it matters only that it was said), it can be interpreted in a number of different ways. Most obviously, Baxter intended to disparage the inquisitors' documentary authority by claiming to possess a superior charter, one that effectively nullified or superseded the one that she was being coerced into producing against herself. The bishop's document may be narrowly incriminating (it might send her to the stake), but hers is more largely redemptive: it will save her not only from temporal fire but also from the devil and eternal punishment. As one reader has proposed, moreover, Baxter may have been posing as a Marian figure harboring the Word in her womb, like a charm, perhaps, thus inuring herself to physical violence.[33]

Baxter's charter of salvation further advertises the impenetrability as well as the sanctity of her bodily enclosure; she is using Christ's charter, in other words, to posit a closed rather than an open spiritual community, or at least one tantalizingly unavailable to the orthodox clergy.[34] This idea of a divine charter openly inscribed on but also mystically contained within Christ's body can be seen in "The Charter of Heaven" from *Pore Caitif*. It warns that

[31] "Images and Pilgrimages," in Hudson, *Selections from English Wycliffite Writings*, 85, ll. 72–74; 87, ll. 159–60.

[32] He argues in "Inquisition, Speech, and Writing" that the trials had become so routine that Excestr was momentarily roused by "outcroppings of idiosyncrasy." Justice dismisses a few important considerations, however: first, that these stray expressions appear only in *reported* speech, either attributed by the defendant to other people or by a witness to a defendant; and second and relatedly, that English could be evidentiary. Any defendant who could not understand Latin had his abjuration recorded in English so that he could swear to its contents. Clearly, in this instance, an English document was as binding and enforceable as a Latin one.

[33] For Baxter as a Marian figure, see Rita Copeland, "Why Women Can't Read: Medieval Hermeneutics, Statuary Law, and the Lollard Heresy Trials," in *Representing Women: Law, Literature, and Feminism*, ed. Susan Sage Heinzelman and Zipporah Batshaw Wiseman (Durham: Duke University Press, 1994), 253–86. For more on women Lollards, see Claire Cross, "'Great Reasoners in Scripture': The Activities of Women Lollards, 1380–1530," in *Medieval Women*, ed. Derek Baker (Oxford: Basil Blackwell, 1978), 359–80.

[34] I am grateful to Bruce Holsinger for helping me to see this point.

Christ's charter is too precious to be locked in a chest: "þis scripture is oure lord Ihesu crist: chartre & bulle of oure eritage of heuene! Locke not þis chartre in þi coffre: but sette it eiþir write it in þin herte," but yet, at the same time, Christ "is þe cofre in whom is closid & loken: al þe tresoure of witte & wisdom of god."[35] In this sense, Baxter is imitating Christ himself as the original preacher and material text of the contract of the Redemption, but, by doing so, she has reframed the idea of a divine charter to counter the trial documents of the institutional Church.[36]

Like the polemical sermons discussed earlier, Baxter's claim implicitly criticizes both the authority and reading practices of the orthodox clergy. It suggests, for example, that textual authority—and particularly the authority to preach—is located not in the documents of the institutional church but in the body of the laity on the one hand (whether individual or corporate), and in Scripture (Christ's charter) on the other.[37] Not only does this suggestion evoke specifically Lollard notions of authority, but also it refers to local practices in which the demand for written texts and secrecy necessitated household-oriented textual communities, which depended, in part, on Lollard women's aural transmission of Scripture. As Ralph Hanna writes about the Lollard women from Norwich, "They embodied texts and transported them in their corporeal persons, gave to them a life beyond mere vellum and thus attained a flexibility . . . of writing that their coreligionists might not have achieved."[38] Baxter's claim suggests even more significantly, however, that the scriptures of the orthodox clergy *are* the literal documents of the law, evidentiary records that must be metaphorically "glossed" by the faithful in order to be transformed into a charter of salvation, a legitimizing and doctrinally significant text. And it is this ironic critique of orthodox hermeneutics that really enabled Baxter to elude her trial, to go beyond what otherwise appears to be posturing and threats. Whatever the consequences of her trial, Baxter's citation of Christ's charter shows how trial documents might be subjected to and might generate infinite glosses. It implies, that is, that the ecclesiastical record does not authoritatively designate subjects—it is not a fundamental text—but rather its supposed subjects continually supply corrective glosses by embodying physically the text of scripture: Christ's original charter. What all these readings make clear is that Baxter was consciously reframing the documentary rhetoric found in contemporary sermons and affective lyric poetry to interrogate and elude the Norwich heresy trials.

[35] Spalding, *Middle English Charters*, 101.

[36] Baxter clearly had a flair for lay *imitatio christi*. According to her witnesses, she once spread her arms out in imitation of the Crucifixion and declared that this was the image of the crucifix that should be worshipped (Tanner, *Norwich Heresy Trials*, 44).

[37] See also Ralph Hanna III, "The Case of the Lollards and the Difficulty of Ricardian Prose Translation," *Modern Language Quarterly* 51.3 (1990): 319–40.

[38] Ralph Hanna III, "Some Norfolk Women and Their Books," in *The Cultural Performance of Medieval Women* (Athens: University of Georgia Press, 1996), 292.

Baxter's deposition suggests how Lollard rhetoric might disrupt the conventions of the written record by invoking an alternate documentary culture—in this instance, the *Charter of Christ* tradition. William Thorpe's 1407 *Testimony* offers a more detailed example of how an unorthodox preacher might manipulate documentary rhetoric to critique and elude his trial. According to Thorpe, his *Testimony* is an accurate transcript of a trial that took place in the palace of Archbishop Arundel, the ostensible grounds for which was Thorpe's unauthorized preaching of heretical doctrine in Shrewsbury. If the trial really took place, it could certainly never have done so in the form reported by Thorpe (Arundel plays an unlikely straw man to Thorpe's erudite martyr), and whether it was conducted in Latin or English—the text survives in both languages—is impossible to determine decisively.[39] The question of historical authenticity aside, Thorpe's *Testimony* is remarkable for the way that it interrogates the language of trial documents, such as those found in the Norwich court-book, and, in doing so, simultaneously excavates a specifically Lollard rhetoric and proclaims the superiority of Lollard exegesis. In this respect, the *Testimony* is strikingly sympathetic to Dominick LaCapra's assertion that "the one thing a trial must repress is the way style . . . may be a politically subversive or contestatory force."[40] Indeed Thorpe, as will become clear, recovers the political and spiritual potency of Lollard "style" by inverting and subverting the written records of the institutional Church.

From the very beginning, for example, Thorpe presents his *Testimony* as an alternative document: a self-made testament to his life and beliefs, but also as a public sermon informing and instructing his present and future audiences. In his prologue he apologizes quite conventionally for revealing the sins of others; he explains that the book is intended to instill virtue in his readers and to comfort those in bad circumstances. He begins his account of his interrogation, moreover, with another conventional literary strategy: "Knowen be it to alle men þat reden or heeren þis writinge byneþforþ þat, on þe Sondai next aftir þe faste Petir þat we clepen Lammasse, in þe ȝeer of oure lord a þousand foure hundred and seuene, I, William of Thorpe . . . was brouȝt bifore Tomas of Arundel, Archebishop of Cauntirbirie and chaunceler þanne of Yngland" (166–71). This salutation suggests that his self-writing has the status of a public proclamation worthy of trust and remembrance. Rita Copeland provocatively asks how Thorpe, as an academic and clerical insider, can offer

[39] Anne Hudson tentatively makes an argument for English based on Thorpe's exhortation to his intended audience in the prologue. See also her comments on the historicity of the text (which she defends) in the introduction to her edition *Two Wycliffite Texts: The Sermon of William Taylor, 1406, and the Testimony of William Thorpe, 1407*, EETS OS 301 (Oxford: Oxford University Press, 1993), xlii–liii. Citations will be given by line in the text. On Thorpe's use of the conventions of standard academic debate, see Fiona Somerset, *Clerical Discourse and Lay Audience in Late Medieval England* (Cambridge: Cambridge University Press, 1998), 179–215.

[40] Dominick LaCapra, "Rethinking Intellectual History and Reading Texts," in *Rethinking Intellectual History: Texts, Contexts, Language* (Ithaca: Cornell University Press, 1983), 47.

a true model of dissent: how can he represent his own life and still speak on behalf of other Lollards?[41] She goes on to demonstrate compellingly that he fashions a dissenting self through intellectual labor, that is, through the violence of his interrogation. It should be added, however, that this salutation offers a more conventional way of representing and reaching out to a larger audience. It may at first seem to perpetuate an orthodox (and in the context of the trials, oppressive) model for public writing, but it actually works to rewrite the heresy documents found in a standard trial. As we saw earlier, first-person English documents were used only for abjurations, and thus the defendant spoke only through an incriminating and coerced confession. By contrast, Thorpe's first-person salutation is close to standard for a patent (i.e., "Sachez ke nus volons et otrions," or in Latin, "omnibus hanc cartam visuris vel auditoris"), not an abjuration, confession, or petition, and thus it effectively reinscribes the dissenting subject into an assertive public document.[42]

Thorpe further invokes and contests documentary culture by forcing Arundel to lay out several trial documents, which Thorpe correspondingly unravels. In fact, he seems to have deliberately provoked each step of the proceedings in order to contest the preaching authority of the institutional Church and to expound on the basic tenets of Lollardy. For example, Arundel begins the interrogation by asking Thorpe to renounce his beliefs in exchange for clemency ("wiþouten ony feynynge knele doun and leie þin hond vpon a book and kisse it, bihoting feithfulli . . . þat þou wolt submytte þee to my correccioun and stonde to myn ordinance" [190–93]). Thorpe uses this opportunity to deliver a suspect version of the Creed, at the end of which he asks if he may lay his hands on the Book. "Of course," says the archbishop, and Thorpe immediately protests that the book is a created thing and therefore cannot be sworn by. He then disingenuously asks Arundel to tell him the procedure by which he must submit (345–48). The archbishop promptly recites a list of formulas, repeating the exact order and language of the Norwich abjurations: Thorpe is to disavow his heretical beliefs, cease from holding them either privately or openly ("priuyli" or "appertli"), stop consorting with or aiding heretics ("neither þou schalt fauoure man ne woman . . . þat holdiþ ony of þese forseide opynynouns"), and deliver the names of heretics to episcopal officers ("þou shalt putten [them] vp, pupblischinge her names, and make hem knowen to þe bishop of þe diocise þat þese ben inne, eiþer to þe bishopis mynystris" [357–60]). Likewise at Norwich, the defendants were first to lay their hands on the Gospels ("Y abjure and forswere, and swere be

[41] Rita Copeland, "William Thorpe and His Lollard Community: Intellectual Labor and the Representation of Dissent," in *Bodies and Disciplines: Intersections of Literature and History in Fifteenth-Century England*, ed. Barbara A. Hanawalt and David Wallace (Minneapolis: University of Minnesota Press, 1996), 199–221.

[42] Compare Thorpe's salutation, for example, with the first few lines of Jack Upland's "petition": "To veri god & to alle trewe in Crist, I Iacke Vplond make my moone, þat Anticrist and hise disciplis bi coloure of holynes wasten & disceiuen Cristis chirche bi many fals signes" (54, ll. 1–3). We see a similar strategy at the beginning of Richard of Bury's *Philobiblon*.

these holy Gospels be me bodely touched"), abjure their heretical beliefs, and promise to hold these beliefs neither "opinly ne prively," nor to give help or favor to those who do so (in Latin, "auxilium vel favore publice vel occulte"). A typical Norwich abjuror likewise ends his retraction with the promise that he will turn over any other Lollards to the authorities: "Yf Y knowe ony heretik or of heresie ony man or woman suspect . . . Y shal late you, worship-full fadir, or your vicar generall in your absens or the diocesans of suche men have soone and redy knowying."[43] What is remarkable in Thorpe's account is not so much his familiarity with these formulas but the way that he deliberately glosses them to extricate himself rhetorically and ideologically from the proceedings. He explains that if he were to swear to what Arundel has set forth, he would undermine the faith of true Christian men, condemn innocent people to their deaths, and damn himself to hell. Thus the abjuration that formed the basis for the heresy trials becomes in Thorpe's *Testimony* an outline for Lollard doctrine.

When Thorpe again refuses to submit, Arundel becomes angry and orders his clerk to take out a certificate sent by the bailiff of Shrewsbury, which has been stored in a cupboard with "dyuerse rollis and other writingis" (621–23). This "litil rolle," as Thorpe calls it, reports the heretical statements preached by Thorpe in Saint Chad's church and is meant to be an intimidating and irrefutable record. Thorpe, however, seems to have goaded the archbishop into taking it out of the cupboard in the first place, and indeed this certificate turns out to be another text from which to launch the Lollard counteroffensive. Arundel reads it aloud, ticking off five stereotypical Lollard positions on the Eucharist, images, pilgrimages, tithes, and swearing, and using the formulas that would become standard in the Norwich trials. Thorpe immediately denies having preached these statements "priuyli ne apeertly" (638), not to protest his innocence but to elaborate on the statements. An improbable dialogue follows in which Arundel puts each of the five statements to Thorpe and allows him five times to rephrase each statement in a more learned and nuanced fashion, in effect, to turn them into mini-sermons. Concerning the third statement on pilgrimage, for example, Arundel asks him, " 'What seist þou now to the þridde poynt þat is certified aȝens þee, preaching at Schrouesbirie opinli þat pilgrimage is vnleeful?' " and Thorpe responds: "Sere, bi þis certificatioun I am acused to ȝou þat I schulde teche þat no pilgrimage is leeful. But, ser, I seide neuere þus. . . . And þerfore, ser, howeuere myn enemyes haue certified to ȝou of me, I toolde at Schrouesbirie of two manere of pilgrimagis, seiinge þat þer ben trewe pilgrimes and fals pilgrimes" (1221–34). Tales of martyrdom are often, of course, about frustrating the legal system, about turning official procedure into a forum for narrative and

---

[43] Tanner, *Norwich Heresy Trials*, 87. Thorpe's version of the abjuration differs only slightly from the Norwich, perhaps because he was loosely translating from or remembering a Latin version; the content of both is remarkably similar.

debate. But by interrogating documentary culture—both the abjuration that Arundel wants him to sign and the certification against him—Thorpe restores doctrinal complexity to Lollard beliefs and proves the irreducibility of Lollard rhetoric. In this way, he inverts the process of the heresy records; rather than letting his sermon be converted into documentary formulas, he converts the language of legal record into a vernacular sermon on Lollard beliefs—a written transcript, that is, of the sermon for which he was arrested!

Thorpe's strategy also reveals a more general concern of his *Testimony*—and, indeed, its ostensible reason for being—that authority can be supported only by the truth of Scripture and the witnessing of true Christian men, not by the prescriptions of prelates. Unlike Margery Kempe, who seems to have spent days on end collecting official letters of credence and safe-conduct, Thorpe wants to prove that his arrest for preaching without a license is doctrinally illegitimate. When Arundel warns that Thorpe had no right to preach because neither he nor any other prelate " 'wol admitte or graunte þee for to preche bi witnesse of her lettris' " (745–46), Thorpe predictably responds that Lollard preachers, unlike the friars, do not want to be bound by the terms of " 'ʒoure lettre neiþer lettris of oþir bishopis writun wiþ enke vpon parchemyne,' " the authority of which is not supported in the gospels (759–62). Furthermore, the evidence of their right to preach consists of the people to whom they preach rather than official letters: " 'ʒhe, þe peple to who we prechen, be þei feiþful either vnfeiþful, schulen be oure lettris that is oure witnesse-berer' " (774–75). Interestingly Thorpe's objection to ecclesiastical letters does not extend to secular letters as well. Later, in a debate about images, Arundel argues in favor of religious images on the grounds that they signify the authority of those whom they represent. As proof, he offers an analogy from secular practice: lords customarily seal their letters with their coat of arms so that their subjects recognize their authority and obey the letters (" 'in worschip of her lordis þei don of her cappis or her hoodis to her lettris' " [1090–91]). Thorpe does not deny the representative authority of secular letters, replying simply that what applies to secular practices does not apply to religious practices: " 'þis worldli vsage of temperal lordis . . . is no symylitude to worschipe ymagis maad bi mannes hond' " (1096–98).

Yet arguably Thorpe is doing much more in his *Testimony* than refuting the authority of ecclesiastical letters and locating authority in Scripture. We have seen that by interrogating legal documents, Thorpe, like Margery Baxter, emancipates himself rhetorically, and consequently sets an example for other convicted Lollards. He further puts the ecclesiastical bureaucracy on trial by opposing a Lollard hermeneutics to what might be called the evidentiary hermeneutics of the archbishop and his clerks. Like Margery Baxter, he attacks the fundamentalism of episcopal officers and, by doing so, ironically turns legal documents into Arundel's *scriptura sola*. If Lollards were accused of interpreting Scripture literally to their own advantage, in the *Testimony*, Arundel's major proof texts become the abjuration and certification to which he adheres literally, and which Thorpe must "gloss" in order to excavate their true sense. In a typical moment in the trial, the archbishop's clerks prompt him to stick to the certification when Thorpe's explication of Holy Church leaves him speechless: " 'Ser, he seide riȝt now þat þis certificacioun þat cam to ȝou from Schrouesbirie is vntruli forgid aȝens him. þerfore, ser, appose ȝe him now here in alle the poyntis which ben certified aȝens him.' . . . And þe Archebischop took þanne þe certificacion in his hond and he lokide þerevpon a while, and so þanne he seide to me . . ." (924–29). Arundel's problem, in other words, is that he and his clerks refuse to distinguish between the literal accusations listed on the certification and Thorpe's subtle exegesis of those accusations. Nor can they reconcile the two truths that Thorpe so plainly exploits: the evidentiary truth of the certification (whether or not Thorpe illicitly preached heretical doctrine at Shrewsbury) and the ontological truth of the statements themselves. In the *Testimony*, Arundel reminds Thorpe that he represents the two spheres of the English "clergie" or "written church": he is *both* archbishop and chancellor, the arbiter of religious doctrine but also the purveyor of legal documents, the means by which doctrinal opinions may be formalized, legitimized, or punished.[44] By performing Lollard exegesis on ecclesiastical documents, Thorpe crucially divides the two spheres of "clergie," the scriptural and the documentary, which Arundel and the heresy trials threatened to conflate.

With Thorpe's *Testimony* we may seem to have gained some distance from the *Charters of Christ* lyrics with which I began. But what all these texts continually suggest, is that documentary language and practices always constitute the matter from which even an anti-establishment agenda may proceed. As in the case of Margery Baxter's deposition or the Lollard sermons, official letters remain in the *Testimony* the dominant points of reference both for establishing an oppositional voice and for contesting orthodox ideas of textual authority.

---

[44] See Justice's illuminating comments on Langland, Ball, and the "written church" in *Writing and Rebellion*, 116–18.

9   The Generation of 1399

Frank Grady

To judge by the evidence of contemporary poetry, heraldic allegory was all the rage in the last years of Richard II's reign. In several poems of
the era the duke of Gloucester, the earl of Arundel, and the earl of Warwick—
Richard's antagonists in 1388 and his victims in 1397—are referred to by
their respective cognizances of the Swan, the Horse, and the Bear. That such
references were utterly transparent we can be sure; John Gower, in the *explicit*
to the *Vox clamantis*, remarks that Gloucester "is commonly called the Swan,"
Arundel the horse, and Warwick the bear.[1] *Richard the Redeless* makes the same
references in unglossed English as Gower does in Latin, and describes how
Henry Bolingbroke—himself represented alternately (and sometimes simultaneously) as greyhound, eagle, and partridge—returned to England after the
deaths of Gloucester and Arundel and released Warwick from his exile on the
Isle of Man:

Thanne sighed the swymmers for the swan failid,
And folwid this faucon thoru feldus and tounes,
With many faire fowle though they feynte were,
And heuy for the hirte that the hors hadde.
Yit they ferkyd [went] hem forth as faste as they myghte,
To haue the Egles helpe of harme that they hadde;

---

[1] "Thomas Dux Glouernie, qui vulgariter dictus est Cignus." I quote the Latin text of the *Vox*
(and, later, the *Cronica tripertita*) from *The Complete Works of John Gower*, ed. G.C. Macaulay, 4
vols. (Oxford: Clarendon Press, 1902), here 4:313. English quotations from the *Vox* (hereafter
VC) and *Cronica* are from *The Major Latin Works of John Gower*, trans. Eric W. Stockton (Seattle:
University of Washington Press, 1962), here 291.

For he was heed of hem all and hieste of kynde
To kepe the croune as cronecle tellith.
He blythid [gladdened] the beere and his bonde braste,
And lete him go at large to lepe where he wolde.[2]

Finally, the anonymous Middle English poem "On King Richard's Ministers," published by Thomas Wright, a poem that never even mentions Richard II, follows the same heraldic routes of Gower and the author of *Richard the Redeless* in recounting allegorically the events of 1397 and 1399.[3] The third and fourth stanzas make the point:

Thorw the busch a swan was sclayn;
Of that sclawtur fewe wer fayne;
alas! that hit betydde!
Hit was a eyrer [swan] good and able,
To his lord ryȝt profitable;
hit was a gentel bryde.
The grene gras that was so long,
Hit hath sclayn a stede strong,
that worthy was and wyth.
Wat kyng had that stede on holde,
To juste on hym he myȝt be bold,
als schulde he go to fyth [fight].[4]

The references to "bush," "green grass," and (in the following stanza) "bag" point to Richard's adherents Sir John Busshey, Sir Henry Greene, and Sir William Bagot in a style of onomastic allegory that falls rather short of even being a pun, and that the author of *Richard the Redeless* also adopts for these characters. Gower tries something similar in the first part of the *Cronica tripertita*, though the result is often an amusingly infelicitous Latinate etymology; for example, he writes "Nova villa Macedo" (1.103)—the "Macedon-

[2] *Richard the Redeless* 3.86–95. All quotations from *Richard* (hereafter *RR*) and *Mum and the Sothsegger* (hereafter *Mum*) are from Helen Barr, ed., *The Piers Plowman Tradition* (London: J.M. Dent, 1993), henceforth *PPIT*. Brackets indicating emendations have been silently omitted, and in most cases I have adopted Barr's word glosses.

[3] *PPIT*, 268 nn. 152–92, notes the connection between the anonymous poem and Richard; John Fisher points out the shared technique in the *Cronica* and the poem in Wright's volume in *John Gower: Moral Philosopher and Friend of Chaucer* (New York: New York University Press, 1964), 110. Stockton cites all three poems, 38 and 337 nn. 99 and 100. Gower claims at the end of part 2 of the *Cronica* that "malicious men" composed a derisive song about the former Appellants that was taken up by "the voice of the fatuous mob . . . in the city": "The Swan does not keep its wings forever, nor the Horse its hide; now the Swan is without wings, the Horse is flayed. The Bear, whom biting chains torment, does not bite" ("Non Olor in pennis, nec Equs stat crine perhennis, / Iam depennatus Olor est, Equs excoriatus, / Vrsus non mordet, quem stricta cathena remordet.' / Sic fatue turbe vox conclamabat in vrbe" [*Cronica* 2.314–17]).

[4] Thomas Wright, ed., *Political Poems and Songs Relating to English History . . . from the Accession of Edward III to That of Richard III*, 2 vols., Rolls Series (London: Longman et al., 1859), 2:363.

ian of the New Town"—for Alexander Neville, archbishop of York.[5] In parts
2 and 3 he wisely tends to stick with the proven winners, the Swans, Horses,
and Bears. In fact, throughout the *Cronica tripertita* the presence of marginal
glosses functioning as an allegorical key—"comitem Oxonie, qui per aprum
designatur," "the earl of Oxford, who is designated as the Boar"—betray the
fact that for all these writers the allegory is more gestural than strategic, or, to
put it another way, it is a function of style.

This essay will show that such wordplay is but one minor feature of a recognizable "Lancastrian" style of writing visible in the earliest fifteenth-century poems, a style that cuts across the formal boundaries usually seen as dividing *Richard's* alliterative long lines from Gower's Leonine Latin
hexameters. These poems share more than a common concern with the public events and political upheavals of the day; they also employ the same strategies for framing and analyzing and moralizing those events, largely through
the adoption of textual models and rhetorical tactics drawn from the bureaucratic and legal culture in which their authors were immersed: parliamentary
reportage, legal instruments, chronicles, and records. "The generation of
1399," then, does not refer to the heroes of the deposition, some group of
Lancastrian retainers enlivening their retirement with hyperbolic accounts of
the landing at Ravenspur. Rather, I use the term to identify the broad range
of texts generated by the accession of Henry IV in the months following his
return from the Continent. A list of these "1399" texts would include the various chronicle accounts dependent on the official "Record and Process" version of the deposition (Walsingham, Cotton Julius B. II, the Evesham chronicle, and others); the *Cronica tripertita* and Gower's other Latin and English
accession poems, including "In Praise of Peace"; its distant cousin, Chaucer's
"Complaint to His Purse"; and the alliterative poems *Richard the Redeless* and,
at a slightly further remove, *Mum and the Sothsegger*.[6] If the study of early fifteenth-century texts—particularly Hoccleve—has become something of a
growth industry in English medieval studies in recent years, and has proven
to be a rich area for the analysis of both royal and poetic self-representation

[5] A. G. Rigg observes that the *Cronica* "shares many of the features of fourteenth-century political poetry: the Leonine rhyme and the fondness for onomastic wordplay" (*A History of Anglo-
Latin Literature, 1066–1422* [Cambridge: Cambridge University Press, 1992], 291).

[6] On the allegiances of Chaucer's poem, see Paul Strohm, "Saving the Appearances: Chaucer's
Purse and the Fabrication of the Lancastrian Claim," in *Chaucer's England: Literature in Historical
Context*, ed. Barbara Hanawalt (Minneapolis: University of Minnesota Press, 1992), 21–40,
reprinted in Strohm, *Hochon's Arrow: The Social Imagination of Fourteenth-Century Texts* (Princeton: Princeton University Press, 1992), 75–94. For Gower, see Grady, "The Lancastrian Gower
and the Limits of Exemplarity," *Speculum* 70 (1995): 552–75. Elizabeth Salter briefly discusses the
similar themes in the alliterative poetry and Gower's work in *Fourteenth-Century English Poetry:
Contexts and Readings* (Oxford: Clarendon Press, 1983), 95–97. One could expand the "generation of 1399" rubric to include the stanzaic verse in MS Digby 102, though these poems are more
broadly moralizing, and less insistently topical, than the ones discussed in this essay. See J. Kail,
ed., *Twenty-Six Political and Other Poems*, EETS OS 124 (London: K. Paul, Trench, Trübner &
Co, 1904).

(especially in the case of Hoccleve) and of the relationship between poetic texts and other contemporary modes of writing, this boom has perhaps come about at the expense of this first generation of Lancastrian texts.[7] In what follows I will focus on three of its representatives, *Mum*, *Richard*, and the poem that has always seemed to me to be *Richard*'s closest analogue among its contemporaries, Gower's *Cronica tripertita*.[8]

In referring to this trio as "Lancastrian" poems, one must acknowledge the interlocking definitions of that adjective. The first, obviously, is chronological or dynastic; from this perspective "Lancastrian" means simply datable after about October 1399. The second denotation has to do with the partisan application of this term, according to which *Richard the Redeless* is a "Lancastrian" poem because it is explicitly critical of the government of Richard II and depicts Henry Bolingbroke as England's savior. *Mum and the Sothsegger* extols Henry personally, though it does find fault with his administration; I would call it more broadly "Lancastrian," though, as will become clear, this appellation is not entirely unproblematic. The movement from one poem to the other is—if I may borrow some language from another originally oppositional discourse—the movement from "we won't get fooled again" to "meet the new boss, same as the old boss."[9] The *Cronica* is perhaps most vehement in its condemnation of Richard II, as a result of its being both a topical poem

---

[7] A notable exception is Helen Barr's *Signes and Sothe: Language in the "Piers Plowman" Tradition*, Piers Plowman Studies 10 (Cambridge: Cambridge University Press, 1994), hence *S&S*. Barr's christening of the *"Piers Plowman* tradition," however—*Richard, Mum, Pierce the Ploughman's Crede*, and *The Crowned King*—indicates the degree to which she is interested here in the continuities between Ricardian and Lancastrian poetry rather than in the potentially unique traits of the latter. For Hoccleve, see Antony J. Hasler, "Hoccleve's Unregimented Body," *Paragraph* 13 (1990): 164–83; Larry Scanlon, "The King's Two Voices: Narrative and Power in Hoccleve's *Regement of Princes*," in *Literary Practice and Social Change in Britain, 1380–1530*, ed. Lee Patterson (Berkeley: University of California Press, 1990), 216–47; Derek Pearsall, "Hoccleve's *Regement of Princes*: The Poetics of Royal Self-Representation," *Speculum* 69 (1994): 386–410; and Ethan Knapp, "Bureaucratic Identity and the Construction of the Self in Hoccleve's *Formulary* and *La male regle*," *Speculum* 74 (1999): 357–76, and "Eulogies and Usurpations: Hoccleve and Chaucer Revisited," *Studies in the Age of Chaucer* 21 (1999): 247–73. A most thoroughgoing account of "the relations between textuality and political process" in the wake of Richard's deposition is Paul Strohm, *England's Empty Throne: Usurpation and the Language of Legitimation, 1399–1422* (New Haven: Yale University Press, 1998).

[8] For a less enthusiastic comparison of the two, see Andrew Wawn, "Truth Telling and the Tradition of *Mum and the Sothsegger*," *Yearbook of English Studies* 13 (1983): 286–87.

[9] The exact relationship between the two poems has been a matter of ongoing speculation. In the first edition of *Mum and the Sothsegger*, Mabel Day and Robert Steele printed both texts and argued that the two were fragments of one larger poem (*Mum and the Sothsegger*, EETS OS 199 [London: H. Milford for Oxford University Press, 1936], xviii–xix). Dan Embree's refutation of this claim is widely accepted; see "*Richard the Redeless* and *Mum and the Sothsegger*: A Case of Mistaken Identity," *Notes & Queries* 220 (1975): 4–12. Helen Barr is of the opinion that there are two poems but one poet; see *PPIT*, 15–16, and "The Relationship of *Richard the Redeless* and *Mum and the Sothsegger*," *Yearbook of Langland Studies* 4 (1990): 105–33. John Bowers has hypothesized that perhaps John But—the Bristol clerk John But—wrote the continuation of *Piers Plowman A, Richard*, and *Mum*; see "*Piers Plowman's* William Langland: Editing the Text, Writing the Author's Life," *Yearbook of Langland Studies* 9 (1995): 88–89. But *Mum* is so much more ambitious and sophisticated than *Richard* that I find it hard to imagine anything but two poems and two poets.

and the last stage of Gower's twenty-two years of moral scrutiny of Richard's reign. His career as a political poet is roughly coterminous with Richard's career as a sovereign, and Gower's downwardly evolving estimation of Richard's potential and character is of course amply evident in the "rolling revision"— M. B. Parkes's phrase—given to the *Vox clamantis* and the *Confessio amantis* throughout the 1380s and 1390s.[10]

The third sense of "Lancastrian" is the one that I will attempt to work out: the sense in which the political allegiances and topical nature of these poems can be correlated with—indeed, enjoin—the use of certain formal poetic devices and structural traits. What I hope to describe, in other words, is a "Lancastrian" poetic that can be defined formally as well as politically, in the way that poems are built as well as in the case they make for Lancastrian legitimacy. Two important traits characteristic of this generation of poems are the disappearance (or in the case of *Mum* the serious curtailment) of the dream-vision as the sign of topical literary engagement with contemporary events, and the concomitant increase of interest in documentary models of discourse, particularly legal texts and representations of parliamentary activity. The two motifs are certainly related; it is logical to assume that a crisis of political authority—the deposition and its aftermath—would present a problem for political poetry trying to speak authoritatively about that crisis. Trading dreams for documents turns out to offer some potential solutions.

Richard and the *Cronica* show the birth of this Lancastrian form immediately after the deposition, while the example of *Mum* a few years later testifies to both its serviceability and, as we shall see, its evolution.[11] And in each case we can point to something like a control group, a pre-deposition analogue against which the poems under consideration can be measured and in contrast to which formal differences can be seen. In the case of the alliterative poems, the control is their great exemplar *Piers Plowman; Richard* and *Mum* are, to borrow Andrew Wawn's phrase, "greatly but not helplessly in Langland's debt,"[12] and there are several ways in which, *pace* the "*Piers Plowman* tradition," both poems depart significantly from Langland's practice (though their innovations are without a doubt significantly enabled by the success and circulation of Langland's poem). For Gower there is the *Vox clamantis*, the

---

[10] M. B. Parkes, "Patterns of Scribal Activity and Revisions of the Text in Early Copies of Works by John Gower," in *New Science Out of Old Books: Studies in Manuscripts and Early Printed Books in Honour of A. I. Doyle*, ed. Richard Beadle and A. J. Piper (Aldershot: Scolar Press, 1995), 86.

[11] Helen Barr dates *Mum* after 1409, seeing an allusion to Arundel's Constitutions of that year in lines 408–14 (a reference to a statute giving friars sole rights to preach). I do not find this claim wholly convincing and would argue for an earlier date, in line with Day and Steele's suggested range of 1403–6. The poem was certainly written after 1402, since it refers to the execution of a group of Franciscans for sedition in August of that year. See *PPIT*, 23; Helen Barr, "The Dates of *Richard the Redeless* and *Mum and the Sothsegger*," *Notes & Queries* 235 (1990): 270–75, in which she surveys various attempts to date the poems; and Day and Steele, *Mum and the Sothsegger*, xix–xxiv.

[12] Wawn, "Truth Telling and the Tradition of *Mum and the Sothsegger*," 271.

poem to which the *Cronica tripertita* is appended as a kind of coda, events after 1397 apparently having advanced past the ability of simple if constant revision to keep pace.

Dreams and the Deposition

Noting that none of these poems is a dream-vision may seem a strange argument to make—after all, they are none of them fabliaux, either, and saying that does nothing to advance our understanding of what they actually have in common. Indeed, that each of these poems should abandon the dream form is in one sense not surprising, since none of them seeks to supply the sort of speculative solutions to contemporary woes offered by their predecessors, the *Vox clamantis* and *Piers Plowman*. The *Cronica*, in fact, is so far from an example of reformist apocalypticism as to be instead a kind of postapocalyptic triumphalism, and its congratulatory conclusion would hardly be enhanced by the distancing device of a dream. Helen Barr, Anne Hudson, James Simpson, Nicholas Watson, and others have described the increasing constraints on political and theological speech in the decades leading up to Arundel's 1409 Constitutions,[13] but there may have been no safer time to engage in direct, undreamed political writing than in the year or so following Richard's deposition—provided, of course, that the sentiments expressed were appropriately Lancastrian.

But the lack of a dream frame in each is significant, because the dream-vision figures largely in the lineage of each, and thus each has to resist considerable generic pressure and historical momentum in order not to be one. Gower and the author of *Richard the Redeless* respond to this pressure in similar ways and with similar solutions; each attempts to maintain the sense of authorial immanence characteristic of the dream-vision by representing the events described in their texts as not just recent but contemporaneous with their composition—even, in the case of *Richard*, as still in the process of unfolding. I will discuss these two texts together before turning at greater length to the more complicated case of *Mum*.

To take the *Cronica tripertita* first: Gower composed it, framed it, and arranged to have it copied as a sort of appendix or conclusion to the *Vox clamantis*, which of course begins with a dream-vision—a rather hard-won vision, in fact, since it takes the poet a good thirty-five lines to fall asleep, de-

---

[13] For Barr, see *S&S*; Anne Hudson, *The Premature Reformation: Wycliffite Texts and Lollard History* (Oxford: Clarendon Press, 1998), esp. chap. 9; James Simpson, "The Constraints of Satire in 'Piers Plowman' and 'Mum and the Sothsegger,'" in *Langland, the Mystics, and the Medieval English Religious Tradition: Essays in Honour of S. S. Hussey*, ed. Helen Phillips (Cambridge: D.S. Brewer, 1990), 11–30; Nicholas Watson, "Censorship and Cultural Change in Late-Medieval England: Vernacular Theology, the Oxford Translation Debate, and Arundel's Constitutions of 1409," *Speculum* 70 (1995): 822–64.

spite a day's worth of *chanson d'avanture* encouragements: birds singing, breezes rustling, flowers blooming. What follows that first terrifying account of the 1381 uprising—the matter of the first book—the poet describes as being derived from his "visus varii," his several visions (*VC* 2. Prol. 80), and in the very last chapter he declares that "While awake, I have set down these my writings which I received during sleep."[14] The *Confessio amantis*, composed after the *Vox*, provides further evidence that Gower thought of the dream-vision as the appropriate form for both moral satire and mirror-for-princes material. The *Confessio*, which describes itself in its earliest recensions as "a bok for king Richardes sake," also demonstrates that for Gower, form trumps language—that is, in both Latin and English the dream-vision represents the instrument of choice for "moral Gower."

Things change, however, around 1400. Gower clearly meant the *Cronica* to function as a sort of conclusion to the *Vox*, which it does in four of the five extant manuscripts, all of which probably date from Gower's lifetime, and all of which include a new concluding paragraph of Latin prose added to establish the transition from the *Vox* to the *Cronica*.[15] This passage, in concert with other revisions Gower performed on the *Vox*, recasts the moral of the earlier poem; instead of serving as a warning to the young king to amend his ways, the *Vox* retrospectively becomes an account of the first stage of the disasters that culminate in the upheaval of 1399—the matter of the *Cronica tripertita*.

But the *Cronica*, by contrast, is not a dream; despite serving as the appendix to a dream, it is always described as a chronicle, in the new *explicit* to the *Vox*, in the prefatory verses that introduce it, and in the first of the Latin marginal notes. This change of mode implies as well a change of voice for the poet. The rhetoric of the dream-vision can be monitory or confessional, as in Gower's earlier long poems, but a dream would make an odd vehicle for the kind of historical reportage the *Cronica* claims to provide, for the relation of events over and done.

To put it another way, the voice of a chronicler is very different from the voice of a dreamer, even a dreamer who tries, as Gower does, to elide his own words with the *plebis vox*, the voice of the people (*VC* 7.25.1469) and, of course—why not?—the *vox Dei*. A chronicle makes different demands of its readers than does a dream-vision; at the most basic level the chronicle, allying itself to the putatively irrefutable authority of the documentary record, typically insists that its readers accept the immanence of that authority in the chronicler's disembodied voice. That voice may only be ventriloquizing earlier texts or other sources, but its authority to do so usually derives from the writer's judiciousness and sagacity rather than his having been physically present during the events recounted. In the dream-vision, however, the authority to narrate derives from the conceit or illusion of authorial presence and au-

---

[14] *VC* 7.25.1461: "Que sompno cepi, vigilans mea scripta peregi."
[15] Macaulay, *CompleteWorks* 4.lix–lxv; and Parkes, "Patterns of Scribal Activity."

thorial experience: the difference between saying "this is what happened" and "this is what happened to me." The *Vox clamantis* stakes its initial claim to our attention and seeks to engage our ethical imagination through the latter remark; the *Cronica tripertita* tries to make the former claim: "this is what happened."

At the same time, though, Gower seems to realize that his retreat from "the unwilled world of vision"[16] leaves a gap of some sort, a weakness in the truth claims of his verse, a failure of the kind of authorial immediacy and immanence implicit in the dream-vision's strategy of address. So he tries to reclaim it, adopting by analogy to the dream-vision the stance of a witness to the events of the *Cronica*. In the opening lines, in fact, he claims to have written it all beforehand, "per ante" (1.9), in anticipation of what it describes, a strategy even he seems to have found untenable, as this is the last time he mentions it. Nevertheless, this claim shows him, I would argue, in search of some sort of authorizing conceit beyond that of simple memorial reconstruction—here a kind of prevenient narrative grace. What Gower eventually adopts, though, is the pretense that each section was composed contemporaneously with the events it describes. Thus part 1, which recounts the triumph of the Appellants in 1388, ends with a prayer on behalf of the three principals (two of whom were in fact already dead): "May there always be glory for the Swan in Christ's banner, and may there be praise in this world for the Horse . . . and may the Bear enjoy honor from the lips of the people" (1.214–16).[17] At the end of part 2, after having described the death of the duke of Gloucester, the execution of the earl of Arundel, and the exile of the earl of Warwick, the archbishop of Canterbury, and Lord Cobham, Gower reviews these events by saying, "In the twenty-first blood-filled year [that is, 1397], during the month of September, savagery held sway by the sword. As I listened in sadness, I entered into the writing of this poem. Lament, you who are alive, now that laments have subsided" (2.340–43).[18]

Finally, in the third part, he adopts a third historical position: "I recently lamented for this broken kingdom overwhelmed by the King's fierceness, but I have ceased my tears since then. I shall now smile upon an unsullied kingdom restored by the probity of its leader, and I shall not refrain from praise of him" (3.3–6).[19] The praise of Henry includes specific reference to the date of his coronation—October 13, 1399—and the account of Richard extends to the Lancastrian fiction that he starved himself to death after the failure of the

---

[16] The phrase is Anne Middleton's, from "Acts of Vagrancy: The C Version 'Autobiography' and the Statue of 1388," in *Written Work: Langland, Labor, and Authorship*, ed. Steven Justice and Kathryn Kerby-Fulton (Philadelphia: University of Pennsylvania Press, 1997), 263.

[17] "In Cristi signo sit semper gloria Cigno, / Laus et in hoc mundo sit Equo . . . / Vrsus et ex ore populi fungatur honore."

[18] "Anno bis deno primo de sanguine pleno / Septembris mense feritas dominatur in ense: / Tristis vt audiui, carmen scribendo subiui: / Plangite, vos viui, quia planctus sunt residiui."

[19] "Nuper defleui, lacrimas set abinde quieui; / Regnum purgatum probitate ducis renouatum / Amodo ridebo, nec ab eius laude tacebo."

earls' revolt in January 1400, and even to his subsequent burial at Langley. This conceit of reportage—and by extension reportorial presence during the events described—shows Gower to be in pursuit of the same authorizing immediacy as the author of *Richard the Redeless*, a work I turn to now.

That the alliterative poem would eschew the dream frame as well is perhaps more immediately striking, given its Langlandian heritage; one thing this suggests is that by about 1400,[20] thanks to the towering example and widespread circulation of *Piers*, and despite that poem's doubts about its own legitimacy and about "makyng" in general, dreams were no longer the necessary marker of serious topical poetry in English alliterative writing. Of course there are, and had been, other formal markers in vernacular verse—rhymed pentameter couplets spring to mind—and in what we usually call the "formal" tradition of the alliterative corpus, the romance histories of Alexander or Arthur never need to be represented as dreams, or as dreamed. What identifies them as literary undertakings is the historicizing prologue, the familiar "after the fall of Troy" rhetoric that displaces the action as it solicits the historical attention of the reader. But in *Richard the Redeless* there are no dreams, simply immediate, contemporary, topical engagement from the opening lines:

> And as I passid in my preiere ther prestis were at messe,
> In a blessid borugh that Bristow is named
> In a temple of the trinite the toune euen amyddis,
> That Cristis Chirche is cleped amonge the comune peple,
> Sodeynly ther sourdid [arose] selcouthe [marvelous] thingis,
> A grett wondir to wyse men as it well myghth,
> And dowtes for to deme for drede comynge after.
> So sore were the sawis [speeches] of bothe two sidis:
> Of Richard that regned so riche and so noble,
> That wyle he werrid be west on the wilde Yrisshe,
> Henri was entrid on the est half,
> Whom all the londe loued in lengthe and in brede,
> And rosse with him rapely [quickly] to rightyn his wronge,
> For he shullde hem serue of the same after.
> Thus talis me troblid for they trewe where,
> And amarrid my mynde rith moche and my wittis eke:
> For it passid my parceit [perception] and my preifis [proofs] also,
> How so wondirffull werkis wolde haue an ende.
> (*RR* 1–18)

The sole copy of *Richard* survives in Cambridge University Library (MS Ll.iv.14), a manuscript from the second quarter of the fifteenth century,

---

[20] *Pierce the Ploughman's Crede*, datable between 1393 and (probably) 1401 (*PPIT*, 9–10), is the first Langlandian poem to dispense with the dream frame; the question of how that poem's Lollard leanings might relate to its formal structure is beyond the scope of this essay.

where it follows a copy of the B-text of *Piers Plowman*, and one might conclude from the poem's first line ("And as I passid in my preiere ther prestis were at messe") that its copyist at least intended it to be taken as a continuation of Langland's dream-vision. After all, the setting of these opening lines—the speaker at prayer in a church during mass—mirrors the situation that introduces the seventh and penultimate vision in *Piers Plowman*, a vision that, significantly, represents the allegorical refoundation of an earthly community and the building of the barn of Unity; *Richard* itself is concerned with the foundation—and reformation—of the English polity. Clearly the author of *Richard the Redeless* is setting us up for some ecclesial dozing in his poem, too.

But we don't get it. The poet describes the "selcouthe thingis" while fully conscious, and indeed fully conscious of their political import. In fact the mention of Bristol in the second line begins at once to militate against the likelihood of a dream, even before the very un-Langlandian direct reference to Richard and Henry in lines 9–11. Though "Bristol" does have a nice Langlandian specificity, like Malvern or Cornhill, it is not a traditional site of uplandish complaint. Bristol, rather, is a place deeply implicated in the events surrounding Richard's deposition; as Helen Barr reminds us, "on 28 July 1399, Sir Peter Courtenay, keeper of the castle, surrendered Bristol to the forces of Henry Bolingbroke and handed over [Sir William] Scrope, Busshy, and Grene, who had taken refuge there. They were executed and their heads sent to decorate the gates of London."[21] Moreover, Bristol was the place to which the rebellious Thomas, Lord Despenser, fled after the failure of the "Epiphany Rising" in January 1400, and the place where he too was beheaded by the populace.

In addition to being in the right place, the author of *Richard* strives, like Gower, to show that he is in the right time, too, by pretending that the events he narrates are not yet resolved, and that he himself writes *in medias res*. He makes this gesture almost at once, with his claim that "it passid my parceit and my preifis also, / How so wondirffull werkis wolde haue an ende." How will it end? the speaker wonders, or rather, pretends to wonder, since it is virtually certain that the poem was composed not simply after Richard's deposition but quite likely after his death, which renders the poem's initial mirror-for-princes conceit purely strategic—a trope rather than a truth claim.[22] The poet may propose to offer Richard "a writte to wissen [advise] him better, / And to meuve him of mysserewle his mynde to refresshe" (1.31–32), but the poem was never intended to be on Richard's reading list as he lay imprisoned at Pontefract. Rather, this fiction of immediacy—the pretended insertion of the text into an environment of putatively unresolved events—seeks to recap-

---

[21] *PPIT*, 247, note to l. 2. As Skeat notes, Bristol was also Richard's point of departure for his campaign against the "wild Yrisshe" (*Piers the Plowman and Richard the Redeless*, ed. W.W. Skeat [Oxford: Oxford University Press, 1886], 2.287).

[22] For evidence that *Richard the Redeless* postdates Richard II, see Barr, "Dates," 271–72.

ture the lost authorial immanence, the authorizing presence, of the speaker in an alliterative, allegorical dream-vision.[23]

Mum and the Sothsegger is a more ambitious and complex poem than either *Richard* or the *Cronica*, and its relationship to its dream-vision lineage is correspondingly more complicated. In the first place, the poem is concerned with truly unresolved events, the troubles of the reign of Henry IV, a reign that, unlike Richard's, was not already over at the time of the poem's composition. At the same time, the shadow of the deposition still looms over the poem, and its influence, I will argue, deforms the one dream that does occur in *Mum*. The *Mum* poet, as we shall see, was fully aware of the problems inherent in an appeal to visionary authority in an era of fundamental political crisis. Finally, *Mum* even more than *Richard* has a multiple generic heritage; its greater debt to the *Fürstenspiegel* tradition also tends to put it at odds with its dream-vision ancestry.

Mum's dream of four hundred–plus lines takes up almost a quarter of the poem as we now have it. It is very reminiscent of *Piers Plowman* in both language and structure; it includes two fully elaborated and apparently unrelated allegories—one on the social organization of the beehive and one of the dwelling place of the "sothe-sigger" in man's heart—that are put into the mouth of a "semely. . . . sage" (954), the superannuated but still hale gardener who oversees the beehive. Moreover, the dream itself is framed by brief passages on the reliability of visions that cite the same authorities (Daniel, Joseph, and Cato) that Will does when he wakes up after the tearing of the Pardon in B passus 7. Both Langland and the author of *Mum* resolve this pro forma skepticism about dreams in favor of their trustworthiness (if not any particular interpretation) by emphasizing the authoritative scriptural examples. But whereas for Langland this passage serves as a jumping-off point for further dreaming, *Mum and the Sothsegger* is done with dreams at this point and turns instead to documents, the famous bag full of books. A closer examination of the dream sequence in *Mum* will reveal the extent of the author's skepticism.

The setting of the dream is a sort of *locus amoenus artistocraticus*, the fantasy version of a "frankeleyn-is fre-holde al fresshe newe" (*Mum* 946), characterized by overwhelming natural beauty, agricultural abundance, ample game ("a swete sight for souurayns, so me God helpe" [*Mum* 931]), and at the center the "gladdest gardyn that gome [man] euer had" (*Mum* 948), overseen by the gardener. The scene represents a seigneurial ideal, a microcosm of a healthy kingdom blessed by both sufficiency and order (and, implicitly, sufficiency because of order). But though most readers agree that the figure of the beekeeper—"An olde auncyen man of a hunthrid wintre . . . sad [grave] of his

---

[23] For a brief but keen account of *Richard*'s attempt to "pass" as a text more dangerous and polemical than it really was, see Kathryn Kerby-Fulton, "Langland and the Bibliographic Ego," in Justice and Kerby-Fulton, *Written Work*, 99–100.

semblant, softe of his speche"(*Mum* 956, 963)—is the most authoritative speaker in the poem, even he cannot offer a satisfying vision of a properly governed commonwealth. His account of how the bees in a hive are of "alle bestz beste . . . y-gouuerned" (*Mum* 997) ought to be a fairly straightforward allegory; it is certainly a venerable image, deriving from Virgil's *Georgics*.[24] The bees' organization is hierarchical and feudal, with the bee-king presiding over an aristocratic class of bees who are evidently devoted to their sovereign and to the good of the hive:

> Thayr dwellingz been dyuyded, I do [prove] hit on thaire combes [honeycombs],
> And many a queynt caue been cumpassid wy-thynne.
> And eche a place hath a principal that peesith [keeps peace in] al his quarter,
> That reuleth thaym to reste and rise whenne hit nedith,
> And alle the principallz to the prince ful prest [ready] thay been at nede,
> To rere thaire retenue to righte all the fautes;
> For thay knowen as kindely as clerc doeth his bokes
> Wastours that wyrchen [work] not but wombes forto fille.
> (*Mum* 1010–17)

But the bee polity is, strikingly, not a self-regulating one, since the wastrel drones who detract from the common profit of the hive have to be destroyed by the beekeeper himself rather than the bee-king or the afflicted bee masses. (The notion of a bee-king, incidentally, is to be blamed on Bartholomaeus Anglicus, the *Mum* author's chief source for this passage.) Even the narrator recognizes this reliance on an outside force as a problem:

> "Yit I mervaille," cothe [said] I, "and so mowen [must] other,
> Why the bees wollen not wirwe [destroy] thaym by tyme,
> And falle on thaym fersly furst whanne they entre,
> For so shuld thay saue thaym-silf and thaire goodes."
> (*Mum* 1074–77)

And though he calls the beekeeper's recital a "wise tale" that "hath muche menyng who-so muse couthe," he concludes that it is "to mistike [mystical/mysterious] for me" (*Mum* 1087–89).

The poet's refusal to interpret the bee allegory, expressed through the narrator's wistful protestation of his incapacity, directly recalls *Piers* again, as Barr notes—specifically the dreamer's unwillingness to explain the meaning of the rat parliament in the Prologue.[25] And like the rat fable (an allegorized account of the Good Parliament of 1376), the bee allegory merits special handling because it too concerns the highest figures in the realm: it is a heavily occluded (and only partly successful) allegory of the deposition.

[24] So notes Barr in *PPIT*, 336 n. 987.
[25] Ibid., 340 n. 1088–89.

Or, rather, the Lancastrian usurpation, since the passage represents not the overthrow of the bee-king but the usurpation of his role as regulator of the drones; the king and his subordinates are powerless to check the drones' abuses, and only an outside force—the gardener—can set the hive on the right track. In answer to the dreamer's question about the bees' inability to police the drones themselves (lines 1074–77, quoted earlier), the beekeeper replies:

> The bees been so bisi . . . about comune profit
> And tendeth al to trauail while the tyme dureth
> Of the somer seson and of the swete floures;
> Thayr wittes been in wirching and in no wile elles
> Forto waite [look for] any waste til wynter approche,
> That licour thaym lacke thair lyfe to susteyne.
> But as sone as thay see thaire swynke [labor] is y-stole,
> Thenne flocken thay to fighte thair fautes to amende,
> And quellen [kill] the dranes quicly and quiten alle thaire wrongz.
> (*Mum* 1078–86)

These lines—not derived from Bartholomaeus[26]—prove too "mistike" for the dreamer because they are a distant but not inaudible echo of the 1399 revolution, when (from the Lancastrian perspective) the country joined with Henry Bolingbroke, "thair fautes to amende," or, to put it as *Richard* does, when "alle the londe . . . / rosse with him rapely to rightyn his wronge, / For he shullde hem serue of the same after."[27] The gardener is a figure for Henry (not the only one in the poem, as we shall see), someone who intervenes from outside the hive (or kingdom) to destroy those who corrupt the polity.

Identifying the gardener as a figure for Henry IV does not exhaust his significance, of course; he certainly has divine associations, and as the resident wise man, he is also the one who authorizes the poet's satiric project at the end of the dream, a most un-Henrician activity. But such a combination of the conventional and the topical is characteristic of the *Mum* poet, whose text throughout is edgier than *Richard*'s, riskier and subtler, in direct proportion to its actual distance from the deposition itself.

Gower sidesteps these issues almost entirely by casting the *Cronica* as history rather than complaint, but both *Richard* and *Mum* confront directly the issue of the authorization of satiric speech and writing. In *Piers Plowman*, of

---

[26] Ibid., 339 n. 1069–86.
[27] Compare *Mum* 143–49:
But whenne oure comely king came furst to londe,
Tho was eche burne bolde to bable what him aylid
And to fable ferther of fautz and of wrongz,
And romansid of the miss-reule that in the royaulme groved,
And were behote helpe, I herde it myself
Y-cried at the crosse, and was the king-is wille
Of custume [and] of coyliage the comunes shuld be easid.

course, this process is fraught with anxiety, contradiction, and displacement, but little of that doubt survives in the later poems, where the question of authorization is much more straightforward. In *Richard*, in fact, the allegorical figure of Reason himself encourages the narrator to persevere in his efforts:

> But yif God haue grauntyd the [you] grace for to knowe
> Ony manere mysscheff that myghtte be amendyd,
> Schewe that to thi souereyne to schelde him from harmes;
> For and he be blessid the better the betydyth [the better it will be for you]
> In tyme for to telle him for thi trewe herte.
> (*RR* 2.72–76)

Reason is of course a much tougher customer in *Piers Plowman*.[28] In *Mum*, the beekeeper's admonitions to the narrator authorize his satiric project:

> Though thou slepe now my soon, yit whenne thou seis [see] tyme,
> Loke thou write wisely my wordes echone;
> Hit wol be exemple to sum men seuene yere here-after. . . .
> I haue infourmed the [thee] faire loke thou folowe after
> And make vp thy matiere, thou mays do no bettre.
> Hit may amende many men of thaire misdeedes.
> Sith thou felys the [feel yourself] fressh lete no feynt herte
> Abate thy blessid bisynes of thy boke-making
> Til hit be complete to clapsyng [clasping] . . .
> (*Mum* 1267–69, 1277–82)

It is true that this advice is given in a dream; at the same time, as we have seen, just what the beekeeper has "infourmed" the narrator remains too "mistike" to be uttered.

James Simpson has argued that while the later poem certainly follows its exemplar in constructing the authority of the satirist, *Mum* does not undo or "deconstruct" that authority in the same way that *Piers Plowman* obsessively does.[29] This much is certainly true, but the situation is a little more complicated. In fact, the later poems can pursue their relatively uncomplicated strategy of authorization because of a generic affiliation that moves them away from *Piers* and toward the *Fürstenspiegel* tradition, which, as Judith Ferster has

[28] Reason in *Piers* is decidedly more reserved on this issue; in the B-text's mirror of middle-earth, he is downright testy in his suggestion that Will get his own house in order before he dare criticize Reason's ordinance of the world, and in the famous encounter in C passus V, Reason and Conscience are openly skeptical of Will's chosen life's work. This passage and its significances are extensively scrutinized in the essays that make up Justice and Kerby-Fulton, *Written Work*. What the author of *Richard* clearly takes from *Piers* is a sense of urgency rather than anxiety, and a confidence in the justification for this sort of topical poetry to be written and disseminated, even without the intervening authorizing function of a dream.
[29] Simpson, "Constraints of Satire," 25.

shown, is subject to its own kind of deconstructive impulse.[30] Both of our poets signal their alliance with this tradition through the conceit of direct address to the monarch; although each poem imagines a readership larger than one, each is also careful to identify the sovereign as a particular recipient of the poem's message.[31]

In *Mum* the beekeeper advises the narrator to "furst feoffe thou therewith the freyst [noblest] of the royaulme" (*Mum* 1284), that is, enfeoff the king with your book, a remark that captures well the transactional nature of the genre. Derek Pearsall has written that "princes welcomed [mirrors for princes] . . . because it was important that they should represent themselves as receptive to sage counsel."[32] Here of course the poet's representation is that the prince will be receptive to his wise words, but in each case it is the gesture—humbly offering advice or graciously receiving it—rather than the content of the advice itself that defines the genre's effects.

But this generic affiliation has consequences, too, because it brings with it the inherent paradoxes of the *Fürstenspiegel* that Ferster has described at length—not just the delicacy of offering advice to one's sovereign, but the paradoxical portrayal of the governor as one who must be governed, and the essential impossibility of giving and taking advice successfully.[33] Such contradictions are visible in *Mum*, where the opening premise of the poem—that the king needs to be alerted to the "comune clamour" (*Mum* 157) and the grievances of his subjects by a truth-teller—mutely implies that the king and his court are entirely out of touch with the kingdom, and can be blamed for being so. And if this implicitly aligns Henry with Mum, the inveterate enemy of truth telling throughout the poem, the connection is made more explicit a little further on by a striking juxtaposition between the two of them. Following a passage that briefly describes the consequences of truth telling—imprisonment, torture, or burning at the hands of some (significantly) unidentified agent—the poet turns to a twenty-six–line encomium of Henry's virtues, par-

[30] Judith Ferster, *Fictions of Advice: The Literature and Politics of Counsel in Late Medieval England* (Philadelphia: University of Pennsylvania Press, 1996).

[31] At the end of his opening discussion of the subject's duties of counsel, the *Richard* poet writes: "And if ony word write be that wrothe make myghte / My souereyne, that suget [subject] I shulde be, / I put me in his power and preie him, of grace, / To take the entent [intention] of my trouthe that thoughte non ylle" (*RR* 1.76–79).

[32] Pearsall, "Hoccleve's Regement," 386. Gower's dedication and direction (and rededication) of poems to sovereigns and patrons is well documented.

[33] *Richard* avoids some of these pitfalls by its conceit of address to the already deposed Richard II, thus further fictionalizing its own undertaking, but the ingrown conflicts of this essentially conservative genre are still visible in some places. For example, in Passus 3, a long diatribe against showy array and the follies of fashion dwindles into an acknowledgment that no one should be blamed for dressing "In comliche clothinge as his statt axith" (*RR* 3.174); a few lines later a condemnation of excessive and expensive mirth turns into a platitudinous remark about how life ought to have both ups and downs (*RR* 3.263–99). This philosophical pragmatism derives precisely from the conventional and conservative nature of a genre that tries to critique the social organization that it would simultaneously preserve, an undertaking that the vexed (and analogous) circumstances of the deposition make even more complicated.

ticularly his martial ones, an example of what David Lawton calls the "antipopulist" loyalty of the *Mum* poet.[34] When this passage of praise begins to
drift into a lament that the covetousness of Henry's council might deter him
from the well-meaning purposes of his own will—when, that is, the poem of
advice to the king begins to suggest that the king might be entirely too susceptible to the wrong advice (a recurrent theme in *Richard*)—Mum abruptly
intervenes, making his first appearance in the poem and changing the subject
from the concrete and topical to a more abstract account of the world's resistance to truth telling.[35]

> But God of his goodnes that gouuernith alle thingz
> Hym [i.e., Henry] graunte of his grace to guye [guide] wel the peuple
> And to reule this royaulme in pees and rest,
> And stable hit to stonde stille for oure dayes.
> But I dreed me sore, so me God helpe,
> Leste couetise of cunseil that knoweth not hymself
> (Of sum and of certayn, I seye not of alle)
> That of profitable pourpos putteth [deters] the king ofte,
> There his witte and his wil wolde wirche to the beste—
> "Nomore of this matiere," cothe Mum thenne
> "For I mervaille of thy momeling more thenne thou wenys [think].
> Saides not thou thyself, and sothe as me thoughte,
> That thees sothe-siggers seruen noon thankes?"
> (*Mum* 223–35)

It is telling that this intervention occurs not just in the middle of a description of the king's household, but in the middle of a description of the king
himself: Henry cannot speak in a poem putatively addressed to him, and
Mum here makes it impossible for the narrator to speak directly of him. It is
more telling still that the interruption occurs after the stability of the kingdom has been introduced as a topic ("And stable hit to stonde stille for oure
dayes"). And, finally, it is a paradigmatic moment in the poem; whenever the
narration verges on a recognizable account of contemporary events, it quickly
veers away again toward the allegorical and the conventional, repeatedly arguing that a resistance to truth telling is characteristic of the world at large,
rather than simply the court environment in which the issue first arises.[36]

[34] David Lawton, "Lollardy and the *Piers Plowman* Tradition," *Modern Language Review* 76
(1981): 789.
[35] Alcuin G. Blamires ("*Mum and the Sothsegger* and Langlandian Idiom," *Neuphilologische Mitteilungen* 76 [1975]: 592) also comments on the abruptness of Mum's appearance, which he compares to Piers's sudden arrival in *Piers Plowman*.
[36] Cf. Strohm, *England's Empty Throne*, 26: "The Lancastrians were no friends to spoken or
written critique. Celebrated occasions of permissible dissent—like Repingdon's admonitory letter—turn out upon closer inspection to be more artfully arranged instances of complicity. This
distaste for criticism was hardly unusual among medieval monarchs. But the innovative element
in the reigns of Henry IV and Henry V is the extent to which, rather than waiting for instances

A related example occurs at precisely that point in the dream-vision at which the narrator declines to unpack the significance of the bee allegory; instead, he reintroduces "the matiere of Mum" and poses to the gardener the question "who shuld haue / The maistry, Mvm or the sothe-sigger" (*Mum* 1096, 1101–2). What ensues is a satirical indictment of how parliament, ruled by Mum, fails to "shewe the sores of the royaulme" and "burst out alle the boicches [boils] and blaynes [blisters] of the heart" so that the sores fester and abscess and "ennoye thaym ther-after" (*Mum* 1120, 1122, 1140). The king is surprisingly—or, rather, unsurprisingly—absent in this account of parliament and its primary function, and this has a double implication: it suggests, echoing the earlier passage, that the king is out of touch with the kingdom's complaints because parliament fails to articulate them properly, and also that the king is somehow complicit in the silence (in part since, as the gardener goes on to observe in a further echo of the earlier passage, his court is full of "coiphes," i.e., coifs, or lawyers, who contribute to the corruption of the process of justice). This passage also proves a bit too alarmingly topical, and the gardener's speech turns quickly to the relationship of Mum and "Lucifer the lyer" and to the quaintly impenetrable allegory of the sothsegger's dwelling in man's heart—turns, that is, to topics more conventionally moral and more broadly allegorical.

Mum's juxtaposition of Henry and its title character—its implication, if you will, that Mum is somehow Henry's alter ego—reveals a profound truth about the poem's own concern with truth telling, and embodies the fundamental constraint on satire in the first turbulent years of the fifteenth century. Mum may be an allegorical representative of the general political climate, but the ultimate source of that climate is the king, and all of the poem's complaints, its almost ritual litany of contemporary abuses (the perils of maintenance, the cupidity of lawyers, the pastoral hegemony of the friars), function to draw our attention away from the unspeakable truth of the moment, the foundational abuse: that is, the fact that Henry is a usurper, that the Lancastrian claim to the throne is illegitimate, that Richard's deposition was spectacularly illegal and his death a political assassination. But Henry can't handle the truth:

> But the king ne his cunseil may hit not knowe
> What is the comune clamour ne the crye nother,
> For there is no man of the meeyne [retinue], more nother lasse,
> That will wisse thaym any worde but yf his witte faille,
> Ne telle thaym the trouthe ne the texte nothir,

of public criticism to arise and responding accordingly, these monarchs regularly attempted preemptive intervention at the imaginative, geographical, and discursive places of insurrectionary possibility." The way the *Mum* poet imagines the relationship between Henry and Mum would seem to be an emblematic literary instance of this practice.

But shony [shuns] forto shewe what the shire meneth,
And beguile thaym with glose, so me God helpe,
And speke of thaire owen spede and spie no ferther,
But euer kepe thaym close for caicching [overhearing] of wordes.
And yf a burne bolde hym to bable the sothe
And mynne [warn] hum of mischief that misse-reule asketh,
He may lose his life and laugh here no more,
Or y-putte into prisone or y-pyned to deeth
Or y-brent or y-shent or sum sorowe haue,
That from scorne other scathe [harm] scape [escape] shal he neure.
(*Mum* 156–70)

Certainly none of the king's "meeyne" is going to tell him tales of "miss-reule," given the consequences cited here. These lines, which precede the praise of Henry's knightly and kingly virtues described earlier, read rather differently through the prism of the deposition—as indeed does the poet's entire encomium, which suddenly seems to be more of an apologia. Disclosing the utterly conventional "truths" told so far in the poem—the fact that justice favors the rich and that taxes are too high—would hardly seem to be a capital crime worthy of imprisonment, torture, or burning, carefully described here as punishments experienced by the offender (*yputte, ypyned, ybrent, yshent*), rather than as strictures imposed by some recognizable agent. But we know who that agent really is. His identity and his interests are made manifest two hundred lines later with the poem's reference to a group of hanged friars—"thaire lesingz [lies] haue led thaym to lolle by the necke; / At Tibourne for traison y-twyght vp [hung up] thay were" (*Mum* 419–20)— which helps to fill in the details of the "comune clamour" that allegedly never reaches the king and his council; the Franciscans were executed for spreading the "lesingz" that Richard was still alive in 1402.[37] One of the poem's few datable references, and the one traditionally used to establish its terminus a quo, forcefully (if briefly) calls to our attention the continuing mortal consequences of the deposition.

Paul Strohm has argued that it is a constitutive condition of Lancastrian texts, gestures, and representations of legitimacy to betray their anxieties about that legitimacy, and to acknowledge (even while endeavoring to repress) its foundation in acts of conquest, repression, and misrepresentation.[38] In *Mum and the Sothsegger* this anxiety is triply evident. It cripples the ability of the dream-vision to provide a visionary solution to the nation's woes by rendering the dream too "mistike"—in the poem's code—for interpretation.

---

[37] Most of the contemporary chronicles describe this incident; a particularly full account appears in J.S. Davies, ed., *An English Chronicle of the Reigns of Richard II, Henry IV . . .* , Camden Society ser. 1, 64 (London, 1856), 24–26. For a modern discussion of the episode, see D. W. Whitfield, "Conflicts of Personality and Principle," *Franciscan Studies* 17 (1957): 326–35.

[38] Strohm, *England's Empty Throne*, passim.

It compromises the poem's portrayal of the king himself by calling attention to what we nowadays would call Henry's political baggage. And finally it renders the poet's appeal to history fundamentally ironic, through its implicit invocation of the bloodier side of contemporary politics.

Nowhere is this clearer than in the *Mum* poet's choice of Genghis Khan as the exemplary historical figure most likely to inspire loyalty in his followers. This passage occurs near the end of the "bag of books" sequence with which the poem breaks off, and about which I will have more to say later on. A "copie for comunes of culmes [items] four and twenty" (*Mum* 1388) describes the quick spread of seditious rumors throughout the country, an obsessive concern of Henry's administration.[39] The passage is linked lexically and thematically to earlier references to Henry by phrases like "king-is courte" and "king-is cunseil," and by the description of "Lesingz . . . / As falsely forgid as though a frere had made thaym" (*Mum* 1404). The antidote to the way people "carpe of the coroune" is the kind of loyalty inspired by "Changwys-is deedes," and at this point the poet briefly retells the story of Genghis Khan's rise to power, probably derived (and slightly modified) from *Mandeville's Travels*. Genghis's success at uniting the seven Tartar tribes rests on "two statuz, as storie of hym writeth, / I herde neuer harder and yit thay holde [held] were" (*Mum* 1431–32): the first, that the "souurayns of the seuene nacions" should slay their eldest sons and heirs, and the second that they should "sese hym in hire londe," that is, give Genghis legal possession of their holdings. Obedience is apparently instantaneous:

> And as the king comandid accordid thay were,
> Consentyng to his couetise with crie alle at oones.
> Thay sparid not to spille blode that spronge of thaymself,
> Ne to lose thayre lordship and lande at his wille.
> Now forto telle trouthe, I trowe hit be no lesyng,
> Who wolde haue griefed for a grote he wold haue grucched there.
> Thus preued [proved] this prince his peuple and thaire hertz,
> And to feil [feel] of thaire fiance [loyalty] ful felly [cruelly] he wroughte;
> And whenne he wiste that his wil was not encountrid [opposed],
> But that he had thaire hertz al hoole at his wil,
> He forgafe thaym thaire graunt and goodely thaym thanked.
> (*Mum* 1440–50)

Assured of the absolute loyalty of his adherents, Genghis embarks on the program of conquest that will turn Cathay into "the richeste royaulme that reyne ouer-houeth [hovers over]" (*Mum* 1456).

The *Mum* poet explicitly intends this exemplum to contrast the selfless loyalty of the Tartars with the grouching and grumbling of the contemporary English. It is difficult, however—even in the postmodern era of business

---

[39] See Barr's note to this passage, *PPIT*, 352 n. 1388–1404.

manuals like *Leadership Secrets of Attila the Hun*—to look past the cruelty and "couetise" of Genghis's methods; even the poet must admit that he acts "ful felly."[40] And of course the passage implicitly and insistently compares Genghis with Henry, not merely because they are both kings seeking the loyalty of their people but because the details of Genghis's program—or pogrom—reflect and refract the themes and circumstances of the deposition.[41] Rightful heirs are slain in a burst of familial violence, and proper lines of inheritance are disrupted in the name of an agenda of conquest, while Lancastrian fantasies of legitimation recur in displaced form: that the Tartars, mired in "diuision," can be united only by a strong, autocratic leader; that their obedience would be characterized by such murderous alacrity; that their new sovereign, once assured of their loyalty, would benignly restore that which he had extracted. Even the claim of divine election, a prominent feature in such celebratory coronation texts as Chaucer's "Complaint to His Purse" and Gower's "In Praise of Peace," reappears in the Genghis Khan story; as in Mandeville (and his source, Hayton's *Fleurs des Histors D'Orient*), the "grete God of goodnes that gouuernith alle thingz" (*Mum* 1417) appears in dreams to instruct the Tartars that Genghis is to be king of all the tribes.

Moreover, the Khan's statutes read as an uncomfortable analogy to Henry's own actions throughout the reign, a long list of politically justified executions of the various rebels to Henry's rule. The earliest months saw the deaths of the Epiphany conspirators, while the battle of Shrewsbury in 1403 was followed by the execution of Thomas Percy, earl of Worcester. Perhaps most recently for the *Mum* poet, Henry and a particularly compliant court of his creation condemned to death both Richard Scrope, archbishop of York, and the Earl Marshal, Thomas Mowbray, for their rebellion in the spring of 1405. In the days prior to the revolt, bills had been posted on churches in York calling Henry a usurper, championing an unnamed rightful heir, and decrying the unjust deaths of the Epiphany rebels and the Percys; the tumults of the early part of the reign had clearly not been forgotten. Henry's execution of an archbishop surpassed even the reputed crimes of Richard II and apparently shocked many (including Archbishop Arundel); the real-world repercussions of that event—for example, reports of miracles taking place at Scrope's tomb—renders the cheerful compliance of Genghis's courtiers all the more fantastical in context.[42] Finally, the Khan's command to his nobles to slay their heirs also looks slyly toward Henry, who kept in close custody the two sons of

[40] Wess Roberts, *Leadership Secrets of Attila the Hun* (New York: Warner, 1991).

[41] As Barr observes, Mandeville describes Genghis's lawmaking at much greater length, whereas the *Mum* poet focuses on these two statutes only (*PPIT*, 354 n. 1431). Day and Steele (*Mum and the Sothsegger*, xxi–xxiii) note the relevance of the Genghis story to the events of the deposition and connect it (as does Barr) to Henry's vexed relationship with the Percys, initially his allies but after 1402 allied with Owain Glyn Dwr in his resistance to Henry's rule.

[42] For the story of the 1405 uprising and its consequences, see J. L. Kirby, *Henry IV of England* (London: Constable, 1970), 185–88.

Roger Mortimer, the late earl of March, who had been Richard's designated heir.[43]

Discovering exemplary figures burdened by undesirable but unavoidable traits seems to have been a specialty—indeed, the inescapable fate—of Lancastrian poets. Certainly Gower has similar troubles in "In Praise of Peace," where the historical models he offers to Henry—Alexander, Solomon, Constantine—turn out to have a host of skeletons in their respective closets.[44] And the *Mum* poet doesn't really help his situation when, in trying to seal off hermetically the potentially unsavory tale of the Tartars with a Latin quotation, he seizes on the first verse of Psalm 132: "Ecce quam bonum et quam iocundum habitare fratres in vnum" (*Mum* 1456a). The line's praise of unity does reconfirm the principle of loyalty that is the ostensible purpose of the Genghis Khan material, but the reference to "fratres," though doubtless meant to be forward-looking, cannot help but look back to the poem's disloyal friars, their seditious "lesingz," and the capital consequences thereof— that is, to the whole recursive complex of Lancastrian paranoia and violence that this anecdote of "fratres in vnum" is designed to repair. The blandness of the next sentence—"Now by Crist that me creed, I can not be-thenke / A kindely cause why the comun shuld / Contre the king-is wil ne construe his werkes" (*Mum* 1457–59)—is blackly (and bleakly) humorous in the context of the "cunseille of Changwys," and nowhere is Lawton's "antipopulist" sentiment more evident. Given the burden of Henry's own history, what's a loyal poet to do?

Poems, Parliaments, Documents

One strategy adopted by all three of our loyal poets in the face of the political instability of the deposition's aftermath is the turn toward legal and documentary modes of discourse. Or perhaps it would be better to say, in each case, that the difficulties posed by the deposition were not so much the material and legislative consequences of political instability (e.g., prosecutions for treason and sedition or statutory censorship) as they were obstacles to thinking clearly and logically about political stability, and to representing the upheaval of the deposition as some sort of contribution to the stability and continuity of the realm. In such circumstances the apparent fixity and unalterable archival persistence of legal documents, chronicles, and statutes would have

---

[43] Kirby (ibid., 182–83), describes how the two boys escaped briefly in early 1405 but were captured before they reached Wales and their uncle Edmund Mortimer, now Owain Glyn Dwr's ally and brother-in-law. The Mortimer claim to the throne through Lionel, duke of Clarence, third son of Edward III, came through the female line, Lionel's daughter Philippa having married Edmund Mortimer, third earl of March. Henry's claim lay in the male line via his father, John of Gaunt, Edward's fourth son.

[44] Grady, "Lancastrian Gower," 561–70.

an undeniable appeal; indeed, such a focus can be seen as one more aspect of the Lancastrian attempt to manage as closely as possible the content and dissemination of official accounts of the deposition.[45]

Certainly Gower wrote under the influence of that Lancastrian master text, the "Record and Process" account of Richard's fall that was copied into the parliament rolls and circulated widely. Despite the pretense of contemporaneous composition that he tries to sustain in the *Cronica*, the finished product represents the triumph of the past tense and of present tendentiousness: the abuses he describes were traits of Richard's administration alone, and they have now been corrected or at least condemned by his successor, "Strenuissimum Principem Dominum Henricum." Gower's idea of what constitutes the narrative of a "chronicle" demonstrates a notably urban, "inside-the-Beltway" bias; both his sense of audience (Archbishop Arundel, for example) and his plan of organization reveal that his "chronicle" was designed to retell a story already familiar to its learned and loyal readers.[46]

In fact, the *Cronica tripertita* is largely organized by its references to parliamentary activity. It begins with the events surrounding the Merciless Parliament of 1388 in part 1, continues in part 2 with the circumstances of the Revenge Parliament in 1397, and concludes—climaxes—with the parliamentary deposition of Richard and Henry's election in part 3. Such attention to matters accomplished, or imagined to be accomplished, primarily in parliament does not necessarily make Gower the constitutional theorist that some have wished him to be, though he is clearly concerned with the legality of each proceeding; the legitimacy of Henry's succession, in both the mind of the lawyer Gower and in the contemporary propaganda, clearly depends on both the irrevocable propriety of 1399 and the complete rejection of 1397. Part of Gower's project in the *Cronica* is thus to deny the legitimacy of both the 1397 body's decrees and the so-called Parliamentary Committee of 1398, which Gower calls "an abomination of the law."[47]

It is in reference to the 1398 parliament that the *Cronica* and *Richard the Redeless* once again intersect. *Richard* (as we now have it) breaks off in the middle of a satirical description of a parliament, and the reference to "a fifteneth and a dyme [tenth]" and "all the custum of the clothe" (*RR* 4.15–16) probably alludes to the lifetime grant of the wool, leather, and woolfells subsidies bestowed on Richard by the 1398 Shrewsbury parliament. In addition to its abrupt termination, this parliamentary passage is interesting for a number of reasons.

First of all, it is a description of a real parliament, not a parliament of rats

---

[45] As described by Strohm in "Saving the Appearances."

[46] Gower wrote a prefatory epistle to the archbishop of Canterbury for a presentation copy of the *Vox* and the *Cronica*. The letter is preserved in All Souls College, Oxford MS 98; Macaulay (*Complete Works*, 4:lxi) thought that this was the very MS presented to Arundel; but see Parkes, "Patterns of Scribal Activity," 92–93.

[47] "Hoc facto regis fuit abhominacio legis" (*Cronica* 3.33).

or birds (or bees, for that matter), or a parliament displaced to ancient Troy, but a contemporary one attended by "knyghtis of the comunete" and "citiseyns of shiris" (*RR* 4.41–42). Bereft of any Aesopian (or Langlandian) disguise, the parliament offers a display of malfeasance, incompetence, and partisanship that seems to look ahead to Dryden, Swift, and Pope as much as to any contemporary models. Indeed, I know of no contemporary models in the vernacular, uninsulated by dream-visions, allegory, or historical distance. Equidistant from literary parliaments on the one hand and real parliament rolls and chronicle accounts on the other, *Richard* offers pure institutional satire. The antics of this sorry gathering—"somme slombrid and slepte and saide but a lite; / And some mafflid with the mouthe and nyst what they mente; / And some had hire [payment] and held ther-with euere; / . . . Some helde with the mo [majority] how it euere wente" (*RR* 4. 62–64, 86)—are briefly interrupted by an unsuccessful ship-of-state metaphor, allegory's last gasp in the poem, before it breaks off incomplete.[48]

Or rather, not just incomplete but incompletable: as the poem tends toward the genre of parliamentary reportage, out of which, as Steven Justice and Katherine Kerby-Fulton have suggested, Ricardian alliterative poetry may have arisen, it ceases to exist.[49] The parliament—whether one sees it as an anxious return to the site of the poem's generic origins, or as an authorized if imperfect alternative discourse of complaint—brings with it, paradoxically, not speaking but silence.

There is yet more to this paradox, however, because the 1398 parliament turns out to have its own complicated *textual* history. That body met in Shrewsbury in January, and toward the end of the assembly Richard established (at the request of the commons, as it is conventionally claimed) a committee of eighteen, twelve lords and six commoners, to continue the business of parliament after its closing. Exactly what Richard had in mind at first for this committee is impossible to recapture; the claim that it was just one more example of his tyranny was one of the charges leveled against him at the deposition, and clearly it did on several occasions serve him as an instrument of revenge, among other things confirming condemnations for treason (in one case a posthumous one). This is also the way Gower describes events in the *Cronica*: "Note how the King secured a committee for himself through subtle deceit so that he, together with certain persons designated by him, could continue the previously instituted Parliament wherever he wished to sit." "Thus, wherever the royal presence sat, it dealt out injury, with the result that no one knew what wicked deeds he stealthily entered into."[50] Just as clearly, though,

---

[48] Here "incomplete" means exactly that: two-thirds of the last page of the poem are left blank, only eleven of the usual thirty-five lines having been written (or composed).

[49] Kathryn Kerby-Fulton and Steven Justice, "Langlandian Reading Circles and the Civil Service in London and Dublin, 1380–1427," *New Medieval Literatures* 1 (1997): 66.

[50] "Nota qualiter rex subtili fraude concessum sibi optinuit, quod vbicumque sedere vellet cum certis personis sibi assignatis, per prius inceptum continuare posset parliamentum." "Sic, vbicumque sedet presencia regia, ledet, / Quod nullus sciuit sceleris que facta subiuit." The first passage is a marginal annotation; the second is *Cronica* 3.31–32.

the group also took up run-of-the-mill governmental business throughout 1398–99—coinage issues, craft disputes, harbor repair, and the like. It may be that the notion of using the committee as a Star Chamber did not occur to the king right away.[51]

One thing is sure, however: once Richard had decided to employ the committee in this fashion, the parliament rolls were amended and recopied so as to provide retrospective justification for its wider scope, as J. G. Edwards's analysis of the three extant copies of the roll has shown. That this took place at Richard's instigation was another charge made at his deposition. Kerby-Fulton and Justice contend that this charge underlies the *Richard* poet's description of the 1398 parliament as a "preuy [secret] parlement" (*RR* 4.25), and that given the "likely Chancery origins of the poem" and the role of Chancery clerks in the official and unofficial genres of parliamentary reportage, "the charge would have been a particularly egregious one for the poet: that Richard was trying to evade and corrupt the documentary supervision of his actions.[52] For Barr, *Richard*'s abrupt conclusion is an instance of imitative form: "Almost as if in mimesis of the breakdown of institutional resources to redress grievances and corruption . . . the supplementary narrative of *Richard* breaks off."[53] But the situation seems to be even more dire: institutional resources have been preemptively coopted to serve "preuy" purposes. Such a "Beltway" reading of *Richard*—the claim that one of the poet's default concerns is the division of labor and the distribution of authority in the civil service—is paradoxically supported by the poem's ostensible west country setting, which actually reveals an insider's knowledge of current events: the first meeting of Richard's parliamentary committee took place in March 1398 in Bristol.[54]

Across the great divide of the deposition, then, these texts mirror each other, Richard II's rewritten parliament rolls and *Richard*'s unwritable parliamentary satire. If the charges made against him in 1399 are true, and Richard was ultimately responsible for rewriting the parliament rolls, then we must credit the king with a keen appreciation of the power of such documents to shape public and institutional opinion, an appreciation more often reserved for his successor. True or not, the appearance of the accusations in the "Record and Process" testifies once again to the acute importance of the control of such texts to the Lancastrian hegemony. And *Richard the Redeless*'s unconventionally literal account of parliament, though incompletely rendered, shows that the poem shares a similar sort of documentary aspiration. Gower attacks the legality and legitimacy of Richard's last parliaments; the author of *Richard* uses allegory and satire in his unfinished attack on them. Both poets

[51] This is the conclusion of J. G. Edwards, "The Parliamentary Committee of 1398," in *Historical Studies of the English Parliament*, vol. 1, *Origins to 1399*, ed. E. B. Fryde and Edward Miller (Cambridge: Cambridge University Press, 1970), 316–28, esp. 320–25.

[52] Kerby-Fulton and Justice, "Langlandian Reading Circles," 78–80.

[53] Barr, *S&S*, 44.

[54] Edwards, "The Parliamentary Committee of 1398," 320.

realize, however, that the control of parliamentary representation and re-portage are one key to the Lancastrian program.

Mum and the Sothsegger has a slightly different set of documentary aspirations. It displays less interest in parliaments, perhaps again because of its greater distance from the events of the deposition. It does share with both *Richard* and the *Cronica* a notable dependence on legal language, which should not be surprising; Gower was himself a lawyer, and *Piers Plowman* certainly bequeathed to *Richard* and *Mum* both a rich legal vocabulary and an interest in the juridical power of various classes of documents: writs, wills, pardons, and the like.[55] Barr, who has amply demonstrated the density and complexity of legal diction and reference in *Richard* and *Mum*, argues that a "founding tenet" of these poems is that "writing corrective poetry is a legal activity, and one that is analogous to prosecuting a suit at law and passing judgment on those found guilty of the charges against them."[56] The logic of analogy implied here seems to me to be substantially correct, though I wish to modify it in a way that will show *Mum* to be both more ambitious and necessarily less successful than Barr holds.

The key passage in *Mum* is of course the bag of books sequence, which occurs immediately after the dream of the beekeeper. Opening a bag of unknown (or at least unstated) provenance "Where many a pryue poyse [secret verse] is preynted withynne / Yn bokes vnbredid [unopened] in balade-wise made"(*Mum* 1344–45), the narrator launches into a catalogue of contemporary abuses "forto conseille the king"(*Mum* 1344–45); the poem breaks off about four hundred lines into the bag. Barr remarks that this is "one of the most self-reflexively bookish moments in Middle English literature. It is a self-conscious proclamation of the political significance of literacy."[57] But there is a particular kind of literacy engaged by this collection. As many critics have observed, almost all of the twelve words used to describe the books actually describe documents with some legal force: there is a "quayer of quitances" (*Mum* 1348), documents recording debts or payments; two "rolles" (1364, 1565) and a "cedule" (schedule, 1734) attached to yet a third roll; a "scrowe" (1489); two "copies" (1388, 1683); a "writte" (1498); and a "title [*Mum*: "lite"] of a testament" (1697).[58] The lexical specificity of the passage reveals the narrator's intimate familiarity with these different kinds of legal

[55] For a discussion of Langland's "documentary poetics," see Emily Steiner, "Medieval Documentary Poetics and Langland's Authorial Identity," in *Crossing Boundaries: Issues of Communal and Individual Identity in the Middle Ages and the Renaissance*, ed. Sally McKee (Turnholt: Brepols, 1999), 79–105.

[56] *S&S*, 164.

[57] *PPIT*, xiv. Richard Firth Green argues that the scene foregrounds "the disruptive potential of literacy," the "unholy alliance between unprincipled authority and literate technology" that is the *Mum* poet's chief target throughout the text (*A Crisis of Truth: Literature and Law in Ricardian England* [Philadelphia: University of Pennsylvania Press, 1999], 280–81).

[58] On the political connotations of "schedule," see Wendy Scase, "'Strange and Wonderful Bills': Bill-Casting and Political Discourse in Late Medieval England," *New Medieval Literatures* 2 (1998): 237.

documents, and his attempt to gather them all under the rubric of "books" (in what must have been one pretty large bag) is a measure of his own ambitions for *Mum and the Sothsegger*. In this last scene, *Mum* is not just a satirical poem about satirical poems about contemporary conditions, a "meta-complaint"; it is a satirical poem about contemporary conditions that aspires to be a kind of satirical document about contemporary conditions. It seeks, in other words, a generically impossible state: *Mum* wants to be one of the "books" in the bag, to be endowed with the documentary, legal, performative force of a writ or a roll or an acquittance.

The narrator has already expressed this ambition in the passage that introduces the bag of books sequence. Inspired by his dream and the beekeeper's encouragement to write, the narrator adopts not a legal metaphor but a medical one to describe his goal:

> Thenne softe [softened] I the soores to serche thaym withynne,
> And seurely to salue thaym with a newe salue
> That the sothe-sigger hath sought many yeres
> And mighte not mete therewith for Mvm and his ferys [companions]
> That bare a-weye the bagges and many a boxe eeke.
> (*Mum* 1338–42)

During the dream-vision the beekeeper had chided parliament for not fulfilling its responsibility to "shewe the sores of the royaulme"; here the narrator sets himself the additional, ambitious task of softening, searching, and salving those sores "with a newe salue." And why not? Mum and his henchmen haven't yet snatched his bag. The beekeeper's remarks about the role of parliament ought to remind us of Gower and *Richard*, and the return of that theme here demonstrates the difference in ambition between *Mum* and the earlier poems. Those texts sought to establish their Lancastrian credentials and to forward Henry's claim to the throne through the representation of parliamentary action, while for *Mum*, even more than for *Richard*, parliament is part of the problem, not part of the solution: it has fallen victim to the eponymous Mum, and Mum as we have seen is no more than the shadow cast by Henry himself. Meet the new boss, same as the old boss.

The narrator thus proposes to take up the sothsegger's task, and even to supersede him, employing a new "documentary poetic" that does not simply tell truths but endows them with the formal properties and performative powers and "material solidity" of rolls and testaments.[59] Of course it is an utterly utopian undertaking, the sort of ambition that comes from taking a little too seriously Shelley's claim that poets are the unacknowledged legislators of mankind. And thus it makes a certain sense that the poem breaks off incomplete at this point, in the midst of an unrealizable project: though the missing

---

[59] The phrase "documentary poetic[s]" is Steiner's ("Medieval Documentary Poetics"). The phrase "material solidity" is Green's (*Crisis of Truth*, 281).

conclusion to *Mum* as we have it is the result of physical circumstances, it is hard to resist the conclusion that a different "logic of the lost leaf" is operating somehow—that the poem ending in the middle of this scene is overdetermined.[60]

Another way to describe what happens at the end of *Mum* would be to say that the poem suffers from a sort of generic overload in the bag of books sequence. Each document, as it is removed and read, turns out to contain a satirical indictment of one or another class of the poet's contemporaries. So the "quayer" and the "penyworth of papir" and the "volume of visitacion" together critique episcopal greed and the shortcomings of ecclesiastical supervision of derelict parsons and priests; the "rolle of religion" decries the aristocratic ambitions of the clergy, and the "paire of pamphilettz" their indulgence in pluralities and concubines; the "copie for comunes," as noted before, attacks the common folks' habit of spreading potentially seditious rumors (and introduces the lengthy Genghis Khan digression); the "scrowe for squyers," the "writte of high wil," and the "raggeman rolle" take up the aristocratic sins of maintenance, feuds among the magnates, and the oppression by the rich of the poor in lawsuits. The list goes on—indeed, it promises to go on past the end of the poem—but its generic affiliation should be clear: it is an estates satire, ticking off first the faults of the clergy, then the commons, then the nobility. This satirical impulse is of course elsewhere evident in *Mum*; the poem begins with an account of the officers of the king's household, and later it gives particularly devastating accounts of the universities and the friars. But at the end of *Mum* the poet comes closest to the standard estates satire schema—and, simultaneously, moves furthest away from it by virtue of his documentary conceit. Traditional estates satire is here kidnapped by the bureaucratic culture that certainly produced both poem and poet; the abuses it catalogues are utterly conventional, but the documentary mode of presentation represents a genuine attempt to renovate a genre much practiced by the poet's contemporaries.[61] If the practical implications of that renewal are not exactly obvious (what is the status, legal or otherwise, of a document embedded in a poem?) nevertheless it is interesting in the context of the other estates satires we know were circulating and being copied in London and Westminster at the same time—not just Langland's, but also Gower's and Chaucer's. Any account of a language policy for Lancastrian England needs room for such unofficial products of official culture as the unsanctioned and probably unsanctionable *Mum and the Sothsegger*, which employs the same

---

[60] The beginning of *Mum* is missing, too—at least two folios. The manuscript is described by Day and Steele (*Mum*, ix–xii).

[61] Chaucer at once springs to mind: Jill Mann claims that when the *Mum* poet puts the phrase "ware and wise" (*Mum* 1716) in the mouth of a corrupt executor, "the phrase seems to indicate the self-interested prudence of Chaucer's Sergeant" (*Chaucer and Medieval Estates Satire* [Cambridge: Cambridge University Press, 1973], 250 n. 23), implicitly reminding us that as a (presumably) younger contemporary of Chaucer's, the *Mum* poet would have been able to look to the *General Prologue* as an example of what could be done with vernacular estates writing.

language (if not the same dialect) and the same generic models as the English texts being recruited to serve the interests of a Lancastrian linguistic nationalism. In its concluding illustration of what Richard Green has called "an unholy alliance between unprincipled authority and literate technology,"[62] *Mum* suggests why such texts might have to be actively conscripted into such a project: not everybody was ready to volunteer.

One thing that the conclusion to *Mum* does make definitively clear is the poem's decisive turn away from the dream-vision; the answer to the dream's own uncertain calls for reform and for an authoritative, written cultural criticism lies not in visionary poetics but in the documents and instruments of the workaday, wide-awake world. This retreat from the dream-vision is one hallmark of the Lancastrian style that I have been describing. The deposition encouraged and naturalized certain formal effects in those texts, both in those eager to celebrate the dynastic change, Gower and the *Richard* poet, and the poet of *Mum*, dealing more skeptically with the aftermath of 1399. The successful legitimation of Henry's usurpation was dependent on the activities of a carefully managed parliament, and on the equally careful management of the texts and documents recording and disseminating that parliamentary activity. Following the logic of the moment, the *Cronica tripertita* allies partisan interest with parliamentary representation in the service of the Lancastrian establishment, while *Richard the Redeless* offers a satirical account of parliamentary doings to delegitimize the assemblies of Henry's predecessor. The poet of *Mum*, full of conventional disillusionment about the parliaments of Henry's reign, turns to documents themselves, and his poem ends (or stops) looking more like a cartulary than a chronicle. Paul Strohm calls Richard's deposition and murder an "empty place," an event that can only ever be partially known and whose significance can only be constructed afterwards through the texts that try to fix its meaning.[63] A study of the first generation of Lancastrian writing confirms that this is not an exclusively modern insight, that while the dust of the deposition was still settling, the writers of the generation of 1399, mindful of the complex and reflexive relationship between political events and political poetry, were remaking text and genre in the Lancastrian image.

---

[62] Green, *Crisis of Truth*, 281.
[63] Strohm, *England's Empty Throne*, xi.

Appendix

History or Narration Concerning the Manner and Form of the Miraculous Parliament at Westminster in the Year 1386, in the Tenth Year of the Reign of King Richard the Second after the Conquest, Declared by Thomas Favent, Clerk

Translated by Andrew Galloway

1. Since, by custom, ancient and long durations fatally seep away from human beings' fleeting present memories, urgent reason has admonished me that, in however childishly inept a way, I should undertake to compose for posterity an account in formal written proceedings[1] of certain extraordinary events that not long ago transpired in England. Let it not be disgusting to bring to mind and commit to memory such things which, if every diligent reader would heed, he would have a mirror, in part, for more easily avoiding adversities, scandals, and the dangers and burning torments of death. I will not therefore allow it to remain delighting in the secret den of silence, how a monstrous sin of this sort, starting from certain people who were smothered in the embers of avarice and burdened by the weight of crimes, thereafter raced through England.

2. During the year of our Lord one thousand three hundred and eighty six, at a time when in the tenth year of his reign King Richard, the second after the Conquest, was cavorting in the glens of his youth, a certain archbishop of

---

Translated from the text edited by May McKisack (*Historia sive Narracio de Modo et Forma Mirabilis Parliamento apud Westmonasterium anno Domini Millesimo CCCLXXXVI . . . per Thomam Favent Clericum Indictata*, Camden Miscellany 14 [London: Camden Society, 1926]; henceforth McKisack), with emendations as noted; numbered paragraphs follow her paragraphs. Tenses have not been made consistent with modern usage. The evidently non-authorial title is misleading, since the bulk of the narrative concerns 1388, with the initial section concerning 1386 drawn from the charges made in 1388, and presented only because it is essential background to the 1388 parliament.

[1] *Processus*, a term of narration used in legal as well as historical writing in the period; *The Westminster Chronicle* also describes one of its accounts of 1388 as a *processus* (ed. and trans. L. C. Hector and Barbara Harvey [Oxford: Clarendon Press, 1982], 278; henceforth *West. Chron.*). Favent describes the trial of 1388 as a *processus*.

York, Alexander Neville by name; Robert de Vere, duke of Ireland; Robert Tresilian, chief justice of the lord king; and Nicholas Brembre, knight and former mayor of the citizens of London, were governors and close councillors of the king, living in vice, deluding the said king, concerned neither with the king's nor the kingdom's business but embracing the mammon of iniquity for themselves through much wickedness. Under their shadow of sins the king is made a pauper, such that, lo! by raising taxations and impositions, the kingdom is lacerated with great wounds. Because of such things, countless adversities were fostered in the kingdom. Perceiving that such things were falling utterly into perversity, the lords of this kingdom, to direct the kingdom into the way of peace, urged the king to hold a parliament on the day after the next Michaelmas.[2] In this parliament the aforesaid Michael de la Pole, chancellor of England, was dismissed from office on the grounds of his usurpations and extortions, and having given back every round ring, he is driven off to Windsor, and all his properties are confiscated in reciprocation for the extortionate fines he devoured. Nonetheless, they did not yet disturb the aforesaid other councillors of the king, but in the same parliament, by the mutual assent of the king and of all the lords, justices, and commons, a commission was given to the below-written lords of the kingdom: to the archbishop of Canterbury; the said archbishop of York; the bishop of Ely, then chancellor of England; the bishop of Winchester; the bishop of Hereford, then treasurer of England; the bishop of Exeter; the abbot of Waltham; the Lord John Waltham, keeper of the privy seal; the duke of York; the duke of Gloucester; Earl Arundel; Lord Cobham; and Richard Scrope and John Devereux, knights: that these, by the power of this commission and of a certain ordinance and statute, succeeding by possession to full power of the king and parliament in this matter, would correct the stupid madness of rebellions and order, counsel, and execute all business of the king and the kingdom, with annual judgments, pledging with their hands on the Gospels that they would observe the aforesaid things well and faithfully. And if anyone aroused the king to contravene the aforesaid ordinance, for the first offense the penalty imposed would be confiscation of all goods; for the second, loss of life and limb. Thus disposing all matters for the better, with the parliament concluded, all departing from there returned to their own affairs.

3. But, one might ask, then what happened? The aforesaid imprudent councillors with others of their companions are inflamed by the torches of wrath on account of the aforesaid things of the parliament being published and ordained. With the parliament's ordinances soon disseminated, they gathered rapidly around the king, and overshadowing him more than usual with illusion, they incited treachery in the heart against all those first moving and ordaining the aforesaid ordinance, commission, and statute to come into being and, according to them, thus derogating the king's prerogative, and by

[2] October 1, 1386.

shredding the royal power even the king would not be as usual able to give gifts by any free will of his to anyone, unless first these had been determined by a council of the commissioners at Westminster. Under pretext of these things, with the devil—who does not forget their ends—persuading them, those hardened by evil days strove iniquitously by clandestine councils through many unheard-of frauds and deceits to nullify all these things, and to have the aforesaid commissioners with their other adherents drawn in the death of traitors, under the form that follows.

4. First,[3] they blinded the guileless king by the conversations from their serpents' mouths, with ambitions, adulations, lascivious words and praises, such that, ensnared by all their poisonous conspiracies and desires, he adhered by agreement, thinking they were disposing everything for the best; and they abhorred the councils and propositions of the said commission at Westminster as if these were treason. Also, the king, struck by love of the praises and illusions of the aforesaid men, begifted them in many ways, as well as their followers under the pretext of receipts of brokerage: he gave John of Blois, the captive heir of Brittany, as he claimed, to the said duke of Ireland and to certain others castles, towns, and lands; to others, however, jewels and monies, all of which sums reached 1,500 marks, in a heavy cost to the king himself and the kingdom. Not even at that point did the devourers themselves give thought to the condition of the king or the kingdom, but thus carrying on in their ways of life, thus depredating with their greedy brokerage receipts, they set up insufficiently competent captains in the said castles and towns, whose naive armed force was totally destroyed, and which finally was seized into the hands of their enemies, an event that had never been seen before, from time out of mind. Also, denigrating the condition of the royal dignity in violation of their allegiance, by which the king alone should be of free condition beyond all others, they swore by the power of a certain oath and made the king submit himself as oath-swearer, that, by the strength of his body and of royal power, in prosperity and adversity, he would sustain and defend them against all who opposed or resisted them. Also, whereas by the ordinance of the aforesaid parliament he was to sit at Westminster with the council of the commissioners at various opportune times, those detractors drew the said king by persuasions to the more remote nooks of the kingdom, to the harm of those faithful commissioners in whose hand then resided the kingdom's power and vitality. Nonetheless, when many—the chancellor of England, the treasurer, and the keeper of the privy seal, and at other times certain others from Westminster with the commissaries of those same officials—made their way over hill and dale toward the king, they could reveal nothing concerning their acts and counsels by informing or speaking to the

[3] As noted above, p. 231, this section on 1386 is little more than summary and elaboration of the charges made against the king's associates in 1388 by the Lords Appellant; see *Rotuli Parliamentorum, ut et Petitones ... Tempore Ricardi R. II*: (London: House of Lords, 1783), 3.230–35. The perspective in this section often reflects its later date and source.

king, publicly or privately, except in the presence of those detractors or their deputies, and thus with the acts and counsels always being reported by those, the detractors were more easily able through this to minimize things contrary to their interests, and to increase with their own elaboration things that accorded with those interests.

5. What more? When, traveling toward the regions of Chester, Lancashire, and Wales, the aforesaid fools took their way making their rounds through all parts to lords, knights, squires, and commons capable of bearing arms, giving golden signs of a simulated sun and silver crowns to retain these men, everywhere at the king's expense the retainers intemperately hasten, so that, prepared in their attack, they might especially assail the said commissaries: the duke of Gloucester, the earl of Arundel, and the earl of Warwick, since these more decisively than the other commissaries were set on curtailing their plans. Also, judging the aforesaid commission and statute to be null, they caused the said duke of Ireland to be ordained chief justice of Chester. Immediately, he along with them sometimes bending to the right, sometimes to the left, framed the order of judgments according to the complaints of money, releasing those deserving punishment, confiscating the goods of others, punishing still others in place of the guilty. Also, through the procurings of scoundrels, through the brokerages and gifts of those who were egregious tormentors, they impeded certain innocents who did not wish to adhere to them, so that they would be less able to prosecute their law, by aggravating them with immense delays, the exhaustion of journeying, and many kinds of expenses. But some, harassed through writs to appear, others through imprisonment, still others through threats of death, they retained under their control, giving them the sign of the aforesaid sun and crown. Also, for destroying the said commissaries and their associates they retained thieves, robbers, and felons, who were illegitimately freed from their convictions of felony and other crimes by charters and patents of pardon. Moreover, notwithstanding that for ages lapsed from memory the land of Ireland was regarded as the patrimony of the king of England, the aforesaid duke of Ireland, baselessly wishing to be sublimely exalted, was created king of the said land of Ireland, for confirmation of which letters of the king were sent to the highest pontiff. Also, the aforesaid Nicholas Brembre, holding the office of mayor of London for a single day, seized by force twenty-two men, some appellants of felony, some convicted felons but chaplains, arresting them under the pretext of diverse transgressions and imprisoning them in Newgate in London, in the silence of night. And having been led, bound fast, in Kent to a place popularly called Foul Oak, by his hot ferocity and without a sound of judgment, mercilessly, in red rivers from their veins they died, through a capital punishment entirely springing from him, except for one man who by chance escaped safe under the guise of an excuse. Also, a certain one of the said detractors, with the king's innocence untainted but nonetheless under his name, went to London at an appointed time, there declaring before certain crafts of the said city

delusory intentions and propositions, led the said crafts by flattery and deceits into vice, by making them swear that they would observe, sustain, and defend the will and proposals of the lord king and themselves, prepared whenever they were asked by the said Nicholas Brembre that they would fight to the death by force and arms to punish all who were disobedient and opposed to the king and to the royal power. With the precipitous decline of the times adding evils to evil, they sent out a royal letter to the mayor of the citizens of London by a courier, the clerk John Ripon, with a certain writ under the king's secret seal folded into the said letter, whose import along with the letter was that the three aforesaid lords, namely, the duke and two earls particularly, and other commissaries were to be indicted in London in the county of Middlesex for high treason and false conspiracy aimed at the king; then they were to be arrested, condemned, and subjected to the cruel death of traitors, and their lineage was then to be disinherited in perpetuity, because the aforesaid ordinance, commission, and statute in derogation of the king's and the Crown's prerogative had been prejudicially ordained through them, and by their goading and ordering the king to consent under coercion to those things. At once the mayor and the aldermen of the said city of London called a common council concerning what should be done about this matter, and these men, with arguments mounted for and against, arrived at unanimity, that it should be well understood that they did not want to accept any part of this thing nor did they want that mandate to be carried out. Meanwhile, since a bad thing leads to worse, and soon by its own weight pulls down another evil onto itself and that evil a third and so on, the aforesaid fools, inflamed by recklessness, clandestinely transmitted by John Golafre, knight, a royal letter to their enemy the king of France, requesting to contract at Calais or somewhere nearby a five-year truce, in this way, namely, that our king of England would there apply himself to deceptively framing the said fraudulent truce, then our king would send for the said duke of Gloucester, the earls of Arundel and Warwick particularly, and certain other commissaries, as if not wishing to do anything without their counsel, and thus surrounded, they would be treasonously slaughtered by horrible torments as false traitors to the king and kingdom. And for ensuring the completion of these things, the said adversary of France would regain in return for this matter all castles, towns, and properties pertaining to the king of England in those regions. And for more fully proving that these things are true, very many safe-conducts from the said king of France, our adversary, were sent here for transporting our king and his favorites there; these safe-conducts, now collected into the hands of the said commissaries, are ready to stand in witness to this at any time whatsoever. Moreover, beyond those letters of that date, other letters of the king directed to the king of France were intercepted from a courier, which are further witnesses. These letters indeed included encouragement to the king of France to make his way into England with a great force, to attack the said three lords and the other commissaries and all those authorizing or

favoring the said ordinance, commission, and statute to be created in derogation of the king's and his rank's prerogative, and villainously to destroy them,
and, by consequence, the English people and language, by surrendering them
to a cruel death. Who has ears for hearing, let him hear.[4]

6. Moreover, laboring in the devil's vineyard with indefatigable minds and
always vigilant, while they were in regions far from Westminster's council in
a castle of Nottingham, they sent by writ for Robert Bealknap, chief justice of
the common pleas; John Holt; Roger Fulthorp and William Burgh, justices of
common pleas; and John Lokton, the king's sergeant at law, striving to make
them associates of their frauds, and when they had compassed these, ignorant
of what they were about to do, there in a council chamber with the king and
said five traitors present and the doors locked they proposed many questions
to them, in the following way. First, whether the new statute, ordinance, and
commission created and published in the preceding parliament at Westminster did not derogate the king's royal prerogative. Also, how those who had
procured it to be made should be punished; and how should be punished
those who had excited and compelled the king to consent to those; and how
should be punished those who impeded him so that he was less able to exercise his prerogative. When these and many other things had been asked, they
responded unanimously to the individual questions that those ought to be
punished either as traitors or that they merit being subjected to capital punishment. To all of this testimony the aforesaid justices, along with John Cary,
then lord chief baron of the Exchequer, compelled as they claimed by a legitimate fear of death, applied their seals for those present, "with these as witnesses: Alexander Neville, archbishop of York; the archbishop of Dublin in
Ireland; Thomas the bishop of Chichester; John the bishop of Bangor; Robert the duke of Ireland; Michael, earl of Suffolk; John Ripon, clerk; and John
Blake, knight. Given on the fourteenth day of the month of September in the
year of our Lord one thousand three hundred eighty seven, and the eleventh
year of the reign of Richard, second after the Conquest." Then the ones who
had been coerced, as they asserted, swore to hide the council, telling nobody
of it under pain of death, and they departed.

7. And when these traitors were scheming these and many other diabolic
things to destroy and enervate the aforesaid ordinance, commission, and
statute, by mutual consent maintained among themselves they affirmed by
oath that they would entirely preserve all these diabolic things. And along
with those, what is worse, they made the king swear with them, that, in his
own person, by his bodily and royal power, insofar as he was able he would
take vengeance against the aforesaid duke and earls and their other adherents
by dragging them to a bitter death. The deeds of all these things may be more
easily recognized if the periods of time and the order are observed. But our

[4] E.g., Matt. 11:15.

Commiserator and merciful Lord, although so many sorrows and torments had been fostered in the kingdom of England on account of the multifarious masses of our sins and crimes, not wishing to take vengeance abruptly but instead to take pity and tolerate still others, as thus driving away our languor, and in order to alleviate the exhausted spirits of the faithful commissaries and cure our anxious sorrows, inspired the hope of strength and understanding in the souls of the said three lords, namely, the duke of Gloucester and the earls of Arundel and Warwick, who, after they had been suspecting for all this time some sort of evils to occur by the said traitors, ordered to be sent cautiously through all parts of England messengers and spies so that they might take and retain all royal letters and their couriers whosoever, to whomsoever the letters were directed or sent, delivering the letters to wherever the commissaries were in England without delay. Once thus done, the outcome of things proved the merits of this, in so much as they examined and understood every counsel for the entire year of those imprudent ones, every traitorous proposal in the substance of the letters recovered—glory to God in the highest, and peace to men of good will on earth![5]—and by this manner of action they considered the kingdom to be at the point of destruction, according to the Gospel saying, "Every kingdom divided against itself will be destroyed."[6] According to the sanctions of law, it is legitimate for everyone to respond to violence with violence; and since it is better to anticipate a problem beforehand than to seek a remedy after a wound has been inflicted, in safeguarding of the king, the kingdom, and their own lives they raised up the people, each of them from his own area, until by everyone's estimate the full number reached twenty thousand men ready for defense, as ones proposing to infringe by force the diabolic propositions of the aforesaid traitors and to soften by explanations their fervid hearts, harder than iron and impervious to divine approval.

8. And since the fame about the earl of Arundel's army was from the first made audible and clear, how with his force he shifted around at night near the regions of London, he lay quiet hiding in woods and forests until a time convenient to him might appear, there awaiting the arrival of his accomplices. Not by injuring anyone did he and all of his men live, but instead they purchased their foods and other necessaries at full market price. They were almost unable to keep the popular community quiet and prevent them from rising with them by their own keen desires, as those bent on destroying the said false lords[7] along with their adherents. Meanwhile, the said false lords, striving to obstruct their purposes with a certain spiritual commission by the

[5] The allusion is to the liturgical piece "Gloria in excelsis Deo," in the preliminary section of the mass.
[6] Matt. 12:25.
[7] *Pseudodomini*, McKisack's emendation of the scribe's various efforts at this word (*pedomnus*, etc.). The word evokes the "false prophets" of, e.g., Rev. 19:20.

power of ancient letters patent in their keeping—the effect of whose proclamations was at that time not at all at the butt-end of things[8] to that extent, but
was only for blinding the people of the city of London—did not fear to have
it proclaimed in the king's name that no one should seem to be so bold, under
pain of forfeiture of all goods, to sell, give, or exchange, publicly or privately,
any goods, any kind of arms, or any other necessities to Richard, earl of Arundel, or any his men, but rather to refuse and reject giving to him and his men,
as rebels to the king, any manner of sustenance, comfort, or refreshment.
Nonetheless, they somewhat feared the scorn of future generations; and both
because the assistance they hoped to get from the mayor and commons of
London might be refused, and because of that new insurrection of men advancing toward them, with turbulent heart they counseled the king to distance himself from the parliament at the next feast of the Purification of the
Blessed Mary, the starting date of parliament that the king and the said commissaries had previously appointed, and not to involve himself in any business
of the kingdom, or himself in any commodious or incommodious matter, any
loss or danger, unless first the three aforesaid lords and the other commissaries would swear an oath that, while holding that parliament, neither they
nor anyone else in their name would propose or put in motion anything concerning the commission against them. And they had it proclaimed through
the city of London that no one, under pain of confiscation of goods, would
seem by any means to promulgate or narrate anything sinister or shameful
about the king or any of his adherents, which was indeed nearly impossible to
prevent.

9. After a brief time elapsed, it happened that the king with the aforesaid
five false lords took their way from the manor of Sheen toward Saint Edward's shrine at Westminster for the sake of fulfilling a pilgrimage. Soon the
aldermen and commons of the said city, in a sizable following of men, en-
countered him on horseback in a gathering, giving him special honor. And
when he had arrived at a place commonly called the Mews, a little ways from
his palace, he made his pilgrimage from there barefoot to Saint Edward at
Westminster, and the chaplain of the said commissaries along with the abbot
and convent of the said monastery met with him in procession, singing.

10. But meanwhile, the aforesaid three lords, that is, the duke and two
earls, with their forces gathered on the same Sunday, that is, the fourteenth
day of November of the same year, at Waltham Cross in Hertford County,
sent for other commissaries remaining with the king in the palace at Westminster. There, in writs, they appealed the aforesaid five false lords, namely,
the archbishop of York, the duke of Ireland, the earl of Suffolk, Robert Tresilian, and Nicholas Brembre, on the crime of high treason, and they volun-

---

[8] *Nichil ad rumbum*, otherwise unattested, possibly corrupt, but more likely to be vividly collo-
quial and whose general meaning, "nothing doing," is clear. Perhaps < ME *rumpe*, Latinized, i.e.,
"end" or "point."

teered that they would prosecute their appeal, and moreover that what they indicted would be legitimately proven, under pledge of their goods and those of competent oath-givers; and they made all the other commissaries to be inserted as part and appellants into their appeal; then they requested them to relate those things to the king. And when a deed of this kind resounded in the king's ears, he sent to them seeking what would be their plan and intention, and they sent a response stating, "It is of concern for the public weal that certain traitors hanging around you be fittingly rejected and punished, since it is better that certain ones die for the people than that the entire nation perish." They also requested that they might converse together coming and going with entire safety. Then the king, with their will understood, in reply ordered them to come; and when they had come to Westminster, and the king was sitting on his throne in the Great Hall in the midst of his commissaries, the said three Lords Appellant with a huge multitude of people entered the hall and there, with both knees bent down, they greeted the king, bowing very submissively three times. And with again the case set forth, in the manner and form by which they had earlier presented it at Waltham Cross, they appealed on the crime of high treason the said archbishop, duke, earl, Tresilian, and Brembre, who at that time were all hidden in the palace, having betaken themselves into obscure strong rooms and shady dens there, just as Adam and Eve anciently did from God, not having the heart to be taken.[9] At once the king accepted the said appeal for trial and prosecution, fashioning for them a day in the aforementioned parliament to be held on the day after the next Purification of the Blessed Mary. But in the meantime, the king put both parties with their goods and their retained men under his special protection, for the purpose that none of the others would cause trouble until the following parliament, a circumstance that was frequently proclaimed publicly throughout all regions of England; and they went away consoled.

11. The aforesaid duke of Ireland, however, with the devil his leader, made his way to the regions of Chester, Lancashire, and Wales and there raised without difficulty from the men in his confiscated retinue a new kind of power in the king's name, numbering six thousand fighting men, for attacking and destroying the aforesaid Lords Appellant. With no royal protection preventing him, he along with his army bent his path toward London with a raging clamor, contemning the peace at the king's expense; his heart, foolish and hateful to God, grazed on vain hopes. Meanwhile, the vigorous and commemorated appellants were apprised about his raging rabble in the nick of time. Adjoining to themselves by reason of affinity the earl of Derby and the earl of Nottingham, and those who had been made consorts of the said appeal, lest one might reckon expensively the long stretches of tireless labors, with their armies they pursued them to a field next to the town of Whitney at the place commonly called Radcot Bridge. In this field the aforesaid duke of

[9] Reading *comprehendi* for the manuscript's meaningless *comperendi*.

Ireland with his army, having a stream of water to their side, prepare themselves for fiercely fighting and destroying the said Lords Appellant, unfurling there the king's standard in violation of the statutes of England. But since those fiercer in the beginning are broken in the end, when they saw the ranks of the said five vigorous appellants everywhere pouring from the hill and turning around them like a swarm of bees, fear seized them. And stupefied when they charged—yet God did not want the spilling of blood or the mutilation of members—they stood as if leaderless, or a herd without a head, giving no occasion or appearance of resisting. Immediately they with all their goods and arms were stripped, and the armies handed them over as if conquered; but since very few were killed and only some drowned while fleeing, the hearts of the cruel ones are instantly softened. The duke of Ireland, however, striking his horse with his spurs, took to the river. He evaded the danger in this way, and amazingly, although certain ones pursued him, they nonetheless lost him. And thus thanks to God, those vigorous appellants in strengthening of the state of the kingdom received the palm of victory in this manner, supported by angelic assistance.

12. When the deed resounded in the ears of the other traitors lying hidden[10] with the king in Westminster, in the hush of night they immediately fled very fearfully along the Thames into the Tower of London for better safekeeping. Nonetheless, the aforesaid Nicholas Brembre, with a stiff and stern expression, in the king's name caused continual watches to be held in order to exclude the said five vigorous appellants from passing through any gate of the city of London by armed force by day or night. However, the said implacable vigorous appellants with their forces headed to London to address the king. Yet when it came to their ears how, through the said Nicholas Brembre, the gates of the said city were guarded by constant watches for repelling them, and when they pondered whether or not the said city would resist them at their arrival, they wavered in mind. In a camp, therefore, behind Clerkenwell in the territory of the same city, on the twenty-seventh day in the month of December of the same year, each of the said Lords Appellant with his army, with a sweet harmony of diverse instruments as prelude, properly prepared himself for the manner of war. They did not wish[11] to enter the city with an abrupt or bold temerity, in a chance event, nor to refrain because of overwhelming fear, but to enter with sober mind, such that wisely and with good deliberation in their own good time they might accomplish all things well. The mayor and citizens of the city through inviting conversation and cheerful expressions, comforting and pleasing them, helped them continually, saying that they might enjoy for their use and at their disposal all things in the city within reason and equity, whereupon the duke of Gloucester said, "Now

---

[10] Reading *latentium* for the manuscript's meaningless *laittiancium*.
[11] The context requires emending *volentes* to *nolentes*, a common minim confusion for the "anglicana" script of this period.

I know truly that no one can prevent liars from telling lies." Soon with mutual consent given, and evening pressing in, for more abundant security each one of the lords was hosted separately with his army before diverse gates around the city. But behold how great an altercation between the king and the said Lords Appellant broke out on each side before they could address in discussion the mutual intentions of their hearts: on the one side, the king shrank from speaking to so great a mass of men, lest perhaps the intolerable savagery or distance between the parties, namely, theirs and the king's, might nearly break out, so he did not want to talk with them beyond the Tower anywhere by any means, and he refused disdainfully to do so. On the other side, the appellants themselves did not wish to address the king there, unless they might be able to enter there with a strong and secure band of men to avoid betrayal and danger. Therefore, the most learned of the other commissaries, after conflicts on each side of the disputations and with documentation of the reasoning, dissolved the hardened heart of the king like ice on a sunny day, such that, adhering to them in that measure, he took care to bend himself to every desire and wish of the vigorous appellants. But nonetheless, the aforesaid lords, lest anything perverse should fraudulently happen, prudently sent a competent band of armed men to investigate in advance every dark hiding place of the said Tower, along with its nooks and corners. Upon their report that no fraud had been found within there, the aforesaid vigorous five, with what one might call a large force, entered the said Tower and, appointing one as doorkeeper and having the doors closed on command, and thus for the time being with those in charge of the said Tower before the king and commissaries, they appealed the said fugitives for the third time and in the manner and form stated above. Driven by this appeal, the king voluntarily offered an oath on his soul that he would adhere by confirmation to them and the counsel of their commissaries, as a good king and just judge, inasmuch as the order of law, reason, and equity demanded. After these things were seen and done, departing the Tower into the city, they returned to their lodgings, keeping continued watch during the nights. And it was proclaimed, not only in the king's presence but also throughout the regions of England, that the aforesaid fugitive traitors, as men definitively summoned, on the established day of parliament, that is, the day after the next Purification of the Blessed Mary, should personally appear ready to respond to the aforesaid falsely deceptive treachery according to the charges.

13. And since the harvest stood seasonably ready at that time for cutting and extirpating thorns, thistles, and tares,[12] by the ratification of the king and the mutual consent of all the said commissaries and appellants, many officials were expelled from the king's household, namely, in the place of John Beauchamp, steward, they appointed John Devereux, knight, one of those appointed from the commissaries, and Peter de Courtney, knight, was ordained

[12] Cf. Matt. 13:30.

in the king's chamber in place of the said duke of Ireland. But the aforesaid John Beauchamp; Simon Burley, vice chamberlain of the king; John Salisbury, doorkeeper of the chamber; Thomas Trivet; James Baret; William Elmham and Nicholas Dagworth, knights; and other clerical officers, namely, Richard Metteford, secretary; John Slake, deacon of the chapel; John Lincoln, chamberlain of the Exchequer; and John Clifford, clerk of the chapel; because they behaved as accomplices in the aforesaid crimes, in that they were informed about them and did not contradict them, and because they desired these things to be done, are mandated to be put under arrest in diverse prisons of England until they would respond in parliament to the things charged. But they dismissed many others, especially their servants and others, as useless and foolish men, throwing them out to be vagabonds. And thus a most filthy nest perched in a certain tree was shattered as completely as possible, and its birds, wounded most foully, dispersed in flight.

14. On the vigil of the following Purification of the Blessed Mary, in the king's chamber at Westminster, by the shared counsel of all the commissaries, the aforesaid Robert Bealknap, John Holt, Roger Fulthorp, William Burgh, John Locton, and John Cary are removed from their offices. Arrested without any debate in order to respond elsewhere fully to the charges, by order of the chancellor they are thrust, stunned and terrified, into the Tower; and in the place of Bealknap, Robert Carleton, in the place of Tresilian, Walter Clopton, are installed in the offices of judges. Then for a brief time, with the new incumbents having been given the burdens of office and accepted by all, and swearing the oaths of office, they departed to take dinner.

15. And since the period of Lent, in accord with the history of this matter, is a time appropriate and acceptable[13] to correct and punish delinquents according to their merits, a great parliament was therefore begun on the second day of the following February in this manner. When everyone of both estates,[14] lords and potentates of this realm, having congregated in the White Royal Chamber at Westminster, the king arrived and took his seat as tribunal; and the five most noble and commemorated appellants, whose own merits of probity resounded everywhere in the land, striving to climax prosperous beginnings with a prosperous outcome, entered the hall with a great multitude in the same suit of golden clothes, each holding another by the arm; and gazing at the king they saluted him in unison, kneeling. There was a single mass of men filling the hall even into its corners. But what bit of the said false lords or of their adherents, prithee, was found anywhere there? Nicholas Brembre,

---

[13] Echoing 2 Cor. 6:2, a passage often used to frame Lenten or penitential sermons. For a late medieval vernacular example, see Andrew Galloway, "A Fifteenth-Century Confession Sermon on 'Unkyndenesse' (CUL MS Gg 6.26) and its Literary Parallels and Parodies," *Traditio* 49 (1994): 259–69; late medieval bilingual English/Latin sermons for Lent using this scriptural passage are noted in Siegfried Wenzel, *Macaronic Sermons: Bilingualism and Preaching in Late-Medieval England* (Michigan: University of Michigan Press, 1994), B-108 (150), O-39 (164), Q-29 and 30 (168), X-09 (201).

[14] I.e., lay and clerical.

having been taken earlier elsewhere, is remanded to be driven savagely into the prison of Gloucester. When therefore according to ancient parliament custom the laity on the left and the clergy on the right of the king had taken their seats, the chancellor standing in full view with his back to the king pronounced a certain speech, touching on the causes and matters of the parliament, categorizing these according to tradition. When this was complete, the aforesaid five lords, rising up, recorded their prefatory words by way of Robert Plessyngton, a prudent knight, who said, "Behold, the duke of Gloucester has come in person, for purgation of himself concerning the treason charged against him by the said fugitives." The chancellor, taking a response from the king's mouth, answered, excusing the said duke, "Lord duke, you would be casting off your origins from so worthy a royal lineage; you are so near to him in collateral line, we find, that for such things to be schemed by you would not be suspected." The aforesaid duke with his four associates, very humbly kneeling on their knees, thanked the king. Then silence was imposed, and the commemorated lords produced in writs the articles of the accusation concerning the aforesaid treachery. Geoffrey Martin, clerk of the Crown, stood before them in the middle of the parliament for a period of two hours, swiftly reading the aforesaid articles. The hearts of some were stricken with sorrow at the horrific contents of the said articles; many had swollen faces with tears on their cheeks. With the reading of the articles concluded, they benignly demanded the king that a just sentence should be imposed, one suited to the aforesaid false deceit according to how it was alleged and to how it would be proven, and indeed that there might be a due execution of this sentence against the persons of the said fugitives; and the king promised these things. So much for the first day. The day after they were stirred by counsels producing nothing, and therefore I will proceed not according to the days but rather I will only touch the larger deeds of the parliament.

16. When therefore on the third day they had come for their proceedings against the said fugitives, the chancellor of England, in the name of the clergy, alleged in full parliament that they would not by any means involve themselves in cases of this sort nor wish to take part in any moment when judgment of blood is pursued. And to confirm these things the clergy issued a written protestation, by which when read publicly they said that they were asserting this not by reason of favor or fear of hatred or of reward, but seeing as the sanctions of the canons and all laws persuade and compel clerks to refrain from impiousness of this sort, they wished to preserve those things. In the chapter house also of the abbey knights of the affinities had gathered to discuss their counsels and materials, for whom they sent to notify them too of the said protestation. Meanwhile, the said protestation notwithstanding, the five aforesaid lords petitioned to pass sentence against the four contumacious ones, condemning them. And when the said lower commons had arrived faster than the word, although the protestation was given out and read through before them too in the same way, the aforesaid five nobles did not

cease to petition against the said contumacious ones. The clergy soon arose, and for the time being departed into the annex of the king's chamber. The king, however, moved by a charitable conscience, discerning that in the work of all things it is good to be mindful of the end, and according to the requirement of law to favor the defendant rather than the plaintiff, carried over the proceedings, to see if something on the part of those absent might meanwhile be alleged or juridically recounted.[15] But the lords, irritated, supplicated the king that no case already in process, or taken up for the first time, or coming up later should be moved by any means, until the present case of treason should be finally put to rest; to whose petition he gave his gracious assent.

17. At length, on the eleventh day of February, when nothing on behalf of those absent might be alleged to prevent that grave sentence of condemnation from being definitively rendered, the aforesaid John Devereux, marshal of the court, holding the place of the king, judged that the aforesaid archbishop, duke, earl, and Tresilian should be drawn from the Tower of London through the city to Tyburn, then without delay hanged on the gallows and all their goods confiscated such that later successors might not rejoice in them.

18. And on the twelfth day of February, which was the first Monday of Lent, when the aforesaid Nicholas Brembre was made to appear, with certain articles proposed and read through before him, he requested a copy, and counsel, and a day for the sake of deliberating better how he would respond to them. And although what he sought was neither an equitable or customary thing, nay further against the rigor of the law, in so grave a criminal case we would have allowed the tiniest matter construably in his favor: had he begged in vain, it would have been imposed on him to answer the charges strictly.[16]

---

[15] Reading *si aliquid pro parte absencium possit interim allegari vel iuritice* [i.e., *iuridice*] *deferri, processum continuavit.* McKisack punctuates *interim allegari vel iuritice, diferri processum continuavit:* emending the text's *diferri* to *deferri,* however (or accepting a common alternate spelling variation), allows a meaningful passive infinitive, and rejecting McKisack's comma between *iuritice* and *deferri* reveals the full parallel construction *interim allegari . . . iuritice deferri.* The Lords Appellant wished to stop the trial and go to judgment and sentencing, whereas Richard wished to continue the proceedings after an interval that would allow for more evidence or testimony.

[16] The text is corrupt here and the edition's punctuation misleading, but both may be readily emended. McKisack prints *et licet neque equam nec usitatam rem desideravit, quinimmo contra rigorem iuris in tam graui causa criminali habuimus adiminicula colorabiliter in sui fauorem pro frustra postulasset, imponebatur ei strictim impositis respondere.* The second long clause as presented in McKisack lacks cogent sense, with two grammatically unsubordinated finite verbs, *habuimus* and *postulasset,* an incomplete sequence of the concessive adverbs *licet . . . quinimmo* ("even though . . . nay, further") without a following "nonetheless," and the incomprehensible word *adiminicula.* The only clear point to emerge from the text McKisack offers is the final phrase, *imponebatur ei strictim impositis respondere* ("it was imposed on him to answer the charges strictly"). In fact, as the following sentences show, Favent presents Brembre's accusers as *not* forcing him to answer the charges strictly, since they both take him up on his challenge for single combat and they allow the delay he has requested. However directly contradicted by other accounts, Favent is seeking to show how lenient and just the proceedings against Brembre were, not the reverse. This is therefore evidently a chief example in the text which led McKisack to note in the preface, "Some passages remain very obscure. . . . Except where a word is obviously misspelled I have not attempted to correct such mistakes" (viii). Yet small corrections produce perfect sense here. The concessive adverbs, which elsewhere Favent uses carefully and correctly, demand a following "nonetheless" clause (even if "nonetheless" is merely implied), which indeed must begin somewhere after *quin-*

For it is read that he answered, "Whoever has charged me with these things, I give witness that I am present here ready to prove by battle with him in the arena that these same things are false." And Brembre said these things terrified that he would die in excruciating pain in the manner of traitors, and would prefer to expire as a knight fighting in arms than scandalously through the parliament's condemnation. Immediately the commemorated appellants with stern visage declared, "And we ourselves give witness and offer ourselves that we are ready to prove by battle with you in the arena that these same things are true." And they threw their gauntlets at the king's feet; and at the same instant from everywhere in the place flew gauntlets like snow from the other lords, knights, squires, and commons, who declared in one voice, "And we pledge a duel for proving on your head that the things said are true." Quicker than speech the king departed for the day. And although these things were not left unconsidered among the sleepers, nonetheless on the next day, as an even heavier matter, appeared many of the crafts of the city of London complaining about many injuries and extortions torturously committed and carried forward against them elsewhere by that same Nicholas Brembre. And since the crafts themselves swore on their souls that they were not corrupted by hatred, fear, or favor of anyone or any reward, nor were they declaring these things maliciously but rather were accusing him concerning the truth, Brembre then stood undone at last.

19. But before they had argued to the finish[17] the end of the trial against Nicholas Brembre, the hapless Tresilian occupied their attention. He had been located above the gutter of a certain house annexed to the wall of the palace, hiding among the roofs for the sake of watching the lords coming and going from parliament. When, however, resolute soldiers had entered that house and, looking around, found no one, a certain knight with intent expression strode to the father of the house and pulled his head up by the hair, drawing his dagger, saying, "Show us where Tresilian is or your days are

---

immo contra rigorem iuris ("nay further, against the rigor of law"); and this "nonetheless" clause must be governed by *habuimus*, requiring a comma before *in tam graui causa* and concluding before the next clause governed by the second finite verb, *postulasset*. The sense of that intervening completing clause, even before any emendation is attempted for *adiminicula*, is therefore "in so grave a criminal case we would have allowed *adiminicula* construably in his favor" (Favent often uses the perfect tense for the apodoses of contrary-to-fact clauses). The following phrases belong to a second, independent set of clauses, *pro frustra postulasset, imponebatur ei strictim impositis respondere*: "had he applied in vain, it would have been imposed on him to respond strictly to the charges." The pluperfect subjunctive *postulasset* confirms the contrary-to-fact construction. This leaves only the meaningless *adiminicula*. The context requires a word or phrase meaning "something of a very tiny portion" in the accused's favor (which the writer claims is always allowed in such grave cases). The solution is to assume simple word misdivision compounding a minim error, the latter common in "anglicana" script, yielding *ad minu[s]cula*: the eight minims of *minu* have been misread as *imini*, and the common spelling alternate of "c" for "sc" needs no comment. Thus the text should here read *et licet neque equam nec usitatam rem desiderauit, quinimmo contra rigorem iuris, in tam graui causa criminali habuimus ad minu[s]cula colorabiliter in sui fauorem. Pro frustra postulasset, imponebatur ei strictim impositis respondere.*

[17] Reading *decertassent* for the manuscript's *deceptassent*, a simple misreading of an original long "anglicana" "r" as "p." McKisack's emendation, *decetassent*, is to be rejected.

numbered." Immediately, the terrified father of the household said, "Behold the place where that man is positioned at this moment," and under a certain round table which was covered for deception with a tablecloth, the unfortunate Tresilian, disguised as usual, was miraculously discovered. His tunic was made out of old russet, extending down to mid-shin, as if he were an old man, and he had a wiry and thick beard, and wore red boots with the soles of Joseph,[18] looking more like a pilgrim or beggar than a king's justice. This event was immediately made clear to the lords' ears, and when, quicker than a word, the aforesaid five appellants under a hasty pretext left the parliament without explaining the reason for their departure, all who remain in parliament were stunned, and many others followed them with passionate zeal. And when at the palace gate they had seized Tresilian, leading him toward the parliament, they proclaimed in a universal voice, "We havet hym! We havet hym!" Meanwhile, interrogated in the parliament how he would excuse himself concerning the false treachery of this kind and other things done by him, he remained nonetheless stock-still and mute, his heart hardened even in the face of death, and he would not confess to the things committed. Immediately parliament was broken for the sake of this matter, and on the grounds of dealing with Tresilian they sent away for the day Brembre, who had remained present. And at once Tresilian was led to the Tower of London so that execution of his sentence might be carried out on his person. His wife and daughters, moaning and imploring weepingly, were present at hand there in that place, and with voiceless requests, kissing him first from one side then the other, they forgave him for one or another of the crimes he had committed. But she, overwhelmed with sorrow in her heart, fell to the ground as if dead. At length Tresilian was bound hand and foot to a hurdle, and along with a vast multitude of lords and commoners, horsemen and pedestrians, he was dragged from the back of horses through the city squares, resting at intervals of about the length of a furlong out of considerations of charity, to see if he wanted to repent anything. But alas, he did not publicly confess, and indeed it is not known what he would say to his friar confessor, nor has it been ours to discover: the friars well treated Tresilian, preserving him from his transgression.[19] And when he had come to the place of Calvary that he might be made defunct,[20] he did not want to climb the stairs, but goaded by sticks and whips that he might ascend, he said, "While I carry a certain something around me, I am not able to die."[21] Immediately they stripped him and found particular

---

[18] In late medieval drama, Joseph, as well as a poor wanderer, is also typically old and doddering, a butt of comedy, especially in his own incredulity at having fathered a child.

[19] A sly reminder that satire about friars' treatment of confessions, and of those they confess, is rampant in the period. Here, the friars are doing their job too well for Favent's and the crowd's tastes.

[20] Cf. Luke 23:33. "That he might be made defunct" (*ut defungeretur*) drops the evangelical tone precipitously. The entire scene carries parodic echoes of the Crucifixion, especially as in Luke.

[21] Late medieval claims of such life-preserving talismans include the description of the green girdle in *Sir Gawain and the Green Knight* (ll. 1851–54), and the claim by Margery Baxter, a fif-

instructions with particular signs depicted in them, in the manner of astro-
nomical characters; and one depicted a demon's head, many others were inscribed with demons' names. With these taken away, he was hanged nude,
and for greater certainty of his death his throat was cut. And it became
night.[22] And he was left hanging until the next day, and, with permission for
carrying away his body sought and obtained from the king by his wife, it was
taken to the Franciscans and is there buried.

20. On the next day a sentence similar to that of the four condemned was
given against Brembre, and when he was drawn from the Tower through the
city on a hurdle to Tyburn, resting at furlong intervals, he gave great penance,
beseeching mercy from God and men against whom he had sinned in past
times, and many commiserating prayed for him. And when the noose was put
on him so that he might be hanged, the son of Northampton asked him
whether the aforesaid things done elsewhere to his father by Brembre were
legally done. For Northampton was formerly a mayor of the city of London,
a richer and more powerful citizen among all those who were in the city, and
through certain ones, associates who were death-bearing plagues, namely,
Brembre, Tresilian and others, was enormously vexed by certain nefarious
conspiracies and confederacies then condemned to death, and with all his
goods stripped hardly escaped alive. And concerning those things Brembre
confessed that neither piously nor justly but with a violent heart for the sake
of destroying Northampton he had infelicitously committed those things.
And seeking forgiveness, hanging by the rope, he died when his throat was
cut. Behold how good and pleasant it is to be raised up to honors![23] It seems
to me better to carry out business at home among paupers than be thus lordly
among kings, and at the end climb the ladder among thieves; since it is more
a matter of onerousness than honor to assume the name of honor.[24] You who
are reading, look down to regard him, and you might be able to consider by
their ends how their works receive results. For in every work be mindful of
the end.

21. Following this they did not proceed to judgments of death of this sort
but instead, until things were riper, undertook business of the kingdom that
they had taken to heart. They ordained for the noble earl of Arundel the admiralty of sea, to resist and intercept enemies if he was able to encounter

---

teenth-century Lollard, that she carried a charter in her womb that would keep her from being
burned; on the latter, see Andrew Galloway, "Intellectual Pregnancy, Metaphysical Femininity,
and the Social Doctrine of the Trinity in *Piers Plowman*," *Yearbook of Langland Studies* 12 (1998):
117–52. Tresilian's executioners appear to have some belief in their possible efficacy.

[22] Cf., e.g., Gen. 1:5, 8.

[23] *Ecce quam bonum et iocundum est sublimari ad honores*. The phrasing and rhythm of the line
echo Psalm 132:1 (Septuagint), *Ecce quam bonum et quam iucundum habitare fratres in unum* ("Behold how good and how pleasant it is for brethren to dwell together in unity"). The psalm appears as an antiphon in the liturgy of feria 5 of the Salisbury Use, one of many liturgical parodies
or echoes in Favent's narrative.

[24] *Cum pocius sit oneris quam honoris assumere nomen honoris*, with paronomasia, homeoteleuton,
and the vestiges of a Leonine hexameter, as throughout the rhythmic prose of these sententious
reflections. The basic pun is very old and widespread.

them by land or by sea; and thus it was done. Also, the bitternesses of heart and the burdened and anxious thoughts between the king and the appellants, if any existed, they graciously swept away by the sweet encouragements of the commissaries, and for the confirmation of this they added by compact that the king would host the appellants at dinner and they would individually host him, as example and notice to the people concerning the firm concord and true friendship that was finally purified between them. And all these things were fulfilled and there was great joy among the people.

22. Returning anew to the fearful judgments of this sort, to the parliament were led Thomas Usk and John Blake, on the fourth day of the month of March, also the fourth holy day of Passion week. These two, although of simple rank, had nonetheless both been forced as accomplices into the aforestated treacheries with the aforesaid potentates. For Usk was a sergeant at arms, and inserted among the traitors in that by his performance in most recent days he had been made sheriff of Middlesex for the sake of indicting the Lords Appellant, and he indicted other commissaries and adherents as traitors in their actions. Blake was Tresilian's adjunct, and was often found coming and going as a referendary on behalf of completing the treacheries and matters of the said five condemned men. And when in judgment they could allege nothing on their behalf to make exception, that grave sentence is given against them and, just as their masters before had earlier made procession to death, they too, fulfilling the same reward of fate, were led to the Tower. At once, at the same time but separately, drenching the neighborhoods with their flesh in the manner usual for traitors, they came to Tyburn and there immediately went to rest between the gallows. But the privilege is given to the truncated head of Thomas Usk, after he was hanged, of being pecked by birds' beaks above Newgate in London.

23. Later in the proceedings, on the sixth holy day of Passion week, they gave attention in parliament to the aforesaid judges, Robert Bealknap, John Holt, Roger Fulthorp, William Burgh, John Locton, and John Cary, lord baron of the Exchequer, concerning their counsel and deed as noted above against all the commissaries and as adherents in the evil hours at Nottingham. And, since it was not necessary to declare single things against them individually, they are condemned all six in a judgment like the prior ones. The clergy, however, while the laity were deciding the death sentence of this kind, rose from parliament and entered the king's private room in order to converse with him. And when a word had been spoken by them about the scandalousness of the death of judges, the archbishop of Canterbury, the bishop of Winchester, the chancellor, treasurer, keeper of the privy seal with the whole group of clergy, with a heavy heart and light foot, appeared in parliament presenting a tearful complaint; and bowing to the king's feet they supplicated him very humbly, exhorting the king and lords of parliament that for the love of God, of the glorious Virgin Mary, and of all the saints, as they themselves in a bitter judgment elsewhere would rejoice in pity, that they cease and desist

totally from the death of those judges present there and most bitterly weeping there, in whose and from whose sense and heads the font, pith, and wisdom of the laws of England thrived, emanated, and was drunk up. There was immense sorrow, especially among the parties of those complaining and those condemned. The duke of Gloucester, earls of Arundel, Warwick, and Nottingham, and many other soft hearts joined with them in mourning. Immediately, by virtue of the complaint of the clergy, the execution against the persons of the judges ceased, and life was given to them again by the king. But what happened after concerning them I will say further below, for they were remanded to the Tower under close guard.

24. Shortly after this, that is, on the twelfth day of March, a Thursday, it happened that the aforesaid knights, Simon Burley, John Beauchamp, James Baret, and John Salisbury, had been led into parliament. The things to be alleged were soon alleged, the things to be proven proven, and they not able to excuse themselves. Yet all the way from that time nearly to the Ascension of the Lord,[25] the parliament was vexed solely by the case of the said Simon. For the united trinity of the three Lords Appellant, namely, the duke of Gloucester and earls of Arundel and Warwick, along with the whole Commons of parliament, insisted that the just judgment in accord with how the matters were alleged and proven against the person of Simon himself should be firmly carried out. From the other side, however, the king, the queen, the earls of Derby and Nottingham, the prior of St. John, his uncle, and many others from the greater members of the lords of parliament labored assiduously on behalf of his life. Therefore, since the said Commons is exhausted by so long a time in labors and expenses attending parliament, and as it was likely that their long expectation in parliament would not be brought to effect, they requested that the king release them so that they might freely depart from parliament for their own business, and in the future, when matters did not pertain to them, not to disturb them by giving the reason for such fatigue in future times that some misfortune had been fostered unexpectedly in the kingdom. There was tumult among the lower commons in diverse regions of England, for example, in Kent and its vicinity: because of Simon, an insurrection had silently risen up. At once everyone on both parties of this Simon, declining from their pleadings,[26] immediately desisted. Finally, on the next Wednesday before Ascension, that is, the fifth day of May, sentence was given against only Simon, namely, that in the manner of his predecessors he be drawn from the Tower to Tyburn and, after being hanged, that his head be amputated from his body. But because he was a Knight of the Garter, powerful and humane in his behavior and pleasing, a relative of the king and always found in his court, therefore, at the urgings of many lords, the king out of his

---

[25] May 7.
[26] Reading *instancionibus* for the manuscript's *instacionibus:* a simple scribal error of omitted suspension.

special grace in imposing the execution of the said sentence relaxed it, mitigating it insofar that Simon was only led to the earth wall at Towerhill in London where, repentant, his head truncated, he suffered his death throes.

25. On the twelfth day of May, that is, on the next Wednesday before Pentecost, were similarly condemned John Beauchamp, steward of the king, James Baret, and John Salisbury, knights of the chamber, whose end, that is, John Beauchamp's and James Baret's, was just like Simon's: with heads truncated, they died at Towerhill. John Salisbury, however, was drawn from Towerhill to Tyburn in the manner of his predecessors, then he received his sentence of hanging. On the same day the bishop of Chichester, the king's confessor, was condemned with them, but on account of his dignity the execution of judgment is entirely relaxed, even so far as preserving his life. But when they began to abhor the horrible torments of this kind, of the death of fellow Christians, they grew mindful of other important matters of the kingdom, such as the war with the Scots and the French, and for the circuit of one year the king's subsidies of customs from wine and wool. Also, concerning certain translations of bishops; since, after it had intoned into the ears of our pope Urban VI that the said archbishop of York was condemned, to remove all suspicions of irregularity in his favor, he decreed that Neville would be archbishop of St. Andrews in Scotland, which archbishopric was indeed under the power of the enemy Scots and at that time in the gift of the antipope. And the pope sought to have granted in tribute to him half of the tithe of England in his subsidy for sustaining his wars, but he was not able to acquire it. He shrewdly recalled, therefore, that something could come to him through certain translations of bishops, and thus in the event he transformed his request concerning a subsidy of this kind into what was construably a common right: he ordered the bishop of Ely, then chancellor of England, to succeed to the archbishopric of York, in the place of his condemned predecessor; and the bishop of Durham into his place, the bishop of Salisbury into his place, and Lord John Waltham, keeper of the privy seal, into his place—all these he wished and mandated to sanctify. And thus by this manner transmuting alternately one into the place of another he provided by canon law for himself the first taxes through translations. When in the same parliament news about this pope's mandates had come to the ears of the English, they debated energetically concerning this matter among other business of the kingdom, because so great an amount of money on the pretext of these translations would be transmuted from England without any remuneration. But their argument did not prevail in parliament since the clergy had not spoken against the pope's mandate.

26. In the Octave of Trinity, that is, on the last day of the month of May, on behalf of closing parliament in the customary manner, the king honorifically convened a parliament at Kennington; then on the Wednesday following they concluded the matters previously touched and not yet put to rest: namely, to Thomas Trivet, William Elmham, and Nicholas Dagworth,

knights, Richard Metteford, John Slake, and John Lincoln, clerks, with worthy pledges given that elsewhere before parliament or the king's council they would be ready personally to appear to respond to charges, free power was given by grace to go in the meantime at their pleasure wherever in England might seem convenient to them. And so far as the aforesaid judges it was discussed and ordained that all six, along with the bishop of Chichester who as is said before was convicted and condemned among them from the day of the order of those present, with *induciae*[27] given up to Saint Peter ad Vincula, should be each located in his region of Ireland, in the manner that follows: namely, that the said Robert Bealknap and John Holt in the town of Drogheda in Ireland should there live not in the role of a judge or an officer, but a derelict and deportee. The said Robert Bealknap could not travel beyond a space of three miles beyond the said town, and John Holt a space of two miles, on pain of execution of the said sentence previously borne upon their persons. The king, from his particular liberality, would contribute forty pounds annually to Robert Bealknap and forty marks to John Holt for their disposition during their lifetimes. Roger Fulthorp by the king's gift would have forty pounds and William Burth forty marks during their lifetimes for sustaining them in the town of Dublin in Ireland where they are deported in a similar manner, except that Roger Fulthorp might enjoy a circle of three miles, William, if he did not stay within two miles, would suffer the penalty noted above. The aforesaid John Cary and John Locton, both with twenty pounds during their lifetimes from the king's retribution, in the town of Waterford in Ireland exist similarly deported, not able to go beyond a boundary of two miles under the penalty noted. The bishop of Chichester to the town of Cork in Ireland in a similar manner then deported exists on forty marks from the king's donation during his lifetime, not exceeding a two-mile limit under the incumbent penalty. Behold men who did not place God before their gaze! You who read, examine how evil things, begun by evil beginnings, hardly are completed in any good conclusion. Wherefore, in all works, remember the end.

27. On the third day of June in the abbey of Westminster, with the arrival of the king, queen, and all lords and commoners of both lay and clerical estates in conclusion of the parliament, the bishop of London (because it was in his diocese) celebrated a mass. With the mass ended, the archbishop of Canterbury delivered a splendid speech concerning the form and danger of oathgiving. With this completed, although the king previously at his coronation had taken on his soul the oath of kings, and the homage and oaths of lords of the realm and community in due manner had been made to him. Nonetheless, partly because he took the oath in a youthful state, partly on account of uprooting and dissipating concerns and stirrings of the heart both on the part

---

[27] The legal term for the time between a defendant's citation and the day fixed for his appearance. The feast of Saint Peter ad Vincula is August 1.

of the king and on the part of the lords, he solemnly renews that same oath in the manner and form by which he took it in his coronation with the homage and oaths of the lords. With these things done, the said metropolitan of England with all the supporters there present, with the candle lit, excommunicated under one cloak all and sundry in themselves or through others contravening or impeding such that by however much the less anything and everything in the said parliament mandated, put to rest, or concluded might not stand firm and be effective in its force and authority; and he extinguished the candle. The chancellor then, extending his hands, made all the Commons vouch in faith and observance of the aforedone things as faithful lieges well and faithfully preserving the aforesaid. And this form of observance of parliament was solemnized through the whole kingdom. On the next day, that is the fourth of June, with mutual greetings held among the king, lords, and commons, each one freely returned to his own affairs in his own region. Now let England, rejoicing, exult in Christ, since by his scars, and by our filthy, bitter remains, the snare [noose] is thoroughly destroyed, and we are free,[28] thanks to God, etc.

[28] Psalm 123:7. In par. 20 Favent uses *laqueus* to mean "noose"; a pun reflecting on the preceding executions may therefore lie in this final prayer. Note also that according to *West. Chron.*, the Lords Appellant allude to a similar phrase, "the snares that spell death" (210), and the phrase appears again at *West. Chron.*, 184. Gower's description of Richard as "he pretends peace, while he weaves bonds of death" (*R. pacem fingit, dum mortis federe stringit* [*Cronica tripertita* 3.469]) may also draw on some pointed circulation of this topos, though it is of course thoroughly conventional.

Index